The Life and Times of
Muhammad

Many books have been written about the life of the Muslim founder, but none is quite like this one by the famous Glubb Pasha. Most have been scholarly tomes or popularized condensations of the tomes written by people who have done their research well. Sir John lived his research, for he was no armchair historian. Most of his adult life was spent in Arabia, and he was almost as fluent in its language as in his own.

It would be of little help in writing about a Roman of the same period as Muhammad (around AD 600) if the writer lived in Italy today. But in the deserts of Arabia, the bedouins have survived into the twentieth century almost as they existed two thousand years ago. Thus, Glubb Pasha has been able to recreate the world of Muhammad and breathe life into the man.

Because the Muslim religion has been a traditional enemy of Christianity, nearly all the biographies of Muhammad have been distorted. Western authors, religious or not, seem to have inherited centuries-old prejudices against the Muslims. Muslim writers, on the other hand, have responded in equally biased, indeed vitriolic, terms. In this recognized classic, Sir John has written the life of one of the most influential figures in history without rancor or bias. He has performed a twofold service: he has given us a major work for readers of biography and a book that has become a standard for students and for all those who want to understand the forces that move the Middle East and reverberate around the world.

D09904351

The Life and Times of Muhammad

John Bagot Glubb
(Glubb Pasha)

Scarborough House/*Publishers*

Scarborough House/*Publishers*
Chelsea, MI 48118

FIRST SCARBOROUGH HOUSE TRADE PAPERBACK 1991

The Life and Times of Muhammad was published in hardcover by
Stein and Day/*Publishers*

Library of Congress Cataloging-in-Publication Data

Glubb, John Bagot, Sir, 1897-
    The life and times of Muhammad / by John Bagot Glubb.
        p.   cm.
    Reprint. Originally published: New York : Stein & Day, 1970.
    Includes bibliographical references and index.
    ISBN 0-8128-1393-6
    1. Muhammad, Prophet, d. 632.   I. Title.
BP75.G58   1991
297'.63—dc20
[B]   91-14433
                                                  CIP

Things are constantly being said, written and preached about the Arab Prophet and the religion he taught, of which an elementary acquaintance with him would show the absurdity. What I wish to do is to enable any one, at the cost of the least possible exertion, to put himself in a position to judge of popular fallacies about Muhammad and his creed.

STANLEY LANE POOLE, *The Speeches and Table Talk of Muhammad*

Nothing is easier than to be stupidly intolerant of the different ideals and principles of other races and other ages. Nothing is easier, as life goes on, than to sink back into well-worn grooves of thought and prejudice from which there is no emergence; ... intellectual sympathy becomes impossible, and without that sympathy there is no possibility of understanding, and without understanding there is no well-wishing and charity becomes an impossibility.

GERALD VANN, *The Water and the Fire*

We may as well tolerate all religions since God Himself tolerates them.

FÉNELON

Introduction

IN the preface to my book, *The Great Arab Conquests*, I complained of the lack of books on Arab history available to the English language reader, although the Arab Empire was half as big again as that of Rome and six hundred years nearer to us. The same objection cannot, however, be raised on the subject of the life of Muhammad. Many biographies of the Prophet have appeared in European languages, English, French, German, Italian and others. In adding to the number of these *Lives*, therefore, I need some better excuse than the absence of other works on the subject.

Such an excuse seems to be all the more essential in that the existing biographies are nearly all the works of learned professors with whose erudition I make no claim to compete. I venture, however, to suggest that men as learned as they were may be too erudite for the general public. Scholars tend to write for scholars and perhaps to look with some condescension on mere "popularisers". Yet today, the general non-technical public are expected to exercise a measure of control over public affairs. It has, therefore, been my object to write a readable book, from which the average educated man or woman can obtain a working knowledge of the subject. I have accordingly economised on learned footnotes and scholarly discussions.

Secondly, it is obvious that no man can devote a lifetime to learned studies and, at the same time, live in intimate contact with the daily life of illiterate tribesmen in the desert. Until I was fifty-nine years old, my life was spent, mostly out-of-doors, in practical activities in the Arab countries. It was beyond my powers to begin at sixty and overtake the scholars whose whole lives had been dedicated to learning.

But although the history of the past has come down to us in books, the most difficult task in the writing of history is not to unearth the "facts" from the volumes in which they are recorded. The most difficult part, in my humble experience, is to place oneself in the mental and spiritual atmosphere of the country and the period of which one is writing.

Now in this respect, the historian of the age of Muhammad is peculiarly fortunate. When we write of ancient Greece or Rome or even of mediaeval Europe, we are limited for our knowledge to the surviving documents. There are no Greek city-states, Roman senates or mediaeval knights in shining armour, whom we can interview to ascertain their opinions. But in the deserts of Arabia, the bedouins have survived into the twentieth century almost as they existed two thousand years ago. The most overwhelming impression I have received from reading the earliest accounts of these events in the original Arabic is that the people there depicted are exactly the men among whom I lived for so many years. I hope, therefore, that my lack of erudition may, to some extent at least, be compensated by my extraordinary good fortune in having lived among the people I endeavour to describe, and in whom thirteen centuries of time had wrought so few changes.

I say advisedly "had" in place of "have", for modern means of transport and the discovery of oil in Arabia have, in the last several decades, shattered this old nomadic world. The student of the future, wafted in an hour or two from London, Moscow or New York to the heart of the Arabian peninsula will no longer find himself carried back to the pre-Islamic tribal world. The mental and spiritual atmosphere, so marvellously preserved for thirteen centuries, will have vanished beyond recall.

One other subject deserves mention before our story can begin. Muhammad was the founder of the Muslim religion which, for one thousand three hundred years, has been regarded as the enemy of Christianity. The enmity, incidentally, has been largely due to political rivalries, not to religious or theological differences, for Islam is closely related to Christianity. These religious prejudices have distorted nearly all the biographies of Muhammad. Western authors, even if not themselves very religious, have nevertheless unconsciously inherited the violent prejudices against Muslims which have become embedded in European culture. Muslim writers, on the other hand, lashed into fury by the bitter criticisms directed against the Prophet by old-fashioned Western writers, have responded in no less vitriolic terms. The result has been not only completely to distort the historical picture but also to increase the hatreds which divide differing races and cultures, now being daily brought into ever-closer contact with one another.

I am a Christian. But I have lived more than half my life among Muslims, sometimes entirely among them with no Christians anywhere near. I know that Islam can produce fine men, and even saints, and that the "image" of Muslims entertained by most people in the West is completely untrue. Yet I have never been tempted to become a Muslim myself.

Modern science has achieved many wonders. Among other things, it has so explored the vastness of space that we are told that our world, in the visible universe alone, is no more than a speck of dust floating in Waterloo station in London. And no one knows how far the universe extends beyond the point which our telescopes can see.

Mediaeval man thought that the Earth was the centre of the Universe and that man was the lord of the earth. He had some reason to be proud. But now that we know that our Earth is but a tiny speck of dust, what pride can be left us? Yet, in all history, few if any communities have been more arrogant than we are. Invisible animalcula on a speck of dust, we announce our indifference to, and contempt for the Creator of the Universe. Poor, poor little fellows! Of all the insane forms which human conceit can assume, the most ridiculous and pathetic must surely be that we alone are on familiar terms with the Almighty. The argument is presumably simple. "I think this or that. God must be a reasonable Being and, therefore, He must obviously agree with me. Consequently, any human being who disagrees with me must be an enemy of God." (I hope the reader will not think such language blasphemous. It is, on the contrary, intended to emphasise the immensity of God and the absurdity of man.)

My position, therefore, is that I am happy to be a Christian, but I have also loved Muslims. Certainly, I do not consider myself entitled to assume the rôle of God and to pass judgement on other men. I have tried to describe the Arabs as I knew them, without passing moral judgements on them, a task for which I am unfit. We have the command on the Highest Authority, "Judge not, that ye be not judged."

Contents

List of Maps

List of Genealogical Trees

Author's Notes

NAMES

ENGLISH-speaking readers always find difficulty with Arabic names, some of which are both long and complicated. The Muslim historians give long lists of names but I have reduced those mentioned to a minimum, in the hope that the reader will remember the important ones. A short note is, however, necessary to explain the various kinds of names.

Let us commence with the name of our hero—Muhammad. The root of the name is the verb *hamada*, he praised. The same root appears in the common ejaculation *Al hamdu lillah*, praise be to God. Muhammad is a form of the past participle of the verb, meaning "the praised". To write Mahomet, substituting a t for the final d, is, therefore, incorrect.

In the seventh century, an Arab was normally known by his own name and that of his father—like John, son of Thomas. The word for son in Arabic is *ibn*, so the simplest name would be Zaid ibn Umar, Zaid, the son of Umar. Important families, however, often employed the name of an ancestor as a family name. Such today is the ruler of Saudi Arabia, Ibn Saud. The Saud concerned is not the father of the ruling monarch but an ancestor two hundred years ago. Since his time, all the members of the present ruling family have used the name of Ibn Saud. Such names as Johnson or Williamson in English are of the same type.

When an Arab had his first son, he often adopted the name of his son preceded by the words "father of". Thus Muhammad's first-born son was called Qasim, with the result that the Prophet could still be called Muhammad or, alternatively, Father of Qasim, Abu Qasim. In some cases, this name entirely superseded the original name, which might be completely lost—thus Muhammad's principal lieutenant was called Abu Bekr. His original name is virtually lost but it is thought to have been Atiq. The feminine form of *ibn* is *bint*—thus we have Ruqaiya bint Muhammad, Ruqaiya, daughter of Muhammad.

I have endeavoured to avoid the use of Arabic words in the text, and have given only the English translations. In the case of place or personal names, I have not used the normal English-Arabic system of transliteration. This system is good for Arabists but, in the case of readers who do not know Arabic, it does not help them to pronounce. I have endeavoured to indicate the pronunciation. In the case of words in which the emphatic syllable is not obvious, I have put an accent on it, the first time the name is mentioned. I have not repeated the accent when the name recurs.

DATES

For various reasons, exact dates for some of the events mentioned cannot be guaranteed. This is, firstly, due to the fact that the seventh-century Arabs used the lunar year of twelve moons, not the solar year. There are basic technical complications in changing these into our calendar, which need not trouble the reader.

Secondly, the early Arab historians often differ, or the same historian will give alternative dates, saying frankly that he does not know which is correct.

Thirdly, on some occasions, the historian only gives the lunar month not the exact day. For example, "In the month of Rejeb". The month of Rejeb in the year in question may have extended, for example, from 15th April to 14th May. In translating this phrase, therefore, one can only write "in April or May".

The possible variations in the dates are comparatively small where major events are concerned. But the dates given for some of the minor incidents vary by a year or two in different writers. But although the Arab historians are not rigidly accurate in their dates, they are extremely voluminous. In many cases, three or four different accounts are given of the same incident as gleaned from different sources, and the reader is left to choose whichever he prefers.

The Muslim historians are extremely fond of anecdotes and do not hesitate to report verbatim conversations. These can scarcely be the result of direct reporting. Writing materials were scarce and casual conversations cannot possibly have been recorded. Nevertheless, they are of considerable value because they undoubtedly represent extremely old traditions of the kind of thing the persons said. More exciting still, to one who has lived among these people, is the fact that many of these conversations, written some thirteen centuries ago are exactly the things these people say today. I have included a few such anecdotes, because they help to bring the narrative to life.

SOURCES

There are in general three sources for the life of Muhammad: the Qoran, the biographies and the traditions. Muhammad claimed that the Qoran was revealed to him by God or by the Archangel Gabriel. After receiving such a revelation, he repeated it to his immediate entourage, who learned it by heart or, in some cases, took notes on any bits of material available to hand. All these different passages were not collated and embodied into one publication until some twenty years after the death of Muhammad.

The text of the Qoran doubtless approximates very closely to the words used by Muhammad. Its value as a source for our narrative, however, is limited, for it consists principally of moral injunctions, denunciations, praises of God and ethical material. It is not intended to be a narrative of events.

The second source at our disposal is the biographies and histories of the first Arab writers. The earliest of these is Muhammad ibn Ishaq, who wrote a Life of Muhammad about a hundred and twenty years after the Prophet's death. The only edition of Ibn Ishaq which has survived is that edited by Ibn Hisham, who died some two hundred years after Muhammad. Another early narrative is the *Al Mughazi* of Waqidi, who died one hundred and ninety-seven years after the Prophet. A few other slightly less ancient narratives have also survived but none written within a century of Muhammad's decease.

The third source of information on the life of our hero is the traditions, called in Arabic *hadeeth*. This word really means a conversation or a verbal report. After the death of Muhammad, his companions took great pleasure in describing him, recounting his sayings and telling of their experiences in his company. New converts listened avidly to these stories and passed them on, until an immense quantity of such anecdotes was in circulation.

The reports of what Muhammad had thought or said on innumerable different subjects soon acquired the force of law. If one of the antagonists in a legal case was able to produce a tradition saying that Muhammad, in a similar situation, had said or done this or that, the judge had no alternative but to give a decision in accordance with the opinion attributed to the Prophet. The result was most unfortunate. Dishonest litigants could not always resist the temptation to invent sayings, which they attributed to Muhammad, in order to support their arguments.

In addition, political parties were active in producing statements alleged to have been made by Muhammad, in support of the policies which they advocated. As a result, the reliability of many of the sayings attributed to the Prophet began to be questioned. In consequence, a new learned profession came into existence, that of the traditionist, whose task it was to distinguish between the real sayings of Muhammad and those false stories which had been forged by interested persons for their own ends.

The two most reliable and most famous traditionists are Bukhari and Muslim. Bukhari wrote his massive work *The True Traditions*, which consisted of ninety-five books or sections, about two hundred and twenty years after the death of Muhammad. Muslim published his book some five or six years later. There have been many other anthologies of traditions, but I have only accepted traditions which appear in Bukhari or Muslim, and preferably in both.

To summarise the situation briefly, the sources are:

1 The Qoran, written down some twenty years after Muhammad's death.

2 The early histories and biographies, the oldest of which were written one hundred and twenty years after the death of the Prophet.

3 The Traditions, the most reliable version of which, by Bukhari, was compiled some two hundred and twenty years after the death of Muhammad.

Innumerable histories, lives and books of traditions have been produced by Muslims all down the ages, but as most of them used the above-mentioned sources, which are available to us as they were to them, it is normally preferable to rely as far as possible on the earliest of the surviving authors.

ACKNOWLEDGEMENTS

I wish once again to express my gratitude to the Librarian of the School of Oriental and African Studies of the University of London, to the Librarian of the Public Library of Tunbridge Wells and to Professor Albert Haurani of St. Antony's College, Oxford.

I

Arabia and Its People

Bedouin society is entirely dependent on the principle of tribal solidarity. The tribe is the self-sufficient cell of the embryonic political and social life. It is the only structure to which the individualistic bedouin will submit. It guarantees support for him in the *bellum omnium contra omnes* which is the law of the desert. It offers him personal protection. It satisfies his vanity and desire for glory with its genealogical and martial traditions.

FRANCESCO GABRIELI, *Muhammad and the Conquests of Islam*
(Slightly abridged)

The slaves of domestic tyranny may vainly exult in their national independence, but the Arab is personally free; and he enjoys in extent, the benefits of society, without forfeiting the prerogatives of nature.

EDWARD GIBBON, *Decline and Fall of the Roman Empire*

An honourable murderer if you will;
For nought did I in hate but all in honour.

WILLIAM SHAKESPEARE, *Othello*

I

IT was March 632. The plain of Arafat outside Mecca was covered as far as the eye could see with a constantly moving mass of human beings, some on foot, some sitting on the backs of their camels. The sky was clear, the sun was shining and the day would have been warm and pleasant but for the pall of dust which hung over the jostling, trampling and fidgeting crowd. All round the plain where this vast mass of humanity was gathered, the bare, arid, rockstrewn mountains of Arabia formed a still and silent backdrop to the restive crowd.

A man rode forward on a camel and a sudden hush fell upon the vast multitude. He was of middle height, with a thick beard in which appeared already a few streaks of grey. The hair around his temples was also beginning to turn white. His eyes were slightly bloodshot, perhaps from the glare of the Arabian sun. His mouth was rather larger than the average, but when he smiled, his face assumed an attractive air of benevolence.

Sitting on the back of his camel, he began to address the immense crowds which surrounded him. "You must remain in harmony with one another," he said. "Every man must respect the rights and the property of his neighbour. There must be no more enmity and no more blood feuds. Usury and extortion are likewise abolished. Be kind to the women whom God has entrusted to you, providing them with such food and clothing as they need. I have left among you God's book, the Qoran, to which if you hold fast you will not go astray. Have I fulfilled my mission?"

The immense crowd broke out into loud shouts, "You have fulfilled it, O Messenger of God." The camel rider spread out his hands, elbows bent, palms upwards. Then raising his eyes to Heaven, he called out three times, "O God, You are witness. O God, You are witness. O God, You are witness." There was a momentary silence, then a tall gaunt negro began to chant the call to prayer.

The ageing Prophet had chosen this day of pilgrimage to bid farewell to his people. Three months later, his mission completed, he was dead. Fired with the wild enthusiasm of the new faith, his followers poured out of their deserts, bent on conquering the world for God.

*   *   *

The peninsula of Arabia is surrounded on three sides by water, the Red Sea on the west, the Persian Gulf on the east and the Arabian Sea on the south. It consists of a range of mountains extending down the whole eastern side of the Red Sea, and two-thirds of the way up the southern coast from Aden in the direction of Muscat. The Hejaz mountains are extended northwards, up through modern Jordan, Syria and Lebanon, at the eastern end of the Mediterranean.

Rain can reach Arabia from either of two directions. Firstly, from the Atlantic and the Mediterranean, from November to March, when moist winds blow in from the west. Secondly, from the monsoon winds which blow northwards from the Indian Ocean on to the southern coasts of Arabia. Unfortunately, however, the mountains of Syria, Lebanon, Jordan and Palestine, which face the Mediterranean, arrest the great majority of the rain coming from that direction, while the mountains of South Arabia stop the rain-laden monsoons which blow in from the Indian Ocean.

As a result of these ramparts of mountains on the west and south, little rain penetrates to the interior of the peninsula, the greater part of which is desert or semi-desert. On the east, it is true, the land slopes gradually down to the valley of the Euphrates and the Persian Gulf. There are no mountain ranges on the eastern side of the peninsula but this fact does not assist the climate, for no moisture-laden winds come from the east.

On the west, the mountains of the Hejaz rise steeply from the Red Sea, leaving only a narrow coastal plain. A hundred miles inland, the altitude averages between two thousand and three thousand feet with peaks rising to five or six thousand. At a hundred and fifty miles inland, the average altitude is some four thousand feet. Thereafter, for a further three hundred and fifty miles, the country consists of the high plateau known as Nejed, which ultimately slopes gradually down to the shores of the Persian Gulf.

The mountain barriers which arrest the rain-bearing winds from the Mediterranean and the Indian Ocean have made the rainfall of the peninsula inadequate for agriculture. This, however, does not mean that it consists entirely of vast sand dunes. There are only two

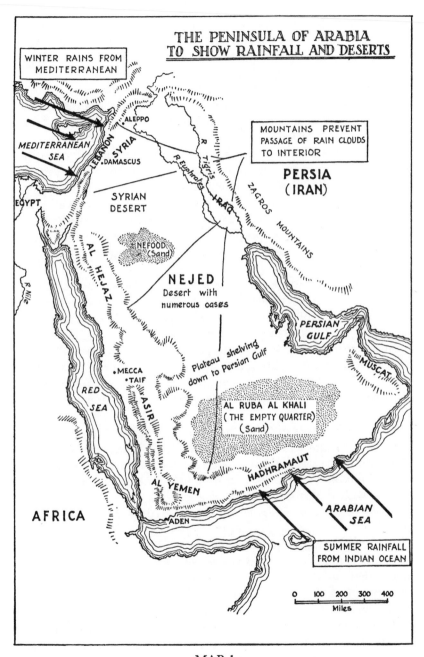

THE PENINSULA OF ARABIA
TO SHOW RAINFALL AND DESERTS

WINTER RAINS FROM
MEDITERRANEAN

MOUNTAINS PREVENT
PASSAGE OF RAIN CLOUDS
TO INTERIOR

ALEPPO

MEDITERRANEAN
SEA

LEBANON
SYRIA
DAMASCUS

R Tigris
R Euphrates
IRAQ

PERSIA
(IRAN)

ZAGROS MOUNTAINS

EGYPT

SYRIAN
DESERT

AL HEJAZ

NEFOOD
(Sand)

NEJED
Desert with
numerous oases

R. Nile

Plateau shelving
down to Persian Gulf

PERSIAN
GULF

MUSCAT

MECCA
TAIF

RED
SEA

ASIR

AL RUBA AL KHALI
(THE EMPTY QUARTER)
(Sand)

AFRICA

AL YEMEN

HADHRAMAUT

ARABIAN
SEA

ADEN

SUMMER RAINFALL
FROM INDIAN OCEAN

0   100   200   300   400
Miles

MAP 1

such areas in Arabia, the Nefood in the north and the Ruba al Khali, the Empty Quarter, in the south. The heart of the peninsula, known as Nejed, is sprinkled with towns, oases and gardens of date-palms, and diversified by local ranges of mountains.

In the north, the desert continues in a triangular-shaped area, known as the Syrian Desert. The apex of the triangle falls just east of Aleppo. This Syrian desert effectively separates the settled areas of Syria from those of Iraq.

In spite of the paucity of the rainfall, there is a considerable quantity of sub-soil water in the peninsula, some breaking out on the surface in springs, in other places near enough to ground level to be drawn up out of wells. The existence of this water allows the cultivation of scattered oases all over Arabia, except in the Nefood and the Ruba al Khali sand deserts. The people of these oases live partly on agriculture, particularly date-palms, partly on domestic animals and partly on commerce.

The great open spaces which separate the oases consist mostly of rolling country, diversified here and there by outcrops of bare mountains, resembling the scenery of Arizona or New Mexico. The surface of the country is covered with many varieties of small thirst resisting bushes and scrub. Whenever a shower of rain does fall, grass and flowers spring to life, painting the fawn-coloured face of the country a pale green shade. When the spring passes into summer, the grass quickly fades and the desert once more resumes its normal beige tint.

These wide spaces dividing the oases were peopled in the seventh century of our era by nomadic tribes, living in black tents woven by their own women from the hair of their goats. The tribal people lived on the milk of their flocks, and on dates, flour or rice which they bought with the proceeds of the sale of their animals, or their by-products of wool or oil. Their herds consisted of camels, sheep and goats.

The variable nature of the rainfall compelled breeders of livestock to follow a nomadic life. So sparse was the grazing, even in good years, that all the grass within reach of any one camp-site was consumed in a few days. Then the tents were struck and the tribes moved on to some area of virgin grazing, discovered by the scouts who had meanwhile been sent out to reconnoitre for another camp.

Each tribe moved normally in a certain recognised area but the wide variations in rainfall made rigid boundaries impractical. Sometimes the annual rains would miss the whole area of a certain tribe, which would be compelled to move in search of grass, perhaps for many hundreds of miles, to the country normally occupied by another tribe. This wandering existence inevitably produced clashes and rivalries between different tribes.

These nomadic battles had occurred from time immemorial and were accepted unquestioningly by the tribes as part of life. Hostilities normally took the form of raids on one another's flocks, until the accidents of grazing and rainfall caused the rivals once more to drift apart. Such wars produced little hatred—nothing certainly to compare with the national rivalries of modern "civilised" nations. Indeed, all nomads regarded themselves as the élite of mankind, treating one another as gentlemen and looking down with contempt on the less hardy breeds of men, who lived in houses and slept in beds at night.

The fertile lands of the north, Egypt, Syria and Iraq, had been endlessly conquered by military invaders of differing ethnic origins, who subsequently settled down and intermarried with their predecessors. As a result, the populations of these countries were ethnically of extremely mixed descent, Aryan, Semitic, African, Turkish or Greek. No invaders, however, had ever been tempted to conquer the desert wastes of Arabia, the inhabitants of which consequently belonged to an ancient and almost unmixed ethnic stock.

Largely cut off from the outside world, this ancient Arab race had evolved a culture of its own. Standing all day watching animals grazing in the vast expanses of the desert was doubtless a monotonous existence. Tribal wars provided the glamour otherwise lacking in their lives. No nomadic tribe waged war in the hope of inflicting any great injury on the enemy, but rather with the object of acquiring glory for itself, by excelling its rivals in courage and endurance.

This pursuit of glory made it necessary to observe certain rules of honour. Treachery, for example, was regarded as shameful. Indeed, two hostile tribes sometimes agreed mutually on the date and place of a battle, weeks or months ahead, to ensure that neither side secured an unfair advantage. In brief, the principal object of warring tribes was honour rather than victory. They had no desire for a "victorious peace", which would have deprived their hard and monotonous lives of glamour and excitement.

To the nomadic bedouin, the sister of honour was poetry. Gifted with ample leisure and a sonorous language, they delighted in the endless composition and recitation of poems, celebrating their own exploits and the deeds of their heroes.

Next to prowess in war, the heroic virtues admired by the tribes and celebrated in their verse were unstinting generosity, lavish hospitality and protection of the weak. Hospitality was doubtless an essential part of desert life. No traveller could ever have crossed the desert at all, if he had been unable to reckon on the hospitality of the nomad tents which were scattered here and there over these vast spaces. But the nomad character was never utilitarian. As in war, so in hospitality, he sought to win fame, glory and the praise of poets by the lavish scale of his entertainment.

The extreme poverty of desert Arabia had never made it feasible to establish a stable government. The absence of such amenities as police, laws and judges, which we accept as a matter of course, left the weak constantly exposed to the outrages of those stronger than themselves. Within the tribe, a democratic community in which all were partners, the weaker members were cared for by the stronger as a matter of course. But when a man, or even more a woman, was for some reason separated from his or her tribe, the individual was at the mercy of the first comer.

It was doubtless this problem which gave rise to the nomad's honourable pride in the protection of the weak. The lonely, the stranger or the oppressed had only to appeal to the nearest tribesman for assistance. The man, or even the woman, thus accosted was obliged to give it. Even if he had no idea of the identity of the person whom he was defending, honour obliged him to save the life and the property of his protégé, if necessary by sacrificing his own.

Another result of the absence of government, less obviously bene-volent than hospitality and protection of the weak, was the blood-feud. If no such institution had existed, a strong man could have killed anybody whom he disliked or whose property he coveted. According to the custom of the blood-feud, however, any member of the victim's family was entitled to kill in retaliation the murderer himself or any member of his family. Thus the murderer, however strong in body and skilled in arms, went in perpetual fear of his life. The feud could eventually be compounded by the payment of heavy compensation, but only if the family of the victim agreed. Should the relatives reject compensation, they had a right to maintain the feud until they had killed their man.

Moreover, although war was carried on in a chivalrous manner, no rules governed the method of obtaining revenge for blood. If such satisfaction had been commonly settled, let us say, by single combat, an accomplished swordsman would always have won and the weak could never have obtained redress. But, according to the rules of the blood-feud, no restrictions were placed on the means used in obtaining revenge for blood. The murderer, or one of his relatives, could be killed in his sleep, by stealth or by a trick.

If the feud had always resulted in the killing of one man in exchange for another and had then come to an end, a certain rough justice would have been applied. But, in fact, the original murderer would sometimes fight back and kill the would-be avenger, thereby committing a double murder. Or the bystanders might join in and some of them be killed also. At times, a member of an entirely different family would be killed by accident, giving rise to a second and independent blood-feud. In tribal warfare, little hatred was felt against a rival tribe, and indeed it was considered honourable to pay a compliment to their gallantry. But the blood-feud gave rise to the bitterest hatreds and to deeds of heartless brutality.

The virtues required of the bedouin cavalier, therefore, were bravery and endurance in war, generosity, hospitality and protection of the weak in peace. These qualities were later to be carried by them to Spain, France and Sicily and to lay the foundation of the mediaeval chivalry of Europe. In one respect, however, the Arab knight differed from our concept of chivalry—he did not aspire to be gentle.

On the contrary, he prided himself on the fact that he avenged every insult or injury with interest, especially in the event of a blood-feud. To be slow to take vengeance would expose him to contempt and dishonour. The abandonment of revenge was an idea which we owe principally to Christianity. The ancient Greeks held the same view as the Arabs, namely, that it was the duty of a good man "to be sweet to friends and bitter to enemies, honourable to the first and terrible to the latter".

"The man of men is he who thinks early and late how he can injure his enemies and do his friends good."[1]

Bedouin gallantry[2] was not mere savagery but a highly organised system, obviously old and well developed. Justice and right were familiar ideas, supported by an elaborate legal system.[3]

---

[1] From the *Hamasa*, quoted by Goldziher, *Muslim Studies*.

[2] The Arabic word is *muruwwa*.

[3] Compare Goldziher, *Muslim Studies*.

The seal of bedouin glory was poetry, endlessly recited in their sonorous language in long rolling verse. The poems dealt chiefly with war, generosity and hospitality, but at times it touched also on love and romance. The bedouin women were free and unveiled and romantic courtship was a recognised institution. In the sixth century bedouin women enjoyed considerable freedom. Young widows, for example, lived in their own tents, where they received suitors as they felt inclined.

*   *   *

While nomadic tribesmen of this nature formed the majority of the inhabitants of Arabia, we have already seen that the peninsula was dotted with oases, which supported a settled population. The town and village dwellers doubtless belonged to the same ancient Arab race[4] as the nomad bedouins, though their manner of life had modified their customs.

Oasis dwellers could be divided into two categories, farmers and merchants. The farmers were chiefly engaged in growing date-palms, dates being a staple food of the bedouins. Beneath the palms secondary crops were raised, small fruit, certain vegetables or fodder for domestic animals. Small quantities of grain were also grown and Taif was famous for its grapes. As all cultivated land was irrigated, usually by water hoisted up from wells, only restricted areas could be brought under cultivation

The cultivators did not normally take part in tribal wars or in raiding. Their laborious lives were spent in extracting a livelihood from the soil. On the other hand, if their settlement were attacked, they would defend it with more obstinacy than the bedouins normaally showed in their battles.

The cultivators, like all the people of the peninsula, were hospitable to travellers and guests, but they normally supplied such meals as were needed, rather than the princely banquets from which the bedouins sought glory. In other words, the cultivators were steady, hardworking people, who watched their income and their expenditure, and observed the laws of generosity and hospitality in a sensible rather than in a glamorous manner. Most of the cultivators lived in

[4] I use the word race as it is defined in the Oxford Dictionary, "a group of persons connected by common descent, regarded as of a common stock". I do not use it in the sense of "a cultural group", as is now sometimes done.

tribes and families and all observed the tradition of the blood-feud in the same way as the nomads.

The other group of oasis dwellers was that of the merchants. The two occupations were not, of course, divided by any hard and fast line. A merchant might own gardens and fields, or a cultivator might occasionally indulge in a commercial venture. Members of the same family might follow one occupation or the other.

Small-scale traders from the oases would visit the nomadic tribes, buy wool, butter,[5] goat-hair or animals on the hoof, and sell small articles to the tribesmen. The more substantial merchants, however, were connected with the transit trade across Arabia to the countries lying beyond the borders of the peninsula, a subject which will be dealt with in a later chapter.

All commercial transactions involved travelling across the desert from one oasis to another or beyond the limits of the peninsula to Egypt, Syria or Persia. The livelihood of the merchant, therefore, depended on the security of travel across the desert where the bedouins were camped. A regular system existed to ensure the security of commerce.

In the absence of any government or central authority, each tribe was a law to itself and acted like an independent nation. The tribes, however, stood in need of the merchants, who imported various articles which they required, including weapons, armour and clothing. The merchants likewise bought camels from the tribes and engaged men to accompany their caravans.

When a merchant wished to take a caravan across the desert, he approached the chiefs of the tribes through whose territory he was to pass. Each tribal chief received a gift or an agreed sum, in return for which he guaranteed the caravan from attack by any member of his tribe. Normally he sent a man of the tribe to accompany the caravan and to warn potential aggressors that it was under his protection. If, after such a warning, marauders plundered the caravan, they had insulted the chief, who would pursue them with all the means at his disposal. Each chief, however, would only be able to give protection from his own tribesmen. Thus a caravan going on a long journey might be obliged to negotiate for its safe passage with six or eight different chiefs, whose tribes might be camped near the route which the caravan was to take.

This procedure seems at first somewhat cumbrous. In fact, how-

---

[5] Arabs made butter from sheep's and goat's milk.

ever, merchants who regularly operated caravans on certain routes
were well acquainted with the tribes and chiefs who camped in the
areas to be crossed. They had standing arrangements with them for
the safe passage of caravans and the payment of the agreed dues to
the tribes.

Before Islam,[6] three months of the year were "sacred", and during
them no raiding or fighting was legitimate. The first of the sacred
months was Rejeb, the seventh month in the Arab lunar year. The
other two were Dhu al Qaada and Dhu al Hajja, the eleventh and
twelfth months of the calendar. Some authorities, however, believe
that there were four sacred months and add to the list Muharram,
the month following Dhu al Hajja and the first of the new year.
These months provided additional security for caravans and merchandise. The sacred months, however, were insufficient to allow free
play to commerce, and, as we shall see, the protection and the
plundering of caravans played a large part in the politics of the
tribes and of the people of Arabia.

*   *   *

A few examples may serve to illustrate the bedouin way of life in
the sixth century better than an abstract description of their customs.

Duraid ibn al Simma was a famous warrior and poet, who lived
into Muslim times as a very old man. One day, when he was still
young, he was leading a raiding party against Beni Kinana. Topping
a pass in the bare mountains of the Hejaz, he saw in an open valley
beneath him a horseman, lance in hand, leading by its headrope a
camel, on which a woman was mounted.

Duraid called up one of his men and told him to overtake the lone
rider and shout to him to leave the woman and the camel and to
escape for his life, as a raiding party was coming down the pass. The
man galloped down into the plain, calling out as he had been
instructed. The rider, however, quietly handed the headrope to the
girl, wheeled his horse, galloped straight back at his pursuer and,
running him through with his lance, flung him violently from the
saddle. Then, cantering after the lady, he took the headrope from
her hands, and the two rode quietly on at a walking pace, as if
nothing had happened.

[6] The name of the religion preached by Muhammad is Islam, or surrender (to God).
A Muslim (vulgarly Moslem) is a person professing the religion of Islam.

As Duraid rode down the pass with the remainder of the raiding party, he lost from sight the two figures of the man and the woman, riding along together on the plain below. As, however, his messenger did not return, he sent after him another horseman, with whom the lone rider dealt in the same manner. Duraid followed him with a third who met the same fate, but on this occasion the lone horseman's lance broke in his hand at the moment of impact. Though he was now unarmed, he once again overtook the lady and the pair rode on quietly together.

As they rode side by side, the rider recited the following verses to his lady.

> Ride on in peace, my lady fair,
> Secure and safe and calm.
> Be confident and debonair
> And free from all alarm.
> I cannot flee before a foe
> Except he taste my arm,
> The boldness of my charge he'll know
> Who seeks to do thee harm.
>
> Horsemen, turn back! Allow my love
> To ride on undisturbed,
> Rabia stands 'twixt you and her
> With visage unperturbed.
> His hand grips firm his shining lance
> Which will not be deterred,
> A wound from it will cast thee down
> To die without a word.

Mystified by the disappearance of his three messengers, Duraid himself galloped out on to the plain. He came upon the body of his first messenger, then that of the second and that of the third. In front of him he could see the horseman, unarmed, riding quietly at a walking pace, leading the lady's camel by its headrope.

Duraid, full of admiration for so gallant a cavalier, even though an enemy, rode up to him and cried, "O horseman, such a man as you does not deserve death. But my men are just behind me, and you are unarmed. Take my lance, my friend, and I will see that my men do not pursue you."

Galloping back to his followers, he told them that the lone cavalier had killed his three messengers and that his lance had broken in the shock of the last encounter. "No one else is to pursue him," he ordered. Duraid subsequently composed some verses to celebrate the fame of this gallant enemy.

> Ne'er have I seen so bold a knight,
> He well his lady served.
> A man 'gainst odds so quick to fight,
> Dark death has not deserved.
> Our horsemen fell before his might,
> Our bravest were unnerved,
> He, calm, rejoined his lady fair
> And rode on undisturbed.

The lone horseman was Rabia ibn al Muqaddam of Beni Kinana and the girl was his young wife, Raita.

Some months later, Rabia was killed by an arrow when riding against Beni Sulaim. Not long after a raiding party, which included Duraid ibn al Simma, was captured by Beni Kinana and taken to their tents. As they were led into the camp, a girl suddenly ran out of one of the tents and threw her cloak over Duraid. "O men!" she cried, "this man is under my protection. He is the one who gave his lance to Rabia, when he was unarmed in enemy country." It was Raita, the widow of Rabia, who was repaying one gallant action by another.

*   *   *

One of the most famous bedouin personalities in the years immediately preceding Islam was Hatim ibn Abdulla of the tribe of Tai. Hatim was an orphan brought up by his grandfather. As soon as he was of age and inherited his father's flocks, he slaughtered so many animals for his guests that he soon found himself a poor man. One day, when visited by three men, he killed three camels for their dinner. It so happened that the three men were famous poets and one of them, Nabigha al Dhobiani, immediately improvised a poem in praise of their young host and his tribe.

"My idea was to do a kindness to you," said Hatim, "but your poem has put me in your debt." Whereupon he insisted that the poets accept as a gift all the camels in his possession.

Soon afterwards, his grandfather hastened to the scene and asked indignantly what had become of his camels. "I gave them away," Hatim replied. "If I had kept them, they would all have been dead in twenty years. But in exchange for them, I have won a poem in praise of our family, which will pass on from mouth to mouth until the end of time."

A reference to the generosity of Hatim is found in *The Rubaiyat* of Omar Khayyam. Urging his lady to forget the famous ones of this world, Omar sings:

> But come with old Khayyam and leave the lot
> Of Kaikobad and Kaikhosra forget;
> Let Rustum lay about him as he will,
> Or Hatim Tai cry 'supper!'—heed them not.

A refinement of bedouin hospitality, still practised, is for the host to stand in front of his tent at the time of the evening meal and call at the top of his voice, "Supper! Supper! Let all come and eat! Anyone who has not yet dined—let him come now!" It is this custom to which Omar Khayyam refers.

Perhaps the most remarkable feature in the character of Hatim was that he is alleged to have vowed never to kill a man. In an age of bloodshed and violence, he was a famous raider, but he always unhorsed or disarmed his opponent without killing him. When he took prisoners, he released them without ransom.[7] Indeed, he had so great a horror of captivity, that whenever he heard of a man who was anywhere being held for ransom, even if he were an enemy, he invaribly paid the sum required of him and sent him back to his home.

Such were the tribesmen of Arabia, who were to form the raw material of Islam. Brave, hardy and enterprising, their battles were often fought in a spirit of chivalry, which they were subsequently to carry to the nations they conquered, from Spain to India. But if their battles were chivalrous, their blood-feuds were savage and ruthless. No sense of generosity or fair play restrained the brutal actions of the avenger of blood.

To such lavish excesses of hospitality and generosity did they give way, that their most famous heroes were always poor. The corollary of this fantastic liberality was ardour for plunder and their lives were

[7] The practice of taking men or women prisoners has now long been abandoned by bedouin raiders.

spent in feats of arms devoted to the looting of the flocks of their enemies, which had no sooner been seized than they were slaughtered or given away.

The crown and seal of their way of life was poetry. Often boastful and bombastic, their verse occasionally breathed a surprising spirit of tenderness and love. The following lines were taken from the *Ode of Antar ibn Sheddad*, which won a prize at the Fair of Ukadh near Mecca, shortly before Muhammad began to preach. The story of Antar and Abla is one of the best known folk romances of early Arabia. The lovers were of the tribe of Abs, a branch of Ghatafan, which will be frequently encountered in this narrative.

It is perhaps a pity that Wilfrid Blunt used blank verse for his translation. The original was, of course, in splendid, sonorous Arabic rhyme, the sound of which might be impossible to reproduce in English.

Truly at first sight I loved her, I who had slain her kin,
Ay, by the life of thy father, not in inconstancy.
Love, thou hast taken possession! Deem it not otherwise!
Thou in my heart art the first one. First in nobility . . .
Then was it Abla enslaved thee showing her tenderness,
White teeth with lips for the kissing. Sweet was the taste of them,
Sweet as the vials of odours sold by the musk sellers,
Fragrant the white teeth she showed thee, fragrant the mouth of her.
So is a garden new planted fresh in its greenery,
Watered by soft-falling raindrops, treadless, untenanted.
Lo, on it rain-clouds have lighted, soft showers (no hail in them),
Leaving each furrow a lakelet bright as a silverling.
Pattering, plashing, they fell there, rains at the sunsetting,
Wide-spreading runlets of water, streams of fertility,
Mixed with the humming of bees' wings droning the daylight long,
Never a pause in their chaunting their gay drinking-choruses.
Though thou thy fair face concealest still in thy veil from me,
Yet am I he that hath captured horse-riders how many!
Give me the praise of my fair deeds. Lady, thou knowest it,
Kindly am I and forbearing, save when wrong presseth me.[8]

*   *   *

[8] Wilfrid Scawen Blunt, *The Ode of Antar*.

The tribes of Arabia before the preaching of Islam are commonly said to have been idolaters. It is, in a sense, unfortunate that the great monotheistic religions, Judaism, Christianity and Islam, all treated idolatry with extreme contempt. To the early preachers of monotheism, idolatry was a real danger and they were not prepared to tolerate any explanations of its possible significance.

In reading of the Arabs before Islam, we are impressed by the fact that many of them were as wise and as reasonable as we are today. It is, as a result, difficult to believe that they can have been so naïve as to worship a stone image made by men, or a natural tree, growing by a well in a mountain valley. In general, the Arabs probably admitted the existence of a supreme God, but they also believed in many spirits, some of which were closely associated with certain localities, such as wells, springs or trees.

Thus it was probably not the well or tree which was worshipped, but the invisible spirit which resided there. It seems possible that the production of stone idols may have been a later development. Perhaps persons who had prayed at the spring or beneath the tree wished for some pious object to carry away with them. Most of the leading families in Mecca before Islam seem to have had small household gods in their homes.

It is interesting that, in some, if not in all, cases of Arabian idolatry, public idols do not seem to have been modelled like human beings, as were those of Greece and Rome. Yet this could scarcely be solely due to lack of skill. In the Yemen, for example, the idols seem to have been almost formless slabs of rock, at a time when the people were highly skilled in architecture, engineering and other arts. Possibly the idol was intentionally rough-hewn, in order not to be like anything living. Idolators in all ages have denied that they worshipped an image made with hands, but have claimed that they prayed to the spirit which dwelt in it.

The Arabic language distinguishes between a monolithic stone, believed to be the abode of a deity, and an idol, which is the carved representation of a living creature.[9] Ibn Hisham states that idolatry, that is the use of stone images carved to resemble human beings, was only introduced to Mecca from Syria in Muhammad's lifetime. Indeed, the Muslim historians do not refer to the unbelieving Arabs as idolaters but as "associaters", persons who associate these local spirits with God.

[9] De Lacy O'Leary, *Arabia before Muhammad.*

In any case, in any religion, worshippers differ widely from one another in their mental conceptions. Doubtless the more simple believed the block of stone to contain magic powers, while the more sophisticated worshippers prayed to the invisible spirit, which perhaps dwelt in the tree or stone. Certainly many Arabs believed that a blessing could be obtained by kissing, touching, or rubbing a sacred object.

It is, incidentally, worthy of note that religions of this kind have often been compatible with very high standards of culture. The philosophy of Plato, studied for centuries by pious Christians, was produced under polytheism. Suetonius tells us that Augustus, having lost some ships in a storm, revenged himself on Neptune by refusing to allow his statue to be carried in procession with those of the other gods at the public games. Yet, for centuries, a polite education in Christian Europe involved profound and reverent study of the age of Augustus.

*   *   *

In 330, some three centuries before Muhammad, Christianity had, for the first time, been officially tolerated in the Roman Empire. The conversion of the Arabs of the Syrian desert began at about the same time. In 375, Christianity became the state religion of the Roman Empire.

Although most of the Arab tribes of the Syrian desert became nominal Christians, however, their new religion seems to have been little more than skin deep. It was doubtless difficult for a people who held such strong views on the honourable duty of revenge to absorb the spirit of a religion which commanded them to love their enemies and to turn the other cheek to aggressors.

Unfortunately, in 420, a monk called Nestorius preached a new interpretation of the Incarnation, which was condemned as heretical by the Council of Ephesus in 431. As a result, the Nestorian Christians migrated in considerable numbers to Persia, where they established themselves chiefly in the Euphrates valley as far south as the head of the Persian Gulf.

A few years later, another monk, called Eutyches, preached another interpretation, which was condemned by the Council of Chalcedon in 451. The followers of Eutyches were known as Monophysites. The majority of the people of Egypt and eastern Syria became

Monophysites, the official faith of the Byzantine Empire being the Orthodox.

Judaism was also widely scattered. Iraq had retained a considerable Israelite population since the Babylonian captivity, some six centuries before Christ. Many of the oases of the western side of Arabia held communities who practised Judaism, though these appear to have been converted Arabs rather than descendants of the Children of Israel.

In brief, in the sixth century after Christ, the majority of the people of Arabia were still pagans, but monotheism was spreading steadily. The time was ripe for the Arabs to abandon their superstitions in favour of a more spiritual and monotheistic conception of God.

II

Kings of Arabia

Petra rose, along with her dependencies, to an incredible opu-
lence . . . Pliny and Strabo both describe the city. Athenodoras
the Stoic visited it, and related with admiration to Strabo his
friend the excellence of the government under a native prince,
and the security with which Romans and other foreigners resided
there. It need hardly be added that this prosperity was entirely
dependent on the caravan trade.

SIR WILLIAM MUIR, *Life of Mahomet*

Arabia in pre-Islamic times was not so self-centred nor so self-
contained, indeed to a great measure its later segregation seems
largely due to the influences of Islam . . . Consequently the
religion of Islam was not evolved amongst remote tribes with
only very slight contact with the outside world, but in the midst of
the general tide of West Asiatic civilisation.

DE LACY O'LEARY, *Arabia before Muhammad*

For some centuries before the appearance of Islam the central
factor in politics . . . was the constant warfare between the
empires of Persia and Byzantium, and this, to a large extent, was
fought out in Arabia. The products of India and further Asia as
well as those of Arabia itself had become necessary to Byzantium
and thus Persia was able to bring economic pressure to bear and
to do this more effectively endeavoured to secure a strong hold
. . . on South Arabia . . . to cut off Oriental products from the
Byzantine markets.

DE LACY O'LEARY, *Arabia before Muhammad*

The collective consciousness of ancient bedouin Arabia revolted
with all its strength against the alternative to the tribal bond,
namely "kingship, the supertribal tyranny of one man".

FRANCESCO GABRIELI, *Muhammad and the
Conquests of Islam*

FROM before the dawn of written history, some three thousand years before Christ, the most advanced civilisations of the world had bordered upon Arabia.[1] The Pharaohs of Egypt, the Assyrians, the Babylonians and the ancient Persians all established empires on the northern borders of Arabia, and the Arab tribes of those days must have been familiar with them.

In 330 B.C., Alexander the Great destroyed the Persian Empire. Thereafter, for some two hundred and seventy years, the countries bordering on Arabia on the north were largely Hellenised. In 64 B.C., the Romans, under the great Pompey, arrived in Syria and Palestine. For the ensuing seven hundred years, Egypt, Palestine and Syria were to remain Roman.

When, therefore, we endeavour to reconstruct the edifice of Arabian society when Muhammad was born in A.D. 570, we have, on the one hand, to consider the tribes already described in the previous chapter. At the same time, however, we must take account of the profound effect produced on the customs and thought of the Arabians by their thousands of years of proximity to, and intercourse with, the most advanced cultures of the ancient world.

Nomadism is a formidable obstacle to cultural progress owing to the practical impossibility of transporting books[2] on camelback or of protecting them in tents. As a result, nearly all bedouins were illiterate, although they cultivated such arts as eloquence and poetry by memory. But in many settled areas on the fringes of Arabia, advanced urban communities existed, ruled by wealthy and powerful dynasties. Some of these Arab states were familiar with the cultures of Greece, Rome and Persia, and, in the centuries before Islam, had already adopted Christianity or Judaism.

Thus, when Muhammad began to preach at the commencement of the seventh century after Christ, the various communities of the Arabic-speaking world differed profoundly from one another. In these days of universal compulsory education, we unthinkingly are

[1] I omit reference to China, which produced its own culture, largely separated from our Western world.

[2] "Books" in the seventh century of course took the form of scrolls, not bound books as we know them.

inclined to expect all the classes of a given people to be at cultural levels not too profoundly separated from one another. That this is a modern development will be realised by a momentary consideration, for example, of eighteenth-century England, "the Age of Reason". Such intellectual giants as Hume, Edward Gibbon, Dr. Johnson, or Sir Isaac Newton lived at a time when the majority of Englishmen could not read or write.

Some indication of the spirit and customs of the tribes having been given in the preceding chapter, a brief description of the cultural and urban communities of Arabia must now be included, under the form of an outline history of the Arab states up to the seventh century A.D.

*   *   *

The earliest organised governments in the peninsula of Arabia seem to have been in the Yemen, and were known firstly as the Minaeans and then as the Sabaeans. The former, of whom our information is scanty, appear to have ruled from about 1500 B.C. to perhaps, 700 B.C. The Minaean inscriptions which have survived depict them as a developed and well organised dynasty. The Minaeans were replaced in about 700 B.C. by the Sabaeans. The Queen of Sheba, who visited King Solomon in about 950 B.C., is believed to have been the ruler of the Sabaeans, although she seems to have lived before her dynasty conquered the Minaeans.

The early wealth and culture of the Yemen was derived from two sources. Of these the first was the cultivation and the export of frankincense and spices. The Pharaohs, the Assyrians, the Babylonians and the ancient Persians all appear to have used incense for their temple worship. The Minaeans had trading posts in the northern Hejaz and Syria for the export of incense.

The second source of the wealth of the Yemen was the transit trade from India, Indonesia and east Africa. Ships from these countries landed the products of the East at Aden, where they were bought by south Arabian merchants and transported by camel caravan to Egypt, Syria and Persia. It is not possible to fix a date for the commencement of the oriental trade. Probably the early Minaeans, about 1500 B.C., lived principally on the export of their own incense and spices. There are traces of an increasing build-up of the oriental transit trade after 600 B.C.

About 315 B.C., an Arab trading people called the Nabataeans had

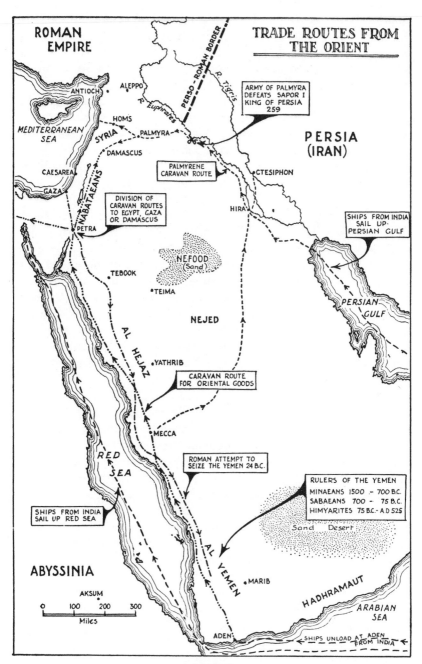

ROMAN
EMPIRE

TRADE ROUTES FROM
THE ORIENT

PERSO-ROMAN BORDER

R. Tigris

R. Euphrates

ALEPPO

ANTIOCH

MEDITERRANEAN
SEA

HOMS

SYRIA

PALMYRA

ARMY OF PALMYRA
DEFEATS SAPOR I
KING OF PERSIA
259

PERSIA
(IRAN)

DAMASCUS

PALMYRENE
CARAVAN ROUTE

CTESIPHON

CAESAREA

NABATAEANS

GAZA

HIRA

PETRA

DIVISION OF
CARAVAN ROUTES
TO EGYPT, GAZA
OR DAMASCUS

SHIPS FROM INDIA
SAIL UP
PERSIAN GULF

NEFOOD
(Sand)

TEBOOK

TEIMA

NEJED

PERSIAN
GULF

AL HEJAZ

YATHRIB

CARAVAN ROUTE
FOR ORIENTAL GOODS

RED
SEA

MECCA

ROMAN ATTEMPT TO
SEIZE THE YEMEN 24 B.C.

RULERS OF THE YEMEN
MINAEANS 1500 – 700 B.C.
SABAEANS 700 – 75 B.C.
HIMYARITES 75 B.C.- A.D 525

Sand   Desert

SHIPS FROM INDIA
SAIL UP RED SEA

AL YEMEN

ABYSSINIA

AKSUM

0   100   200   300
Miles

MARIB

HADHRAMAUT

ARABIAN
SEA

ADEN

SHIPS UNLOAD AT ADEN
FROM INDIA

MAP 2

appeared in the north. Their capital was at Petra in southern Jordan. The exact form of commercial relations between the Sabaeans and the Nabataeans is not known. Perhaps the Sabaean merchants handed over their caravans to the Nabataeans at one of the oases in the northern Hejaz.

Both the Minaeans and then the Sabaeans passed away and were succeeded by the Himyarites. The first Himyarite king recorded was a certain Al Harith, who was reigning about 75 B.C. Later Himyarite kings of the Yemen extended their suzerainty over Central Arabia or Nejed, and even invaded Persia. In 24 B.C., in the reign of the Emperor Augustus, the Romans sent an expeditionary force under Aelius Gallus to conquer the Yemen. It marched down the eastern shore of the Red Sea, suffering intensely from heat, thirst and exhaustion. Although it reached the Yemen and survivors returned, the enterprise ended in fiasco and was never repeated.

According to tradition, the irrigation of the Yemen depended on a dam built at Marib, a place mentioned by Strabo and Pliny as Mariaba. About A.D. 120, the dam is alleged to have collapsed, a disaster which gave rise to a large-scale emigration of tribes from the Yemen to the northern parts of the peninsula. It does not, however, appear to have destroyed the prosperous economy of the Yemen, which perhaps was relying more and more on the transit trade.

There can be no doubt that the civilisation of the Yemen at this period was well advanced. Agriculture was highly skilled, great care was devoted to irrigation and the hills were systematically terraced and maintained. The Yemenites were extremely competent as masons and erected very tall buildings, constructed of stone so carefully dressed that the joints were scarcely visible.

From A.D. 200 to 236,[3] we read of a Yemenite king called Asad abu Qarib, who is alleged to have conquered all Arabia up to the Euphrates. During his campaigns, he captured Yathrib,[4] an oasis in the Hejaz, many of the inhabitants of which professed Judaism. Asad was deeply impressed with Jewish monotheism, and took two rabbis with him back to the Yemen. As a result, he and many of his subjects renounced idolatry and adopted Judaism.

*   *   *

[3] Hereafter the use of B.C. and A.D. will be discontinued. All dates will be A.D. unless otherwise stated.

[4] Map 2, page 43.

Mention has already been made of another civilised, commercial state, that of the Nabataeans with their capital in Petra, where the caravan route from the Yemen divided into three. One road turned westwards to Egypt, another led to the port of Gaza, a third to Damascus.

The Nabataeans first appear in history about three hundred years before Christ, possibly at a time of confusion in the Yemen. They grew rich and luxurious by handling the oriental trade. For some centuries they controlled the eastern part of Syria, including the ancient and sophisticated city of Damascus, and were in intimate relations with the Romans. In 106, the Nabataean kingdom was abolished by the soldier-emperor Trajan, and its territories annexed to the Roman Empire as the province of Arabia Petraea.

With the destruction of the Arab Nabataean kingdom, the eastern trade route from the Yemen seems to have languished. The Nabataeans had been in the habit of going down into the Hejaz, perhaps to the Yemen, to bring up the oriental merchandise on their camels, a task of which the Romans themselves were incapable.

Another Arab oasis, Palmyra, in the Syrian Desert, succeeded to the wealth of Petra. The Palmyrenes descended to the head of the Persian Gulf with their caravans, bought the oriental goods which arrived by sea and transported them to Palmyra, whence they were distributed to Syria and the West.[5]

The first Arab prince of Palmyra of whom we have cognisance appears to have been a certain Udhaina, called by the Romans, Odenathus. He was made phylarch of eastern Syria and the Jezira about 150, in the reign of Marcus Aurelius Antoninus. He was raised to this rank forty-four years after the destruction of Petra by Trajan, a period probably sufficient to allow Palmyra to gain wealth and importance by taking over the trade formerly handled by Petra.

The most famous Odenathus, the great-grandson of the first, received the name of Septimius, probably in acknowledgement of favours received by the family from the Emperor Septimius Severus, who reigned from 193 to 211. The Roman Empire at this time was no longer governed by Italians, but had become a multi-racial Mediterranean state.

For six centuries the happiness and prosperity of northern Syria and the Jezira had been constantly threatened by the endless wars and rivalries of Rome and Persia. In 257, Sapor I, King of Persia, invaded

[5] Map 2, page 43.

Syria, defeated the Roman army and carried away the Emperor Valerian as a prisoner to his capital of Ctesiphon.

Flushed with victory, Sapor returned with a fresh army and occupied Antioch. All this time, Odenathus and his Arabs had remained quietly in their oasis in Palmyra, surrounded by deserts impassable to the Persian army. But when Sapor was returning once more, marching down the valley of the Euphrates, the Arabs of Palmyra suddenly poured down upon his army, threw it into confusion and captured a large part of his plunder,[6] including even some of the wives of the Great King. Moreover, this was no mere tribal frontier incident. Odenathus pursued the Persian King to the gates of Ctesiphon, his capital, and on two occasions laid siege to the city. "The majesty of Rome," writes Gibbon,[7] "oppressed by a Persian, was protected by an Arab of Palmyra." As a reward for these services, the Prince of Palmyra was awarded the title of Augustus and donned the imperial purple in his desert oasis. But the glory of Septimius Odenathus Augustus was short-lived. In 267, he was assassinated by his own nephew in Homs.

His wife, the famous Zenobia,[8] succeeded to his throne and conquered Syria, Asia Minor and Egypt. But a new and capable emperor, the martial Aurelian, had assumed the purple in Rome and had restored discipline throughout the empire. Zenobia was not wise enough to conciliate him in time. Marching on Syria, Aurelian defeated the army of Palmyra at Homs. After a long and difficult siege, the city was taken and the beautiful Zenobia, bound in golden chains, was led through the streets of Rome in Aurelian's triumph.

The impression that the Arabs were mere savages at the time of Muhammad is contradicted by the fact that four Roman Emperors had been Syrians from Homs, and two, Philip the Arabian and Septimius Odenathus, had been Arabs of the desert.

*   *   *

Mention has already been made of the collapse of the great dam of Marib in about A.D. 120 and of the consequent northward migration of a number of Yemenite tribes. One such community, bearing the name of Ghassán,[9] seems to have reached the deserts of Syria about

[6] Map 2, page 43.
[7] Edward Gibbon, *Decline and Fall of the Roman Empire*.
[8] The Arabic name was Zainab.
[9] The nearest approach most English-speaking people can make to the pronunciation of the initial gh is by pronouncing it like r, Rassán.

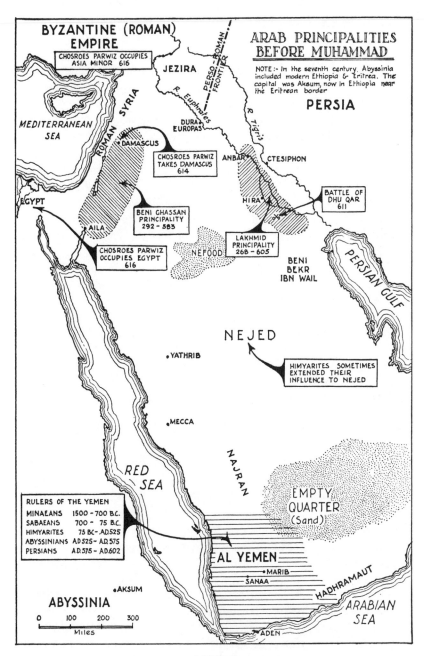

MAP 3

250, when the dynasty of Palmyra was at the height of its glory. The fall of the family of Odenathus was followed by the appointment of other chiefs by the Roman authorities. In about 292, however, Thalaba ibn Amr[10] of Beni Ghassan, was made phylarch of the Arabs of eastern Syria. The family were to retain their prominent position until the Muslim conquest in 636.

At almost the same time as Beni Ghassan arrived in Syria, other Yemenite tribes appeared in the desert west of the lower Euphrates. In 268, Sapor I, King of Persia, appointed a certain Amr ibn Adi, of the tribe of Lakhm, as prince of the Arabs of the deserts west of the Euphrates. Amr the Lakhmid, who ruled from 268 to 288, occupied the Euphrates town of Hira as his capital. Like Beni Ghassan in Syria, the Lakhmids of Hira were to retain their position until a few years before the Muslim conquests in the 630's.

Throught this period, Rome and Persia were to remain constantly in a state of either hot or cold war. In 475, the Western Roman Empire was overrun by barbarians, but the Eastern half continued with its capital in Constantinople. After the separation, the Eastern Roman Empire is often called the Byzantine Empire, though the Byzantines themselves claimed the title of Romans. The frontier between the two empires extended, with a few variations, from Dura Europas on the Euphrates to Armenia and the Caucasus. This imperial border was heavily fortified by both sides but neither empire erected any fortifications along the edge of the deserts of Arabia.

Both adopted the same policy of protecting their southern flanks by the employment of Arab satellite dynasties, Beni Ghassan in Syria under the Romans and the Lakhmids on the Euphrates under Persia. The two Arab dynasties fought one another in the interests of their respective imperial suzerains. These Arab princely dynasties were familiar with the imperial courts of Constantinople and of Ctesiphon, then the capital of Persia. At home, however, their subjects consisted largely of those nomadic tribes already described, to whom something of the culture of Rome and of Persia was transfused through the medium of the courts of the Arab princes.

At the time of the establishment of the Arab dynasties of Beni Ghassan and Lakhm, the Himyarites were at the height of their glory in the Yemen and controlled the greater part of the Arabian peninsula. There were, therefore, after the middle of the third

[10] Caussin de Perceval, *Histoire des Arabes avant l'Islamisme*.

century, three Arab dynasties, the Himyarites in the Yemen, the Lakhmids at Hira and Beni Ghassan in Syria.[11]

A distinguished member of the Lakhmid dynasty was Naaman I, the One-eyed, who ruled from 390 to 418. His reign was brilliant, victorious and wealthy and Hira became a city famous for its culture. The King of Persia, Yezdegird I, sent his son Bahram to the court of Naaman to be brought up and educated, a remarkable tribute to the refinement and politeness of these early Arabs.

On the death of Yezdegird I in 420, while Bahram was still at the court of Hira, another of the king's sons, Chosroes, seized the opportunity afforded by his brother's absence to usurp the throne. But Mundhir I of Hira, who had succeeded his father Naaman I, assumed the rôle of king-maker, marched on Ctesiphon and placed Bahram on the throne of Persia.

Bahram was passionately fond of hunting, a sport he had learned from the desert Arabs who, down to our own times, have always taken great pleasure in their hawks and their greyhounds. Readers of Omar Khayyam will remember his verse:

And Bahram, that great hunter—the wild ass
Stamps o'er his head, and he lies fast asleep.

*　　*　　*

Having told how Beni Ghassan and the Lakhmids established themselves in the north, we must now return once more to the Yemen, where we have already seen that the great Himyarite, Asad abu Qarib, had introduced Judaism. At the beginning of the sixth century, the ruler of the Yemen, Dhu Nuwas, was a fanatical Judaiser. Not long before, a Christian monk from Syria had introduced Christianity to Najrán,[12] thereby rousing the indignation of Dhu Nuwas. The latter, as a result, invaded and conquered Najran. He dug an enormous trench which he filled with burning faggots, and into which he threw the Christians to be burned alive.

A fugitive Christian from Najran reached Constantinople and appealed for help to the Byzantine Emperor, Justin I. The empire was incapable of sending an expeditionary force to the Yemen, but the Emperor wrote to the Christian Emperor of Abyssinia, urging him to avenge the martyrs of Najran. The Abyssinian invasion is thus

[11] Map 3, page 47.　　[12] Map 3, page 47.

ascribed by tradition to religious motives. But South Arabia, as we have seen, was the landfall of the ships bearing the rich Oriental trade to the Byzantine Empire and to the West. It is not impossible that economic interest, in addition to religious obligations, impelled the Abyssinians and the Byzantines to come to the aid of the persecuted Christians of Najran.

In 525, the Abyssinians landed in the Yemen, Dhu Nuwas was killed and the Himyarite dynasty came to an end. The Abyssinians thereupon took over the country, which they were to rule for more than fifty years. The most famous Abyssinian viceroy of the Yemen was Abráha, who governed the country from 537 to 570. In the latter year, he led a military expedition northwards with a view to the capture of Mecca. Once again, tradition ascribes a religious objective. Mecca possessed an important idol temple, whereas Abraha is said to have built a Christian cathedral in his province, to which he hoped to persuade all the Arabs to resort. The later Muslim historians allege that Abraha was about to capture Mecca when his army was attacked by vast flights of birds, which dropped pebbles on the Abyssinian troops. As a result, the army beat a hasty retreat, Abaha himself dying before reaching his headquarters in the Yemen. It has been suggested that an epidemic of smallpox may have caused the withdrawal of the invaders. Tradition relates that Abraha came to Mecca riding on an elephant, with the result that the year 570 was long remembered by the Hejaz Arabs as the Year of the Elephant. It was in this year that our hero, Muhammad, was born.

Abyssinian prestige seems to have been weakened by this military fiasco and the Yemenites grew increasingly rebellious. In 574, Saif dhu al Yazan, a prince of the deposed Himyarite royal family, went to Hira, where he complained to the Lakhmid prince against the tyranny of the Abyssinians. The prince took him to Ctesiphon, to lay his petition before the King of Persia, Chosroes Anushirwan.

The king summoned his councillors to a discussion, but all agreed that the Yemen was too far away and too poor to warrant Persian intervention. Saif dhu al Yazan was given ten thousand silver dirhems and told that the king could not help him. As he left the palace, the Yemenite prince allegedly distributed the ten thousand dirhems in tips to the royal servants. When Chosroes heard of this conduct, he summoned Saif once again to his presence and enquired why he had behaved in such a manner. "What should I do with silver?" asked the Yemenite prince in a bored tone, "the stuff is valueless in my country. We have whole mountains of silver and gold, from which we can extract an inexhaustible supply."

The King of Kings was impressed, and decided to send an army to "liberate" so wealthy a country. The Persian expeditionary force engaged in war against the Abyssinians, after declaring Saif dhu al Yazan to be king under Persian protection. For the ensuing twenty years, the country remained in anarchy, Persians, Abyssinians and Arabs being involved in endless wars, all against all. In 597, however, Chosroes Parwiz sent another Persian army, which succeeded in establishing order. The Abyssinians and the Himyarite royal family disappeared from the scene and a Persian satrap ruled the Yemen.

There were at this time three religions in the country. The majority of the public still preferred idolatry. Saif dhu al Yazan, however, practised Judaism, together with a powerful element in the royal family and among the inhabitants. The Christians were a small minority. In Najran, on the contrary, practically all the population was Christian.

Communications between the Yemen and Persia were, however, too long and precarious for effective control to be exercised. Moreover, in 602, Chosroes Parwiz declared war on the Byzantine Empire and invaded Syria. The war was to last twenty-six years, during which time the Great King was too preoccupied to give a thought to the Yemen. Anarchy, fighting and confusion resulted and the Persian troops eventually married locally and became absorbed in the population of the Yemen.

The country remained in a state of disorder until its annexation by the Muslims in 633. It was, however, never to recover the culture and wealth which it had enjoyed before the Abyssinian invasion, and it has to this day remained in a condition which has changed but little since the seventh century.

*   *   *

Having brought the history of South Arabia up to the period of the life of Muhammad, we must now return to the north. Here the Arab dynasty of Beni Ghassan ruled eastern Syria from Mount Hermon, immediately west of Damascus, to Aila, at the head of the Red Sea—the modern port of Aqaba.[13] With the rank of patricians

[13] Map 3, page 47.

of the Byzantine Empire, they were responsible for the administration of their province and for defence against attacks from the desert, whether on the part of the Lakhmids, the Arab allies of Persia, or by desert marauders in search of plunder.

On the Euphrates, the Lakhmids, with their capital at Hira, were responsible to the Persian King of Kings for the Arab population within the empire and for defence against the Arab allies of Rome or the independent raiders of the desert. The River Euphrates, from the latitude of Anbar southwards, was itself the boundary between the desert and the sown. From the Euphrates to the east, the alluvial valley of Iraq was cultivated by a peasant population of largely Persian origin. The Arabs roamed in the desert west of the river. North of Anbar, however, the Arabs had crossed the Euphrates into the Southern Jezira.

*   *   *

The official religion of the Byzantine government was Orthodox Christianity. In the fifth century, however, a new heresy, known as the Monophysite, was adopted by the Egyptians and the Arabs of eastern Syria. In 581, the Prince of Beni Ghassan was arrested and carried to prison in Constantinople. His arrest is alleged to have been due to his adherence to the Monophysite heresy. The Arabs of eastern Syria rose in revolt but were suppressed. In 583, the dynasty of Beni Ghassan was abolished, though in fact its members seem to have continued to exercise authority because they commanded the loyalty of the tribes, even without official recognition or government subsidies.

*   *   *

On the eastern side of the desert, the last scion of the Lakhmid house was Naaman V abu Qaboos, who was converted to Christianity. He reigned with distinction for twenty-two years, from 583 to 605, and enjoyed great prestige in Arabia. Of him, a contemporary Arab poet sang,

> You are the sun, all earthly kings but planets;
> When you shine forth, their lights are lost to sight.

Naaman V, however, incurred the displeasure of Chosroes Parwiz, King of Persia, as a result of a court intrigue. Warned of the anger of the king, Naaman V took refuge with his family with the desert tribe of Beni Bekr ibn Wail.[14] Leaving his women and his treasure for safekeeping among the tribesmen, he gave himself up to Chosroes Parwiz, who immediately put him to death. He was the last of the Lakhmid dynasty, which had reigned in Hira for three hundred and thirty-seven years. A Persian satrap was appointed as governor of Hira.

Chosroes Parwiz then summoned Beni Bekr to hand over the treasure and the royal women and children who were in their custody. He was, however, unable to coerce the tribe while it was camped far out in the desert. In the summer of 611, Beni Bekr camped at Dhu Qar,[15] only a few miles from the Euphrates. Seizing the opportunity, Chosroes sent against them a column consisting of two brigades of Persian cavalry and two brigades of the army of Hira. An Arab emissary was sent ahead of the column to require the handing over of the family of Naaman V. The protection of the weak, particularly of helpless women, was, as we have seen, a point of honour among the tribes. Beni Bekr sent back the emissary with a message rejecting the Persian terms.

Handhala ibn Thalaba, having been elected to lead the tribes, gave the order next morning to advance against the Persians. He had given instructions for the tribal women, mounted on camels, to follow the warriors. When the Persians came in sight, Handhala is alleged to have sent men to hamstring the women's camels, leaving the wives and daughters of the tribesmen standing, a forlorn and helpless group, in the open desert. "Now," he shouted, "let every man defend that which is dearest to him in all the world." After a succession of furious charges and counter-charges, both Persian brigade commanders were killed, the troops broke and were pursued by the triumphant Arabs to the Euphrates.

The Day of Dhu Qar seems to have been in June or July 611. It immensely strengthened the morale of the Arabs against the Persians and thus was an important factor in initiating the Arab invasion of Persia twenty-four years later. By abolishing the Lakhmid dynasty, the King of Kings had alienated the Arab tribes, whom he was not strong enough to subjugate by force.

Thus, by a remarkable coincidence, both the Byzantine and the

[14] Map 3, page 47.

[15] There is a well, now called Abu Ghar, twenty miles from the Euphrates, which would fit the description of Dhu Qar, but I have no proof of its being the same place, though I once lived there for several months.

Persian Empires quarrelled with their Arab satellites, only a few years before Muhammad began his preaching. When the Battle of Dhu Qar was fought, Muhammad the future Prophet, was already forty-one years old. The year before the battle, in 610, he had seen his first celestial vision. Two years after the battle, he began to preach.

The factor, however, which, more than any other, was to facilitate the Muslim conquests was that, in 602, the King of Persia, Chosroes Parwiz, invaded the Byzantine Empire. In 614, he took Damascus, and, in 616, he simultaneously occupied Egypt and all Asia Minor. Not until 628 was peace restored, on the basis of the frontiers of 602. After twenty-six years of war, both of the great empires were in a state of bankruptcy and anarchy.

*   *   *

From this brief description of events in Arabia in the centuries before Islam, it will have appeared that the Arabs, in war, politics and diplomacy, operated, as it were, on two distinct levels. The upper level was that of what may be called the Principalities and the Powers. Arabia had always produced her own dynasties of princes, such as the Sabaeans, the Himyarites, the Lakhmids and Beni Ghassan. Nejed, the central part of Arabia, was poor and rarely able to support its own dynasty. The dynasties arose rather on the circumference, the Yemen, eastern Syria or the lower Euphrates, and to a great extent owed their wealth to trade.

In addition to the Principalities, however, there were the Great Powers surrounding Arabia. The poverty and the vast extent of the peninsula made it impossible to conquer. Yet the whole peninsula was placed in a geographical situation which gave it immense strategic importance, because it lay between the world of the Indian Ocean and that of the Mediterranean. The exchange of the products of these two vast areas had produced the world's most important trade route, which flowed across, or round the shores of, Arabia.

The Great Powers of those days, therefore, avoided the arid wastes of the interior with their warlike inhabitants, and endeavoured to establish control of strategic outposts on the circumference, in Aden and the Yemen, Petra and Trans-Jordan, Palmyra, or the Persian Gulf. Almost all these considerations apply today as they did two thousand years ago.

The major Great Powers during the period which we have been

considering were Rome—later **Byzantium** or East Rome—and Persia. Today, they are the United States and Russia. Abyssinia played the part of an ally of Byzantium. Both Great Powers made use of treaties with Arab rulers to protect their own interests, the Romans with Beni Ghassan, the Persians with the Lakhmids. At the end of the sixth century, both Great Powers grew tired of their Arab allies, who seemed to be more trouble than they were worth. The result was to be disastrous to the Byzantines and the Persians alike.

The many centuries of existence of these Arab Kingdoms is of great interest from the cultural angle, as well as from that of power politics. The Sabaeans and the Himyarites had been both rich and civilised. The high quality of their work in irrigation and architecture show them to have been as up-to-date as perhaps any other country in the world, in those sciences at least. Their textiles and embroideries were also in great demand in other countries. The Abyssinian and Persian invasions, however, ruined the Yemen, which has never recovered.

On the northern fringes of Arabia, the Nabataeans and the Palmyrenes were at home in the Roman world. The Beni Ghassan kings and their subjects were frequent visitors to Constantinople, Asia Minor and Syria. The latter had, for a thousand years, been one of the most wealthy and civilised provinces of the Roman Empire.

Hira, on the Euphrates, was only seventy miles from Ctesiphon, the capital of the ancient and cultured empire of Persia. The Lakhmids must have been as cultured as the Persians themselves, as is proved by the fact that one of the Kings of Persia entrusted the upbringing of his son to the Arab King of Hira. In view of these facts, the suggestion that the Arabs were before Islam a race of savages cannot be maintained.

*　　*　　*

So much for the upper tier of Arab diplomacy, politics and war—the level concerned with kings, governments and foreign countries. But, inside Arabia, another world existed, where the basic loyalties of men and women were held by the tribe and the family.

It is essential firmly to grasp the fact that the tribe held for the pre-Islamic Central Arabians the position held by the nation for the peoples of the West today. The tribe was the object of that emotional and moral devotion which the peoples of Britain, the United States,

France or Germany now give to their countries. To betray the tribe was as disgraceful as for an American, let us say, to spy for Russia.

Except to their own immediate retainers, the princes did not inspire any such emotion. Whether the tribe joined this prince or that, or kept clear of all such entanglements, was a mere matter of political expediency at any given time. To renounce such an alliance, or to enter into an agreement with a different ruler, involved no more moral ignomiy than is entailed when a modern government supports or opposes the United Nations, for the emotional loyalty of the citizens is not given to the United Nations but to their own country.

The princes of Arabia, like the United Nations, were supernational (or rather super-tribal) political organisations, which it might or might not be advisable to join, but which carried only a minor emotional appeal. Such diplomatic attachments were left to the discretion of the tribal chiefs, who periodically visited the princes to conclude political agreements, just as the heads of states of the modern world visit the United Nations.

The princes were often in competition with one another to secure the adhesion of the tribes, the military support of which increased their power and prestige. When the tribal leaders came to visit him, therefore, the Arab ruler would welcome them warmly, make a lavish display of hospitality and finally send them away clad in rich robes of honour and with valuable presents in cash. In the same manner, when the chiefs arrived back in their tribes, wearing the embroidered robes presented to them by the prince, their prestige was enhanced among their own tribesmen. This system, which is doubtless in Arabia far older than history itself, continued almost unchanged into the twentieth century.

European writers, to whom a king, as head of the state, seems to be the natural authority to whom men should feel emotional loyalty, have often denounced the treachery of bedouins in frequently changing from one prince to another. It is therefore essential to appreciate that the tribe, not the prince, represented for the bedouin what his "country" is to a modern citizen of the West.

These peculiarities are of importance when we come to consider the career of Muhammad. When it became clear that the Prophet had become a man of political and military authority, the bedouins saw him, not so much as a Messenger of God, but as a new prince, similar to the Lakhmids and Beni Ghassan. They visited him, were entertained, received gifts and departed, discussing among themselves the advisability of joining his movement.

Finally, it is interesting to notice the difference between warfare between princes and warfare between tribes. Princes waged war to win, to increase their power, to bring more tribes under their control or, if they were satellites of Rome or Persia, to raise their prestige with their suzerain. In pursuit of these ambitions, the princes could be both brutal and treacherous. Tribal warfare was caused by no such ambitions. One tribe did not expect, or even desire, to exterminate or subjugate its rival.

Often princely wars and tribal wars went on simultaneously, each on its own plane, so that two tribes which both had agreements with a certain prince were nevertheless at war with one another. The ordinary tribesmen greatly preferred their own tribal wars to the campaigns of kings in which they might be obliged to join. Tribal wars involved no discipline, the tribesman coming and going as he wished. Moreover, a point on which they felt strongly, each man in a tribal raid kept the loot he took. Princes had an unpleasant habit of collecting all the loot and dividing it up themselves.

NOTABLE DATES[16]

Minaean Rule in the Yemen	1500–700 B.C.
Conquest of the Middle East by the Persians under Cyrus	538 B.C.
Sabaean Rule in the Yemen	700–75 B.C.
Conquest of the Middle East by Alexander The Great	330 B.C.
The Nabataean Kingdom	315 B.C.–A.D. 106
Himyarite Rule in the Yemen	75 B.C.–A.D. 525
Bursting of the Dam of Marib in the Yemen. Northward Migration of Yemenite tribes	120
Asad abu Qarib, King of the Yemen Introduction of Judaism to the Yemen	200–236
The Golden Age of Palmyra	150–272
Lakhmid Dynasty of Hira, satellite kingdom of Persia	268–605

[16] *Note:* Some of the principal dates are repeated at the end of each chapter, to give the reader a summary of the course of events without referring back.

Beni Ghassan dynasty, Phylarchs of East Syria under the Romans	292–583
Collapse of the Western half of the Roman Empire	475
Dhu Nuwas of the Yemen massacres the Christians of Najran	524
Abyssinian Conquest of the Yemen	525
Abraha Abyssinian Viceroy of the Yemen	537–570
Year of the Elephant Birth of Muhammad	570
Saif dhu al Yazan the Himyarite asks Persian help against the Abyssinians	574
Civil war in the Yemen	574–597
Deposition of the dynasty of Beni Ghassan	583
Deposition and death of the last Lakhmid King, Naaman V	605
Muhammad's first vision	610
Day of Dhu Qar	611
Commencement of Muhammad's preaching	613
War between the Byzantine and Persian Empires	602–628

PERSONALITIES

Asad abu Qarib, the great Himyarite King	200–236
Septimius Odenathus, Augustus and Prince of Palmyra	258–267
Zenobia, Queen of Palmyra	267–272
Abraha, Abyssinian Viceroy of the Yemen	537–570
Naaman V, last Lakhmid King of Hira	583–605
Chosroes Parwiz, King of Persia	590–628

IMPERIAL RULERS

Byzantine Emperors		*Kings of Persia*	
Justinian	527–565	Chosroes Anushirwan	531–579
Justin II	565–574		
Tiberius	574–582	Hurmizd IV	579–590
Maurice	582–602	Chosroes Parwiz	590–628
Phocas	602–610		
Heraclius	610–641		

III

Mecca and Quraish

The Koreishites, who reigned in Mecca, were conspicuous among the Arabian tribes, but their ungrateful soil refused the labours of agriculture and their position was favourable to the enterprises of trade.

EDWARD GIBBON, *Decline and Fall of the
Roman Empire*

The ritual of Meccan religion centred in the Kaaba . . . and the well Zemzem. Probably the original nucleus was this well for there is nothing else to explain why this sterile valley should be a sacred place.

DE LACY O'LEARY, *Arabia before Muhammad*

Did you not see how my Lord dealt with the people of the elephant? Did he not cause their effort to end in confusion? And He sent down upon them flocks of birds, which threw down upon them stones.

Qoran CV, 1 to 4

For the protection of Quraish, to prosper them in their winter and summer journeys. So let them worship the Lord of this house.

Qoran CVI, 1 to 3

THE little town of Mecca, near the Red Sea coast of Arabia, was of some importance in the sixth century for two different reasons. On the one hand, it was an important centre of idol worship, to which many of the nomadic tribes of Arabia made pilgrimages. In addition to its religious prestige, however, Mecca was also an active centre for commerce.

The fact that the wealthy oriental trade was carried by camel caravan up the eastern shore of the Red Sea has already been mentioned. Throughout the centuries, this lucrative trade had been operated first by the Minaeans, then by the Sabaeans and the Nabataeans and finally by the Himyarites, who, however, in 525, had been conquered by the Abyssinians. Finally, the Persian invasion of the Yemen in 575 and the ensuing anarchy had so impoverished the Yemenites that they could no longer handle the trade on which their prosperity had depended for many centuries.

In the sixth century, the people of Mecca profited by the disasters of their predecessors to take over this extremely lucrative business. Mecca was approximately half-way between Aden and Syria, and had probably always been a halting place for caravans. But the Meccans do not seem to have become the capitalists, who actually handled the trade, until after the collapse of the Himyarites in the Yemen in the sixth century.

The site of the little town of Mecca seemed to possess few advantages except for the existence of some shallow wells in the stony bed of a narrow valley, some six hundred yards wide and a mile and a half long, between bare, rocky mountains. There was no water for gardens or cultivation and the steep slopes of the mountains which enclosed the site were denuded of vegetation.

The wells, however, were of value in so barren and desolate a country, and their owner was also the guardian of the idol fane. According to tradition, the site had, in remote antiquity, belonged to a tribe called Jurhum, alleged to have been related to the Amalekites of the Old Testament. At a date impossible to decide, the tribe of Jurhum are said to have been superseded by Khuzaa. A tribe by the name of Quraish had apparently originated in the country north of Mecca, being an offshoot of a larger group called Beni Kinana.[1]

Possibly about 235, Fihr, the then chief of Quraish, married the daughter of the chief of the Khuzaa tribe, who was warden of the idol temple of Mecca, known as the Kaaba.

About 420, a descendant of this Fihr, called Qusai, likewise married the daughter of the Khuzaa chief of his time. Qusai, an active and intelligent youth, made himself useful to his father-in-law, who often employed him as his deputy in the performance of the rites of the idol temple. As a result, when the Khuzaa chief died, Qusai attempted to assume the guardianship of the temple. Khuzaa objected, claiming for their tribe the hereditary right to the post, and took up arms. But Qusai had planned his little coup d'état. Calling on his relatives for their support, he defeated Khuzaa in battle and drove them out.

As a result of this successful usurpation, Quraish became the owners of the valley of Mecca and Khuzaa sank into a subordinate position, living in the country north-west of the site of the wells.

It seems probable that Khuzaa had lived in tents in the valley and that the Kaaba, the idol shrine, consisted only of four walls without a roof. Rain is of rare occurrence in Mecca, but on windy days the grit and sand which blow along the surface of the ground cause intense discomfort. It is quite possible that Khuzaa had lived in tents but had surrounded them with low walls, to protect themselves from the sand and wind.

Qusai was a man of remarkable character and intelligence. He persuaded Quraish to build houses, grouped around the Kaaba and in the narrow tributary valleys. The tribe is alleged to have consisted of thirty-six clans and must therefore have been in existence for several centuries. It appears, however, that only the more important clans, or those closely related to Qusai, built houses round the Kaaba. The others lived further away, still doubtless in tents, while some remained nomadic in the desert.

As a settled community, Mecca attracted various types of individuals, not themselves of Quraish. When, in the sixth century, the members began to play a leading rôle in the oriental trade, some families grew rich and acquired retainers. They gathered round them slaves and domestic servants, guards to accompany the caravans, artisans, carpenters, sword- and arrow-makers, weavers and workers in leather. A growing community also attracted fugitives, tribesmen

[1] Map 7, page 176.

GENEALOGICAL TREE:
TO SHOW THE CLANS OF QURAISH

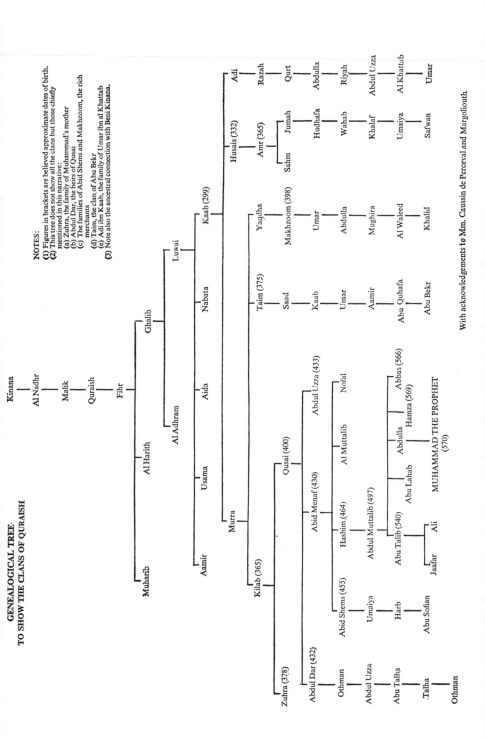

NOTES:

(1) Figures in brackets are believed approximate dates of birth.
(2) This tree does not show all the clans but those chiefly mentioned in this narrative:

   (a) Zuhra, the family of Muhammad's mother
   (b) Abdul Dar, the heirs of Qusai
   (c) The families of Abid Shems and Makhzoom, the rich merchants
   (d) Taim, the clan of Abu Bekr
   (e) Adi ibn Kaab, the family of Umar ibn al Khattab

(3) Note also the ancestral connection with Beni Kinana.

With acknowledgements to Mm. Caussin de Perceval and Margoliouth who had fled from their tribes owing to blood-feuds and were glad to marry and settle down in Mecca. An urban society began to grow, no longer confined to one tribe.

Qusai organised the pilgrimage to the idol temple. He divided his descendants into categories, to each of which he allotted specific duties. The custodianship of the Kaaba he entrusted to his eldest son and to that son's children. His name, Abdul Dar, or Slave of the House, presumably referred to these duties.

The annual pilgrimage to the shrine lasted three days, during which large numbers of Arabs from all over Arabia came to Mecca. Qusai decided that Quraish should provide the poor pilgrims with food and water during this period, for which purpose he collected a tax known as *rifada*. Although the religious rites of the pilgrimage lasted only three days, a series of fairs were held at various sites in the neighbourhood during the preceding weeks. As Quraish gradually changed from stock-breeders to merchants, these fairs offered them an opportunity to sell the articles brought by their caravans.

A remarkable reform introduced by this extraordinary man was connected with the calendar. The Arab tribes had hitherto employed the lunar months, an easy system for an illiterate people in a country where the phases of the moon are rarely concealed by clouds. Unfortunately, the lunar year of twelve months is approximately eleven days shorter than the solar year.

The pilgrimage was held in the twelfth month of the lunar year and thus moved back eleven days each year in respect of the solar year. Thus, in the course of thirty-three years, the pilgrimage moved completely round the calendar.

Qusai decided that the best idea would be to have the pilgrimage take place in the autumn. He accordingly persuaded the Arabs to accept an intercalary month every third year, in order to make the lunar year match the solar. The system was not quite accurate but was nevertheless a remarkable effort on the part of a primitive tribal chief in the deserts of Arabia.

Another custom instituted by Qusai was the presentation by himself of a lance with a piece of white cloth tied to it, to the leader of any tribal war party which set out on an expedition. This banner served as a rallying point in a fight. This ritual was to survive as a revered ceremony in some of the world's most mighty Muslim empires.

Arab nomadic tribal chiefs have never exercised autocratic

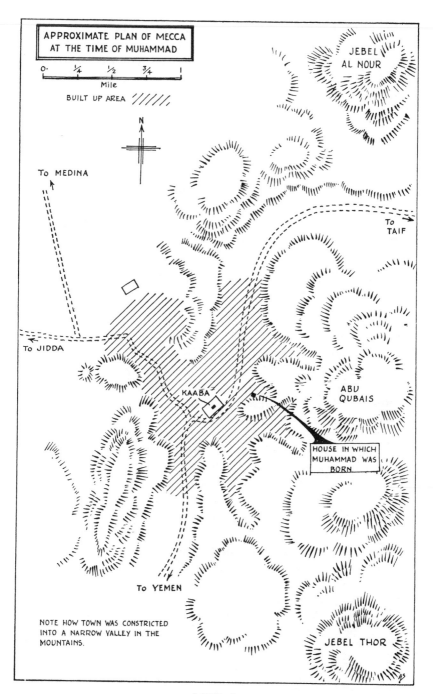

APPROXIMATE PLAN OF MECCA
AT THE TIME OF MUHAMMAD

0   ¼   ½   ¾   1
Mile

BUILT UP AREA ///////

N

JEBEL
AL NOUR

To MEDINA

To TAIF

To JIDDA

KAABA

ABU
QUBAIS

HOUSE IN WHICH
MUHAMMAD WAS
BORN

To YEMEN

NOTE HOW TOWN WAS CONSTRICTED
INTO A NARROW VALLEY IN THE
MOUNTAINS.

JEBEL THOR

MAP 4

powers and tribal policy is always discussed in public, usually in the chief's tent. If tradition be correct, however, Qusai seems to have given these public discussions an unusually formal aspect by erecting a building immediately opposite the Kaaba called Dar al Nedwa, or House of Consultation. We must not be deceived by so dignified a name into visualising a stately public edifice. The Dar al Nedwa was probably a single room built of rough stones laid in mud mortar and roofed with palm logs or brushwood.

Qusai died sometime between 450 and 460, bequeathing his position to his eldest son, Abdul Dar. Probably in the second generation, however, the descendants of Abdul Dar do not appear to have been capable of exercising undisputed authority. The descendants of Abid Menaf[2] disputed the leadership. Eventually a compromise was reached. The clan of Abdul Dar retained the guardianship of the temple and of the House of Consultation, and the right to carry the tribal banner in war. The clan of Abid Menaf was given the duties of collecting the *rifada* tax, and of providing food and water for the pilgrims.

A number of other public duties were also distributed to branches of the family. One such hereditary task was that of controller of divination, a process which was practised by throwing down a quiver of arrows in front of a male idol called Hubal. The oracle's answer was interpreted from the manner in which the arrows fell.

Probably owing to the anarchy in the Yemen caused by the Abyssinian and then the Persian invasions and the disappearance of the Himyarite kings, Quraish only seem to have become the capitalists of the oriental trade in the second half of the sixth century. During this period, however, certain clans, such as the descendants of Abid Menaf and of Makhzoom,[3] became extremely rich, while other families remained in poverty. The majority, however, acquired something of the commercial spirit and even the humblest inhabitants of Mecca would invest in trade whatever modest savings they could collect. Some would club together and send one of their number with a caravan to trade with their money and share out the profits on his return.

Thus the leading men of Mecca were not mere camel caravaners but capitalists. They went down in person to meet the Indian ships in Aden, purchased the articles and transported them, first to Mecca,

---

[2] Abid means "slave of". Menaf was the name of an idol.

[3] Genealogical tree, page 63.

and then to Syria, Gaza, or Egypt. In Damascus or in Egypt, they bought goods of local manufacture and brought them back to Mecca, where they sold them to the Arab tribes at the fairs held in connection with the annual pilgrimage.

The fact that a branch caravan route led from Mecca to the lower Euphrates, passing south of the Nefood sand desert, gave the Meccans an additional commercial advantage.[4] Nevertheless, the main trade route was that which bore the commerce of the East from Aden to Syria and Egypt.

Obviously a community which could buy the products of India and China, and sell them at a profit in the Byzantine or Persian imperial territories, must have possessed a considerable degree of organising capacity, education and knowledge of the world.

Of the sons of Abid Menaf,[5] the eldest, Abid Shems, or Slave of the Sun, was extremely active in business and made a considerable fortune. Constantly preoccupied with his money-making ventures, he did not undertake any public duties in Mecca, owing to his frequent long absences on business journeys.

As a result of the unwillingness of Abid Shems to assume local responsibilities, Hashim, the second son of Abid Menaf, undertook the family duties. He also had made a good deal of money and he earned fame and popularity by his lavish provision for the pilgrims. In the course of one of his business trips, he married a woman of the Beni al Najjár clan in Yathrib, an oasis some two hundred and fifty miles north of Mecca. Selma was apparently a lady of remarkable personality who, in 497, gave birth to a son best known to history as Abdul Muttalib.

Hashim, the son of Abid Menaf, is said to have been the first to organise the two annual caravans which the Meccans were thenceforward to utilise. One went to the Yemen to purchase the goods from India and return to Mecca; the second went from Mecca to Syria. Hashim died in Gaza where he had gone with a merchant caravan, and the next senior brother, Al Muttalib, took over the duties of feeding and watering the pilgrims.

Hashim's widow, Selma, returned to her people in Yathrib, taking her small son with her. When the boy was old enough to leave his mother, his uncle Al Muttalib rode to Yathrib and brought him back to Mecca, riding pillion behind him on his camel. Seeing Al Muttalib entering the town with a boy, the bystanders imagined that he had

[4] Map 2, page 43.   [5] Genealogical tree, page 63.

bought a new slave. The name Abdul Muttalib, Slave of Al Muttalib, stuck to him all through his life. His real name was Shaiba.

Al Muttalib subsequently died in the Yemen. The distant deaths of the leaders of Quraish, in Yathrib, Gaza or the Yemen, testify to the amount of time they spent on their long business journeys. Of all the sons of Abid Menaf, only Abid Shems died in Mecca. The youngest, Nofal, died at Sulman, a desert well on the caravan route to Hira on the Euphrates.

Abdul Muttalib succeeded his uncle, Al Muttalib, in the family duties of feeding and watering the pilgrims. The later Muslim historians allege that it was Abdul Muttalib who dug the sacred well of Zemzem, in the courtyard of the Kaaba, from which pilgrims have drunk ever since. There were already a number of wells in the valley of Mecca but Zemzem retains a peculiar sanctity, as being in the courtyard of the Kaaba.

Abdul Muttalib is alleged to have been a prominent personality in Mecca, at the time of the advance of Abraha, the Abyssinian governor of the Yemen, in 570, the Year of the Elephant.[6] Quraish made no attempt to defend the town, which they evacuated with all their belongings. According to tradition, Abdul Muttalib prayed to God to defend the Kaaba with the result that He sent birds who dropped pebbles on the Abyssinian army. It is possible, however, that Abdul Muttalib's apparently monotheistic prayer dates from after Islam and was attributed to him, for he was to be the grandfather of Muhammad.

We have, however, already noted that the idolaters seem to have recognised a single supreme God, although they normally prayed to their local gods and goddesses. Moreover, as we have seen, both Judaism and Christianity had already penetrated Arabia to some extent.

One member of Muhammad's family, Waraqa ibn Nofal, was a professed monotheist and is alleged to have translated portions of the Gospels into Arabic. Waraqa's sister also is mentioned as a regular reader of the Gospels.

*   *   *

Abdul Muttalib, who was born about 497, had ten sons. As a young man, he had vowed to the gods of the Kaaba that, if he had

6 Page 50.

ten sons, he would sacrifice one of them. When he actually did have ten, he was haunted by anxiety concerning this vow and eventually decided that he must fulfil it. He cast lots among his sons, and the lot fell upon Abdulla, a youth as yet unmarried. But Abdul Muttalib could not make up his mind to kill his son and had recourse to a local sorceress for advice. She recommended him to offer the gods a number of camels as blood-money in lieu of his son's life. If the gods refused, he could go on increasing the number of camels until they agreed.

This procedure was carried out by the process of throwing down marked arrows before the idol Hubal, in the square in front of the Kaaba, with the assistance of the official diviner. Abdul Muttalib first offered ten camels in lieu of the life of his son, but, according to the diviner, the arrows were unfavourable. Hubal had rejected the offer.

The anxious father raised his bid by ten camels at a time. At the tenth throw of the arrows, the diviner stated that Hubal had accepted one hundred camels to release Abdul Muttalib from his vow.

The whole incident is interesting, especially in its distant resemblance to the offering up of Isaac by Abraham. Later, Muslim tradition was to modify the story of Abraham and Isaac, claiming that Abraham had offered Ishmael, his son by Hagar, not Isaac. The offering took place on the site of the Kaaba, where Abdul Muttalib offered his son, Abdulla. Ishmael was released by Abraham at the command of God, as in the case of Isaac in Genesis, a sheep being found in the vicinity as a substitute. Some Muslim traditionists, however, believe that it was Isaac, not Ishmael, who was offered by Abraham.

Abdulla subsequently married Amina, a woman of the Beni Zuhra clan of Quraish. A few months later, however, he died in Yathrib where he had gone on business, leaving his young wife pregnant. She gave birth to a boy called Muhammad, the future prophet. The year was 570, the Year of the Elephant.

It was the custom of Quraish to give their babies to be suckled by women of the nomadic tribes outside Mecca, the pure desert air being considered more healthy than the dusty alleyways of the settlement of Mecca. One day, a party of women of the Beni Saad clan of the Hawazin tribe came to Mecca to look for babies to suckle.

The young widow, Amina, offered her baby to them but all the women refused to take him when they heard that his mother had lost her husband. It was the custom for the father to give the foster-mother a generous tip, whereas widows were normally less generous. Eventually all the women had found babies except one, called Haleema. As the whole party were preparing to return to the desert, Haleema, unwilling to return home empty-handed, accepted the unwanted orphan. Many miracles were subsequently recounted about the stay of the infant Muhammad with Beni Saad, the most striking being the appearance of two Beings clad in shining white who threw the little boy on the ground, took out his heart and washed it and then replaced it in his breast.

We need not discuss these miracles, because Muhammad himself was later on to admit that he could not work miracles. Moreover, his inability to perform miracles was to be used by his enemies as an argument that he was not a real prophet. If all the miracles of his childhood which were subsequently told had been known when he was preaching, the sneers of his detractors could easily have been contradicted.

The young Muhammad remained with his foster-parents until he was six years old. By day he used to go with Haleema's other children to take the sheep to graze. Later in life, when he had become famous, Muhammad used to say, "There is no prophet but has worked as a shepherd. I herded sheep as a boy."

In 576, at the age of six, Muhammad returned to his mother Amina in Mecca, but before the end of the year she also died, leaving him an orphan of both parents. For a short time, he was cared for by a slave girl. Then he was taken in by his grandfather, Abdul Muttalib, who became extremely fond of him and used constantly to pet him and play with him.

Two years later, however, in 578, Abdul Muttalib died, and the poor little orphan's life was once again disrupted. Before his death, however, his grandfather charged another of his sons, Abu Talib, to look after the child. Abdulla, Muhammad's father, had been the brother of Abu Talib by both their father and mother. Abdul Muttalib's other sons had apparently come from different mothers.

At the age of twelve—other accounts say nine—Muhammad accompanied his uncle Abu Talib on a commercial trip with a caravan to Syria. The Muslim historians delight to relate that he was seen by a Christian monk in Syria, who foretold that one day he would be a prophet. The story may well record some meeting between the boy Muhammad and a Christian hermit, of whom there were many at this time on the borders of the Syrian desert.[7]

Muhammad appears to have been a serious child. The insecurity of his infancy may have made him quiet and thoughtful beyond his years. In such circumstances, it is not improbable that he may have engaged in conversation with a Christian recluse who, noticing his serious demeanour, may have foretold for him a life of exceptional quality.

* * *

At some date between 584 and 590, when Muhammad was between fifteen and twenty years old, war broke out between Quraish and their allies, Beni Kinana, on the one hand, and the tribe of Hawazin on the other. The cause of the dispute was so typical of sixth-century life in Arabia that it may be worthy of mention. Naaman V abu Qaboos, the Lakhmid King of Hira, wished to send a caravan to deliver merchandise for sale at the fair of Ukadh, one of the markets which were held in the vicinity of Mecca at the time of the pilgrimage.

As has already been explained, caravans passing through tribal areas provided themselves with guides from the tribes in question. The guide was under an obligation to protect the caravan from his fellow-tribesmen. In this manner, Naaman V had provided himself with a guide from Hawazin.

A certain man of Beni Kinana, an outlaw noted for his crimes, had hoped to secure the job but had been rejected. He nevertheless accompanied the caravan when it left Hira for Mecca. One day, when the Hawazin guide was off his guard dozing during the midday halt, the outlaw murdered him and robbed a part of the merchandise.

The murderer was not only of Beni Kinana but was also a client of Harb ibn Umaiya of Quraish.[8] The crime was all the more flagrant in that it was perpetrated in the sacred month preceding the Meccan pilgrimage, during which all acts of violence were forbidden. The resulting war between Quraish and Hawazin was consequently called the Sacrilegious War. It was to last for five years, involving a pitched battle every year.

---

[7] At the beginning of the fourth century, St. Anthony had initiated the first Christian monasticism, in caves in the Egyptian desert.

[8] Genealogical tree, page 63.

It seems probable that Muhammad was only fourteen years old when the war began, for he subsequently related that he had gone to the first battle to help his uncles. He picked up the spent arrows which came from the enemy and handed them to his uncles to shoot back.

*　　*　　*

Few details are known of Muhammad's life as a young man. Although his grandfather, Abdul Muttalib, was an important man in ·Mecca, Muhammad's uncle, Abu Talib, was apparently poor. Presumably the large number of Abdul Muttalib's sons had resulted in only a small inheritance for each. For a time, the boy was obliged once again to work as a shepherd. When he grew to adolescence, he apparently engaged in commerce, like most of the members of his family. A tradition has survived that he accompanied his uncle, Zubair, on a business journey to the Yemen.

He seems to have been a quiet, pensive youth and is said to have been nicknamed "the trustworthy" in Mecca. In later life, he claimed that he had never been guilty of sexual immorality in his youth.

Khadija[9] was a rich widow of Quraish, who had been twice married. She was a business woman, engaged in the caravan trade, and managed her own affairs. In 595, when Muhammad was twenty-five years old, Abu Talib seems to have recommended his nephew to her. As a result, she asked him to take charge of a caravan of hers which was to go to Syria.

He was told that he would be expected to sell the merchandise and to buy Syrian piece-goods with the proceeds, for subsequent resale at the Meccan fairs. It is possible that the influence of Abu Talib procured him the appointment but it is obvious that Muhammad must already have possessed some business experience and a reputation for honesty, or the rich widow would not have confided her caravan to his management.

Tradition relates that, on the northward journey, the caravan one day halted to rest during the noonday heat. Muhammad went to sleep under a tree, when a Christian monk arrived and asked who he was. "None but a prophet ever sat beneath that tree," he is said to have remarked. The story is not particularly probable. There are so

---

[9] Pronounced Khadeeja.

GENEALOGICAL TREE
TO SHOW RELATIONSHIP BETWEEN MUHAMMAD AND KHADIJA AND
WARAQA IBN NOFAL, THE MONOTHEIST

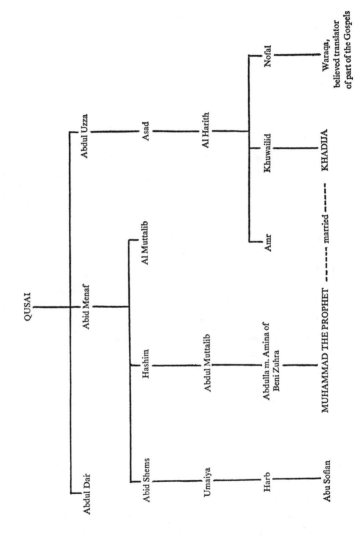

few trees in those parts and the summer sun is so hot that every tree must be used for shade many thousands of times. The numerous traditions associating Muhammad with Christian monks in Syria are, nevertheless, worthy of note. The tree in question is still shown in Jordan, north of Amman.

The results of Muhammad's management of the caravan seem to have been highly satisfactory. Khadija is said to have been delighted with the profits realised. "Now Khadija was a determined, noble and intelligent woman," writes Ibn Ishaq, "so she sent to Muhammad, saying, "O son of my uncle,[10] I like you, because we are relations, and also for your good reputation among the people." She then added a proposal of marriage.

This incident is of interest, not only because it was a milestone in the life of Muhammad, but also because it illustrates the position occupied by women in pre-Islamic Arabia. Khadija was an independent woman running her own business and it was she, not her future husband, who suggested the marriage. Muhammad consulted his uncles on the matter. They advised acceptance.

Khadija's father had been killed in the Sacrilegious War. Her uncle Amr ibn Asad was head of the family, and his consent was necessary. Abu Talib, and perhaps Hamza, another uncle, accompanied Muhammad to Khadija's house, where a party had been arranged. The lady had not, it seems, broken the news to her uncle and he was unaware of the significance of the occasion. However, Khadija plied him diligently with wine until he was slightly confused. Abu Talib then made a brief speech, asking the consent of the uncle of the bride. Waraqa ibn Nofal, whom we have already seen as the translator of the Gospels, seconded the request.

The bride's uncle is alleged to have made no reply. Silence was accordingly assumed to mean consent. Some hours later, the old man woke up and asked what was going on. The guests told him that they were celebrating the wedding of his niece Khadija to Muhammad ibn Abdulla. Uncle Amr, however, replied to the effect that it was all rubbish, and that he would never consent. "But it was you who gave me away," exclaimed Khadija, in apparent astonishment. As the old uncle could not quite remember what he had been doing for the previous two or three hours, he decided that perhaps the best course would be to leave it at that.

Tradition alleges that Khadija was forty years of age, though one

[10] There is no word for cousin in Arabic.

writer alone says that she was twenty-eight.[11] As she was to bear him six children, two sons and four daughters, it seems unlikely that she could have been already forty years of age. Nearly all their children died young, none of them reaching the age of forty. Both the sons died in infancy.

In every other way, however, the marriage was a complete success. The young husband—Muhammad was only twenty-five—confided all his anxieties to his somewhat middle-aged bride, who combined for him the love of a wife with the maternal tenderness of the mother whom he had lost in infancy.

Though normally quiet and reserved, Muhammad, like most Arabs, was devoted to children. In the privacy of his family and his intimates, he was often relaxed and happy, sometimes even playful and humorous.

NOTABLE DATES

Marriage of Qusai to the daughter of the chief of the Khuzaa tribe	420
Qusai seizes Control of Mecca	440
Birth of Abdul Muttalib, grandfather of Muhammad	497
Year of the Elephant ⎫ Birth of Muhammad ⎭	570
Death of Abdul Muttalib ⎫ Muhammad cared for by Abu Talib ⎭	578
Marriage of Muhammad to Khadija	595

PERSONALITIES

Qusai, founder of Quraish ownership of Mecca	Died *circa* 455
Hashim, great-grandfather of Muhammad	
Abdul Muttalib, grandfather of Muhammad	497–578
Waraqa ibn Nofal, cousin of Muhammad, translator of the Gospels	
Abu Talib, Muhammad's uncle and foster-father	
Khadija, Muhammad's first wife	

[11] Ibn Habib, quoted by Muhammad Hamidullah, *Le Prophète de l'Islam.*

IV

The Call

Khadija, some years older than himself, . . . finally offered herself to him in marriage. This woman, no longer in her first youth, remains the most sympathetic feminine figure in the Prophet's biography. The slow maturation of the religious unrest in Muhammad's soul naturally escapes precise dating. One thing is certain: that in about 610 . . . there exploded within him a crisis, of which a sufficiently clear and reliable tradition has been preserved.

FRANCESCO GABRIELI, *Muhammad and the Conquests of Islam*

The message of the Arabian Muhammad was a parallel of the message of the Hebrew prophets of the Old Testament. God is one. He is all-powerful. He is the creator of the universe. There is a judgement day. Splendid rewards in Paradise await those who carry out God's commands, and terrible punishment in hell for those who disregard them. Such was the gist of his early message.

P. K. HITTI, *The Arabs*

It is well said, in every sense, that man's religion is the chief factor with regard to him.

THOMAS CARLYLE, *Heroes and Hero-Worship*

I have immortal longings in me.

WILLIAM SHAKESPEARE, *Antony and Cleopatra*

IV

AFTER his marriage, Muhammad seems to have remained in business for some time. We are not clearly told whether he assisted his wife to manage her affairs or whether he worked independently. All their relatives were in business and Muhammad knew no other way to earn a living. Many passages in the Qoran use business language to point moral issues, such as "those who buy error make a bad bargain".

When Muhammad was thirty-five years old, that is in 605, Quraish decided to roof the Kaaba, which, it appears, had hitherto consisted only of four walls with no covering. An examination of the masonry, however, inspired doubts as to whether the existing walls would carry a roof. It was suggested that the walls be demolished and that the whole edifice be rebuilt, in order to make it strong enough to support the additional weight.

There was some fear, however, that the gods and goddesses might resent this action and vent their anger on the workers. At length, one man, bolder than the rest, advanced against the wall with a pickaxe, crying aloud meanwhile, "O goddess! Don't be afraid! O goddess! We intend only what is for the best." The good people of Mecca lay awake that night, wondering if some thunderbolt from the gods would strike down the sacrilegious demolisher of their shrine. As, however, he arrived on the work again next morning with his pickaxe, the Meccans assumed that their gods were pleased with the enterprise, and were looking forward to the occupation of better accommodation.

It so happened that a ship belonging to a Greek merchant had been wrecked, possibly on the coral reefs off Jidda. The ship's timbers were taken for the roof of the new building, which a Copt[1] in Mecca, who happened to be a carpenter, undertook to erect.

The story of roofing the Kaaba sheds an interesting light on contemporary conditions in Mecca. The fact that the temple itself had no roof increases the probability that the "houses" of Mecca consisted in many cases merely of tents with walls round them. The same possibility is suggested by the fact that only the wreck of a ship on the Red Sea provided the timber for the roof and that the services of an

---

[1] Copt merely means an Egyptian, the same word with a hard g.

Egyptian were necessary to construct it. Obviously no such roundabout methods would have been needed if the Meccans themselves lived in houses with roofs.

It is, of course, possible that the absence of roofs did not involve a comparable backwardness in other respects—it scarcely ever rained in Mecca, and tents or awnings could keep off the sun. No trees large enough for roofing grew in the Hejaz, and long baulks of timber could not be carried from the Yemen or Syria by camel. The lack of timber had naturally resulted in the non-existence of carpenters.

These peculiarities of Mecca, however, were not common to all the Arabs of the time. We have already seen that, a thousand years before, the people of the Yemen lived in stone houses several stories high, built in beautifully cut masonry. Beni Ghassan were familiar with the ancient cities of Jerash, Jerusalem, Damascus and Antioch, with their classical colonnades and marble temples. The ruins of Ctesiphon still attest the wonderful skill of the Persians, among whom lived the Arab Kings[2] of Hira.

A large black stone, possibly a meteorite, had been built into the wall of the primitive Kaaba building and was regarded with peculiar veneration by the Meccans. When the rebuilding of the walls reached the level on which the black stone had formerly been incorporated in it, each of the clans of Quraish demanded the privilege of placing the stone in position. The debate waxed hot and an outbreak of violence seemed imminent.

The Abdul Dar clan, who, it will be remembered, had been appointed guardians of the House by Qusai, loudly claimed their pre-eminent rights. They brought a bowl of blood and called on their supporters to dip their hands in the blood and swear to support their claim.

Abu Umaiya of the clan of Beni Makhzoom, allegedly the oldest man of Quraish, suggested a solution. He proposed that all present should agree that the first man who entered the court of the Kaaba after that moment should be asked to judge the dispute. The idea was accepted and the first man to enter a few minutes later was Muhammad. Informed of the cause of the quarrel, he called for a cloak, spread it on the ground and laid the black stone upon it. He then ordered a representative of every clan to take hold of the edge of the cloak and to raise the stone together to the required height.

[2] The other countries which we now call "Arab", such as Egypt and North Africa had, of course, no connection with Arabs in the early seventh century.

Thereupon, with his own hands, he laid it in position in the wall.

The idol shrine of Mecca was hedged with taboos, which may well have stretched far back into antiquity. It was laid down, for example, that pilgrims from outside Mecca could not bring "profane" food into the courtyard. The ritual of pilgrimage required the pilgrim to walk round the Kaaba seven times, but "profane" clothes were not allowed in the temple courtyard. Those desirous of circumambulating the House were obliged to obtain fresh clothing from the custodians. Persons too poor to procure "sacred" clothing must needs perform their circumambulation naked.

During these years after Muhammad's marriage but before the commencement of his Ministry, four men in Mecca are mentioned as having withdrawn from the idol worship of the Kaaba. One of these was Waraqa ibn Nofal,[3] Khadija's cousin, whom we have already seen as a student of the Gospels. Another was later to become a Christian in Abyssinia. A third migrated to Constantinople, where he also became a Christian.

The fourth of these seekers after monotheism was Zaid ibn Amr ibn Tufail, who had rejected the idolatry of his relatives, but who had adopted neither Judaism nor Christianity. Many years later, Asma, the daughter of Abu Bekr, Muhammad's first successor, used to say that she remembered Zaid as a very old man, sitting in the courtyard of the Kaaba and praying, "O God, if I knew how you wished to be worshipped, I would so worship you; but I do not know." Ridiculed by his family, he travelled through Iraq and Syria, questioning monks and rabbis. On his return journey to Mecca, he was killed by bandits.

These examples will suffice to show that, at least to some extent, new ideas were stirring in Mecca. There was no religious prejudice or persecution, with the result that occasional Jews and Christians were to found living in the town or passing through on business. Moreover, the constant journeys undertaken by the men of Quraish to Persia, Syria and Egypt, where they mixed with Christians, Jews and Zoroastrians, had begun to inspire them with contempt for their own primitive idols.

In a sense, therefore, the business interests of the Meccans had resulted in a feeling of religious malaise. In addition to the four seekers after truth already described, there were philanthropists in Mecca who helped the poor, protected unwanted baby girls, released prisoners, or bought slaves in order to set them free. But these

[3] Genealogical tree, page 73.

charitable persons were not united by any religious dogma.

Much has been made by writers of the alleged Arab custom of burying baby girls immediately after birth. The evidence on this subject is conflicting and some tribes seem to have welcomed the birth of a daughter. Other accounts allege that the motive for disposing of baby daughters was the fear of family dishonour, if they grew up immoral. The marriage of girls at eight or nine years of age may likewise have been intended as a protection against scandals. It is also conceivable that later Islamic writers tended to paint too dark a picture of the times before Muhammad, the more to emphasise the benefits brought by Islam.

On the other hand, there are many signs of chivalry and romantic love, particularly among the nomadic tribes. Khadija, as we have seen, managed her own business. Women, moreover, sometimes exercised considerable influence as prophetesses or as poetesses. At the annual fairs in the neighbourhood of Mecca, particularly the fair of Ukadh, poetical competitions were held, attracting vivid popular enthusiasm. In some cases, women entered with the men for these poetical contests and recited their verses in public.

Another quality of Arab society, even in primitive times, was courtesy. Two factors contributed to this peculiarity, the first the Arab jealousy of personal honour, the second the absence of any form of police. The touchiness of Arab honour meant that the least discourtesy might be violently resented. The absence of police resulted in the instant settlement by bloodshed of an insult.

Perhaps the explanation for these contradictions can be found in the existence of a largely illiterate society, spread over vast areas of desert, giving rise to many local variations. As a result, we find in early Arabia deeds of savagery, mingled with acts of chivalry, baby girls buried alive and stories of romantic courtship, crude pagan ceremonies and the search for a spiritual God by such as Zaid ibn Amr ibn Tufail.

These wide diversities may for us be difficult to appreciate, for our modern society has been made uniform by ease of travel, newspapers, radio and television. Yet this has only happened in the last fifty years or, at any rate, since the introduction of universal compulsory education. We must, therefore, be cautious how we generalise regarding the Arabs before Islam.

*   *   *

The fifteen years which followed his marriage, from 595 to 610, had been spent by Muhammad in quiet routine in Mecca. Part of his time was passed in business, not too strenuously pursued and not apparently involving many distant journeys. Khadija's money had presumably put an end to his financial anxieties.

That he was aware of his good fortune, which he was later to attribute to God's favour, is perhaps proved by the words of Chapter XCIII of the Qoran, believed to be one of the earliest passages revealed in Mecca. "Your Lord has not forsaken you nor become displeased . . . Did He not find you an orphan and give you shelter? And find you wandering and guided you; and find you in want and made you free from want."

Only two events of this period need be recorded. As a penniless orphan, Muhammad had been cared for by his uncle, Abu Talib. The latter was now growing old and was in poor financial circumstances. Muhammad, who was now comfortably off, decided to repay his debt to the old man by relieving him of one of his sons. Ali, a son of Abu Talib, left his father's house and was virtually adopted by Muhammad who, though in reality his first cousin, was old enough to have been his father.

Zaid ibn Haritha was a Christian boy, born in southern Syria. As a child, he had been kidnapped by bandits and sold as a slave. A nephew of Khadija, on a business trip to Syria, had bought the boy and given him to his aunt in Mecca. Muhammad after his marriage found Zaid in Khadija's house, and became fond of him, with the result that she gave the child to him as a gift.

Some time later, Zaid's father, who had been searching for him for many years, located him in Mecca and offered a large sum to buy his freedom. Muhammad called the boy and offered him the choice of returning to his father or of remaining in Mecca. Zaid chose to remain in Muhammad's household. The latter, moved by the youth's devotion, hastened with him to the Kaaba, where he publicly manumitted him from slavery and adopted him as his son. Thus, although his two sons by Khadija had died in infancy, Muhammad's family now included two youths, Ali and Zaid, both of whom looked upon him as their father.

As the years passed, the future prophet devoted an increasing amount of time to meditation. Escaping from the distractions of business and from the crowded alleyways of Mecca, he would retire to the bare mountain slopes which overlooked the little settlement. Here he would take refuge in some lonely cave, where he could think without worldly interruptions. Perhaps the memory of those Christian hermits, whom, on his trips to Syria, he had seen living in caves in the desert, may have suggested such ideas to his mind.

In fact, however, this kind of asceticism was already practised to a limited extent by the idolaters of Mecca. The exercise known to them as "tahannuth" seems to have resembled the modern idea of a religious retreat—a temporary withdrawal from worldly surroundings for the purpose of religious meditation. It seems as if those idolaters, whom we regard with so much contempt, were moved by spiritual promptings as genuine as those of religious people in our own times.

Muhammad's grandfather, Abdul Muttalib, is alleged to have been in the habit of spending the month of Ramadhan every year in a cave in the mountains. Other Meccans, we are told, before Islam practised fasting, abstention from alcohol and other forms of self-denial.

Muhammad's thoughts seem to have dwelt largely on the forms of eschatology of which he had heard from conversations with Jews and Christians. The natural scenery around Mecca, the rocky mountains bare of vegetation, and the flaming heat of the midday sun, perhaps encouraged the mind to dwell on thoughts of catastrophe, of hell-fire and of an avenging God. Returning home with his mind filled with these speculations, he would unbosom himself to the faithful Khadija, always a willing and sympathetic listener.

Aisha, whom he was to marry after the death of Khadija, later said of this period that "solitude became dear to him and he would go to a cave on Mount Hira to engage in meditation there for a number of nights, before returning to his family. Then he would go home for a short time to procure provisions for another stay."

Suddenly, one night in the month of Ramadhan 610, a vision came to him. "At length," says Aisha again, "unexpectedly the Truth came to him and said, 'O Muhammad, thou art the Messenger of God'." "I had been standing," Muhammad himself is alleged to have said, describing the incident, "but I fell to my knees."

"Read!" the Vision cried, but Muhammad replied, "I cannot read." The Vision then enfolded him, pressing him so tightly that he could not breathe. A second and a third time, the same process was repeated. A complication arises here, for owing to the idiosyncrasies of Arabic, the two words normally translated, "I cannot read", *ma aqrau*, can also mean "what shall I read?" The interpretation "I cannot read" has been commonly adopted by Muslim commentators, as proving that Muhammad was illiterate,[4] a fact which, if correct, increases the miraculous nature of the Qoran. Scholars have also traced the origin of the word *qara* to one used by Syrian Christians at the time, meaning to recite, not to read.

Whatever interpretation is adopted does not affect the validity of the vision but only goes to prove whether or not Muhammad was illiterate. After the third repetition of the question and answer, the Vision replied:

> Read in the name of thy Lord who created,
> Who created man of blood coagulated.
> Read! Thy Lord is the most beneficent,
> Who taught by the pen,
> Who taught what they knew not to men.[5]

The Vision was gone, leaving Muhammad in agitation and mental confusion. "I will go to the top of the mountain and throw myself down, that I may kill myself and be at rest," he thought in his terror. "When I was midway on the mountain," he said, recalling the experience later, "I heard a voice from Heaven, saying, 'O Muhammad! Thou art the Messenger of God.' I raised my eyes to Heaven and lo! He stood in the form of a man, with his feet astride the horizon. I continued standing there until he departed, and I returned to my family in Mecca. I went in to Khadija and sat by her thigh and drew close to her." The cave on Mount Hira is only two or three miles from Mecca, so he could be home in less than an hour.

It may be of interest to note that visions have sometimes been classified as either visionary or auditive, something seen or something heard. The first call of Muhammad and perhaps his visit to Jerusalem, described below, may be classed as visionary. But the revelations which came to him throughout the rest of his life, and which when collected constituted the Qoran,[6] were auditive. He heard but he did not normally see.

On arriving home, still in great perturbation of mind, he told Khadija what he had seen and heard, pouring out to her his fears and his mental confusion. He was afraid of going out of his mind or of

---

[4] It seems curious that Muhammad should be unable to read, when most Meccan merchants could do so, especially as he had been in charge of a caravan going to Syria. As he was brought up by Abu Talib, his education may have been below the average.

[5] Qoran XCVI. This translation is by Guillaume.

[6] The word Qoran is derived from the word *qara* already mentioned. It means the Reading or the Recitation.

being possessed by an evil spirit. Sorcerers, diviners, oracles and persons who claimed to possess occult powers were well known in the Arab world, and Muhammad feared that he would be thought to be one of them.

But Khadija rose gallantly to the occasion. "Rejoice, O son of my uncle," she cried, "and be of good cheer, verily by Him in whose hand is the soul of Khadija, you will be the Prophet of this People. God will not bring you to shame for He knows your sincerity and your truthfulness."

When he was somewhat pacified, she got up, put on her cloak and hastened out to the house of her cousin, Waraqa ibn Nofal, who, it will be remembered, was one of the seekers after a spiritual God, and who had adopted Christianity and translated the Gospels. Khadija told him all that Muhammad had heard and experienced, begging him to give his opinion. "If all you have said be true," replied Waraqa, "the Spirit has appeared to him, as he appeared long ago to Moses. Tell him to be of good heart, for he is to be the Prophet of his people." So Khadija returned to her husband and told him what Waraqa had said, as a result of which his fears were somewhat calmed.

In the account of this experience given by Ibn Ishaq and Tabari, the Being seen by Muhammad is stated to have been the Archangel Gabriel. Scholars, however, have pointed out that there is no mention of Gabriel in that portion of the Qoran revealed in these early years in Mecca. As already mentioned, Aisha is alleged to have said that "the Truth" came to him. I have, therefore, omitted the name of Gabriel in the above account.

This first call of the Messenger of God[7] is mentioned in several places in the Qoran. For example Chapter LIII, verse 4, reads:

It was a revelation revealed.
The Lord of great strength taught him.
He stood in the high Heaven,
Then He came lower and lower
Till He was two bowshots away or less,
Then He revealed to His servant what He revealed.

*   *   *

[7] In his lifetime, Muhammad was most frequently called "the Messenger of God" by his followers. Alternatively, we may call him the Apostle of God, the word apostle meaning messenger. The title "the Prophet" came into general use later—I have used all three expressions.

The interpretation of Muhammad's mission which has been current in the Western world has varied considerably from time to time. In the Middle Ages, he was thought of almost as a devil incarnate. In the eighteenth century, the Age of Reason, he was visualised as a wise man and a legislator or, conversely, as a deliberate impostor. In our own times, in the Soviet Union, the rise of Islam has been explained as a revolt of the working classes of Mecca against the capitalists. In each case, Western writers seemed to explain the Prophet's career in terms of the thought fashionable in the age when they were writing.

Whatever opinion the reader may form when he reaches the end of this book, it is difficult to deny that the call of Muhammad seems to bear a striking resemblance to innumerable other accounts of similar visions, both in the Old and New Testaments, and in the experience of Christian saints, possibly also of Hindus and devotees of other religions. Such visions, moreover, have often marked the beginnings of lives of great sanctity and of heroic virtue.

To attribute such phenomena to self-delusion scarcely seems an adequate explanation, for they have been experienced by many persons divided from one another by thousands of years of time and by thousands of miles of distance, who cannot conceivably have even heard of each other. Yet the accounts which they give of their visions seem to bear an extraordinary likeness to one another. It scarcely appears reasonable to suggest that all these visionaries "imagined" such strikingly similar experiences, although they were quite ignorant of each other's existence.

The analysis of Muhammad's first call and of his subsequent revelations[8] is a subject involving both psychological and theological problems, which cannot be discussed in this book. Suffice it to say that the first "call" which he received was apparently of a different nature from the regular "revelations" from which originated the text of the Qoran.

One point, however, is of considerable importance and should, I think, be known to the reader before we continue any further. After the death of Muhammad, Islam and Christianity became involved in mutual warfare for a thousand years. The causes of these wars were political, originating in the rivalry between the Arab and the

---

[8] I use the word "revelations" as being the term normally employed to describe these phenomena. I do not thereby wish to imply any particular opinion as to their origin, one way or another.

Byzantine Empires, rather than in religious or theological differences. These long centuries of war between Muslim and Christian governments produced intense and fanatical hatreds, which gave rise in Europe to the most profound prejudices against Muhammad.

The best proof that these hostilities were political and not religious lies in the fact that, throughout the whole period, Christian populations continued to live in Muslim countries without being persecuted, although foreign Christian governments were regarded with intense hostility.

One of the results of these hatreds, however, was that Muhammad was for many centuries represented in Europe as a conscious impostor. Only in recent years have Western scholars attempted to break away from this tradition, and to engage in a sincere and unprejudiced search for the truth concerning the origins of Islam.

Far from Islam being the essential enemy of Christianity, it sprang from the same sources as both Christianity and Judaism. Indeed, Islam has even been described by some authorities in recent years as no more than a Christian heresy—a form of Christianity which has diverged in some respects from the teaching of the Church. The main principles announced at the beginning of Muhammad's mission could certainly have formed the basis of any contemporary Christian sermon.

1. The blessing of God freely bestowed on men, in nature, in the creation of the human race, in the rain, the growth of vegetation and so on.
2. The consequent duty which is incumbent upon men to serve God.
3. The ultimate judgement and punishment of men who refuse to do so.

The object of this book, however, is to record history. For this purpose, complete impartiality is essential. When, therefore, the revelations of Muhammad are discussed, I make bold to ask the reader to do all in his power to divest himself of conscious or unconscious prejudice.

NOTABLE DATES

Birth of Muhammad	570
Marriage of Muhammad	595
The Great War between Byzantium and Persia	602–628
Muhammad's Call	610

PERSONALITIES

Waraqa ibn Nofal ⎫
Zaid ibn Amr ibn Tufail ⎭   Monotheists in Mecca

Abu Talib, Muhammad's uncle

Ali ibn abi Talib, Muhammad's cousin, whom he brought up

Zaid ibn Haritha, Muhammad's slave, then adopted son

V

The Years of Ridicule

Lord, how are they increased that trouble me; many are they that rise up against me. Many there be which say of my soul, "There is no help for him in God." But Thou, O Lord, art a shield for me.

Psalm III, vv. 1, 2 and 3

Woe to every backbiter and slanderer, Who heaped up riches and counted them. He thinks his riches make him immortal.

Qoran CIV, 1 to 4

The friends and some of the relatives of Mahomet listened with reverence to his admonitions . . . The great body of the Quraish were careless and indifferent. As Mahomet passed by the knots that clustered about the Kaaba discussing the events of the day, they would point disdainfully at him as a half-witted creature.

Sir William Muir, *Mahomet*

V

KHADIJA was Muhammad's first convert. From the moment of his call, until her death nine years later, she never faltered. Whenever he encountered mockery or contradiction, he was sure, when he returned home in the evening, to find a cheerful and loving comforter. She was always ready by her confident equanimity to restore his courage and to lighten the burden of his fears.

The original call was followed by an interval during which there were no messages, visions or revelations, and the Messenger of God became fearful and anxious. The length of the interlude is not clearly stated but has been estimated as having lasted for between two and three years. It is thought to have been ended by a revelation which now forms the beginning of Chapter XCIII of the Qoran, of which the title is "The Early Hours of the Day".[1] In verse 3 it is stated, "Your Lord has not forsaken you, nor has He become displeased", referring to the doubts and anxieties which had grown up in the mind of the Apostle since his first call.

* * *

This may perhaps be a suitable place in which to insert a note on the Qoran. The book is a compilation of the revelations received by Muhammad. Unlike the Bible, therefore, the Qoran is a single homogeneous work, which purports to record the words of God as revealed to His Messenger, Muhammad, over a period of twenty-two years.

The earliest revelations were received by the Prophet when he was as yet unknown and had virtually no following. These were presumably retained in his memory or in that of his close relatives, Khadija, Ali or Zaid ibn Haritha, his slave and then adopted son.

Later on, when he became great and famous, many writers would gather to record the revelations. The notes which they took were not,

---

[1] The Qoran does not consist of books and chapters like the Bible but of chapters only. Each chapter has a number and a title and is divided into verses.

however, immediately embodied in a book but were retained by such persons as had taken them down. Proper writing materials appear to have been scarce, and the records of the revelations were written on odd bits of material, perhaps papyrus, textile material, bits of leather or the shoulder-blades of sheep. Each writer kept his own notes and the whole mass of this material was only co-ordinated into a single book several years after the death of the Prophet.

When the collection and compilation of the many individual records were eventually made, it was found impossible to arrange the various revelations in chronological order. As a result a purely arbitrary system was adopted. The chapters were arranged in the order of their length, the longest being at the commencement of the book and the shortest at the end. This, in fact, was almost the reverse of the chronological order. The first revelations, received in Mecca, were brief, poetic and passionate. But when, in later life, the Apostle of God had become a political and military, as well as a religious leader, the revelations grew longer and longer and consisted largely of detailed instructions and regulations for the ordering of every detail in the life of a Muslim. Moreover, it is not certain whether or not each chapter embodies a single revelation. The same chapter often deals with a number of different subjects. Each such section may or may not have been originally a separate revelation.

As time went on, the Prophet sometimes forgot the text of past revelations, which some of his followers still remembered. In other cases, new revelations came down which seemed to cancel earlier ones. In answer to questions, or perhaps criticisms, of these changes, Qoran Chapter II, verse 106, was revealed. "Whenever[2] We suppress a verse or cause it to be forgotten, We bring one which is better or similar. Do you not know that God is Almighty?"

It is apparent that the Messenger of God had never attempted to define God in philosophic terms, as modern theologians attempt to do. It is not, indeed, the task of the prophet to know *about* God and to formulate a scientific description of His attributes. Rather is it the rôle of the prophet to know God and to obtain some form of contact with Him. The Apostle, in this instance, seems to consider God as an All-Powerful Ruler, who is perfectly entitled to change or modify orders previously issued.

After the death of Muhammad, when Muslim thinkers came in contact with theologians and philosophers in other countries, a

---

[2] God is speaking.

dogma appeared to the effect that the Qoran had existed in Heaven from all eternity, a theory which seems far removed from the simple mentality of Muhammad himself.

The Messenger of God passes equally lightly over the vexed problem of Free Will and Predestination. In one place he seems to say that God has predestined some men to be righteous and others to be wicked. Elsewhere, however, he states that man's salvation depends on his own efforts. Prophets, it must be admitted, are never theologians; the two types are incompatible.

Finally, it must be understood that the Qoran is not a classified textbook of faith or morals. In the course of his ministry, which lasted for twenty-two years, 610 to 632, the Apostle suffered many vicissitudes and encountered a great many problems. When faced with some difficulty, he often claimed to have received a revelation in which God instructed him how to deal with the particular situation which confronted him.

The revelation in question, however, although it came as a solution of a specific problem, was subsequently incorporated in the Qoran and thereby became Islamic Law. Thus a woman complained to Muhammad that she had been deprived of her inheritance. The ensuing revelation laid down the proportion of the inheritance which the plaintiff was to receive but it also became the Muslim law for all female inheritance ever since.

In order, therefore, to understand the Qoran, it is necessary to have a knowledge of the vicissitudes of the Prophet's life. A student who is not a Muslim, and who reads the Qoran through from beginning to end without any knowledge of the events of the Apostle's life, will understand very little from it.

But while the reading of the Qoran today may make little impression on Western students, there is evidence to show that the contemporary effect produced was overwhelming. When the Qoran was read aloud, the listeners were at times overcome with fear and trembling. Bearded warriors burst into tears, fainted or fell into a spiritual ecstasy, in which they temporarily lost consciousness of the world around them. Many stories have come down to us of men falling dead when they heard some verse describing the fate of the wicked in hell. Whatever allowances we make for exaggeration, there can be no doubt of the profound impression produced.

Such phenomena are not unknown in the history of religious revivals, especially among emotional peoples. I have personally known bedouins remain completely calm in an emergency, when Europeans were showing signs of panic. The normal demeanour of the Central Arabians is one of quiet dignity. But beneath this outwardly calm appearance, there seem to be deeply submerged moods of passion and emotion more profound than those experienced by Europeans.

In addition to the enthusiasm which it provoked, the Qoran inspired its hearers with intense fear. The seventh century Arabians had simple and direct minds, devoid of cynicism. They believed that what they heard were the actual words of God, describing with vivid homely details the unbearable tortures of hell-fire which awaited them. The shock often produced such terror that the hearers fainted or fell dead, possibly from a heart attack.

*   *   *

There can be no doubt that Muhammad himself was profoundly alarmed at the prospect of hell, and that the early passionate revelations on this subject were the product of his personal emotions. In some places also, he seems to foresee the occurrence of an earthly catastrophe, an earthquake or fire from Heaven, as a punishment on the wickedness of Mecca.

It has become fashionable in recent years among Western Christians to deprecate fear of hell. Traditionally, however, "fear" was always considered to be an essential quality of Christians. According to Tor Andrae, the homilies of Ephraim, a preacher of the Nestorian Christian Church in the sixth century, resemble Muhammad's descriptions of hell in the actual expressions, phrases, formulae and manner of words used.

It may almost be said that fear of hell was the original basis of all the Prophet's teaching, and that he owed much of his language on the subject to Syrian Christianity. He believed that the pious *should* be afraid.

As has already been stated Muhammad's first "call" was followed by an interval of possibly two or three years, during which he received no further visitations. Once the revelations recommenced at the end of this interlude, they continued until the end of his life. The Prophet claimed that the revelations were the words of God himself. It is essential, in reading the Qoran, to remember throughout that the speaker is God.

Various writers have attempted to classify under a number of heads the manner in which Muhammad received his revelations.

Firstly, there is a tradition that, when asked how a revelation came, the Apostle replied that sometimes it came to him with a sound like a bell. When it left him, he knew what it had said. This description does not suggest that he heard precise words but rather that, on the conclusion of the experience, he found certain ideas imprinted on his mind.

Secondly, some traditions seem to assert that God spoke to the Prophet, as it were from behind a veil. On these occasions, he appears to have heard actual words, which he was able to commit to memory and subsequently to repeat.

Thirdly, the Apostle is said to have stated that sometimes God spoke to him through an angel in the form of a man. This figure seems to have normally been assumed to be the Archangel Gabriel.

It appears that, in general, the Apostle knew when a revelation was coming. Normally he lay down and was covered with a cloak or a quilt. At times he perspired profusely, even in cold weather. At the end of the revelation, he sat up and repeated the message received. At times, however, it appears that a revelation, or perhaps an inspiration, came to him instantaneously when he was riding, or perhaps at a public gathering in answer to a question.

*　　*　　*

It is interesting to compare the form in which Muhammad received his revelations with similar passages in the Old Testament. For example, Numbers XV, verse 1, says:

> And the Lord spake unto Moses, saying,
> "Speak unto the Children of Israel and say unto
> Them, when ye be come into the land . . . "

Or again, Leviticus XXII, verse 1:

> And the Lord spake unto Moses, saying,
> "Speak unto Aaron and to his sons, that they . . . "

Qoran V, verse 4, says,
> They ask you as to what is allowed them. Say:
> The good things are allowed to you . . .

or again:

> Ask the Children of Israel how many clear signs
> We have given them . . .

The whole Qoran consists solely of what God said to Muhammad,
so there is no necessity to introduce each passage with the words,
"The Lord spake unto . . ." Otherwise, however, the style is strikingly similar, as also are the details of day-to-day practical affairs
concerning which, in both cases, God is represented as giving direct
orders. There is more mention of Moses in the Qoran than of any
other individual and there is no doubt that Muhammad regarded
himself as a divine messenger in the same category.

*   *   *

Mention has already been made of Ali ibn abi[3] Talib, whom the
Messenger of God had taken into his household in order to help his
father, Abu Talib, with his expenses. Ali was ten years old when the Call
came to Muhammad, and he became the first male convert to Islam.

It appears to have been about this time, not long after his Call, that
Muhammad began some form of ritualistic prayer, preceded by formal ablutions. According to Aisha, who later became the Prophet's
wife, God first commanded him to make two prostrations in the course
of each prayer, though the number was subsequently increased to
four. The prostration consisted in first assuming a kneeling attitude,
and then bending forward until the nose and forehead touched the
ground.

Tradition relates that the Messenger of God, accompanied by Ali,
used to slip out of Mecca and take refuge in some small secluded
valley in the surrounding mountains in order to perform the ritual
prayers. One day, Abu Talib came upon them unawares and asked
what they were doing. The Prophet is alleged to have replied that God
had sent him as a Messenger to mankind to teach them His religion,
which he was now practising. He begged his uncle, Abu Talib, to
accept his guidance and to help him to disseminate the new faith.
But the old man replied that he could not give up the religion of his
fathers. Nor, he added, could he join in exercises which necessitated
his placing his backside above his head—referring to the prostrations

[3] Abu becomes abi in the genitive.

which he had witnessed. Muhammad, however, could rest assured that he would not himself oppose him.

This little story, which we owe to Aisha, seems surely to smack of truth. It illustrates vividly the rough, outspoken character of Abu Talib, too old and conservative to change his ways. Yet he had a heart of gold, which impelled him always to stand by his nephew, without, however, taking much interest in his new-fangled ideas.

The third person to accept Islam, after Khadija and Ali, was Zaid ibn Haritha, whom we have already seen as a slave boy, given by Khadija to Muhammad, and then manumitted by him and adopted as his son.

The fourth convert was a man of middle age. His real name seems to have been Atik, but he was universally known as Abu Bekr, the son of Abu Quhafa, of the Taim clan of Quraish.[4] Abu Bekr was a prosperous merchant, though not among the richest of Quraish. He was a man of kindly disposition and was generally popular. Genealogy was a hobby of his and he appears to have been widely accepted as an expert on the subject.

There are many indications that Muhammad was by nature a man of a somewhat retiring disposition, hesitant and anxious to avoid publicity. He had agreed with Khadija and with the two boys, Ali and Zaid, to keep his religion secret. But Abu Bekr, once converted, became an active proselytiser. In 610, Abu Bekr was thirty-seven years old, while Muhammad was three years older. As compared to the majority of the early converts, Abu Bekr was a mature man of the world. Another of the first proselytes was Zubair ibn al Awwám, a cousin of the Apostle, who was still in his teens, and Saad ibn abi Waqqás, an apprentice arrow-maker, who was seventeen. As we shall see again later, Islam was distinctly a "youth movement".

A number of modern writers have attributed this feature to economic reasons. Quraish had originally been a nomadic tribe and many of the clans were still in that condition—in fact, some have continued so until our own times. Others had settled down in Mecca, as we have seen, under the guidance of Qusai, some two hundred years earlier. To commence with, however, they had merely assumed responsibility for the pilgrimage.

Probably only after the overthrow of the Himyarites by the Abyssinians in 525, Quraish had begun to play as increasing part in the wealthy oriental trade. As a result, certain sections of the tribe,

[4] Genealogical tree, p. 63.

particularly Beni Makhzoom and Beni Abid Menaf, had become rich, while some others were still in their original tribal poverty. This new contrast between wealth and poverty, it has been suggested, had given rise to a feeling of uneasiness among the younger generation. These conjectures are too manifestly a mere copy of recent ways of thought in Europe to command much credence. In addition, I have myself lived a great part of my life among Arabs, much of it with the poorest elements of the population, but I have never noticed among the poor any jealousy of their richer fellow-citizens.

It may well appear incredible today in the West that people should exist anywhere who do not attach primary importance to money. Yet such was and is largely the case. To attribute to these people in the sixth century the present materialistic outlook of the Western world is entirely to misread history. Arabs have always been jealous people, but wealth was not the object of their jealousy.

We may, however, readily admit that the change in social conditions in Quraish, as the result of a partial abandonment of nomadism for a settled life, may have unconsciously led a number of young people to question the traditions of an earlier age.

In the Western world of today, economics play so large a part in life and thought that we are satisfied with any explanation which attributes the troubles of past ages to economic causes. The East, however, has never attached so much importance to economics. With perhaps truer insight than we possess, differences of wealth were accepted as a matter of course, and it was realised that the rich, in practice, were no happier than the poor. Moreover, and this may be a major factor, their poverty was akin to nature, they lived in great open spaces with their animals, and were not confined to the sordid surroundings of man-made slums.

It is true that, apart from a few boys of Quraish who were cousins or relatives of Muhammad, many of the earliest converts were slaves or from the poorer classes. But this applies to nearly all new religious movements. The great and the powerful are in general more engrossed in worldly duties, not necessarily money-making, but glory, study, power, rule, administration, art and family pride. "Not many wise men after the flesh, not many mighty, not many noble, are called," writes St. Paul of the early Christians, "but God hath chosen . . . the weak things of the world to confound the things which are mighty."[5]

[5] 1 Corinthians I, 26.

Of course, if the new movement is a success and wins wide popular support, Mr. Worldly Wiseman will join it and work himself up into an influential and lucrative position. This, thirty years after the Apostle's death, was to happen to Islam. At the time of which we are now writing, however, not many mighty had as yet rallied to the side of the new Prophet.

*   *   *

Islam began, then, with the conversion of Khadija and Abu Bekr, a few youths mostly related to the Apostle and a handful of poor people and of slaves. All were bound over to strict secrecy. When he wished to recite the ritual prayers, Muhammad retired to some spot where he would not be seen. Abu Bekr was more open and, through him, a few people heard of these new cranks. But as they did no one any harm, nobody worried about them.

Three years passed in this manner. The order to preach publicly came to Muhammad after this interval of doubt and timidity. Chapter XXVI of the Qoran, verses 213 to 218, are believed to refer to this occasion:

So call not upon another god but God, lest you be of those who will be punished. And warn your nearest relatives and be gracious to those who believe. But if they disobey you, then say, "Surely I am innocent of what you do". And rely on the Mighty One, the Merciful, who sees you when you stand up.

Or Chapter LXXIV:

O thou who art wrapped in a cloak,[6] arise and warn, magnify your Lord, cleanse your clothing and shun uncleanness.

Tradition relates that Ali subsequently gave the following account of what occurred. "The Apostle of God called me and said, 'God has ordered me to warn my family and my nearest relatives, and the task is beyond my strength. I knew that, when I made this message known to them, I should meet with great unpleasantness, so I kept silence until Gabriel came to me. He told me that if I did not do as I

[6] This sentence refers to the fact that Muhammad lay down and was covered with a cloak or quilt when he felt a revelation coming.

was ordered, my Lord would punish me. So get some food ready with a leg of mutton and fill a bowl with milk and get together the sons of Abdul Muttalib, so that I can address them.' "[7]

A minor point about this tradition is the extraordinarily inadequate hospitality offered, although Muhammad, after marrying Khadija, was in comfortable circumstances. The Arab custom has always been to kill an animal for guests, even if it were only a kid of the goats. Ali, indeed, is made in the tradition to comment on the inadequacy of the food, which he says one man could have eaten, yet forty men came and all had as much as they could eat. The explanation probably lies in the desire to attribute a miracle to the Messenger of God. In fact, Muhammad always denied that he had the power to work miracles, but this has not prevented the traditionists from attributing them to him.

As soon as the meal was over, Abu Lahab, one of the Prophet's uncles,[8] dismissed the company, before he could deliver his address. However, the same company was invited to come again and, on this occasion, the Apostle was able to say, "O sons of Abdul Muttalib, God has ordered me to call you to Him. So which of you will help me and be my successor?" This short speech was received with complete silence, until Ali, who was then only thirteen years old, cried out, "O Messenger of God, I will be your helper!" This outburst was greeted with general laughter and the company broke up still chuckling among themselves at the absurdity of the whole affair. As a naturally shy man, the shame which Muhammad suffered at this fiasco can well be imagined.

The impression created in the minds of the Meccans who now, for the first time, began to hear of Muhammad's message, seems to have been that he was mad. Some thought, however, that he was possessed by a jinn or an evil spirit. Such a view might provoke sympathy or ridicule, but it did not immediately give rise to opposition.

*   *   *

As has already been indicated, the task of arranging the chapters of the Qoran chronologically, in the order of their revelation, is a difficult one. While endeavouring to do so, commentators have made

---

[7] Ibn Ishaq. Trans. Guillaume.
[8] Genealogical tree, p. 63.

use of the assumption that the Apostle's preaching did not immediately arouse strong opposition. The Qoran might almost be called a diary of the Prophet's mission. When he was heckled by his opponents, the answers which he was to make were revealed to him and were subsequently recorded in the Qoran.

If this reasoning be correct, then the earliest chapters of the Qoran are those in which no heckling is mentioned. Judged on this basis, the first revelations consisted largely of positive statements, praising the power of God, using the wonders of creation as evidence, and contrasting the Divine Majesty with the weakness and the insignificance of man. Above all, these early chapters carried a warning to the latter of his fate, if he failed to submit to God.

Who is more unbelieving than man? Of what did He create him?
Of a tiny particle He created him and gave him power. Then He
made his way easy. Then He caused him to die and buried him.
Then, if He willed, He raised him to life again.[9]

Or again:

Glorify the name of the Lord, the Most High, who created and
made, gave power and guided.[10]

One of these early chapters makes a special appeal to Quraish, whom the Apostle, at this period, was particularly addressing:

For the protection of Quraish,
Their protection on their winter and their
                              summer journeys,
Let them worship the Lord of this house,
Who feeds them lest they hunger,
And gives them security against fear.[11]

The reference is, of course, to the long caravan journeys to the Yemen and Syria.

It is interesting here to note that God is referred to as the Almighty and the Creator without further explanation, as if the idea were already familiar to his hearers. The pagan Arabs were, indeed, ready

[9] Qoran, Chapter LXXX, 17 to 22.   [10] Chapter LXXXVII, 1 to 3.
[11] Qoran, Chapter CVI, 1 to 4.

to admit the existence of a Supreme God—Muhammad's father had been called Abdulla, Servant of God. They regarded their idols (or perhaps the spirits who indwelt the idols) as minor deities, whose intercession with Almighty God might be invoked.

Such statements, at any rate, seem to have aroused no opposition. Any laughter or ridicule at this stage can probably be attributed to the claim of such an apparently commonplace fellow-citizen to be a special Messenger of God. Prophets have no honour in their own countries.

*   *   *

Ibn Ishaq tells us that Muhammad's descriptions of the glory and power of God did not cause Quraish to turn against him until he began to denounce their idols. When, however, they heard their gods attacked, the Meccans were indignant.

Tabari quotes an early letter addressed to Abdul Malik ibn Merwan, who was khalif[12] from 685 to 705, which reads as follows:

"Now as for the Messenger of God, when he summoned his tribe to accept the guidance and light revealed to him, . . . they did not hold back from him when he first called them, but almost hearkened to him until he mentioned their idols . . . then the body of the people turned back from him and left him."[13]

The use of the expression "turned back" seems to suggest that, at the very beginning of his public mission, the Apostle met with a certain sympathy from his hearers.

When opposition increased, a number of prominent men of Quraish went as a deputation to Muhammad's uncle Abu Talib, who was apparently recognised as the head of the family of the descendants of Hashim. The principal members of the deputation were two brothers, Utba and Shaiba, the sons of Rabia. With them were Amr abu Jahal, the head of the clan of Beni Makhzoom, and Abu Sofian ibn Harb, of the descendants of Abid Shems, the elder brother of Hashim,[14] and a few others. In general they represented tne richer families engaged in the caravan trade.

"O Abu Talib," Ibn Ishaq reports them as saying, "your nephew has cursed our gods and insulted our religion . . . Either you must

---

[12] Or caliph.   [13] *See also* W. Montgomery Watt, *Muhammad at Mecca.*
[14] Genealogical tree, p. 63.

stop him or you must allow us to deal with him." The old man gave them a conciliatory reply. The Apostle, however, continued to publish his religion and to call men to join him.

Their first effort having produced no result, the delegation returned a second time and lodged an even more strongly worded protest. Moreover, they now had a further cause of complaint in the fact that the Messenger of God had stated that the ancestors of Quraish, having been in their lifetime idolaters, were now suffering torments in hell-fire.

"We are not prepared to tolerate that our ancestors be reviled and our gods insulted," the second deputation said. "You, Abu Talib, enjoy a respected position among us, but unless you restrain your nephew or get rid of him, we will be obliged to take action against both of you together."

Abu Talib was deeply alarmed and distressed by this scene. We need not think of the members of the deputation as particularly evil and unscrupulous men. With one or two exceptions, they were wise, respectable and public-spirited citizens, the most prominent and successful business men in the community. As such, they were anxious for stability and security, and were disturbed by agitators propounding new-fangled and revolutionary ideas. Abu Talib was very much of the same type. Today he would be like a respectable professional man, perhaps the manager of the local branch of a bank, whose nephew was a preacher of red revolution. His uncle was fond of Muhammad, but the latter's activities were really making his situation extremely embarrassing.

Abu Talib sent for his nephew and told him what the notables of Mecca had said. "Spare me and yourself," the old man begged. "Do not put on me a burden greater than I can bear."

The Apostle of God was completely taken aback by this appeal, imagining that his uncle was about to withdraw his protection and leave him to his fate. "O uncle!" he cried, "by God, if they were to put the sun in my right hand and the moon in my left, on condition that I abandon this course, until God has made it victorious or I perish in it, I would not abandon it." Turning away to leave, he suddenly burst into tears.

The old man was deeply moved at his nephew's emotion. "Come back, O son of my brother," he called. "Go out and say what you please, for, by God, I will never give you up, come what may."

Two statements made by Muhammad had particularly angered the Meccans. The first of these was his denunciations of the local gods and the second the emphasis which he laid on the Last Judgement, and the eternal punishment of idolaters in hell-fire. These oft-repeated themes had provoked the Meccans to enquire what had become of their fathers and their ancestors, who had lived in idolatry. When the Apostle answered unhesitatingly that all of them were already suffering in hell, the Meccans were moved to indignation. A tenderness and respect for their ancestors has perhaps always been a feature of the people of Arabia. Sitting among the nomads in their tents, I have often heard a man endeavour to calm another by saying soothingly, "May your father be in Heaven!"

The possession of many sons has always been thought in the Middle East to be the strength and glory of old age. Ibn Ishaq tells a (to us) curious story of a third deputation of notables to Abu Talib, which brought with it a young man. The elders pointed out that the youth in question was the strongest and the most handsome young man in all Quraish. "Adopt him as your son," they said, "and give up to us the son of your brother, who has opposed your religion and mocked our way of life." But the stout-hearted old man refused to consider so cold-blooded a transaction.

The failure of the three deputations to Abu Talib greatly exacerbated the situation. The indignant notables whose demands had been rejected now began openly to speak against the Apostle and against the handful of persons whom he had converted. But tribal solidarity was almost an instinct among these people, just as national loyalty is among Europeans today. Even if we disapprove of the government of our country, we still feel obliged to stand by our compatriots if they are threatened with attack by foreigners.

Abu Talib was the recognised head of the descendants of Hashim and the members rallied to support his attitude, although the great majority of them were still idolaters. It was the recognised duty of a clan to protect all its members, even if they were in the wrong or had committed crimes of which their fellow tribesmen disapproved. Any man who used physical violence against Muhammad would therefore have incurred a feud with all Beni Hashim. The poets were soon in action to defend the clan:

> Quraish summoned all the world to force us;
> They failed, and jealous fury filled their breasts.
> We have never bowed to those who would coerce us,
> Nor submitted to the proud in their behests.

As we have already seen, however, a number of the first converts to Islam were slaves, clients or strangers, with no fellow-tribesmen in Mecca to protect them. Upon these men the Prophet's enemies were able to inflict not only reproaches and recriminations but actual physical violence and imprisonment.

The attachment of the pre-Islamic Arabs to their ancestors was not merely filial affection, still less pigheaded conservatism. Nevertheless, Muhammad's condemnation of their ancestors seems to have provoked them more than his denunciation of their idols. The explanation may lie in their belief in heredity. They took immense trouble in the breeding of their horses and their camels, because they were convinced that the offspring would inherit the qualities of the parents.

Applied to human beings, this meant that brave, noble and knightly ancestors would produce equally splendid descendants. When a tribe gloried in the virtues of its ancestors, it was thus indirectly praising their living descendants. Conversely, when the Messenger of God condemned the ancestors of Quraish, he condemned also their offspring, the living members of the tribe.

It is interesting to consider that our modern theories of human equality tend to discredit heredity. We like to think that all babies are born "equal", must all receive the same education and, as a result, will all prove as good as one another in adult life. Yet it is doubtful if this is really true. The son of a musician will probably inherit a facility for music, the son of a fine soldier is likely to do well in a military career. Many other factors, of course, affect the issue. If the Arab belief in heredity was an over-simplification in one direction, our own popular neglect of it may be equally erroneous in the other.

Perhaps also the Arabs realised that knowledge of the great deeds performed by his ancestors constitutes a strong incentive to a young man to live up to their example.

*   *   *

Mention has been made of the fact that tribesmen from all over Arabia were in the habit of coming on pilgrimage once a year to the idol temple of Mecca. The pilgrimage took place during the sacred months of truce and was preceded by a number of fairs held in the vicinity. The time of the annual fairs and of the pilgrimage was now approaching. The year was 613, and Muhammad was forty-three years old.

The leaders of Quraish were anxious lest visitors from other parts of Arabia be persuaded by Muhammad that the idols of the Kaaba were undeserving of worship. We may credit the Meccans with a genuine hereditary loyalty to the customs of their ancestors but, in addition, it is to be noted that the prestige of Quraish and the financial success of the fairs accompanying the pilgrimage depended on the public veneration for the temple. To destroy the reputation of the Kaaba for sanctity would be to strike at the very root of the power and prosperity of Quraish.

Before the commencement of the pilgrimage season, therefore, some of the notables discussed measures to prevent Muhammad from persuading the pilgrims that the idols were no longer worthy of veneration. They agreed all to use the same argument. Visitors were to be told that the Apostle was a magician, who was able by his spells to cause dissension between a man and his father, his son or his brother, or between him and his wife. The fact that the converts to Islam had hitherto been mostly individuals who had thereby incurred the anger of their relatives lent colour to the charge. In the seventh century, belief in sorcery of this kind was widely held all over the world.

This suggestion is alleged to have come from Al Waleed ibn al Mughira, one of the wealthy merchants of Quraish.[15]

Qoran, Chapter LXXIV, verse 24 onwards, is believed to refer to this incident.

> He said, "This is nothing but enchantment.
> This is only the talk of a human being."
> I will cast him into hell.

The speaker in the last line, of course, is God. The reference to "the talk of a human being" was intended to contradict the Apostle's claim that his messages were received from God.

From this period onwards, much of the Qoran consists of answers believed to have been dictated to Muhammad by God Himself, instructing him how to reply to his hecklers, or denouncing the actions of his enemies.

[15] Genealogical tree, p. 63. Khalid, the son of this Al Waleed, was to become a famous Muslim commander.

The Prophet's opponents accordingly accosted the pilgrims who came to Mecca, warning them against his words the object of which was, they said, to sow dissension among them. It is quite possible that this campaign of defamation did the Apostle more good than harm. Modern publicity seems to have discovered that the first essential to success is to become known to the public, whether as a criminal or as a hero is only of minor importance. The hostile remarks which the Quraish leaders took such trouble to disseminate among the pilgrims may perhaps have served to enhance Muhammad's importance and to carry his name to distant parts of Arabia.

NOTABLE DATES

Birth of Muhammad	570
Marriage	595
The Call	610
The Interlude	610–613

PERSONALITIES

Notables of Quraish

Utba and Shaiba, sons of Rabia

Abu Jahal Amr ibn Hisham, chief of the Beni Makhzoom clan

Abu Sofian ibn Harb, of the Abid Shems clan

Abu Talib, Muhammad's uncle

VI

The Emigration to Abyssinia

There is none that understandeth, there is none that seeketh
after God . . .
Their throat is an open sepulchre; with their tongues
they have used deceit;
The poison of asps is under their lips . . .
There is no fear of God before their eyes.

Romans III

They said, "you are only mortals as we are. The Merciful God has
not revealed anything to you. You are only liars."
They replied, "Our Lord knows that we are indeed sent to you as
messengers. Our only duty is to deliver a clear message."
O the tragedy of men. No apostle comes to them but they mock
him.

Qoran XXXVI, 15 to 17 and 30

VI

T HE most active opponents of Muhammad at this period were Abu Jahal, the leader of Beni Makhzoom,[1] and the Prophet's own uncle, Abdul Uzza, more commonly known as Abu Lahab. Abu Jahal was apparently a respected citizen with a reputation for sagacity and a valued member of the council of elders. Abu Lahab was a less respectable personality.

In a certain sense, the charge directed against the Messenger of God of being a divider of families was justified. We have seen that many of the new converts were young men, sometimes under twenty, and that their activities often aroused the indignation of their parents. An early Quraish convert, Khalid ibn Saeed, for example, seems to have been turned out of his father's house and to have been obliged to live with the household of the Apostle.

It is difficult to assess the exact degree of persecution suffered by the new converts. Arabs, on the whole, are kind and easy-going people, and the Meccans of the seventh century seem to have been no exception. Undoubtedly a good deal of ridicule and sarcasm was directed at the Apostle, but this can scarcely be called "persecution", as it has been practised throughout history by the more brutal peoples of Europe and Asia. The Romans crucified their victims. Under Nero, the Christians were burned alive or thrown to the lions. The Tartars exterminated their enemies by thousands. In mediaeval Europe, heretics were burned at the stake or tortured on the rack. No such methods were used, or even dreamed of, by the Meccans against the first Muslims.

Nevertheless, the continual sneers must have been exasperating. Ibn Ishaq has an interesting passage which is worthy of quotation on how the Messenger of God was treated by Quraish at this period. It is a tradition stated to have come from Amr ibn al Aasi, who was still at that time an idolater, though he was later to become the conqueror of Egypt for Islam.

Asked what was the worst thing which Quraish did to the Apostle, he replied, "I was with them one day in the square outside the Kaaba and the Messenger of God was mentioned. Some of them

[1] Genealogical tree, p. 63.

said that they had never known anything like the trouble which they had suffered from this fellow, who had reviled their religion and divided the community against itself."

"While they were thus discussing him, the Apostle came towards them, kissed the black stone and then passed by them as he walked round the temple.[2] As he passed they said some injurious things about him. I could see this from his expression. He went on, and as as he passed them for the second time, they once again attacked him in the same manner. Then he passed the third time and they did the same. He stopped and said, 'Will you listen to me, O Quraish? By Him who holds my life in His hand, I bring you slaughter.' This word so struck the people that not one but all stood silent and still. Even one of them, who had hitherto been most violent, spoke to him in the kindest way possible, saying, 'Depart, O abu al Qasim[3] for, by God, you are not a man of violence'."

The same tradition goes on to relate how, the next day, a group was discussing him when the Messenger of God appeared. They surrounded him, asking, "Are you the man who said such and such against our gods?" The Apostle replied that he had said that. One of them seized him by his cloak but Abu Bekr intervened, weeping and saying, "Would you kill a man for saying 'God is my Lord'?" Then they left him. "That", Amr ibn al Aasi is reported as saying, "was the worst that I ever saw Quraish do to him."

One day Abu Jahal, the chief of Beni Makhzoom, met the Messenger of God in the street and loaded him with abusive remarks and with sarcasms on the subject of his new religion. Muhammad, however, passed on without replying and joined a group of Quraish in the space outside the Kaaba. Shortly afterwards, one of the Apostle's uncles, Hamza ibn Abdul Muttalib[4] passed by, with his bow hanging from his shoulder. He was an athletic man, of great physical strength, and was extremely devoted to hunting.

A freedwoman, who had heard Abu Jahal's abuse of the Messenger of God, accosted Hamza and described the incident to him. Hamza was furious and hurried to the Kaaba, where he saw Abu Jahal sitting among a group of men. Raising his bow, Hamza struck him on the head shouting, "Will you insult him when I too follow his religion? Hit me back if you dare!"

[2] He was performing the customary ritual circumambulations of the Kaaba.

[3] To call a man father of his son was to show respect. Qasim was the name of Muhammad's first son, who had died as a baby.

[4] Genealogical tree, p. 63.

Some men of his own clan, Beni Makhzoom, ran to Abu Jahal's assistance, but the latter said quietly, "Let him alone, for I did insult his nephew." Whether Hamza had previously intended to declare himself a Muslim, or whether he did so out of pique on the spur of the moment, we do not know. But his accession to the little group of Muslims greatly strengthened Muhammad's position, for Hamza was a famous warrior and many people were afraid of him.

A story exists, but of doubtful credibility, that the elders of Quraish one day approached the Messenger of God and offered to give him a large sum of money, or even to make him the ruler of the town, if he would give up attacking their gods. The story seems improbable because, at this period, the Meccans were not really afraid of Muhammad. He was, they thought, a troublesome agitator, though with only a small following of less than a hundred people, in a town of some ten thousand inhabitants.

That they should offer a money bribe is possible, though in that case they must obviously have badly misunderstood their man. But it is not reasonable that they should have offered to make him their ruler. The episode may perhaps have been misunderstood. Quraish might well have accused the Prophet of wanting money or of wishing to make himself ruler of Mecca.

A favourite approach adopted by his opponents was that of asking for a sign. They would believe him, they said, if he would bring down an angel to confirm his claims. Or if he would ask God to give him palaces and gardens and gold and silver. "Let the heavens fall down upon us in fragments," said one, "and we shall believe you." Others claimed that they had discovered that the Prophet had been taught what to say by a man from Yemama in Nejed. "The Apostle", Ibn Ishaq tells us, "went away sad and grieved."

A man of Quraish called Al Nadhr had lived for some time at the court of the Lakhmid Kings of Hira. Here he had learned the old Persian romances, which told of the stirring deeds of such mythical heroes as Rustum and Isbandiyar. When the Apostle sat in the midst of a group of people and spoke to them of the ancient prophets and of how they too had warned people of God's anger, Al Nadhr would sit a short distance away. Then he would call out, "I can tell you better stories than he can, so come over here to me". Chapter LXVIII[5] probably refers to this man, where it says in verse 15, "when

[5] The Qoran was not collected into one book and divided into chapters and verses until after the Prophet's death. The quotations given in this narrative were presumably in Muhammad's lifetime, taken from his memory or the mass of notes taken by his followers.

our verses are recited to him, he says, 'These are stories of the ancient peoples'."

Like the Old Testament prophets, Muhammad laid great stress on the coming punishment of the wicked, whether in this world or in the next. To illustrate this theme, he made use of many Old Testament stories, notably that of Moses, his warnings to Pharaoh and the ultimate drowning of Pharaoh in the Red Sea. His accounts of the events told in the Old Testament, however, are sometimes inaccurate, and, in some cases, incomprehensible to us.

Chapter XIX of the Qoran tells the story of Zacharias in the temple and of the birth of John the Baptist, of the annunciation to the Virgin Mary and of the Virgin Birth of Christ. In this account, the Virgin is described as the sister of Aaron. The Arabic for Mary is Miriam and the Virgin Mary is called in Arabic, Miriam the Virgin. Much discussion has raged round the fact that the Apostle called Miriam the Virgin the sister of Aaron—the majority of Western commentators have expressed the view that he confused the two women, whose lives were separated by some 1300 years.

Maulana Muhammad Ali, however, in his commentary on the Qoran, states that "only a limited acquaintance with the Arabic language has made men call this an anachronism". He claims that Jews were often called sons of Moses and that the expression "sister of Aaron" was of a similar nature.

In fact, the Apostle's references to Old Testament stories present a number of such difficulties. To the impartial observer, the deduction would possibly be that he had heard these stories from Jews and Christians, but had failed to memorise all the details correctly. In view of the fact that Muslims insist that the Apostle of God could not read or write, this is not surprising.

The correct and exact record of "facts" is a process to which modern scholarship attaches great importance but concrete facts may be of no significance, where the inculcation of moral lessons is the object in view. For example, if Christ's parable of the Good Samaritan had been reported in one place as "a certain man went down from Jerusalem to Jericho", and in another place "from Jerusalem to Damascus", the moral teaching would not have been affected. We should merely accept that one of the copyists had made a slip. If, therefore, Muhammad had made errors of fact due to failure of memory, no significance need have been attached to them.

A problem arises, however, owing to the Muslim belief that the

Qoran contains the actual words of God. Many passages begin "Say". "Say: I am only a mortal like you." God Himself is telling the Apostle the exact words which he is to repeat to the people. Any allowance for human error could be thought to weaken the authority of such a message. In the face of these difficulties, we can perhaps best use the formula which the Muslims themselves used, when confronted by similar problems—"God knows the truth".

Ibn Ishaq tells us that, at this period, the Meccans sent two men to the large Jewish colony at Yathrib, some two hundred and fifty miles north of Mecca, to enquire their opinion of Muhammad. According to this account, the Jews told the Meccans to ask Muhammad about the legend of the Seven Sleepers and of "the mighty traveller who reached the confines of the East and West". The messengers duly returned and propounded the two riddles to the Apostle in public. He promised to reply the next day but, in fact, he brought the answer only after fifteen days. He then recited Chapter XVIII of the Qoran, referring to the story of the Seven Sleepers and their dog, and explaining the mighty traveller as "the man with the two horns", a sobriquet for Alexander the Great. The fact that these riddles were, in actual fact, put to the Messenger of God to test his claim to be a prophet seems to be proved by this chapter. It seems, however, unlikely that the questions had been suggested by Jews. Both problems seem to have a strong Greek flavour.

One day the companions of the Apostle came together and somebody remarked that Quraish had never heard the Qoran read aloud distinctly. A slave called Abdulla ibn Masood, a recent convert, offered to read it in public. Those present, however, pointed out that it would be better for a man of good family to make the attempt, as his relatives would be bound to protect him from physical violence. But Abdulla insisted. "Let me go," he pleaded. "God will protect me."

The next morning, Abdulla took up his position in the open space outside the Kaaba and began in a loud voice to recite a passage from the Qoran. The spectators at first looked at him with curiosity. "What on earth is this son of a slavewoman saying?" they asked one another. Soon, however, they realised that he was reciting some of Muhammad's revelations, and they surrounded him and began to beat him, and to strike him in the face, but he continued to recite as long as he could.

Eventually he was obliged to stop and returned to his companions, his face bruised and bleeding. "This is just what we feared would happen to you," they said, but he replied ecstatically that he would do it again the next morning. But his friends answered, "No, you have done enough. You have made them listen to something they did not want to hear."

Meanwhile, Quraish were intensifying their opposition. Tribesmen of Quraish who had been converted were dealt with by their families, some being beaten, abused and even denied food. If this were done in the family, fathers to their sons or elder to younger brothers, no inter-clan feuds resulted. Slaves, menial persons, clients or refugees, who enjoyed no local tribal protection, were, however, exposed to actual physical violence.

Bilal ibn Ribah, a tall African slave, was taken out every morning by his master, Umaiya ibn Khalaf, and made to lie on his back in the scorching heat of the midday sun with a large rock on his chest. "You will stay here," he told him, "until you deny Muhammad and acknowledge Al Lat and Al Uzza." But Bilal was made of sterner stuff. Whenever his owner asked him if he were now ready to recant, he replied only, "One God! One God!"

One day, Abu Bekr passed by while Bilal was being treated in this manner, and said to his master, "How long are you going to continue maltreating this poor fellow?" "It was you who corrupted him," replied his tormentor angrily. "I have a black slave," answered Abu Bekr, "who is stronger than Bilal and is still an idolater. I will exchange him with you for Bilal."

No sooner was the transaction completed than Abu Bekr, now his master, freed Bilal from slavery.

*   *   *

The Messenger of God who, as we have seen, was a kind, rather hesitant personality at this stage of his life, was deeply distressed by the vexations borne by his followers of Quraish and, even more so, by the actual physical sufferings of his humbler converts.

"It might be better for you if you went to Abyssinia," he said to some of them. "The people there are friendly and the king rules with justice, for it is a Christian country. You could stay there until God relieves us of victimisation in this country." It is interesting to note that at this period, the Apostle regarded the idolaters of Mecca as his enemies, whereas Christians and Jews he looked upon as more or less allies.

According to Ibn Ishaq, who mentions them all by name, eighty-three men took up the Prophet's suggestion and left for Abyssinia, a number of them accompanied by their women and children. Prominent among them was Othman ibn Affan, of the clan of Beni Umaiya and a cousin of Abu Sofian, of whom we shall hear more. Othman was married to Ruqaiya, a daughter of Muhammad and Khadija.

The list seems to have included very nearly all the persons who had accepted Islam and the Messenger of God must have remained with a much reduced group of adherents, among the generally hostile inhabitants of Mecca, a situation which proves him to have possessed a considerable degree of moral courage and conviction. Ali and Zaid stayed with him and the ever faithful Abu Bekr. The emigrants did not all go ostentatiously together but in small parties of eight or ten.

The Arabs of Mecca were not unfamiliar with Abyssinia, a country with which they occasionally did business. Moreover, as has already been related, the Abyssinians had ruled the Yemen for some fifty years, from 525 to 574. It seems probable that the arrival of the handful of Meccan refugees gave rise to little public interest in Aksum, the Abyssinian capital. There appears to have been freedom of worship in the country and the Muslims were able to practise their new religion without let or hindrance. How they earned their living in Abyssinia has not apparently been recorded. As some of them were in the future to remain voluntarily in Abyssinia after they could have returned safely to Arabia, we must assume that most of them did find a comfortable means of livelihood.

A modern authority,[6] however, has suggested that the emigration to Abyssinia may have been at least partly due to internal schisms inside the Muslim group, which were subsequently hushed up by Muslim historians. It appears impossible at this date to discover all the motives which inspired the emigration.

Another suggestion, based on the study of the list of names given by Ibn Ishaq, is that the majority of the emigrants to Abyssinia were of the clans of Abid Shems and Beni Makhzoom. These were the families to which belonged the richest merchants and many of the leaders of Quraish, and who formed the strongest elements in the opposition to Muhammad's "innovations". It may be deduced from this that Muslim converts from these clans met with ostracism and

[6] W. Montgomery Watt, *Muhammad at Mecca.*

GENEALOGICAL TREE
THE DESCENDANTS OF ABID MENAF, THE NEAREST RELATIVES OF MUHAMMAD

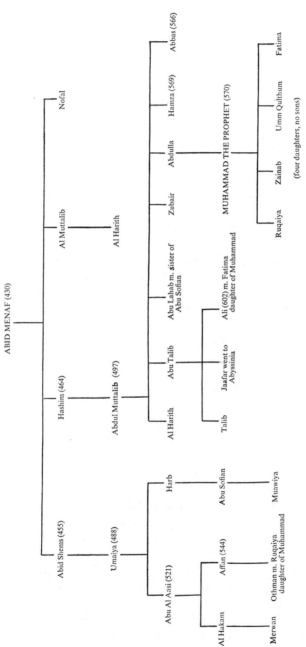

NOTES:

(1) Abdul Muttalib had ten sons, but three are omitted.
(2) The descendants of Hashim and Al Muttalib were the victims of the boycott.
(3) Abu Lahab, who refused to stand in with Beni Hashim, was married to the sister of Abu Sofian of Beni Umaiya, and went with his "in-laws".
(4) Most of these men had many more sons, omitted for lack of space.

persecution in their domestic circles. Members of less wealthy families, such as Beni Hashim, Al Muttalib, Zuhra or Taim perhaps suffered less domestic opposition, with the result that few of them went to Abyssinia. The reasons for the emigration may have been varied but it is impossible to be entirely positive on the subject.

Mecca did a certain amount of trade with Abyssinia, particularly in leatherwork, and the peoples of the two countries seem to have known one another. Some scholars have speculated that Muhammad himself had been to the country and knew the Negus, or Emperor, personally. There is, however, no proof of this theory.

When the leaders of Quraish realised that a large proportion of Muhammad's followers had gone to Abyssinia, they sent a deputation to the Negus to ask for their extradition. The two delegates sent were men of outstanding capability and intelligence, Abdulla ibn abi Rabia and Amr ibn al Aasi, later to become one of the most famous of Muslim conquerors. It might appear curious to us that Quraish should want the emigrants back. If they had been making trouble in Mecca, their departure might have been thought to have been a victory for the opposition. Two possible explanations may perhaps be offered. The first is that amicable relations with the Negus were important to Meccan business. The second, and perhaps the more probable, was that tribes reckoned their power in men. They, therefore, instinctively resented the departure of a tribesman to join another community in a distant country.

Leatherwork seems to have been a valued product of Mecca and the delegates took with them a considerable consignment. They were instructed on arrival to bribe the courtiers and the Abyssinian leaders and to persuade them to use their influence with the Negus on their behalf. Abdulla and Amr then requested a royal audience, at which they said that some people from Mecca had taken refuge in the dominions of the Negus. "They have forsaken our religion and not accepted yours but have introduced a new religion which they have invented." They begged the Negus to send them back to Mecca. The notables of the court, who had accepted the bribes, advised the Emperor to comply.

The latter, however, refused to expel them until they had had an opportunity to state their case. Summoned to the royal presence, the refugees had agreed that Jaafar ibn abi Talib, the brother of Ali, should be their spokesman.[7] He commenced the defence by saying

[7] Genealogical tree opposite.

that they had previously been worshippers of idols, living immoral lives, but that God had sent them an Apostle, who had taught them to worship one God, to abandon idols and to live honestly. Asked by the Negus if they had any of God's revelations with them, Jaafar recited Qoran, Chapter XIX, presumably verses 1 to 40, in which is told the story of Zacharias and the birth of John the Baptist, followed by the Virgin Birth of Jesus.

Verse 35 of this chapter, however, reads: "It beseems not God that He should take to Himself a son." It is possible therefore, that Jaafar stopped at verse 34. Professor Margoliouth, on the other hand, suggests that this verse may have been added later, when the Muslims had clashed with the Christians in Arabia. At any rate the Negus seems to have received the impression that the Muslims were a Christian sect and categorically refused to hand them over to idolaters.

But Amr ibn al Aasi was not yet defeated and next day he requested a second audience at which he begged the Emperor to send for the Muslims again and ask them whether or not Jesus was a creature. Summoned to the royal presence again to answer this question, Jaafar is alleged to have replied, "We say about Him that which our Prophet says, namely that He is the Servant of God, and His Apostle and His Spirit and His Word, which He implanted in Mary, the Blessed Virgin."

It is possible that this scene was invented by later historians, who were sophisticated theologians. If, on the contrary, this anecdote is historical, it shows the Meccans, Muslims and idolaters alike, to have possessed a considerable knowledge of the niceties of the Christian dogma. This is by no means impossible. It will be remembered that a cousin of Muhammad, Waraqa ibn Nofal, had translated portions of the Gospels into Arabic.

The Negus was satisfied with the answer given by Jaafar, and Abdulla and Amr ibn al Aasi returned empty-handed to Mecca.

*   *   *

A young man of Beni Makhzoom by the name of Al Arqam had been converted to Islam and had made his house available as a meeting-place for the Muslims. Being at Al Safa, outside the streets of the little town, it was in a quiet situation, where meetings of the faithful would not attract much attention.

One of the most violent opponents of Muhammad was a certain

Umar ibn al Khattab, of the Adi ibn Kaab clan.[8] A fierce, aggressive man, he was a good deal feared in Mecca. One day this Umar left his house with his sword by his side, with the intention of breaking up a Muslim meeting, attended by some forty people, including women, which he had heard was being held in the house of Al Arqam. Striding up the lane, he met a man of his own clan who asked him where he was going. "I am going to break up this meeting and to kill Muhammad," Umar replied hotly.

"Wouldn't it be better if you went back and dealt with your own family first?" enquired his interlocutor.

"Why? What's wrong with my family?" asked Umar.

"Your brother-in-law Saeed and your sister Fatima have become Muslims. You'd better deal with them first," said the other.

Umar turned on his heel and hurried back to the house occupied by his married sister. The information which he had just received was correct. His sister Fatima and her husband had become Muslims, but had concealed their conversion from Umar. At the time when the latter reached the door of their house, Khabbab, an early convert, was reading to them Chapter XX of the Qoran, a copy of which he had brought for the purpose. Hearing Umar's voice at the door, Khabbab, who was a slave and could have been killed or maimed by Umar, ceased reading and ran to hide in the back of the house.

Umar had heard the sound of reading aloud and burst into the room, crying:

"What's all this nonsense going on?"

"Oh, nothing," said the couple lamely, as people do on such occasions.

"By God, I heard it," shouted Umar, "and I have been told that you have joined Muhammad's religion." He seized his brother-in-law by his clothes as though he would hit him but Fatima tried to intervene to prevent her brother striking her husband, whereupon he hit her in his rage.

"Yes, we are Muslims," they now cried aloud, "we believe in God and His Messenger and you can do what you like!"

When Umar saw the blood running down his sister's face where he had struck her, his anger suddenly evaporated. "Give me what you were reading just now," he said, "so that I can see what Muhammad says." But Fatima, who had hidden the manuscript in her clothes, replied courageously,

[8] Genealogical tree, p. 63.

"O my brother, you are an idolater and unclean, and only the clean can touch it." So Umar went out and washed and when he returned he asked for it again, swearing to give it back.

Umar was well educated and was able to read easily. The chapter in question opened with God addressing the Prophet.

We have not revealed to you the Qoran that you may fail;
—It is a reminder to him who fears,
A revelation which has come down from the Creator of the
    earth and of the high heavens.

"What splendid words are these," Umar is alleged to have said.

Hearing these words, Khabbab the slave emerged from his hiding place and cried, "Come to God, O Umar, come to God, for God's Messenger has been praying for your conversion."

So Umar seized his sword once more and hurried back to the house at Al Safa, where the meeting which he had intended to break up was still in progress. When he knocked at the door, one of the Muslims peeped through a crack and saw him. Turning back to Muhammad, he said in alarm, "It is Umar with his sword on." Fortunately Hamza, the mighty hunter, was in the congregation. "Let him in," he said grimly. "If he wants to make trouble, we will deal with him."

The Apostle went to meet him at the door and, seizing his cloak, said "When will you cease your persecutions, O Umar?" But Umar replied meekly, "O Apostle of God, I have come to you to believe in God and in His Apostle." Such is the generally accepted version of this event, though, in the account Umar himself used to give, the incident of hitting his sister was not mentioned.

The conversion of Umar was a great event in Islam. The Muslims felt more confident with two such champions as Hamza and Umar on their side. The fear generally felt for Umar was perhaps expressed in a saying attributed to the Apostle, "If Satan himself saw Umar coming, he would get out of his way".

Umar was ten years younger than the Messenger of God. As a youth, he was reputed to have been a heavy drinker. The Prophet's second successor, he was to see the little sect of Mecca expand into a world empire. In spite of his violent character, Umar was to become a truly sincere Muslim and a passionate admirer of the Apostle. His character was the opposite of that of Abu Bekr, who always advocated gentleness, whereas Umar invariably recommended the use of force. At home he used to beat his wife.

*   *   *

The conversion of Umar was a severe shock to the opposition. In spite of the departure of the emigrants to Abyssinia, the new ideas were still spreading, even if slowly. The refusal of the Negus to send back the refugees was also an unexpected rebuff to the wealthy merchants. As a result of a meeting held by the notables, a new policy was introduced. Sanctions were to be imposed on the Messenger of God and his near relatives.

A solemn agreement was drawn up according to which all the other clans of Quraish were to impose a ban on the descendants of Hashim and of his brother Al Muttalib.[9] They were to refuse to marry the daughters of these two families or to give their daughters in marriage to them, nor were they to buy from them or sell to them. To add further to the solemnity of the undertaking, a written deed was drawn up and hung in the Kaaba.

As soon as the boycott was enforced, members of the two banned families moved to the alley where Abu Talib lived, in a little valley on the edge of the town, beneath the surrounding mountains. According to one source, some four thousand people came under the ban, but this figure would appear grossly exaggerated if we accept as the total population of Mecca the estimate of ten thousand already given. Perhaps four hundred is a more probable figure, including women and children, clients and slaves.

The ease with which all those people seem to have moved and gathered round their chief seems further to support the theory already mentioned[10] that Quraish were still partially living in tents. Only Abu Lahab, the Apostle's uncle and bitter opponent, abandoned Beni Hashim and joined the opposition. The remainder of the two families stood by Abu Talib, although only a minority of them believed in Muhammad's mission.

Abu Lahab's wife had been in the habit of bringing bundles of thorns and strewing them outside the house of the Messenger of God, so that he trod on them when he stepped out of his door. Chapter CXI of the Qoran refers to Abu Lahab and his wife.

[9] Not Abdul Muttalib, but his uncle Al Muttalib, the brother of Hashim. Genealogical tree, p. 120.

[10] Chapter III, p. 62.

Destruction overtake the hands of Abu Lahab and he will
                                                    perish;
His wealth and his profits will not save him;
He will burn in a fire of flame
Together with his wife the bearer of firewood,[11]
A fibre rope tied round her neck."

The sanctions imposed on the families of Hashim and Al Muttalib
can scarcely be described as a boycott, because they prohibited only
buying, selling and marrying. In other respects, the members of the
family moved freely about the town. The Messenger of God, however,
suffered increasingly from abusive language cast at him. In spite of
this hostility, he seems to have continued to walk about the streets
and to sit, read and argue in the public square, without being exposed
to physical violence.

*   *   *

These years in Mecca, indeed, appear to have consisted of endless
arguments, often followed by new revelations denouncing those who
opposed the Apostle, rather than of persecution in the usually
accepted physical sense of imprisonment, torture and martyrdom.
In the Qoran and the Traditions, we have the arguments used by one
side in the debate only, the idolaters' theses being often only deduc-
ible from the replies given to them in the Qoran.

There is no means today of understanding precisely what were the
beliefs of the idolaters, but it would appear that they were prepared
to admit the existence of a single supreme Deity, if their various idols
were admitted as intermediaries between the Almighty God and men.
The crudity of their statuary does not necessarily mean that they
worshipped stones or trees, any more than Christians worship
plaster figures or painted canvases depicting the saints. It seems
probable that the greater number at least appreciated that the idols
were merely representations of spiritual beings. In view of the fact
that Muhammad himself recognised the existence of angels and jinn,
a number of the Meccans may genuinely have thought that some
compromise would be possible.

There seem to be indications that some at least of the pagans were

[11] The allusion may be to the thorns she scattered, or the expression may be figurative—
she kindled the fire of scandal.

ready to admit the possibility of the survival of human personality in another life but that they disbelieved in a revival of their earthly bodies. One man took an old bone to the Messenger of God and said, "Muhammad, do you say that God can bring this to life again after it has decayed?" "Yes, I do say that," he answered. "God will bring it and you to life again. Then He will send you to hell." The man crumbled the bone between his fingers and blew the dust in the Prophet's face.

Muhammad was basically a quiet, peaceable and friendly character. He loved the people of Mecca, Tabari tells us, and sought anxiously for some kind of formula which would enable him to be reconciled to his people. According to Tabari and Waqidi, the Apostle was one day reciting Chapter LIII of the Qoran in public. He reached verse 18 (in which God bears witness to Muhammad's claims), "He saw of the greatest signs of his Lord. Have you then considered Al Lat and Al Uzza and Manat, the third, the other?"

At this point, Satan put into the Prophet's mind to insert the words, "These are exalted females, whose intercession is to be hoped for." When his recitation was completed, Muhammad prostrated himself, as did also the Muslims who were present. The idolaters, delighted at the mention of their three goddesses as intercessors, prostrated themselves also, so that everyone in the square of the Kaaba, Muslims and non-Muslims alike, bowed down in worship together. The people then dispersed, Quraish congratulating one another that a formula for reconciliation seemed to have been found.

Many Muslim writers, including Ibn Ishaq, omit this passage altogether. Modern Islamic commentators have at times denounced Christian authors for referring to it and accused them of deliberately seeking to discredit the Apostle. Yet entirely to omit it would scarcely be honest. Muhammad himself never claimed to be infallible and the very friendliness of his character would make his estrangement from his own people all the more painful to him.

A further point which may be taken to strengthen the probability of the incident is the statement that the news of a reconciliation between Muhammad and Quraish reached the emigrants in Abyssinia, some of whom actually returned to Mecca on the strength of the report. Ibn Ishaq even gives a full list of the names of those who returned after hearing of the reconciliation, though he does not mention the affair of the Satanic verses, as the "diabolic interven-tion" in the Apostle's recitation is commonly called.

If, indeed, a compromise was reached between the Prophet and the idolaters, it must have lasted several days, perhaps weeks, if it was long enough to persuade some of the refugees to return from Abyssinia. Tabari, however, who mentions the Satanic verses, seems to suggest that Muhammad repented of the compromise the same day. A modern writer, Dr. Muhammad Hamidullah, claims that the Apostle did not pronounce the Satanic verses but that the idola-ters distorted his words.

In so far as the Apostle's infallibility is concerned, another incident is reported to have occurred at about the same time. He was engaged in a long discussion with an influential Meccan, whom he was most desirous to convert, when an old blind man came by and asked him to recite a passage from the Qoran. Muhammad was annoyed at being interrupted, made no reply and eventually walked away, frowning.

Chapter LXXX of the Qoran is believed to refer to this occasion. In it, God reproves the Apostle in the verse, "He frowned and turned away when the blind man came to him." This incident seems to emphasise his readiness to admit his own fallibility. But his con-science continued to reprove him concerning his recognition of the three goddesses as intercessors. At length Gabriel appeared to him and told him that it was not he but Satan who had put the offending verse into his mouth, as had indeed been his custom with all former prophets. The Satanic words were expunged from the chapter, the reconciliation with Quraish was ended and opposition was resumed.

*   *   *

Meanwhile, the sanctions were still in force, but like similar economic sanctions in our own times, they failed to produce the desired effect. Several people were ready to run the blockade, some of them being apparently people of other clans, connected with Beni Hashim by marriage. Often at night, camels loaded with foodstuffs could be seen slipping out of the town and following the alley leading to Abu Talib's little valley.

Those Muslims who did not belong to Beni Hashim had meanwhile remained in their families and were thus not exposed to the sanctions. However, the rising tension resulted in their suffering from increasing insults and abuse. Some of them even placed themselves under the protection of distinguished men from among the idolaters.

Even Abu Bekr, whose relatives, it appears, had disowned him, obtained permission from the Apostle to emigrate. On the way, however, he met a certain Ibn al Dughunna, who was head of a tribal group which seems to have acted in some capacity as allies of Quraish or escorts of their caravans. Informed that Abu Bekr was leaving Mecca, he enquired the reason, in view of his status as a respectable citizen, known for his kindliness and charity. It is interesting to note that this man, to some extent prominent in public life, appears to have been unaware of the trouble in Mecca. Perhaps later Muslim writers have overemphasised the stir caused by the preaching of Muhammad at this stage.

Eventually a party of Quraish sympathetic to Beni Hashim began to demand the termination of sanctions, which in any case had failed to achieve their object. Abu Jahal, the chief of Beni Makhzoom, was the only voice raised to oppose the proposal. When the deed, which had been nailed up in the Kaaba, was examined, it was found to have been entirely destroyed by worms, except for the words, "In Thy Name, O God . . ." with which it began. This fact turned the scales and it was generally agreed that the ban be raised. It had lasted some three years, from 616 to 619.

Professor Margoliouth, on the other hand, suggests that the ban may have been raised on the occasion of the compromise resulting from the Satanic verses. The incident remains obscure and we can only once again take refuge in the formula used by the Muslims— "God knows the truth".

NOTABLE DATES

Birth of Muhammad	570
Marriage to Khadija	595
The Call	610
The Interlude	610–613
Commencement of Public Preaching	613
Persian Occupation of Syria, Egypt and Asia Minor	612–628
The Emigration to Abyssinia	615
The Boycott of Beni Hashim	616–619

PERSONALITIES

Muslims

Muhammad, the Apostle of God
Khadija, his wife
Ali ibn abi Talib, his cousin
Zaid ibn Haritha, his adopted son
Abu Bekr, his best friend
Hamza ibn Abdul Muttalib, Muhammad's uncle
Othman ibn Affan, Muhammad's son-in-law
Bilal ibn Ribah, an African slave
Khabbab, a converted slave

Leaders of the Opposition

Abu Jahal, the chief of Beni Makhzoom
Amr ibn al Aasi, Quraish delegate to Abyssinia
Abu Sofian ibn Harb
Abu Lahab, Muhammad's uncle

Other Personalities

The Negus (or Emperor) of Abyssinia

VII

The Pledge of Aqaba

When Quraish became distressed by the trouble caused by the enmity between them and the Apostle . . . they stirred up against him foolish men, who called him a liar, insulted him and accused him of being a poet, a sorcerer, a diviner and of being possessed. However, the Apostle continued to proclaim what God had ordered him to proclaim.

IBN ISHAQ [trans. Guillaume]

Among the Arab tribes, the efforts of the Prophet had not been happier than at Taif. It was from Yathrib that the solution came.

EMILE DERMENGHEM, *Muhammad*

O people worship your Lord who created you and your forbears, that you may understand perfectly. Who made the earth a resting place for you and the sky a covering. Who sent rain from Heaven and brought forth fruits to support you. Do not, therefore, set up rivals to God.

Qoran II, 21 and 22

RITUAL prayers had been introduced by the Messenger of God at an early stage of his mission, although it is not exactly known at what date he gave them their final form, which is still in use. It is important to realise that these prayers were intended as a tribute of praise to God and do not include personal petitions, for which a different Arabic word was used. The ritual prayers perhaps most closely resembled the Christian singing of psalms, although the Muslim prayers are only said, not sung. The Messenger of God did not like music, and forbade it to his followers.

The ritual prayers are divided into sections, called *rakaa* or prostrations. A prostration consists of the following procedure.

1. The worshipper stands facing Mecca, raises his hands to his ears and says, "God is most great".

2. The hands are then joined on the breast and the worshipper says, "Glory be to Thee, O God, Thine is the praise, blessed is Thy Name, exalted is Thy Majesty and there is no god but Thee. I take refuge with God against the devil who is stoned."

3. Then the opening chapter of the Qoran called the *Fátiha*, is recited.

> In the name of God, the Merciful, the Compassionate.
> Praise be to God, the Lord of the Worlds,
> The Merciful, the Compassionate,
> Ruler of the Last Day.
> We worship Thee and we ask Thy help.
> Guide us in the straight path.
> The path of those on whom Thou hast bestowed Thy Grace,
> Not those with whom Thou art angry,
> Nor those who have gone astray.
> Amen.

4. A chapter of the Qoran, which the worshipper knows by heart, may then be recited. (Some of the short chapters consist of only three or four lines.)

5. This recitation over, the worshipper says, "God is most great", and bows forward from the waist, placing the palms of his hands on his knees. In this position, he says three times, "Glory to my Lord, the Great".

6. The standing position is then resumed, with the words, "God hears him who praises Him. O Lord, Thine is the praise."

7. The worshipper then prostrates himself, falling first on his knees and then bending the body forward until the forehead touches the ground. In this position, the following words are repeated three times, "Glory to my Lord, the Most High."

8. The worshipper then straightens up his body, but remains for a few seconds in a kneeling position sitting back on his heels. He then repeats the prostration, his forehead on the ground.

The worshipper has now completed one *rakaa*. He resumes the standing position and recommences at the beginning, for his second *rakaa*.

This, very briefly, is the ritual of Muslim worship today. It has to be repeated at least five times a day, the number of prostrations varying on different occasions. It is preceded by a ritual ablution, and and the whole service may be terminated by two or three final prayers and a greeting of peace. It is, however, unlikely that these details had been elaborated at the time in the life of the Apostle with which we are now concerned.

It will be seen that this ritual is, in reality, almost solely a service of praise. Indeed, to use the word prayer to describe it gives most English-speaking people a wrong impression. The whole service does not contain a single petition, unless the phrase, "Guide us in the straight path", from the *Fatiha* be considered as such. This ritual of praise, repeated five times a day is called in Arabic *Salat*. A petition offered to God is called *dua*.

The Messenger of God did not lay down any ritual for the public or private offering of petitions to God, but tradition relates that he frequently referred to specific supplications of this kind. Qoran, Chapter XL, verse 60, has the phrase, "Your Lord has said, 'Call upon Me and I will answer you'."

The Apostle also laid emphasis on the duty of remembering God during the busy occupations of the day, a task which has also been frequently enjoined upon Christians. Muslim, the famous traditionist, quotes an alleged saying of Muhammad, "People will not sit remembering God without the angels surrounding them, mercy covering them, peace descending upon them and God mentioning them among those who are with Him." The same authority also reports a traditional saying of the Apostle, "A Muslim's supplication for an absent brother receives an answer".

More spiritual is another saying attributed to the Messenger of God, "God says, 'I am present when my servant thinks of me, and I am with him when he remembers me'."[1]

The Prophet himself seems to have made considerable use of ejaculatory prayer, and Muslims do the same to this day. For example, a Muslim setting out in the morning will say, "O God! I trust in Thee!" When starting on a journey, "We have placed our confidence in God!" and many other such phrases. Indeed, their use has become so frequent and so general, that they have almost lost their religious significance.

The Messenger of God, however, approved of repetition. One tradition states that he said "If a man says 'Glory be to God' a hundred times, a thousand blessings will be recorded for him or a thousand sins will be removed from him." Penitence also received a place in these ejaculatory prayers. To this day, pious Muslims will frequently sigh, and repeat again and again, "I ask pardon of God, I ask pardon of God!"

During the years spent by the Prophet in Mecca, the ritual prayers gave rise to more opposition than almost any part of his teaching. This resistance was particularly marked among the bedouin tribes, whose free and unrestricted lives made regular duties peculiarly obnoxious, especially if they were to be carried out with a specific drill and at fixed times. In addition, the universal Arab attachment to human dignity caused objections to be raised to the physical movements involved, such as kneeling, bowing and prostrating themselves.

But while the bedouins opposed, or merely neglected the ritual prayers, they willingly made frequent use of ejaculatory prayers, even addressing God in human terms of endearment, such as *Ya rubaibi*,[2] "O my dear little Lord", when asking a particular favour.

As already indicated, during these years of persecution and opposition in Mecca, the Messenger of God regarded the idolaters of Quraish as the enemies of his mission, but looked upon Jews and Christians as his natural allies. His sermons, and the chapters of the Qoran revealed hitherto, made frequent use of Old Testament stories, from which he drew moral lessons. As we have seen also, he recommended the persecuted to emigrate to Abyssinia, because it was a Christian country.

[1] This tradition is reported by both Bukhari and Muslim.
[2] Goldziher, *Muslim Studies*.

Ever since he had begun to recite formal prayers, he had faced towards Jerusalem to do so, for Jerusalem was the Holy City of his religious friends, the Jews and the Christians. One morning, at about this period, the Apostle announced that he had visited Jerusalem during the previous night.

According to one account, the Archangel Gabriel woke him during the night, and mounted him on Buraq, an animal "whose every stride carried it as far as its eye could reach".[3] Accompanied by Gabriel, the Apostle reached the temple in Jerusalem, where he found Abraham, Moses and Jesus awaiting him. They all prayed there together.

Tradition relates that from Jerusalem the Apostle mounted up to the seven heavens, where he met Adam, Noah, Moses, Abraham and Jesus. Passing beyond all these until even the Archangel Gabriel dared go no further, he found himself in the presence of God. He also was allowed a glimpse of Paradise and a glance into the infernal regions. On this occasion also, he received detailed orders regarding the ritual prayers already described. Thence, remounting Buraq, he returned in a few minutes to Mecca.

The next morning, the Messenger of God announced in the public square outside the Kaaba that he had been to Jerusalem and back during the previous night. According to Ibn Ishaq, "most of the people said 'By God, this is a plain absurdity! A caravan takes a month to go to Syria and a month to return and can Muhammad do the journey both ways in one night?' "

Many Muslims are said to have given up their faith as the result of this affair. It has, indeed, provided a fertile field for discussion and speculation among Muslims ever since. Ibn Ishaq quotes a statement attributed to Aisha, later to become Muhammad's wife, to the effect that, "the Apostle's body remained where it was, but God removed his spirit by night". "Only God knows how the revelation came and how he saw what he saw," says Ibn Ishaq, summarising the various accounts, "but whether he was asleep or awake, it was all true and actually happened."

*   *   *

The year 619 was one of disaster and bereavement for the Apostle of God. To begin with, Khadija died. For nine years, since his first Call,

[3] Ibn Ishaq.

she had been his ever-ready confidante, his strengthener, his support and his first convert. He revealed all his doubts and his troubles to her, and her steadfast encouragement enabled him to persevere, in spite of seemingly endless difficulties and discouragements. He had remained for twenty-four years faithful to his middle-aged wife and he spoke of her with affection to the end of his life.

A few weeks after the death of Khadija, the Apostle married Sauda bint Zamaa. This marriage seems to have been little more than a matter of domestic convenience. The Prophet was now forty-nine years old, and Sauda herself seems to have been middle-aged and rather fat. Muhammad's daughters were married and he lived with the two youths, Ali and Zaid. Perhaps Sauda, who was a widow, was little more than a housekeeper. She remained with Muhammad until his death, but is rarely mentioned by his biographers.

Shortly afterwards, his uncle, Abu Talib, also lay dying. A number of Meccan notables, including Utba and Shaiba, the sons of Rabia, and Abu Jahal of Beni Makhzoom, visited his bedside during his last illness. According to Ibn Ishaq, they spoke as follows: "You know what trouble exists between us and your nephew. We want you to call him, so that we can come to an agreement, that he will let us alone and we do the same for him."

The Apostle of God was sent for, and the old man told him what the others had said. "Let them give me one word," Muhammad replied. "Let them say, 'There is no god but God and Muhammad is His Messenger'." The visitors turned to one another, saying, "This fellow is not going to give us anything we want", and left the room in annoyance.

The Apostle made great efforts to persuade Abu Talib to repeat the Muslim witness of faith, but the old man only lay silent, making no response, until he passed away. Abu Talib seems to us an attractive character. Outspoken, loyal and sympathetic, he endured many worries, losses and contradictions in order to protect his nephew, although he did not believe in his preaching. He is not considered a hero by Muslims, for he died in unbelief. Nevertheless, if it had not been for the staunch courage with which he stood by his nephew, Islam might have died in its cradle.

Muhammad was daunted at the formidable hostility which faced him in Mecca after the deaths of Khadija and Abu Talib. It occurred to him that to emigrate might be the wisest course and he decided first to try Taif, a small town some fifty miles east of

Mecca. Taif was famous for its fruit gardens and its cool climate, in contrast with the dust, glare and heat of Mecca. The inhabitants of Taif were of the tribe of Thaqeef, but a number of rich Meccans also owned property, orchards, and vineyards there.

Some accounts allege that the Messenger of God went alone, others that he was accompanied by his adopted son, Zaid ibn Haritha. On reaching Taif, he asked for and was granted an interview with the three headmen of the town, who were brothers. They received him kindly, but when he began to urge their conversion, they laughed outright. "If God needed a messenger, could not He have found someone better than you?" enquired one. "If you are really an apostle," said another, grinning, "you are much too important to speak to a person like me."

Muhammad felt utterly crushed. "If that is how you feel," said he, "at least do not tell anyone what I said to you," a request which seems once more to lay stress on his natural timidity and reserve. The shaikhs of the town, however, did not comply with his request but seem on the contrary, to have noised abroad in Taif the ridiculous conversation which had passed between them and their visitor.

Once more, if the preaching of Islam in Mecca had made such a furore as the historians suggest, we are surprised that the people of Taif do not seem to have known about it. At any rate a crowd quickly collected, and the Prophet was stoned and chased until he succeeded in taking refuge in a vineyard. According to tradition, this vineyard belonged to two men of Quraish, the same Utba and Shaiba, the sons of Rabia, whom we have just seen at the deathbed of Abu Talib. It so happened that, at this very moment, they were working in their vineyard. Moved with pity at the abject state to which Muhammad was reduced, they sent him a plate of grapes by a young Christian slave in their service.

The Apostle on this occasion is said to have prayed, "O God, I complain to Thee of the feebleness of my strength and of my insignificance before men. O Most Merciful! Thou art the Lord of the weak and Thou art my Lord." Afraid to return to Mecca now that he no longer enjoyed the protection of Abu Talib, he sent a messenger to several leading idolaters, asking their protection. Two refused but eventually Mutim ibn Adi, chief of the Nofal clan of Quraish, agreed to protect him. Next morning, he, his sons and his nephews went fully armed to the public square of the Kaaba, and announced that Muhammad was under their protection.

Although the protection of Mutim ibn Adi enabled the Apostle to return to Mecca, he seems to have despaired of preaching any more to Quraish, or perhaps Mutim, the idolater, only gave his protection on this condition. Muhammad decided, for the time being, to limit his efforts to attempts to convert the tribesmen who visited Mecca from time to time. At the season of the annual fairs, a considerable number of tribesmen pitched their tents in the surrounding districts, profiting by the months of truce.

The principal gatherings of this kind took place in the six weeks preceding the day of the great pilgrimage, beginning on the first day of the lunar month of Dhu al Qaada, which, like its successor, Dhu al Hajja, was a sacred month. The first twenty days were occupied by the great fair of Ukadh, at which the famous poetical contests took place. The ensuing ten days were occupied by the Fair of Mujanna and the last eight days by that of Dhu al Majaz.

Muhammad visited the nomadic encampments in turn, endeavouring to convert the tribesmen to his monotheism, but Abu Jahal, the Beni Makhzoom chief, followed him round, telling his audiences that he was mad and advising them not to take any notice of him. Probably at about this time, a man called Tufail ibn Amr, of the Daus tribe, came to Mecca, was converted and offered the Apostle sanctuary among his kinsmen. The offer, however, seems to have been refused, but we do not know the circumstances.

Muhammad was, this year, at the very lowest point in his fortunes. The Meccans must have thought that his whole mission had failed. Perhaps as a result, they were more tolerant, though somewhat contemptuous. Some Muslim traditionists allege that it was at this time that the leaders of Quraish offered him wealth, power and the position of chief of Mecca, if he would renounce his claim to be a prophet. This version, however, seems unlikely, as the Apostle must have seemed too weak and friendless to cause his enemies any anxiety. If such offers were ever made, it is more likely that this occurred during the lifetime of Abu Talib.

Another unfortunate development was that Abu Lahab, one of the bitterest enemies of the Messenger of God, had succeeded his brother, Abu Talib, as the head of the clan of Beni Hashim. Immediately after the death of Abu Talib, Abu Lahab seems to have changed his tone and promised to protect his nephew[4] but a short time afterwards he returned to his former attitude of hostility. Thus Beni Hashim, his

[4] Genealogical tree, p. 120.

own relatives who had protected him so staunchly hitherto, were no longer reliable.

The bedouin tribesmen doubtless listened with curiosity, if not with amusement, to the sermons of this apparently eccentric crank, but little positive result was visible. One tribal shaikh is alleged to have offered to fight for him and give him victory over his enemies, if Muhammad promised to make him his lieutenant and to share with him his authority. The Apostle evaded the demand by replying that only God could give authority. The bedouin, however, with the brutal frankness of his kind, replied that he wanted a straight promise, and no vague excuses.

*   *   *

The oasis of Yathrib, some two hundred and fifty miles north of Mecca, has already been mentioned. Four hundred years before, the Himyarite King of the Yemen, Asad abu Qarib, had captured the place and taken to the Yemen two Jewish rabbis, who had converted some of the people of South Arabia to Judaism.

The settlement of Yathrib differed fundamentally from the township of Mecca. The latter, as we have seen, possessed only a few shallow wells in a dry watercourse, the water of which was frequently insufficient even for drinking purposes. It possessed no vegetation, agriculture was impossible and the little settlement was enclosed by bare, rocky mountains, shimmering beneath a scorching sun. There was nothing in Mecca to live on and the people were obliged to earn their livelihood elsewhere, by trade to the Yemen, Egypt, Syria or Persia. Mecca was to them little more than a *pied-à-terre*, a base from which they set out on their caravan journeys and to which they returned.

The economy of Yathrib was entirely different. An ample water supply and a wide valley between the mountains gave full scope for agriculture. The whole valley was pleasantly green with crops and was well planted with gardens of date-palms. The inhabitants of the Yathrib oasis lived principally on agriculture and on a limited number of domestic animals. The population still retained its tribal organisation. Each small tribe owned its own area of cultivation, in the centre of which it had built its own little fortified village. The valley, therefore, appeared green and refreshing, dotted here and there with small villages, a peaceful and soothing scene.

In the year 620, Yathrib was inhabited by five small tribes. Three of these, which were those which had been the longest in possession, professed the Jewish faith. The people of Arabia in the seventh century were not interested in ethnology. No records exist as to whether these peoples were the descendants of the tribe of Judah from Jerusalem, or whether they were ethnically Arabs who had been converted to Judaism, as were the Jews of the Yemen.

To all outward appearance, they were Arabs. Their tribal organisation and their customs were the same as those of the local inhabitants and their mother tongue was Arabic. More significant, still, their names were all Arabic names. Wherever Jews travel over the world, they nearly always take some of their personal names with them. Moses, Aaron, Abraham, Jacob, Joseph, are found among Jews in every land, but such names seem to have been extremely rare or non-existent among the Jews of Yathrib.

It is impossible now to know the origin of these three "Jewish" tribes. The probability, however, seems to be that several centuries earlier, a rabbi or a party of rabbis had come to Yathrib and had converted the local Arabs to their monotheistic faith, superior as it was to the superstitious idolatry of the tribesmen. We know that, at the time of Christ and for some centuries afterwards, the Jews were extremely active proselytisers.

The other two tribes of the Yathrib oasis practised the popular paganism of Arabia, and yearly sent large convoys of worshippers to the pilgrimage at the idol shrines of Mecca. These two tribes, known as the Aus and the Khazraj, had formed part of that large group of Yemenites alleged to have migrated northwards at the time of the bursting of the great dam at Marib.

Reaching the Yathrib area, the Aus and the Khazraj had found the "Jewish" tribes in possession, but had succeeded in forcing their way into the oasis and in taking over an area of gardens and cultivation. By the year 620, the two pagan tribes had achieved the upper hand and the tribes which practised Judaism had been forced into a subordinate position. Members of both groups, however, mixed on terms of equality. The Judaistic tribes, indeed, as the result of their superior religion, were better educated than the idolaters, just as Christians, say, in Central Africa often are in comparison with pagans.

Also, as practising a more enlightened religion, the Judaistic tribes worked as artisans in various crafts, and were probably much richer than their pagan neighbours. They were also money-lenders. In a military capacity, however, they were dominated by the idolaters and one of their tribes, Beni Qainuqa, were clients of the Khazraj and paid them tribute The other two Judaistic tribes, Beni al Nadheer and Beni Quraidha do not seem to have paid tribute, though they were in some way affiliated to pagan tribes.

The Judaistic tribes had schools, where the Torah and the Jewish scriptures were taught. Presumably all, or nearly all, of their men must have been able to read and write. At the annual fairs, they competed with the bedouins in the poetic contests. The pagans of Yathrib, being farmers, not merchants, rarely travelled and knew little of the world outside.

The Aus and the Khazraj were in general poor. They borrowed money from the Judaistic tribes. When the Messenger of God died twelve years later, his armour is alleged to have been in pawn to a Jew. There was only one set of bridal clothing and ornaments in the whole oasis. When a pagan girl was to be married, the necessary finery had to be hired from a Jew.[5]

Probably in 616, a feud had broken out between the two pagan tribes, the Aus and the Khazraj. As was so often the case, the quarrel arose over a question of "protection". A man of the Aus had given his protection to a bedouin of Dhobian who was visiting the oasis. A tribesman of the Khazraj paid a Jew to smack the bedouin's face in one of the Jewish settlements. His protector from the Aus hurried to the scene to defend his protégé and killed the Jew who had struck him. The Khazrajite then pursued the Ausite, but, failing to overtake him, killed another man of the tribe.

A series of battles ensued between the Aus and the Khazraj, culminating in the so-called Day of Buath, when the Aus were victorious. A notable fact, tending perhaps to show that the "Jews" of Yathrib were Arabs, was that two of the Judaistic tribes fought for the Aus, while the third took the part of the Khazraj.

Life in Yathrib continued precarious, for all the warring tribes lived quite close to one another. A certain Khazraj chief, a man of moderate views and peaceful temperament, had refused to take part in the fighting and had used every effort to end the fratricidal strife. His name was Abdulla ibn Ubay, and we shall hear more of him.

*   *   *

[5] An early predecessor of Moss Bros of London.

Meanwhile, the Messenger of God, as we have seen, had been obliged virtually to limit his preaching to nomadic tribesmen and to the strangers who visited Mecca or neighbouring fairs at pilgrimage time. In the year 620, he took the opportunity of the arrival of the pilgrims from Yathrib to engage them in conversation. A group of seven or eight men, all but one of them apparently of the Khazraj were impressed by his words. They knew that the Jews were expecting the arrival of the Messiah and they may have considered the possibility that Muhammad might be he. Or the Khazraj may have thought that he could be used as a mediator or peacemaker in the oasis. At the end of the pilgrimage they returned to Yathrib, meditating on these possibilities.

During the ensuing year (620–621), Muhammad's fortunes seem to have been at their lowest ebb. There were apparently no new converts, nor did he attempt to preach in Mecca. At length the pilgrimage season came round again. The seven men from Yathrib with whom he had spoken the preceding year had brought five more with them. In a little valley in the mountains just outside Mecca, the Apostle met and talked with the twelve and recited to them portions of the Qoran.

The twelve Yathribis declared themselves convinced and entered into a pledge that they would not henceforward associate other gods with God, nor steal, commit fornication, bury their female babies, slander their neighbours, nor disobey the Messenger of God in what was right. In return, they were promised ultimate admission to Paradise. These pledges are of interest, as they were presumably typical of what Muhammad asked of all his converts at that time. It may be noted, firstly, that the commands were all negative, and, secondly, that the prohibitions were all against actions, like the Ten Commandments on Sinai. There are no rules governing thoughts or emotions, telling the converts to love or to hate, for example.

This pledge has been called the first pledge of Aqaba or the pledge of women, because it involved a promise of loyalty but without an obligation to fight. When the twelve returned to Yathrib, the Apostle sent with them Musaab ibn Umair, an early convert belonging to the descendants of Abdul Dar ibn Qusai. He was to read the Qoran to them, pray with them and instruct them in the faith.

Muhammad waited in some anxiety for another year until, in March 622, the pilgrimage season came round once more. A large party of idolaters from Yathrib came to the pilgrimage, among whom

were mingled the new Muslim converts. The night after the completion of the idolatrous ceremonies the Yathrib Muslims slipped away
secretly, when their pagan companions had gone to sleep. They
forgathered surreptitiously in the same valley of Aqaba where the
first pledge had been taken the year before. They consisted of
seventy-three men and two women.

The little group sat silently together under the stars until at last
Muhammad appeared, accompanied by his uncle, Abbas, who,
though still an idolater, was perhaps anxious for his nephew's
safety.[6] According to Ibn Ishaq, Abbas spoke first, telling the Yathrib
pilgrims that Muhammad was prepared to live among them, if they
would undertake to protect him.

Thereafter the Messenger of God himself spoke and recited passages
from the Qoran, adding, "I invite your allegiance, on condition
that you undertake to protect me as you would your own families".
The chief of the party, Al Bara ibn Maroor, replied that all were
willing to give their allegiance and that they would protect the
Apostle with their weapons, as they protected their own women.

One of the notables, however, expressed the fear that, if they
fought for Muhammad and made him victorious, he would then
return to Mecca and live there and abandon Yathrib. The Apostle
immediately promised to transfer his loyalty to them. "I am of you
and you are of me," he said. "I will war against all who fight against
you and I will be at peace with those who are at peace with you."
Twelve leaders were then selected, nine from the Khazraj and three
from the Aus. Finally, the Yathribis asked what reward they would
receive in return for their loyalty. "Paradise," replied the Messenger
of God simply.

"Hold out your hand," said the men of Yathrib, and they filed
past one by one, each striking the Prophet's hand to pledge his
faith. This oath was called the second pledge of Aqaba. After the oath,
those who had sworn stole away in small parties and lay down
quietly among their sleeping companions of the Yathrib caravan.
But in spite of these precautions the news leaked out and in the
morning a Meccan deputation visited the encampment before the
Yathrib caravan moved off, and accused the leaders of conspiring
with Muhammad. The leaders, however, swore an oath that the

---

[6] The principal Muslim historians wrote at a time when the descendants of Abbas were
khalifs and emperors. Reports associating Abbas with Muhammad's early activities may
have been inserted by these writers to please the then ruling dynasty.

story was untrue, for they were idolaters and were, in fact, unaware of the pledge.

The caravan set out for home, but meanwhile the leaders of Quraish obtained further confirmation of the meeting and a party of men was sent in pursuit. They failed to overtake the main caravan but captured a straggler called Saad ibn Ubada, who had not only taken the pledge but was also one of the twelve leaders who had been selected. Him they seized and dragged back to Mecca, beating him on the way, though he was a respected man and one of the chiefs of the Khazraj. Saad, however, had had business relations with a certain Jubair, the son of Mutim ibn Adi, who had given his protection to Muhammad. On entering Mecca as a prisoner, Saad shouted loudly, "I am under the protection of Jubair ibn Mutim". Somebody ran and told Jubair, who came and released the prisoner.

* * *

Presumably just before the second pledge of Aqaba, the Apostle had received a revelation authorising the Muslims to fight and to shed blood. Hitherto he had merely been told to call men to God, to endure their insults and to forgive the ignorant. Now, he said, he had received authority to fight against those who had wronged him. According to Ibn Ishaq, the first orders revealed to him authorising resistance were contained in Chapter XXII of the Qoran, verses 39 to 42. "Permission to fight is given to those who are being killed unjustly and God is well able to give victory. Also to those who have been unjustly turned out of their country, merely because they said, 'God is our Lord'. Had not God used some men to resist others, the wicked would before now have demolished the cloisters, the churches, and the places of prayer and worship where the name of God is constantly remembered."

This authorisation of the use of force is, it will be seen, couched in terms of defence. The people of Yathrib having accepted this obligation of armed defence, the Messenger of God gave orders to his followers in Mecca to emigrate to Yathrib and there to establish contact with their fellow Muslims, who had sworn to protect them. Some Meccans tried, rather half-heartedly, to prevent the departure of the Muslims. A small number were forcibly detained by their relatives. In general, however, all who really wanted to go succeeded in doing so.

As on every other occasion in their relations with the Apostle, Quraish were half-hearted in their opposition. It was nearly always the Muslims who took the initiative, while the Meccans limited their action to attempts to prevent them doing as they wished to do. The ineffectiveness of their resistance may perhaps be attributed firstly to the fact that the Quraish leaders were business men with other preoccupations. Secondly, the Muslims were inspired by a new and revolutionary idea, by which they were deeply stirred. The idolaters took up a purely negative stand—they tried to prevent anything being changed—an uninspiring formula. Thirdly, the Muslims, on the average, were young, the Meccan leaders were old.

Muhammad was fortunate in not being opposed to a highly organised religious hierarchy, such as that of the Jews before Christ or of the Roman Catholic Church during the Reformation. Arab idolatry was casual and confused. There was no sacerdotal class and no organisation whose duty it was to defend it.

The majority of the Muslims who migrated from Mecca to Yathrib were well received and provided for by their new co-religionists, many of whom behaved with great generosity. A place for prayer was marked out on the ground at Qoba, a settlement at the southern end of the oasis, where a number of the Meccans found accommodation. Abu Bekr urged the Messenger of God himself to migrate but, not without courage, he stayed on in Mecca, where now only Abu Bekr and Ali seem to have remained with him.

Quraish were alarmed at these new developments. Their lives were based upon family loyalty which, in the absence of an organised government and a police force, was the only security on which any man could rely. Muhammad was preaching an entirely new loyalty, a bond uniting his converts to one another. The movement had, already disrupted many families, and, in some cases, young men seduced by Muhammad had behaved with gross disrespect to their parents. If this kind of thing were allowed to continue, they thought, the very foundations of civilised society would be undermined.

In addition to these subversive activities, these aggressive young men had now gone off to Yathrib, where they had bound themselves to the members of other tribes by some kind of pledge, which apparently envisaged the possibility of war. Were they going to make war on Quraish, their own fathers, brothers and cousins, who had brought them up from childhood with loving care and solicitude? The public anxiety might perhaps be compared to that which would be felt today in England, if a party of Oxford graduates, some of them the sons of British Cabinet ministers, should defect to Moscow and swear to fight for Russia against all the world.

* * *

Before closing our account of the years spent by Muhammad in Mecca, we may notice the bitter experiences which he had suffered. Neither he nor his converts had, it is true, been crucified, tortured on the rack, or burned alive. Nevertheless, the Apostle himself must have suffered psychologically the very depths of depression and despair.

For ten years the whole of his life had been dedicated to preaching the cause, which was now the principal object of his existence. All these devoted and courageous efforts had seemingly ended in utter fiasco. The handful of persons whom he had converted had scattered to the winds. He was ostracised by his relations and his fellow-citizens, and was everywhere loaded with ridicule and contempt, so that he scarcely dared to show his face. Could anybody ever be a more total failure than he was?

Yet he had borne all this depression and despair with exemplary patience. His resentment may have found a perhaps subconscious outlet in his descriptions of the agonies of hell to which his tormentors would be consigned, but, in other respects, he accepted his own apparent failure with stoicism. His endurance of these manifold discouragements, however, seems to contradict the opinion, formerly often expressed by Western writers, that he was a mere unscrupulous adventurer. Looking only at his final triumph, it is easy to say that this had been his objective throughout, forgetting that, twelve years after his call, his whole work seemed to have ended in a ludicrous fiasco.

In a similar manner, we must surely make allowance for the years of ridicule, if we feel ourselves inclined to criticise his first vindictiveness when the tide ultimately turned.

NOTABLE DATES

PERSONALITIES

Abu Talib, Muhammad's uncle and protector. Died 619

Abu Lahab, another uncle, succeeded to the leadership of
Beni Hashim. Hostile to Muhammad

Abbas, another uncle, but friendly to Muhammad, though
an idolater

Utba ⎫ Sons of Rabia, moderate men but hostile to
Shaiba ⎭ Muhammad

Abu Jahal ibn Hisham, chief of the Beni Makhzoom clan,
bitterly hostile to Muhammad

Abdulla ibn Ubay, moderate minded chief of the Khazraj
tribe in Yathrib

Musaab ibn Umair, Muslim missionary sent by Muhammad to Yathrib

VIII

Helpers and Emigrants

The support of the Medina adherents, and the suspicion of an intended emigration, irritated the Quraish to severity; and this severity forced the Moslems to petition Mahomet for leave to emigrate. The two causes might co-exist and react on one another; the persecution would hasten the departure of the converts, while each fresh departure would irritate the Quraish to greater cruelty.

Sir William Muir, *Life of Mahomet*

There were two periods in which persecution was the most severe; the period before the emigration to Abyssinia and the period following the second pledge of Aqaba.

Tabari

A deputation of about seventy-five men invited him to make Yathrib [al Madinah] his home . . . The Jews, who were looking forward to a Messiah, had evidently predisposed their heathen compatriots in favour of such a claimant as Muhammad. Having allowed two hundred followers to elude the vigilance of Quraish and slip quietly into Al Madinah . . . he himself followed and arrived there . . . Such was the famous *hijrah*—not entirely a "flight" but a scheme of migration carefully considered for some two years. Seventeen years later, the Caliph Umar designated that lunar year [beginning July 16, 622], as the official starting point of the Muslim era.

P. K. Hitti, *History of the Arabs*

I have loved justice and hated iniquity: therefore I die in exile.

Bowden, *Life of Gregory VII*

THE notables of Quraish held a meeting to discuss the defection of the Muslims to Yathrib. As usual, they acted too late, when the new converts had already left. There was an old saying that, "other nations obeyed a government or a single ruler, but the Arabs knew no such institution, for every Arab thought himself fit to be a king and was unwilling to endure a rebuke from any other man". The Meccans were just such an equalitarian democracy.

As we have found in our own experience, democracies are pleasant to live in but, in an emergency, they are at a great disadvantage compared to more authoritarian systems. If Mecca had been ruled by a dictator, Islam might have been suppressed long before. But the endless discussions of the notables rarely resulted in action. The Muslims, on the other hand, were few but were under the orders of one man.

The result of the deliberations of the elders was that the only course left was to kill Muhammad, a suggestion attributed by Ibn Ishaq to Abu Jahal, the chief of Beni Makhzoom. In order to avoid a blood-feud, it was agreed that one man from every clan of Quraish would plunge his sword into the body of the victim.

A single assassin, secretly briefed by a local dictator, would doubtless have murdered the Apostle. As in the modern Western democracies, however, the claim that everyone has a right to be consulted on matters of policy makes secrecy and swift action impossible. The council of notables did not have a limited and specified membership. Any adult man could be present at its deliberations. Scarcely had the elders reached their decision than the Messenger of God was fully informed of all that had passed. One report alleges that Abdulla, the son of Abu Bekr, had been present at the session. Another version, however, states that the Prophet received warning from Raqiqa, an aunt of his who was married to a man of the Beni Zuhra clan.

The Apostle thereupon left his house and went to that of Abu Bekr. Before doing so, he told Ali to lie on his (the Apostle's) bed and that no harm would befall him. This Ali did, wrapped in the Prophet's cloak to complete the deception. According to the usual account, the assassins assembled outside the Apostle's house, but God deprived them of their sight. They consequently remained outside the house until the morning, when they discovered that Muhammad had left and that only Ali was there.

We may perhaps classify this narrative among those other miraculous tales with which the devotion of the faithful has decorated the life of the Prophet. It is, however, easy to imagine that a party of assassins consisting of one man of every clan would not be easy to organise, and could not be made ready the same night.

It would be natural, however, for the conspirators to place spies to observe the Prophet's house and these might well have peered in and, seeing Ali sleeping in Muhammad's cloak, have assumed that their intended victim was still there. In fact, it seems highly probable that Abdulla ibn abi Bekr was present in the council when the decision to picket the Apostle's house was taken. This would account for the speed with which Muhammad moved to Abu Bekr's house as soon as he had received Abdulla's report. It would also explain how the Apostle was able to assure Ali that no harm would come to him— he knew that only observers were to be posted that night and that the murder was to be carried out the next day.

It is frustrating that the historians present us only with a miracle, instead of giving us a factual account of the events of this dramatic night. For this, in that faraway, hot, dusty little valley beneath the bright Arabian stars, was a night pregnant with history. How utterly different the world would be today if the elders of Quraish, instead of their ludicrous plan for a representative company of assassins, had hired some bravo to go straight to Muhammad's home with his dagger.

Meanwhile, as soon as it was dark, the Apostle and Abu Bekr slipped out of the latter's house by a back way, scrambled up the rocky slopes overhanging the little town and took refuge in a cave on Mount Thor, a mountain about three miles south of the town, that is, in the opposite direction to the track leading to Yathrib. Pursuers, it was thought, would most likely imagine that the Apostle had left to join his followers in the northern oasis.

Abu Bekr, the careful merchant, had brought with him a bag containing five thousand dirhems. This sum was all that he had left of his original fortune of forty thousand dirhems, the remainder having been spent by him in assisting poor converts, or in buying and manumitting slaves who had become Muslims. The Prophet himself had brought no money at all.

Abu Bekr's son, Abdulla, the same who had listened to the discussion at the council of notables, stayed in Mecca with the women of Abu Bekr's family. He was to observe events and to bring news each night to the two fugitives in the cave. Ali also remained in Mecca with the Apostle's wife, Sauda.

A certain Aamir ibn Fuhaira had been a slave and had been converted to Islam. Abu Bekr had bought him and released him from slavery, to save him from persecution. This man, grateful to his patron, agreed to bring his flock of sheep each morning at dawn and lead it past the mouth of the cave, thereby obliterating the tracks of persons who visited the cave during the night.

It must be admitted that the Apostle had shown considerable courage in remaining alone in Mecca after the migration of all his followers to Yathrib. Abu Bekr had previously begged him several times to escape but he had refused. On the evening when he took refuge in Abu Bekr's house, he is said to have greeted the latter with the words, "God has now given me leave to emigrate". We are left to assume that he had previously been convinced that God did not approve of his flight and had only authorised him to leave when the notables had decided on his assassination.

As soon as Muhammad's escape became known, a reward of a hundred camels was offered for his apprehension, but no very energetic measures seem to have been taken to organise the pursuit. Some of the leaders of Quraish, indeed, seem rather to have welcomed this solution, by which they hoped to get rid of a troublesome agitator without shedding blood. As usual, the elders were not agreed, no one man was in a position to take charge and the result was that nothing was done.

Abu Bekr, who had foreseen the possibility of having to escape with God's Messenger, had previously bought two riding camels which he had placed with a bedouin retainer of his called Abdulla ibn Arqat of Beni Kinana, who was still an idolater. On the third night, Abdulla, the son of Abu Bekr, came to the cave and reported that the hue and cry in Mecca had subsided. He recommended that the two fugitives leave immediately.

Their three-day concealment in the cave had been a period of great tension and anxiety. Abu Bekr showed signs of strain, but the Apostle kept assuring him that God would protect them. The Qoran refers specifically to this nerve-wracking time of waiting. "God certainly helped him when he was driven out by the unbelievers. He was the second of two when they were in the cave, when he said to his companion, 'Mourn not, for God is surely with us'. So God sent down his peace upon him."

Abdulla ibn Arqat, meanwhile, had arrived with Abu Bekr's two riding camels and with one of his own. Asma, one of Abu Bekr's daughters, had come with her brother Abdulla, carrying a bundle of food which she had cooked for the fugitives to take with them. She had forgotten to bring a rope to fasten the bag on to the saddle, so she took off her belt and tied it with that.

Abu Bekr had arranged for Abdulla ibn Arqat to act as their guide. We are all too apt to lump all Arabic-speaking peoples together, just as they, until recent years, called all Europeans Franks, not troubling to distinguish between French, British, Germans or Italians. Not only, however, do the peoples of the Arabic-speaking countries differ completely from one another today but, even inside the peninsula, the townspeople differ greatly from the nomads.

Even so famous a writer on oriental subjects as Professor Margoliouth writes that[1] "experiences as a caravan boy taught him (Muhammad) the art of scouting . . . sufficient to stand him in good stead when he became a captain of banditti". I believe this statement to be entirely erroneous. The merchants of Quraish were not desert-dwellers and, with their caravans, they travelled the desert as passengers, guided and escorted by the nomadic tribesmen. They were no more natives of the desert than a business man who flies the Atlantic in an airliner is a pilot. He relies entirely on the airline officials to convey him from place to place.

Thus we see that Muhammad and Abu Bekr were obliged to engage a bedouin idolater to guide them on their journey from Mecca to Yathrib. It is true that they might have accomplished this short trip alone if they had followed the main caravan route. But the possibility of pursuit made it essential for them to avoid the highroad and to travel by circuitous ways through the arid mountains of the Hejaz. Abu Bekr took with him his freedman, Aamir ibn Fuhaira, riding pillion behind him on his camel, to serve the Apostle and himself on the journey. It was 18th or 19th June, 622.

The very next morning, the fugitives were overtaken by a horse-man of Beni Kinana, who had actually ridden in pursuit of them, in the hope of winning the reward of a hundred camels which Quraish

[1] Margoliouth, *Muhammad and the Rise of Islam.*

had offered for their apprehension. But they persuaded him to leave them alone and not to report their location.

Only after two days riding did they reach Usfan, which is not more than fifty miles from Mecca, whereas a riding camel can do eighty to a hundred miles in twenty-four hours. It is possible, however, that they hid in the mountains during daylight and travelled only at night. At Arj, a little further on, they found a camp of Aslam, a section of Khuzaa. By chance, a baby daughter of Abu Bekr was with a wet nurse in this camp. The tribesmen accordingly welcomed him and provided a riding camel for the Messenger of God, whose mount seemed rather weak.

* * *

When the fugitives had whispered goodbye to Abu Bekr's son and daughter outside the cave on Mount Thor and the camels had padded silently away into the darkness beneath the sharp Arabian stars, the curtain rose on one of the greatest dramas of human history. How little did Caesar or Chosroes, surrounded by their great armies and engaged in a long and bitter war for world supremacy (as they thought), realise that four ragged Arabs riding silently through the bare mountains of the Hejaz were about to inaugurate a movement which would put an end to both their great imperial dominions.

Abdulla ibn abi Bekr and his sister Asma were left standing forlornly on the bare mountain outside the cave. It had been agreed that they would, for the moment, remain in Mecca. Next morning, a number of leaders of Quraish came to Abu Bekr's house to find out where the Apostle of God and Abu Bekr had gone. Asma went out to them and they asked her about the two men. When she replied that she did not know where they were, Abu Jahal, a rough man according to Ibn Ishaq, slapped her face so violently that one of her earrings fell off.

Abu Bekr had left Abu Quhafa, his father, in Mecca. He was very old and quite blind. Hearing that Abu Bekr had gone, he came round to the house and said to his grand-daughter Asma that he thought that her father should have left her some money. How were they going to manage? "I told him," the brave girl subsequently reported (she was still in her early teens), "that he had left us plenty of money. I took some stones and put them in a niche where Abu Bekr kept his money; then I covered them with a cloth and took his hand

and said, 'Put your hand on this money, grandpa.' He did so and said, 'There is nothing to worry about; he has done well to leave you enough money'. In fact, Abu Bekr had left them nothing at all.''[2]

The bedouin guide had not taken his charges in the direction of Yathrib but westwards towards the coast and up to Usfan, as we have seen. Still going north, he passed Qudaid, after which he bore away to the north-east through the mountains.

The Muslims who had already migrated to Yathrib had heard the news of the Apostle's disappearance from Mecca, but, receiving no reports of his whereabouts, had remained in great anxiety. At dawn every day, they would ride out to the top of the pass through which the track from Mecca descended to the oasis of Yathrib. There they would remain until noon, scanning in vain the empty valleys and mountains to the south for a party of camelmen approaching. At noon, when the blazing sun made the bare shadeless pass into a furnace, they would abandon hope for that day and return anxiously to the houses of Qoba, the most southerly village in the oasis.

On the 28th June, 622, about noon, when the watchers had already returned sorrowfully from their morning vigil, three weary camel riders topped the pass and looked out over the green smiling oasis of Yathrib, which had opened suddenly beneath them. Picking their way down the stony descent, they dismounted to rest in the shade of a palm tree on the outskirts of the settlement of Qoba. A Jew had been the first to see the travellers and called to the Muslims that the man they were expecting had come. Hurriedly they ran out from the huts and buildings of the settlement, calling joyfully to one another, "He has come! He has come!" Many of the spectators did not at first know which was the Messenger of God and which was Abu Bekr, until they saw the latter arranging his cloak on a stick so as to shade Muhammad from the sun's scorching rays.

A certain Qulthoom ibn Hidm, who lived near by, invited the Apostle to stay as a guest in his home, while Abu Bekr was accommodated in another house near by, where a number of Muslim refugees from Mecca were already living. The first stage of the Prophet's mission was over. No longer the persecuted and humiliated victim of his jealous fellow-townsmen, he was now gradually to become the mentor, and subsequently the suzerain of all Arabia.

*   *   *

[2] Ibn Ishaq.

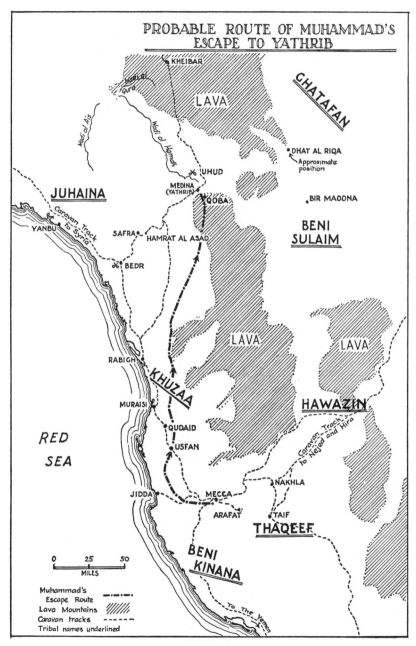

PROBABLE ROUTE OF MUHAMMAD'S ESCAPE TO YATHRIB

KHEIBAR

GHATAFAN

LAVA

Wadi al Qura

Wadi al Ais

Wadi al Hamdh

DHAT AL RIQA
• Approximate
position

✕ UHUD

MEDINA
(YATHRIB)

QOBA

JUHAINA

BIR MAOONA

YANBU

Caravan Track
to Syria

SAFRA •

HAMRAT AL ASAD

BENI
SULAIM

✕ BEDR

RABIGH

KHUZAA

LAVA

LAVA

MURAISI

HAWAZIN

QUDAID

USFAN

Caravan Track
to Nejed and Hira

RED
SEA

JIDDA

MECCA

NAKHLA

ARAFAT

• TAIF

THAQEEF

BENI
KINANA

0   25   50
MILES

Muhammad's
  Escape Route
Lava Mountains
Caravan tracks
Tribal names underlined

To The Yemen

MAP 5

The Messenger of God rested for three days in Qoba, at the end of which Ali arrived from Mecca, where he had settled a few outstanding financial affairs which the Prophet's hasty departure had not allowed him to complete. Ali was twenty years old at this time.

The Apostle was unable to sleep for several nights, although he had now reached comparative safety—the fear engendered by the danger of assassination in Mecca, the strain of the three anxious days in the cave, and the vicissitudes of his escape, had told heavily on his nerves. Gradually, however, the tension relaxed and he was once more able to sleep.

Quraish, with their usual half-heartedness or perhaps with an Arab sense of honour, had not descended so low as to detain or persecute the relatives or the women of the fugitives, as certain European dictatorships have done in our times. Sauda, the wife of Muhammad, Ali ibn abi Talib, and Abdulla, the son of Abu Bekr with his sisters, had all escaped from Mecca unmolested, except for Asma's smack in the face from Abu Jahal. As all the Muslims had now left Mecca, however, their pagan relatives in some cases sold their houses and property and kept the money. Many Meccan idolaters welcomed the era of peace and concord ushered in by the disappearance of the Muslims and the termination of religious controversy.

Muhammad had meanwhile sent word of his arrival to Asad ibn Zurara, one of the first Yathribite converts. Asad had been present and had taken the Pledge at the first meeting at Aqaba and had then been one of the twelve leaders chosen at the second Pledge of Aqaba. He was of the Beni al Najjar clan of Khazraj, to which Selma, the wife of Hashim, Muhammad's great-grandfather, had belonged. The Apostle was, therefore, in a position to claim family relationship with Beni al Najjar.

The Messenger of God had arrived in Qoba on a Monday. On the ensuing Friday, he mounted his camel and rode to the north towards the centre of the oasis. Tradition reports that many families along his route came out and invited him to stay and live with them. Muhammad, however, doubtless anxious to avoid giving offence, replied that he would dismount wherever God guided his camel to stop. This perceptive animal came to a halt in the settlement of Beni al Najjar, the Prophet's relatives, in front of a shed used for the storage of dates.

The camel having knelt down and refusing to rise again, the Prophet dismounted. A young man called Khalid ibn Zaid of Beni al Najjar took the baggage into his house and invited Muhammad to be his guest. He had been one of the early converts to Islam and had taken the oath at the Second Pledge of Aqaba. Some other Muslims came out and pressed the Messenger of God to stay with them, but he replied, "A man should never be separated from his baggage".[3] This had already been carried into the house of Khalid. The Apostle enquired to whom the date barn belonged and was told that it was the property of two orphan boys. Their guardian offered to sell and the deal was soon concluded. Abu Bekr paid the money from what was left of his cash, and work began on the building of the world's first mosque.

With his pleasant facility for giving nicknames, the Apostle had called the refugees from Mecca the Emigrants, and the Yathrib converts the Helpers. Willing volunteers from both communities now set to work, levelling, cutting mud bricks and erecting buildings, the Messenger of God himself working with them.

> If we sat down while the Prophet worked
> It could be said that we had shirked,

sang one of the volunteers.

Arabs often sing together when working, repeating the same couplet until one of their number invents a new one. The chorus then picks up the new words and repeats them once or twice, until a fresh couplet is improvised.

> There is no life but that to come, O Lord!
> Spare Emigrants and Helpers with Thy Word.

Then Ali produced new lines:

> There's one who labours night and day
> To build a mosque of bricks and clay,
> And one who turns from dust away.[4]

It used to be said that the shirker who turned away from the dusty work was Othman ibn Affan, who had married the Apostle's daughter, Ruqaiya.

[3] Any old soldier in the British Army will be familiar with the motto "Never be separated from your kit".

[4] Ibn Ishaq.

Ammár ibn Yásir, a former slave, staggered up with a load of bricks, saying in mock distress, "They want to kill me! They couldn't carry that load themselves." Umm Salama, a woman who was later to be one of Muhammad's wives, used to tell how she saw the Apostle pause in his work, run his fingers through his hair and say, "It is not these men who will kill you, Ammar, but a band of wicked men." Many years after the Prophet's death, Ammar was killed fighting for Ali in a civil war, and his death was hailed as a fulfilment of this prophecy.

The Apostle was strongly opposed to the expenditure of money on buildings although, later on, Islam was to erect magnificent mosques, palaces and castles. In Yathrib, the climate was hot and rain infrequent. The rooms next to the mosque, for the accommodation of Muhammad's family, were built of mud bricks or of mud daubed on to wattle. Wood was scarce. Some of the rooms had doors, while others merely had a strip of sacking hung up to screen the entrance.

Nearly a year elapsed before the completion of the mosque and the building of the rooms beside it for the Prophet and his family. His wife, Sauda, was installed in a room and, soon after his arrival in Yathrib, he also married Aisha, a daughter of Abu Bekr. She was nine years old, while the Apostle was fifty-three. When she was married she brought her toys with her to her room in the Apostle's house, where she used to sit playing with them on the floor. Until the end of his life, Aisha was to be the dearest of his wives.

The establishment of the Prophet in Yathrib was later on to lead to a change in its name. Hereafter it was to be known as the Prophet's City, *Medinat al Nebi*, more often abbreviated to Medina, a name by which we shall refer to it in future.

The Messenger of God had now eluded his enemies and was established among a small group of friends. His future, however, was still highly problematical. Some seventy Meccan Emigrants were now in Medina, some with their families, while others had left their wives and children in Mecca. The number of Helpers, that is to say converts of Medina, was now considerably greater, but the majority of the Aus and the Khazraj, the Arab tribes of the oasis, were still idolaters. In addition, the Jewish tribes, though fewer than the idolaters, constituted an unknown factor.

One of the principal considerations which had inspired the hostility of the leading men of Quraish in Mecca may well have been the realisation that a man who claimed direct and frequent revelations from God could not but be involved in government and politics, whether he wished it or not. No other man could undertake to rule the community, if he felt himself exposed at any moment to a divine revelation condemning his policy. It will be remembered[5] that the Aus and the Khazraj, the two Arab tribes of Yathrib, now Medina, had been engaged in a private war, but that one of the chiefs of the Khazraj, Abdulla ibn Ubay, had refused to join in the fighting.

The wisdom and moderation of Abdulla ibn Ubay had led to a reconciliation, as a result of which both tribes had agreed to recognise his leadership, making him thereby the chief man in the oasis. Now the Messenger of God had arrived on the scene and an enthusiastic band of supporters was collecting round him. Inevitably the arrival of this new and striking figure—human nature being what it is—provoked the jealousy of Ibn Ubay. Nevertheless, we must remember, in mitigation of his jealousy, that he was a man of peace, of moderation and of wisdom.

Faced with this somewhat precarious situation, the Messenger of God inaugurated two measures. Firstly, he arranged a plan of adopted brotherhood between the Muslims of Medina and the Meccan refugees or, in Muslim terms, between the Helpers and the Emigrants. Thus Abu Bekr became the "brother" of one Kharija ibn Zuhair of the Khazraj. Umar ibn al Khattab became brother to Itban ibn Malik of the Khazraj, and so on. It will be appreciated that, in a country with no government or police, everyone needed some protection in order to feel secure. This protection was normally provided by the tribe but the Meccan Emigrants had abandoned their tribes. It was, therefore, essential that they be "adopted" by the tribes of Medina. Soon after the arrival of the Apostle in Medina, Asad ibn Zurara, the chief of Beni al Najjar, died.[6] It will be recollected that the Prophet's great-grandmother was of this clan. On the death of their chief, they accepted Muhammad as his successor, thereby further strengthening his position in the oasis.

The next step was to conclude an agreement with the Jewish tribes. The Messenger of God claimed that the religion he preached was the original faith of the Patriarch Abraham. We have already seen that Old Testament stories had figured in the Qoran and that the example of Moses was frequently cited.

The assumption was that the Jews had in some way lapsed from

[5] Page 142.   [6] Page 158.

the pure faith of Abraham and that the Apostle had come to rectify errors which had crept in. He claimed that the religion he preached was the original, the pure "Judaism" of Abraham. In any case, in contrast to the idolaters of Arabia, Muslims and Jews alike were monotheists. When the Messenger of God introduced the ritual prayers, he laid down that Muslims, when praying, were to face Jerusalem. Moreover, it had been from Jerusalem that he had gone up to Heaven and had seen the vision of God. All these factors had combined to inspire the Apostle with the hope that the Jews would be his allies, perhaps even that they would accept him as their Messiah. Indeed, at the beginning of his residence in Medina, their attitude appears to have been friendly.

Ibn Ishaq has preserved for us a document alleged to have been an agreement drawn up between the Emigrants, the Helpers and the Jews of Medina. It reads rather more like a draft for a *modus vivendi* between the three communities than an agreement between them. Here are a few extracts from this instrument.

"In the name of God, the Compassionate, the Merciful, this is a document from Muhammad the Prophet, concerning the believers and the Muslims of Quraish and Yathrib, and those who followed them. They are one community to the exclusion of all other men."

The document is lengthy and repeats itself, and a few brief quotations must suffice. "A believer shall not slay a believer for the sake of an unbeliever." This provision refers to tribal blood-feuds. If an unbeliever were killed, a near-relative of his, who would normally avenge his death, must not do so, if he be a believer. As has been repeatedly emphasised, the basis of all Arab society was tribal loyalty and the protection which the tribe extended to all its members. Membership of tribes, however, cut right across membership of the Islamic community. As a result, the Apostle wished to replace the tribe by the Muslim community. Muslims were to abandon their obligations to their tribes and assume virtually identical obligations to the group of believers.

"To the Jew who follows us belong help and equality. He shall not be wronged nor his enemies be aided . . . The Jews shall contribute to the cost of war, so long as they are fighting alongside the believers . . . The Jews of the Beni Auf are one community with the believers— the Jews have their religion and the Muslims have theirs." "The contracting parties are bound to help one another in the event of an attack on Yathrib." "Loyalty is a protection against treachery. He who acquires anything acquires it for himself. God approves of this document."[7]

The "agreement" is long and rambling. Ibn Ishaq heads it, "The Covenant between the Muslims and the Jews", but there is no mention of signatories. In fact, this document has the appearance of having been a combination of two which were perhaps discovered and put together by later historians. The first articles deal with relations between the Emigrants and the Helpers, intended to consolidate the unity and the brotherhood of the Muslim community. The second half of the document is concerned with relations between the Muslims and the Judaistic tribes.

Although the Jews of Yathrib were probably ethnically Arabs, with perhaps a small admixture of Jewish blood from the missionaries who first settled among them, their way of life was now similar to that of many other Jewish communities. They had accumulated considerable wealth by industry, commerce and usury—Jews in Medina, as we have already seen, often figure as money-lenders. These similarities between the way of life of the Jews of Medina and in other parts of the world do not necessarily imply any ethnic connection. Africans converted to Christianity often similarly adopt European customs, in contrast to their non-Christian fellow-countrymen.

Although the Jews were better educated than the idolatrous Arabs of Medina—there was at least one Torah[8] school in the oasis—their mother tongue was Arabic, of which they had so great a command that their poets competed on equal terms with those of the pagan Arabs.

It will be seen from the subjects treated in the "Covenant with the Jews" that the Messenger of God, immediately on his arrival in Medina, had been drawn into politics, administration and justice. As the executive leader of a growing community which was obliged to provide for its own survival and security, this development was probably inevitable. Nevertheless it marked a complete change in the Apostle's way of life. The patient, dedicated and persecuted Prophet had changed almost overnight into the politician and statesman. The change may, of course, have been more apparent than real. It is probable that he had long since foreseen that his mission would lead him into politics.

The agreement with the Jews was of short duration. The Arabs spent many hours a day sitting in their guesthouses and talking,

[7] Ibn Ishaq.   [8] The Torah is the Hebrew word for "the Pentateuch".

and the way of life of the Jews in Medina was the same in this respect
as that of the Arabs. The Jewish rabbis, at such public gatherings,
took pleasure in cross-questioning the Apostle on the subject of the
Old Testament stories which he had been accustomed to use. They
did this with a view to revealing his ignorance and making him
appear ridiculous. It will be remembered that the rabbis in the
Gospels followed the same method. "Then went the Pharisees, and
took counsel how they might entangle Him in His talk."[9]

One such question addressed to the Prophet was a request to
describe the nine plagues with which Moses had afflicted the Egyptians. On another occasion, it having been suggested that Muhammad might be the Messiah, the Prophet whose advent had been
foretold, the Jews pointed out that the Messiah was to be a descendant of David and therefore that Muhammad was not eligible.
Sometimes these questions were deliberately intended to make the
Messenger of God look foolish and ended in angry scenes or minor
acts of violence. One or two Jews, however, admitted that Muhammad was the expected Messiah and announced their conversion to
Islam.

Ill-feeling between Jews and Muslims continued to increase,
sometimes leading to an exchange of blows. One day, Abu Bekr was
making a collection for poor members of the Muslim community,
using as a slogan a quotation from the Qoran "Who will lend God a
good loan?" A passing Jew remarked facetiously, "If God wants a
loan, He must be in distressed circumstances." Abu Bekr, usually
a man of mild temper, replied with a blow.

Meanwhile, conversion to Islam proceeded at a fairly rapid pace
among the idolatrous Arabs of the Aus and the Khazraj. It is impossible from the written records of history to recapture the secret of the
personalities of great men. There seems to be no doubt, however,
that the Messenger of God possessed some extraordinary power of
winning over and influencing other people. Many cases are reported
of unbelievers who came to mock but who, after a short interview
with Muhammad, accepted Islam and remained devoted Muslims
for the rest of their days.

The rising success of the Apostle was naturally unwelcome to
Abdulla ibn Ubay, who, before the arrival of the Muslims, had been
the chief man in the oasis. Nevertheless, as we have seen, he was a
wise and prudent man and was careful to conceal his pique. Before

[9] Matthew XXII, 15

long, he too declared himself a convert. Nevertheless, he remained, to some extent, a figurehead for those Arabs of Medina who, openly or secretly, sneered at the Prophet's teaching and complained of the confusion and the danger which the coming of the Muslims had brought to Medina.

Such professed but in reality insincere converts are known in Muslim tradition as the *munafiqeen*.[10] This word is normally translated into English as "the hypocrites" but the translation does not completely convey the sense. I have preferred to use the phrase "the false Muslims", even if it be somewhat cumbrous.

Revelations frequently came to the Apostle, answering the questions put to him or denouncing the false Muslims. A certain Nabtal ibn al Harith, for example, used to come to the Apostle and talk to him and listen to his preaching, and then recount all that he had heard to the false Muslims. He was alleged on one occasion to have said that Muhammad was all ear and believed everything he was told. Chapter IX, verse 61, of the Qoran is thought to have been a reply to this man:

"There are some of them who annoy the Prophet and say that he is all ear, and believes anything. Say:[11] he is a good ear for you. He believes in God and trusts the believers, and is a mercy for those of you who believe. And there is a painful punishment in store for those who annoy God's Messenger."

NOTABLE DATES

Birth of Muhammad	570
The Call	610
The Commencement of Preaching	613
The Death of Abu Talib	619
The Visit to Taif	619
First Pledge of Aqaba	621
Second Pledge of Aqaba	622
The Migration	622
Escape of Muhammad from Mecca	18th June, 622[12]
Arrival of Muhammad at Qoba	28th June, 622

[10] The correct classical nominative plural ends in -oon, but I have used the more familiar colloquial case-ending employed today.

[11] This is an imperative. God is telling the Apostle what to say.

[12] Others have calculated that the Migration took place in September 622.

PERSONALITIES

Muslims

Abu Bekr ibn abi Quhafa
Abdulla ibn abi Bekr
Ali ibn abi Talib
Asad ibn Zurara, first Muslim leader in Yathrib

Muslim Women

Sauda, Muhammad's wife
Aisha, daughter of Abu Bekr, Muhammad's third wife
Asma, elder daughter of Abu Bekr

The Opposition

Abu Jahal, chief of Beni Makhzoom, Quraish
Abdulla ibn Ubay, chief of Yathrib

IX

Bedr

They bore within their breasts the grief
That fame can never heal—
The deep, unutterable woe
Which none save exiles feel.

WILLIAM AYTOUN

Muhammad accomplished his purpose in the course of three small engagements: the number of combatants in these never exceeded a few thousand, but in importance they rank among the world's decisive battles. The first step was the most difficult for it was no easy matter to persuade the Medinans to attack their old friends in Mecca . . . and the Meccan imigrants, too, must be persuaded to take up arms against their heathen kinsmen. Blood relationship . . . was a sacred tie recognised by all Arabs . . . By the preaching of war as a sacred duty Muhammad gradually induced his followers to attack the Meccans.

ALFRED GUILLAUME, *Islam*

The truth is that the strangest inconsistencies blended together [according to the wont of human nature] throughout the life of the Prophet. The student of history will trace for himself how the pure and lofty aspirations of Muhammad were first tinged and then debased by a half-unconscious self-deception.

SIR WILLIAM MUIR, *Life of Muhammad*

IX

THE Emigrants had found their first few months in Medina something of an ordeal. To begin with, the ample water supply and the irrigated gardens of Medina bred mosquitoes and fever. In Mecca, where water was so scarce, there had been no fever and the Meccans, who presumably had little resistance, nearly all succumbed to it in Medina.

Many of the Emigrants were penniless, having abandoned all their possessions in Mecca. Some men had been obliged to leave their wives and children behind them and found themselves in Medina, not only without money, but without shelter or family. Fortunately the climate was warm and it rarely rained, and they were able to sleep in the open or in the mosque.

The Messenger of God, it is true, had arranged for some of the Helpers to adopt an Emigrant each, as a brother. The two families lived together and helped one another. But the Helper naturally expected his Meccan brother-Muslim to work. The Emigrants, however, had no idea of agricultural work, which was the only form of employment available in Medina. In Mecca, there was no agriculture and the people lived on commerce.

One of the earliest Muslims, Abdul Rahman ibn Auf, was cordially welcomed by the "brother" to whom the Apostle had allotted him. "Here are my worldly goods," the Medini said, "you can take half and leave half to me. I have two wives—choose which of them you want, I will divorce her and you can marry her."

"May God's blessing be on you and your family," replied Abdul Rahman. "All I ask of you is to show me the market." Borrowing a small sum, he bought an article and resold it at a profit. Repeating the process again and again, he accumulated enough money not only to buy a house, but to marry a girl of Medina and give a party on his wedding day. The story illustrates vividly the difference between the farmers of Medina and the businessmen of Mecca.

The Apostle himself got into trouble owing to his ignorance of agriculture. The principal source of the livelihood of the people of Medina was their date palms. These trees, like some others, have male and female. To produce a crop of dates, the men climb the male tree, extract the pollen and insert it in the female tree. This process was repugnant to Muhammad and he forbade the Muslims to follow it. But when the date harvest came round, the believers had no fruit, and the Apostle was obliged to admit that he had made a mistake. The Muslims soon appreciated the Prophet's position to the effect that when he received a divine revelation, it must be instantly obeyed; but that, where there was no revelation, he was liable to make as many mistakes as other men did.

A tradition from Bukhari alleges that there were, about this time, some one thousand five hundred Muslims in Medina. According to Muhammad Hamidullah,[1] the population of the whole oasis was about ten thousand souls, of whom the idolaters were rather more numerous than the Judaistic tribes. Such figures are doubtless unreliable, but the Muslims in any case were still a small minority.

The only pseudo-Christian mentioned in Medina at this time was a certain Abu Aamir of the Aus, nicknamed the Monk. To what extent he was a Christian is not known. Abu Aamir rejected Muhammad's claims to prophethood and went to live with the Meccan idolaters to escape him.

*   *   *

Seventeen or eighteen months after the arrival of the Apostle in Medina, the increasing friction with the Jews led to a significant ritual change. We have already seen that, ever since the Prophet's night visit to Jerusalem, the Muslims had been ordered to face the Holy City to say their prayers. Now, as if to mark the abandonment of the attempt to co-operate with the Jews, the direction of prayer was changed from Jerusalem to Mecca.

Another and similar modification was the abandonment of Saturday as the Sabbath and the substitution of Friday as the special day of the Muslim week. The Apostle did not, however, follow the Jews and Christians so far as to forbid all work on Friday. The day was to be marked only by a special noonday service in the mosque.

During the first year of the Apostle's residence in Medina, Islam had become a small, closely-knit community of perhaps a thousand or fifteen hundred souls. It seems to have been during this period that several of the bases of Islam were established. Among these bases are the five daily prayers, though it is not certain at what date these

[1] Muhammad Hamidullah, *Le Prophète de l'Islam*.

assumed their final form. Some commentators, however, believe that there were only three daily prayers during the lifetime of the Apostle.[2]

The second duty laid upon the Muslims at this period was that of giving alms. Alms, in the Islamic community, is a strictly defined proportion of certain types of wealth, and has come more closely to resemble a tax than a charitable gift. In early Islam, the alms was distributed among the poorer members of the community.

The third of the bases of Islam inaugurated at this time was the fast of Ramadhan. Some western authorities believe that the Apostle introduced fasting when he came to Medina in imitation of the Jewish fast of ten days, which precedes the day of Atonement. When, however, the breach with the Jewish tribes took place, he instituted a fast lasting the whole month of Ramadhan, in order to make it different from the Judaistic procedure.

Equally significant is the general fact that prayer, alms and fasting were the bases of Judaistic religious practice. In Matthew VI, where the hypocrisy of the Pharisees is denounced because they pretend to be pious in order to be seen of men, the three examples given are prayer, almsgiving and fasting. Whereas Western commentators may attribute these institutions to imitation of the Jews, the Muslims would reply that Islam is the religion of Abraham, who was the first Muslim. It is, therefore, natural that Islam and Judaism should resemble one another.

The procedure followed in the ritual prayers has already been described. Believers were allowed to perform the rites alone or in company. Those who were able to come to the mosque for prayers ranged themselves, rank upon rank, behind a leader, who stood in front of the congregation. Behind him, the believers recited, bowed and prostrated themselves in unison. Some modern psychologists have seen, in these precise and synchronised movements, the virtue of inculcating discipline and comradeship, in the same manner as military drill.

When considerable numbers began to attend the daily prayers at the Prophet's mosque, the need was felt for a time-signal to enable them all to line up simultaneously. The Jews made use of a trumpet for the same purpose and the Messenger of God at first considered following their example. The idea was abandoned when tension increased between the Jews and the Muslims.

[2] *Encyclopaedia of Islam. Salat.*

Christians were in the habit of using a bell or clapper, but this method also was considered and rejected. A man of the Helpers came to the Messenger of God one day and told him that in a dream he had seen a man who had suggested the use of the human voice. The Apostle liked the idea and decided to try it. Bilal, the old negro slave who had been tortured by his owner in Mecca,[3] was chosen as the first *muedhdhin*, or caller to prayer. The formula selected, which is still the same today, ran as follows: "God is most Great! God is most Great! God is most Great! I bear witness that there is no god but God, I bear witness that Muhammad is the Apostle of God. Come to prayers, Come to prayers. Come to good works.[4] Come to good works. God is most Great! God is most Great! There is no god but God."

Bilal used to climb on to the roof of the nearest house to call the people to prayer. The minaret, which has since become typical of Muslim architecture, did not appear until long afterwards.

*   *   *

Within a few months of their arrival, many of the Emigrants were starving, and the original generous welcome extended to them by the Helpers was beginning to wear thin. Some of the Meccans are said to have been obliged to live largely on herbs. Their clothing was scarcely sufficient decently to cover their nakedness.

The former merchants of Mecca, most of whom had lost all their money, tried to return to business. We have already seen that Abdul Rahman ibn Auf was making money. Abu Bekr sold clothes in the bazaar. Othman ibn Affan bought and sold dates. Ali, on one occasion, carried buckets of water for a man who was making bricks. At the end of the job, he was paid sixteen dates.

The Messenger of God shared fully in these privations and often suffered the pangs of actual hunger. His family rarely ate anything but dates washed down with water. If Muhammad received presents of food, he shared it with the destitute Muslims who lived in the mosque. When he was married to Aisha, there was no wedding feast. There was nothing in the house to eat.

*   *   *

[3] Page 118.

[4] Professor Guillaume believes the word employed to be derived from an Aramaic word for "worship", but if so, the original meaning is now lost.

Seven months elapsed after the arrival of the Apostle in Medina before hostilities began. It is not clear whether the decision to raid the commercial caravans of Quraish was taken principally for economic reasons, the Muslims being destitute, or whether there was a long-term strategic plan to make war on Mecca. Some Muslims had acquired an attitude of patient resignation in the service of God, and were somewhat taken aback at being told that they must kill their cousins and brothers.[5]

The second Pledge of Aqaba, which had been taken by the Muslims of Medina, was couched in purely defensive terms. They had undertaken to protect the Apostle from his enemies but they were not bound to join in offensive operations against Quraish. As a result, the first raiding parties which went out to intercept Meccan caravans consisted only of Emigrants.

European writers, unfamiliar with the details of life in Arabia, have at times regarded Quraish as just another tribe, like Ghatafan, Hawazin or Tai. It must, however, be remembered that bedouin tribes regarded perpetual warfare as a desirable, or at least an inevitable, concomitant of human existence. War was, indeed, their chief interest in life. Quraish, on the contrary, were merchants. Bitten with the idea of commerce producing wealth, they were chiefly interested in making money and had no desire for battle honours. War, in fact, interfered with business and they were anxious to be at peace with all Arabia. Moreover, as we have already seen, they did not know the desert and were obliged to take bedouin guides when they went on journeys.

An amusing story, though admittedly dating from several centuries after the Messenger of God, serves to emphasise the continuing mutual dislike between bedouins and townsmen. Qirwash ibn Muqallad, of Beni Uqail, who camped in the desert near Mosul in the tenth century, was charged with laxity in his religion. In reply he claimed that in battle he had killed only five or six bedouins. As far as city-dwellers were concerned, he added, God would scarcely take him to task on their behalf.

When the Arab historians and traditionists wrote their books, Quraish had become khalifs and emperors, and authors were well advised to show them all due respect. There are, however, hints

[5] T. W. Arnold, in *The Preaching of Islam*, claims that the Muslims did not initiate hostilities with Quraish before Bedr. The early Muslim historians, however, do not seem to support his view. It is principally in recent years that "aggression" has been denounced as a crime. In most previous ages, aggression in a good cause was considered commendable.

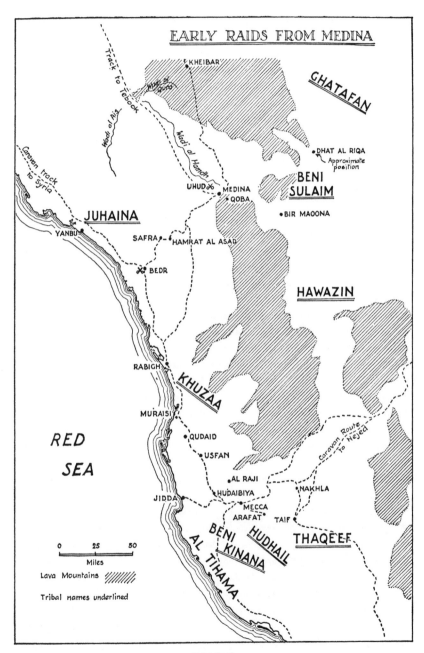

EARLY RAIDS FROM MEDINA

Track to Tebook

Wadi of Ais

Caravan Track to Syria

Wadi al Quna

Wadi al Hamdh

KHEIBAR

GHATAFAN

DHAT AL RIQA
Approximate position

UHUD ⚔ • MEDINA
• QOBA

BENI
SULAIM

• BIR MAOONA

JUHAINA

YANBU •

SAFRA • — HAMRAT AL ASAD

⚔ BEDR

HAWAZIN

RABIGH •

KHUZAA

MURAISI •

RED
SEA

• QUDAID

• USFAN

• AL RAJI

• NAKHLA

Caravan Route to Nejed

JIDDA •

HUDAIBIYA

MECCA
ARAFAT • TAIF •

BENI
KINANA

HUDHAIL

THAQEEF

AL TIHAMA

0   25   50
Miles

Lava Mountains /////////

Tribal names underlined

MAP 6

dropped in anecdotes here and there which indicate that the tribes looked on Quraish with some contempt as mere townsmen and shopkeepers. The Meccans, of course, regarded the tribes with equal condescension as being wild and ignorant. It is, therefore, not surprising to find that the first attempts at raiding by the Emigrants were far from successful.

A glance at the map will show that Medina was ideally situated as a base for the interception of caravans going north from Mecca to Syria. Probably in January 623, the first Muslim raid set out, under the command of Hamza, the Prophet's uncle. He was accompanied by thirty riders and his objective was to seize a caravan commanded by Abu Jahal. Hamza overtook the caravan near Wadi al Ais but the chief of the local tribe, Juhaina, mediated between the two parties, who separated without fighting.

In February 623, a Muslim raiding party of sixty riders intercepted a Quraish party led by Abu Sofian ibn Harb near Rabigh. The two sides again parted without fighting, though Saad ibn abi Waqqas,[6] an early convert, shot off a quiverful of arrows at Quraish. These were the first arrows shot in Islam.

In June 623, the Apostle set out on his first raid, in the hope of capturing a Quraish caravan. No enemy was encountered. The party, however, found the Beni Dhamra clan of Beni Kinana. Instead of fighting, the Prophet held consultations with their chief, and concluded a treaty of friendship with him. As we shall see, Muhammad was not interested in fighting and the charm and persuasiveness of his manner were vastly more useful to Islam than was his sword. The raiders were absent from home for fifteen days. Three or four others raids went out between June and October 623, looking for Quraish caravans, but all returned empty-handed. In November 623, some of the camels of Medina were successfully raided by bedouins.

The futility of these first expeditions may be partly attributed to the instinctive hesitation of both sides to engage in fratricidal strife, for all the men of both parties were of Quraish. The Helpers of Medina took no part in these early enterprises.

It must now have become apparent to the Muslims that no plan of injuring Quraish by intercepting their caravans could be made effective without the co-operation of the bedouin tribes. The system by which each tribe agreed to protect the caravans passing through

6 Page 99.

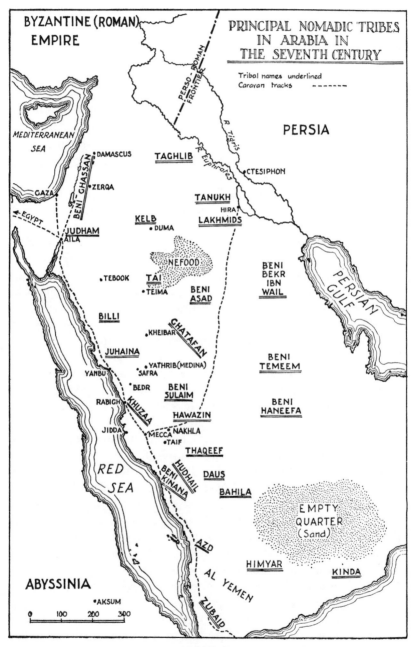

MAP 7

its territory was proving extremely effective.[7] The Muslims could not attack the caravans unless they could first win over the tribes. For this reason, the Apostle's treaty with Beni Dhamra is something of a milestone in the operations between the Muslims and Quraish.

In September 623, the Apostle went with a hundred and fifty men to intercept a Quraish caravan going to Damascus at Dhi al Ushaira, near Yanbu. They missed the caravan but again the Prophet took advantage of the occasion to make a treaty with the Mudlij tribe.

In addition to their lack of experience as raiders, the Emigrants were unable to conceal their plans. When they gathered for an expedition, everybody knew about it. The Apostle appears to have realised this, for the next raid set out with sealed orders. In November 623, a party of eight Muslims started out under the command of one Abdulla ibn Jahash. The Messenger of God gave Abdulla a letter, telling him to open it after travelling east for two days.

When he did so, he found an order to proceed to Nakhla, on the road from Taif to Mecca and to ambush Quraish caravans. When subsequent complications arose, it was said that the orders were only to observe caravans, but it seems somewhat unreasonable to suppose that so much trouble and danger would be incurred, merely to observe the passage of caravans. Before the raiders had been long in ambush, a small Meccan caravan came down the track, travelling from Taif to Mecca, and loaded with the produce of Taif, dried raisins, skins and wine. The little convoy was escorted by four men. It was the last day of Rejeb, one of the sacred months of truce among the Arabs, during which to fight was an act of impiety. Nevertheless, after a brief consultation, the Muslims attacked. One of the men with the caravan, Abdulla ibn al Hadhrami, was killed, two were taken prisoner and one escaped. The caravan was brought back to Medina as booty.

The Arabs were taken aback by the Muslim breach of the sacred month, the observance of which was thought by the idolaters to be a religious duty. It is true that the observance of the four sacred months had long been bound up with the idolatrous worship of the Arabs, but, in the endless warfare of Arabia, the sacred months were also a very great relief to the general public and a valuable protection for commerce. The infringement of the sacred month, therefore, came as a considerable shock to Muslims and to polytheists alike.

Consequently, there was something of an outcry in Medina when

[7] Page 29.

Abdulla ibn Jahash returned with his plunder. It is impossible now to know whether the Apostle of God had considered the question of the month of Rejeb when he sent the raiders out. On their return, he refused at first to accept his official share of one-fifth of the booty.

Another curious aspect of this affair was that the sealed orders included a provision that anybody who did not wish to go on, should be allowed to return to Medina. Was this a loophole for "conscientious objectors", who did not want to infringe the sacred month, or was it based on the danger incurred in so small a party going so far afield? Nobody asked to turn back but two men subsequently absented themselves. They returned to Medina some days later making the excuse that they had lost their riding camel.

The Muslims in Medina remained in a state of suspense, for some days, until it was terminated by the revelation of Chapter II of the Qoran, verse 217.

"They ask you about fighting in the sacred month: Say:[8] Fighting in it is an important matter, and preventing men from following the way of God and denying Him and the sacred mosque and turning its people out of it—these with God are more important still, and schism is more important than killing. They will not cease fighting you until they turn you from your religion, if they can. And any of you who recant from your religion will die a pagan."

The violation of the sacred month is half admitted to be an offence but is negligible in comparison with the crimes committed by Quraish.

Amid the violent recriminations which resulted from the breach of the sacred month, the fact must not be forgotten that the killing of Abdulla ibn al Hadhrami marked the first blood shed by the Muslims. Unfortunately the man was a client of Utba ibn Rabia, one of the moderate and respected leaders of Quraish, whom we have already met.[9] As we have seen, questions involving the obligation of the strong to protect the weak were fruitful causes of hostilities among the Arabs. Utba ibn Rabia was in honour bound to avenge the death of his protégé.

The seizure of the caravan and the killing of Abdulla ibn al Hadhrami greatly exacerbated relations between the Meccans and the Muslims and soon resulted in a state of open war.

*   *   *

[8] God is speaking to Muhammad.   [9] Chapter V, p. 104 and Chapter VII, p. 137.

In the autumn of 623, the annual Quraish caravan to Syria and Gaza had passed up the coast of the Red Sea west of Medina. The caravan consisted of a thousand camels laden with priceless oriental merchandise and was under the command of Abu Sofian, one of the leaders of the opposition to the Apostle's preaching in Mecca. The Muslims failed to intercept it.

The caravan was expected to leave Damascus in January 634 and the Messenger of God determined to seize it. The operation was one of considerable importance. The caravan represented a large part of the annual income of all Mecca for, although the rich merchants owned much of it, almost everyone in the town had some share in the venture. By corollary, of course, if the Muslims were able to capture the caravan, they would become wealthy overnight and their war chest would be correspondingly strengthened.

So inexpert, however, were the believers at this stage at concealing their plans that Abu Sofian received news of the Muslims' intention, while he was still at Zerqa,[10] a hundred miles south of Damascus. He immediately sent a fast camel rider to Mecca, calling upon Quraish to send out an armed force to meet him, sufficient to escort him past Medina.

On 8th March, 624, Muhammad set out from Medina with three hundred and fourteen men, eighty-three of whom were Meccan Emigrants and two hundred and thirty-one Helpers. So poor were the Muslims that only seventy camels and two horses could be found to carry them. Every three or four men took it in turns to ride one camel. The Apostle shared his camel with Ali ibn abi Talib and Zaid ibn Haritha, his adopted son. These conditions were a terrible handicap in the vast areas which had to be crossed in desert warfare. In the present instance, however, the distance was only some eighty miles and, by taking turns to ride, the raiders were able to cover it.

The bedouin messenger sent by Abu Sofian rode posthaste. Arriving early one morning in Mecca, he couched his camel below the Kaaba, turned the saddle back to front, tore his clothes, and called at the top of his voice, "O Quraish! The caravan, the caravan! Muhammad and his comrades are lying in wait to seize your wealth which is with Abu Sofian! You will not be in time to save it! Help! Help!"

This alarm produced consternation in Mecca. Men rushed right

---

[10] Zerqa, today in Jordan, was to become an Arab Legion army camp in 1948. Map 7, p. 176.

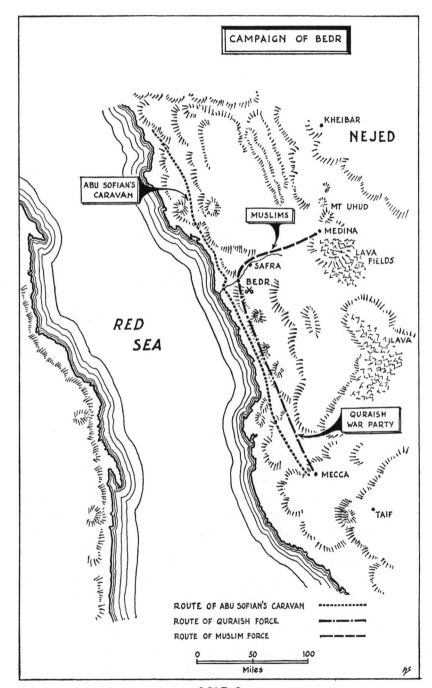

CAMPAIGN OF BEDR

KHEIBAR

NEJED

ABU SOFIAN'S CARAVAN

MT UHUD

MUSLIMS

MEDINA

LAVA FIELDS

SAFRA

BEDR

RED SEA

LAVA

QURAISH WAR PARTY

MECCA

TAIF

ROUTE OF ABU SOFIAN'S CARAVAN ·········

ROUTE OF QURAISH FORCE — · — · —

ROUTE OF MUSLIM FORCE — — — —

0   50   100
Miles

MAP 8

and left, arming and mounting. Scarcely a man stayed behind, and those who, for one reason or another, were unable to go, hired a substitute to take their place. The Prophet's uncle, Abu Lahab, one of his bitterest critics, was one of those who sent a man in his place. An old man called Umaiya ibn Khalaf, who was so fat as to be almost incapable of riding, was sitting in the public square, when another man, seeing him inactive, presented him with perfume, saying, "Scent yourself with this, for you belong to the women!" The old man struggled to his feet and joined the war party, only to be killed, as we shall see, in the battle.

Meanwhile, the Apostle had set out from Medina. The war banner was carried in front by Musaab ibn Umair, the first missionary to Medina.[11] The Messenger of God was preceded by two black flags, one borne by Ali, the other by a man of the Helpers. The Muslim plan was to surprise the caravan while it was watering at Bedr. For this purpose two bedouins of the local tribe, Juhaina, were sent on ahead to scout. Once again it is to be noticed that tribesmen had to be used for scouting, an art in which the townsmen of Mecca and Medina were inexpert.

The two bedouins couched their camels near the wells of Bedr and went forward with a water-skin to draw water.[12] On the wells were two local girls and a man of Juhaina, also drawing water. While the two bedouin scouts were ostensibly waiting their turn at the well, they overheard the two girls discussing the fact that the caravan was expected to water there on the following day. Armed with this information, the two scouts returned and reported to the Prophet.

Meanwhile, the caravan was approaching the wells from the north. Abu Sofian was very uneasy. If the Muslims were going to attack the caravan, the wells of Bedr would be the obvious place. He had still received no message from Mecca as to whether or not Quraish had sent an escort to meet him. He decided to ride on ahead himself and reconnoitre the wells. When he reached Bedr, he found the same bedouin of Juhaina who had been there when Muhammad's scouts had come shortly before. Abu Sofian enquired of this man if he had seen anybody. "Nothing particular", replied the Juhani, "only two camelman who stopped here a short time ago to fill their water-skins."

Abu Sofian walked over to where the two scouts had couched

their camels, picked up some of the dung and rubbed it between his
fingers. In it, he found some undigested date stones. The examination of the dung of unknown camels is to this day a normal scouting
technique among bedouins. The camels of the nomadic tribes live by
grazing. Only camels kept in a town would be fed on dates. Abu
Sofian instantly reached the correct conclusion. These camels had
come from Medina and, therefore, the two men were not passing
bedouins but Muslim scouts. Hastily remounting his camel, he rode
back at a swinging trot until he met the head of his caravan. Divert-
ing it westward to the seashore, he pressed forward at full speed and,
having marched all night without a halt, was well to the south and
already out of danger by the next morning.

The Muslims in the meantime were approaching from the east.
After passing Safra, the Apostle called a halt. Here news was received
that Quraish had left Mecca to meet and escort their caravan, but
there was no news of the arrival of the latter. Muhammed collected
the men of his party and explained the situation to them all. Abu
Bekr, Umar and the Emigrants announced their readiness to follow
him, whatever he decided.

The Messenger of God, however, was anxious concerning the
Helpers. Since the second pledge of Aqaba, on which their obligation
to him was based, had been a purely defensive undertaking, it was
uncertain whether they would consider themselves bound to support
Muhammad in an offensive raid against the Quraish caravan,
eighty miles away from Medina. Addressing himself to a group of
Helpers, he said, "Give me your advice, O men."

Saad ibn Muadh, one of the chiefs of the Aus, replied emphatic-
ally, "We believe in you, O Messenger of God, we witness that you
have brought us the truth, and we have given our pledge to obey
you. If you plunged into the sea, we would plunge into it behind
you. We are ready to fight your enemies tomorrow."[13] The Apostle
was greatly relieved to hear this declaration of loyalty from the men of
Medina. "Forward, then, in good courage," he cried. "For God has
promised us one of the two parties," meaning either the caravan
or the Quraish escort force. After marching another six or seven
miles, the force bivouacked a short distance from the wells of Bedr,
which all three parties were now approaching, each unaware of the
movements of the others.

After dark, a reconnaissance party was sent forward to the wells,

[13] Ibn Ishaq, slightly condensed.

where they found a party of camelmen drawing water. They seized two prisoners and brought them back to the Apostle for cross-questioning. The men proved to be from the Quraish war party which, they alleged, was bivouacked two or three miles to the south. After further interrogation, it became evident that the force was about a thousand strong. All the principal leaders of Quraish were present. This report produced considerable disappointment among the believers, who had hoped for an easy victory and ample loot from the caravan, the escort of which consisted of only thirty or forty men.

As soon as Abu Sofian was clear of danger, he sent a messenger across to inform the Quraish escort of his position and to tell them that the caravan had passed Bedr safely. When the war party received Abu Sofian's report, their counsels were divided. Tribal feeling was strongly opposed to a battle, the Muslim Emigrants being from all the different clans of Quraish. To shed the blood of kinsmen was deeply abhorrent to the Meccan pagans.

The Beni Zuhra clan, to which Muhammad's mother had belonged, turned about and set out for Mecca immediately. Talib, the eldest son of Abu Talib, Muhammad's uncle, with a party of Beni Hashim idolaters, did the same. Another clan, Beni Adi ibn Kaab, the relatives of Umar ibn al Khattab, also absented itself and turned back.

Utba and Shaiba, the sons of Rabia, whom we have already met at Mecca and Taif, were the two principal leaders of Quraish. They were steady and reliable citizens, moderate and respectable. Utba, whose own son was with Muhammad, opposed the shedding of the blood of fellow tribesmen. But, it will be remembered, Abdulla ibn al Hadhrami, killed with the caravan at Nakhla, had been his client. Amr, the brother of Abdulla, taunted him with his duty to avenge the blood of his protégé.

Abu Jahal of Beni Makhzoom, however, a younger man, whom we have often met as the Apostle's bitterest enemy, insisted that they must go on and fight, and his forcefulness won the day. Quraish mounted and rode northwards towards Bedr.

If their deeply-rooted family loyalties made Quraish hesitate to engage in battle with the Emigrants, the latter had no such inhibitions. It was a basic feature of the Apostle's policy to destroy tribal loyalties, and to replace them by devotion to the Muslim community, and many dedicated young Muslims had adopted the new outlook with enthusiasm. Moreover, they were bitterly resentful at having been obliged to leave Mecca and had suffered intensely from poverty and destitution during their first year as refugees in Medina. Most of them were still desperately poor. Many had been separated from their wives and children. They had nothing in the world but their swords, which they burned to use to avenge their grievances.

Meanwhile the Muslims had also moved forward and had halted north-east of the wells. The believers, as we have already noted, always distinguished sharply between the Prophet's divine revelations, which were infallible, and his private opinions, which could be quite wrong. A certain Hubab ibn al Mundhir came up to him and said, "Is this a place which God has ordered you to occupy, so that we can neither advance nor retreat, or is it just your idea?" When he was told that it was just Muhammad's idea, he suggested that they move forward and occupy the wells. The water would then be denied to the enemy, while the Muslims would have all they needed. The Messenger of God immediately adopted this proposal.

A booth made of palm fronds was then erected in which the Prophet could shelter, and his riding camels were couched behind it. "If we are defeated," said Saad ibn Muadh, the Aus chieftain, "you could escape on your camels to Medina." At this moment, the forces of Quraish were seen moving down the slope of a hill opposite the Muslim position and making for the wells. It was sunrise on 15th March, 624. When the Messenger of God saw the Meccans advancing, he cried out passionately, "O God, here come Quraish in their vanity and pride, fighting against Thee and calling Thine Apostle a liar. O God, grant the help which Thou hast promised me. Destroy them this morning."

The two war-parties[14] were now halted close to one another, and time was allowed for single combat between champions, as was the Arab custom. The Apostle had meanwhile drawn up the Muslim line, facing towards the west. The sun, which had just risen, was behind them, but shone into the eyes of the Meccans who were approaching from the direction of the sea.

Among the seventh century Arabs, it was thought to be a point of honour for the commander to challenge the enemy to single combat. The Quraish leader, Utba ibn Rabia, the wise and moderate citizen who had opposed fighting, now stepped forward. On his right was his brother Shaiba,[15] on his left his son Al Waleed. The three then

---

[14] It seems to be misleading to refer to these gatherings of tribesmen as armies.
[15] Page 138.

challenged three champions from the Muslims to come forward. Three men of the Medina Helpers stepped out of the ranks but the Quraishites asked who they were. When they replied, Utba answered, "You are noble warriors, but we want our own men." Then raising their voices they cried, "O Muhammad! Send against us our equals of our own tribe."

The Messenger of God then called upon his uncle Hamza, and his cousin and son-in-law, Ali ibn abi Talib, who had married Muhammad's daughter, Fátima.[16] The third of the party was one Ubaida ibn al Harith, a man already middle-aged. Ubaida engaged Utba, each simultaneously delivering a fatal sword cut to his adversary. Hamza and Ali were both outstanding swordsmen. Hamza quickly killed Shaiba, while Ali slew Al Waleed. The dying Ubaida was carried back to the Prophet, crying, "Am I not a martyr, O Messenger of God?" Muhammad's words, "Indeed you are, Ubaida," enabled him to die happy.

The defeat of their champions probably did much to undermine the morale of Quraish, for the Prophet had already claimed that God was fighting on his side. Many of the Meccans may suddenly have feared that their opponents really were receiving supernatural assistance. Meanwhile the Messenger of God himself, accompanied by Abu Bekr, had retired to the arbour of palm branches which the Muslims had made for him. "O God," he cried, "if this faithful band perish today, there will be none left to worship Thee."

After a time, Abu Bekr intervened. "O Messenger of God," he said, "your repeated entreaties will annoy your Lord, for surely God will fulfil His promise to you." The Prophet then left his arbour and approached the men, calling out that every man killed that day would be instantly admitted to Paradise. A young man beside him was eating some dates. "What!," he cried, "is there nothing between me and Paradise but to be killed by these men?" Throwing away the dates and seizing his sword, he plunged into the battle and fought till he was killed.

All this time, a confused and furious sword fight was in progress. The tribesmen had little conception of tactics and their battles consisted in a wild mêlée of sword-slashing. Quraish suffered a number of tactical disadvantages. They had advanced against the Muslims across soft sand dunes, while the believers awaited them

---

[16] This name is pronounced Fáatima, not Fateema. In English, it might be spelt "Fartimmer", the r's being silent.

standing on firm soil. Just as the lines were about to engage, a violent squall of wind whipped up the sand in the faces of the Meccans. "Gabriel," cried the Prophet ecstatically, "with a thousand angels is falling upon the enemy."

Suddenly stooping, Muhammad picked up a handful of gravel and threw it at the Meccans, crying out, "Confusion on their faces." For some time the fight had swayed back and forth without either side gaining a clear advantage. Now Quraish began to waver and then to give ground. Then suddenly they broke and fled in a wild rout.

Meccan losses were variously estimated at between forty-nine and seventy dead, and a similar number of prisoners. The Muslims admitted only fourteen killed. Among the leaders of Quraish who met their death was Abu Jahal, chief of the clan of Beni Makhzoom, the Apostle's bitterest enemy. Muhammad sent his servant to search the field for his corpse. When he found it, he cut off his head and threw it down at the feet of the Apostle who cried ecstatically, "The head of the enemy of God. Praise God, for there is no other but He!"

*   *   *

The Messenger of God had given orders that one of the Quraish leaders, Abu al Bakhtari, should not be killed because, though an idolater, he had restrained the people of Mecca from persecuting him. He was taken prisoner with a companion, one Junáda, who had shared his camel on the march. When the Muslims captured Abu al Bakhtari, they told him that Muhammad had ordered them to spare his life. "And what of my comrade, Junada?" he asked. "We are not going to spare him," the Muslims replied. "The Apostle only gave orders about you." "In that case," said the old man, "I will die with him. The women of Mecca shall not say that I forsook my friend to save my own life."

Umaiya ibn Khalaf, the fat old man who was given the perfume in the public square of Mecca, was taken prisoner by Abdul Rahman ibn Auf, one of the early converts. The two men had been close friends in Mecca before the preaching of Islam had divided them. Abdul Rahman now accepted the sword of Umaiya and led him away to the Messenger of God. But, on the way, they met Bilal, the tall, gaunt negro who gave the call to prayer. Bilal had been Umaiya's slave and the latter had tormented him by tying him up in the sun when he became a Muslim, to make him recant.[17]

[17] Page 118.

As soon as Bilal saw his former tormentor, he ran up at full speed, shouting, "The infidel! The enemy of God! Umaiya ibn Khalaf! May I not live if he lives!" But Abdul Rahman ibn Auf protested. "He is my prisoner," he said. "I accepted his surrender. He is under my protection." But Bilal continued to shout, "The infidel! The enemy of God! O God's Helpers!" A crowd gathered and Umaiya was hewn to pieces, in spite of the protests of his captor.

This was one of many similar incidents. We have seen on several occasions what immense importance the Arabs attached to the duty of protecting men who asked for their help. This and many other similar customs may be said to have constituted a code of chivalry observed by the nomads of Arabia from that day to this. Throughout these fourteen centuries, all these customs have been preserved, except at periods of religious enthusiasm. Whenever a religious revival has occurred, the codes of honour have been abandoned. The service of God has provided a pretext, for who could be blamed for killing the "enemies of God"?

The Apostle ordered that a great pit be dug and that the bodies of the unbelievers who had been killed should be thrown into it. When the body of Utba ibn Rabia, one of the most respected leaders of Quraish, was dragged up, his son, who was a Muslim, was standing beside the Messenger of God. Seeing the expression on the young man's face, Muhammad said, "You feel deeply your father's death." "I used to know my father as a wise, virtuous and cultured man," said the youth. "I hoped he would become a Muslim. It saddens me that he died in unbelief."

As the bodies of Quraish were thrown into the pit, the Prophet himself addressed them. "O people of the pit," he cried, "have you found that what God threatened is true? For I have found that what my Lord promised me was true."

Meanwhile the victorious Muslims had begun to quarrel among themselves about the booty. Those who had killed a man and taken his weapons claimed the right to keep them. Others, who had been guarding the person of the Messenger of God, had had no opportunity to plunder but demanded a share of the loot. The Apostle ordered that all the booty be collected in one place and be distributed equally among the believers. This incident established the procedure which was to be followed in all succeeding Muslim wars.

Having sent messengers to ride posthaste ahead of the column to carry the good news to Medina, the Messenger of God then led the triumphant Muslims slowly eastwards. Between Safra and Medina he was met by deputations from the oasis bringing their congratulations on the victory.

One of the prisoners taken in the battle was Al Nadhr ibn al Harith the man who, when the Apostle preached in Mecca, had followed him, telling stories from the ancient legends of Persia. "Are not my stories as good as his?" Al Nadhr used to ask his audiences. When the column passed Safra, the Messenger of God ordered Ali to strike off Al Nadhr's head. There is no recorded explanation why he was not killed with the others after the fighting. A little further on, the Apostle gave orders for the decapitation of another prisoner, Uqba ibn abi Muait. "But who will look after my children, O Muhammad?" cried Uqba in anguish. "Hell fire," replied the Prophet coldly.

The many stresses and strains set up by the slaughter of the leaders of Quraish at and after Bedr is emphasised by the story told by Sauda, the Apostle's wife. She had been visiting a family of Muslim Emigrants from Mecca, to console with them over the deaths of two relatives, when she heard that the prisoners had arrived in Medina. ("This", Ibn Ishaq reminds us, "was before the introduction of the veil", after which Muslim women coul ɩ no longer freely visit their neighbours, male or female.)

"I returned to my house," continues Sauda's narrative, "where the Apostle was. There was Abu Yazeed Suhail ibn Amr in a corner of the room with his hands tied to his neck. I could hardly contain myself when I saw him in this state and I said, 'O Abu Yazeed, you surrendered too easily. You should rather have died a noble death!' Suddenly the Prophet's voice startled me, 'Sauda, would you stir up trouble against God and His Apostle?' 'By God,'[18] I answered, 'I could hardly contain myself when I saw Abu Yazeed in this state and that is why I said what I did.' "

Chapter VIII of the Qoran was revealed after the Battle of Bedr. We may end the present chapter by quoting some relevant passages from it.

"They ask you about the profits acquired in battle. Say: The profits belong to God and to the Apostle.[19] So render your obligations to God and settle your disputes, and obey God and His Apostle if you are believers . . . When God promised that one of the two

---

[18] Muslims do not consider it blasphemous to swear by God.

[19] This is apparently a reference to the fact that the Muslims quarrelled over the loot. There is some doubt over the meaning of the word used, but this seems to be the intention.

groups[20] should be yours, you hoped that which was unarmed should be yours but God wished by His word to confirm the truth and to cut off the unbelievers . . . When you implored the help of your Lord, He answered you: 'I am reinforcing you with a thousand angels one behind the other' . . . When your Lord said to the angels: 'I am with you, so make the believers to stand firm. I will throw fear into the hearts of the unbelievers, so strike them upon their necks . . .' O you who believe, when you meet the unbelievers advancing to battle, do not turn your backs. He who turns his back on that day . . . shall meet with the anger of God and his abode will be hell."

NOTABLE DATES

Arrival of Muhammad in Medina	June 622
First Muslim raid under Hamza	January 623
Muslim raid near Rabigh. Saad ibn abi Waqqas shoots the first arrow in Islam	February 623
Beni Dhamra raid. Muhammad makes a treaty with them	June 623
A number of small unsuccessful Muslim raids	June to October 623
Dhi al Ushaira raid. Muhammad makes a treaty with Mudlij	September 623
Nakhla raid under Abdulla ibn Jahash. Abdulla ibn al Hadhrami killed, first death inflicted by Muslims	November 623
Breach with the Jewish tribes. Direction of prayer changed from Jerusalem to Mecca	October 623 to
Friday substituted for Saturday as the special day of the Muslim week. Institution of the Fast of Ramadhan	January 624
Battle of Bedr	15th March, 624

PERSONALITIES

Muslims

Abu Bekr, the Apostle's first lieutenant
Umar ibn al Khattab, his second lieutenant

[20] Either the caravan or the relieving force.

Ali ibn abi Talib, the Apostle's cousin
Zaid ibn Haritha, the Apostle's "son"
Abdul Rahman ibn Auf ⎱ Early converts
Saad ibn abi Waqqas   ⎰
Saad ibn Muadh, leader of the Aus

Leaders of Quraish

Utba   ⎱ Sons of Rabia
Shaiba ⎰
Amr abu Jahal, chief of Beni Makhzoom
Umaiya ibn Khalaf
Abu al Bakhtari
All the above were killed at Bedr

Abu Lahab, the Apostle's uncle
Abbas, the Apostle's uncle
Abu Sofian, leader of the Quraish caravan

X

Uhud

War, war is still the cry,—war even to the knife.

LORD BYRON, *Childe Harold's Pilgrimage*

However unimportant in itself as a military engagement, this skirmish laid the foundation of Muhammad's temporal power. Islam had won its first and decisive military victory; the victory itself was interpreted as a divine sanction of the faith. True, in the following year the Meccans avenged their defeat . . . but their triumph was not to endure.

P. K. HITTI, *The Arabs*

Destroy Thou them, O God; let them fall by their own counsels . . . for they have rebelled against Thee. But let all those that put their trust in Thee rejoice: let them ever shout for joy, because Thou defendest them; let them also that love Thy name be joyful. For Thou, Lord, wilt . . . compass them as with a shield.

Psalm V, 10 to 12

The Messenger of God said:
A morning or an evening battle in the Path of God is better than the world and all that is in it."

Tradition recorded by both Bukhari and Muslim

X

IT is difficult for us now to realise what an amazing and complete revolution the victory of Bedr made in the position and mentality of the Muslims. From being a despised and persecuted sect, they were changed in a few hours into victorious military conquerors. With almost the sole exception of Abu Sofian, who had been with the caravan, all the leaders of the Quraish opposition to Islam had been killed. The Meccans who had scorned and persecuted them had been utterly humiliated. It is not surprising that, for a time at least, the Muslims were drunk with victory. Such is human nature. We have seen examples of it in our own times.

It is impossible to deny that the Messenger of God himself showed signs of vindictiveness, for he too was a man, as he himself had been the first to admit. As he grew older, he was to become more urbane and more clement in his later triumphs. But at Bedr all the insults and humiliations which he had suffered were still fresh in his memory. By a remarkable coincidence, Abu Lahab, the Apostle's uncle, one of his bitterest opponents, who had not gone out with the force to Bedr, died of illness in Mecca soon afterwards.

Another of the Prophet's uncles, Abbas,[1] had been taken prisoner at Bedr, fighting for the idolaters. Muhammad ordered that he be held until an adequate ransom be paid for him and for two of his nephews. "But I was a Muslim," Abbas protested. "The people of Mecca obliged me to fight." "God knows best about your being a Muslim, uncle," the Apostle answered, "but to all outward appearance you were fighting against us, so pay your ransom."

Among the prisoners also was Abu al Aasi ibn al Rabia, the Apostle's own son-in-law, married to his daughter Zainab, who was still in Mecca. Abu al Aasi had been a nephew of Khadija, the Prophet's first wife, and it was at her request that Muhammad had given him his daughter, before his call to be an apostle. Zainab now collected the money for her husband's ransom and sent it to her father, and with it she sent a necklace which had been a wedding present from her late mother, Khadija. When the Messenger of God saw the necklace, he was overcome with emotion and asked the

[1] Genealogical tree, p. 120.

Muslims to agree to the release of Zainab's husband without a ransom.

These and innumerable other stories have come down to us, showing the tragic family divisions which resulted from Bedr, as from all civil wars. The fact that the majority of Muslims were young men has already been mentioned. In many families, a younger son had been converted, while the parents and perhaps the eldest son had remained in Mecca. Some of these young Muslims had been remarkably callous where family ties were concerned, and had even urged their fellow-Muslims to kill their own fathers, if they met them in battle.

Yet this very callousness had been an extraordinary tribute to the persuasiveness of the Prophet's teaching. The whole of Arab life at the time was based on family solidarity. We have seen how Beni Hashim stood by Muhammad during the blockade, although most of them were still idolaters. The Messenger of God had preached against family loyalty and had insisted that it must be replaced by loyalty to Islam. The relationship of one Muslim to another was to be that of brotherhood, annulling the ties of natural sonship and brotherhood, which had previously been considered to possess overriding importance.

But by far the most important result of Bedr was the extraordinary rise in prestige and morale which it gave to the Muslims. However, the material gains were not to be despised. The plunder taken on the battle field is said to have consisted of a hundred and fifty camels, ten horses, and the weapons and armour of the dead and the prisoners. The ransoms obtained from the prisoners were much more valuable. Rich prisoners were made to pay a ransom of four thousand dirhems, though poor prisoners were released for less. As we have seen, Chapter VIII of the Qoran had stated that all the profit belonged to God and His Apostle. Ultimately, however, the Prophet retained one-fifth, the remaining four-fifths being distributed among the Muslims.

It is interesting to notice that the Meccan prisoners, while waiting for their ransoms, were made to teach the Muslims of Medina how to read and write. This fact once again emphasises the difference between the merchant community of Mecca and the uneducated agriculturalists of Medina.

Bedr transformed the whole situation of the Muslims. If victory had gone to Quraish, the whole Islamic movement might have come to a violent end. Ever afterwards, those who had fought at Bedr were to be looked upon as the heroes and princes of Islam. The Apostle, however, attributed the victory to divine assistance. Chapter III, verse 123, of the Qoran claims that three thousand angels fought on the Muslim side at Bedr.

One of the first results of the victory was a tightening-up of discipline in Medina. The Messenger of God always attached great importance to the sarcasms of poets, who played a rôle somewhat similar to that of the press in our time. It was the poets who held up the rulers to ridicule. Asma bint Merwan, a married woman with five children, possessed the gift of poetical satire, which she directed against the Apostle. She was murdered by the Muslims, when in bed with her children. Soon afterwards a male poet called Abu Afek met the same fate.

Many Western historians have denounced these assassinations, and others which were to follow, as sheer terrorism. One point in this connection may be worthy of mention. The use of assassination as a political weapon is indefensible in a country which possesses a constitution, laws, a judicial system and a police force. In seventh century Arabia, however, none of these things existed. Security depended on family solidarity, a time-honoured system which enabled the Arabs to live, to them, satisfying lives. But the Apostle had destroyed family solidarity in order to build the Muslim community. This left no means of enforcing authority other than violence.

It may be of interest here to include a quotation from a review, written by the historian, Sir Charles Petrie, on the subject of the judicial murder of Sir Thomas More by Henry VIII in 1535, nine centuries after Muhammad. "It must not be forgotten," writes Sir Charles, "that it was a belief almost universal in that age that force was a necessary and effective prophylactic against dangerous opinions."[2]

Muhammad was dedicated to the propagation of a religious movement which he believed had been revealed by God. The poets were making his efforts appear ridiculous. There were no legal means of dealing with them. We may consider that the poets, accused of fomenting disloyalty, should have been arrested and tried. But an accused person cannot be arrested if there are no police, nor "tried" if there are no laws which he can be accused of breaking.

[2] *The Illustrated London News*, "Books of the Week", 21st December, 1968.

The Messenger of God, however, adopted one other method of dealing with the satirical poets—he engaged one of them to defend him. Hassán ibn Thábit was middle-aged and had already achieved fame as a poet. He had spent some years at the court of the Beni Ghassan princes in eastern Syria. Asked by the Apostle if he could defend him from the attacks of his enemies, he replied by putting out his tongue. "There is no armour which I cannot pierce with this weapon," he said.

*   *   *

The satires of the Arab poets were not the only opposition encountered by the Prophet in Medina. The Jews had become increasingly hostile to him as time passed. We have seen that the Messenger of God had originally hoped for Jewish support against the idolatrous Arabs, even if they refused to accept him as their messiah. He made lavish use of Old Testament stories, he prayed facing Jerusalem and borrowed many minor practices from Judaic ritual.

If the Jews of Medina had been men of wide outlook and generous wisdom, it is possible that they might have discovered a method of peaceful co-existence, for, ironically enough, the Jews were to become the allies of the Muslims against the Christians for many centuries after the Apostle's death. But how could the Jews of Medina be men of broad-minded wisdom? As we have seen, they were themselves probably early Arab converts to Judaism and their daily lives in their desert oasis were spent as market gardeners or small artisans.

It is true that there were among them rabbis and that many of them had an intimate textual knowledge of the Pentateuch. But it was this very knowledge which was to prove their ruin. They could not resist the temptation to show their superior cleverness by pointing out the factual inaccuracies in the Apostle's versions of the Old Testament stories. Thus they made the same mistake as the satirists —they made the Messenger of God look ridiculous by catching him out on points of detail. Unprepared to fight, they were foolish enough to goad the Muslims to rage by their clever pinpricks.

The immense rise in prestige and in self-confidence acquired by the Muslims as a result of their astounding victory at Bedr inspired the Messenger of God to adopt a stronger line against his Jewish tormentors. Chapter III, verse 11, of the Qoran seems to refer to this particular moment.

Say to those who disbelieved: "You will be defeated and driven together to hell, an evil resting place. There was a sign for you in the two parties which fought one another: one party fighting in the way of God and the other disbelieving"

—an obvious reference to Bedr.

The first Jewish community against which the Muslims proceeded was the tribe of Beni Qainuqa. This group are said to have been goldsmiths by trade and were probably the wealthiest of the Jewish tribes. Their numbers are given as three hundred armed men and four hundred unarmed. They also made armour but owned no fields or gardens. A short time after Bedr, an altercation in the market of Beni Qainuqa, involving Hamza and Ali, provided a *casus belli*. Ibn Ishaq gives an alternative version, alleging an indecent act by a Jew towards an Arab woman.

As in most of the other settlements in the oasis, the houses of Beni Qainuqa were built in a single compact group, forming a little fortress. The Muslims had no means of battering down masonry walls and confined themselves to a close siege of the settlement. None of the other Jewish tribes moved to support their co-religionists. There does not appear to have been any fighting and after a siege of two weeks the Jews surrendered.

Beni Qainuqa had two tribal allies from among the Aus and the Khazraj. Both had professed Islam. The first was Ubáda ibn al Sámit of the Aus. He went to Muhammad and said, "O Messenger of God, I take God and His Apostle and the believers as my friends. I renounce my agreement and friendship with these unbelievers."

The other ally of Beni Qainuqa was Abdulla ibn Ubay of the Khazraj, a man, as we have seen, with a reputation for a dislike of bloodshed. During the war between the Aus and the Khazraj he had remained neutral and, as a result, had been accepted as chief of the whole oasis, until Muhammad had come. Abdulla had, nevertheless, professed Islam.

As soon as he heard of the surrender of Beni Qainuqa, Abdulla went to the Apostle. "O Muhammad," he said, "deal kindly with my allies", but the Apostle turned his back. He thereupon caught hold of Muhammad's cloak. "The Apostle was so angry", says Ibn Ishaq, "that his face became almost black." He said, "Confound you, let go of me." But Abdulla replied, "No, by God, I will not let you go until you deal kindly with my clients. Four hundred men unarmoured and three hundred in armour protected me from my enemies.[3] Would you cut them down in one morning? By God, I am a man who fears that circumstances may change." Suddenly the Apostle relented. "You can have their lives," he said.

The phrase attributed to Abdulla by Ibn Ishaq, "Would you cut them down in one morning?" implies that the Jews were about to be put to death. Muslim writers have been severe in their judgement of Abdulla ibn Ubay, who was believed to have been the chief of the "hypocrites". We, however, can perhaps see his difficulty in the light of the revolution which Islam had introduced. To fulfil tribal obligations had been a debt of honour among the Arabs. Abdulla, over and above this consideration, seems to have owed his own life to these Jews. Yet Abdulla had professed Islam and the Messenger of God had abolished tribal obligations. When, moreover, we remember that Abdulla's plea was only for mercy, we may perhaps take a more lenient view of his action than do the Muslim writers.

Chapter V, verse 51, of the Qoran is believed to date from this occasion.

"O you who believe, do not take Jews and Christians as friends. They are friends of one another. Whoever of you takes them as friends is one of them. But you will see those in whose heart is a disease hastening to them, saying 'we fear a change of circumstances'."[4]

Verse 57 of the same chapter may well explain something of the Apostle's resentment against the Jews of Medina.

"O you who believe, do not take as allies those who received the Books before you, but who now treat your religion as a joke and a game."

Eventually Beni Qainuqa were ordered to migrate from Medina to Syria. They left most of their property behind them, but were able to take sufficient animals to carry them on their journey. There were other Jewish settlements on their route to the north, where they were able to rest and where some of them may have remained.

The expulsion of Beni Qainuqa was of immediate benefit to the Muslims. Firstly their wealth and houses were distributed among the Emigrants from Mecca, many of whom had until then been living on charity. Their fate also alarmed the other hostile elements in Medina, both Jews and polytheists.

*   *   *

[3] It appears that Beni Qainuqa saved Abdulla's life during the war between the Aus and the Khazraj.

[4] Or "a reversal of fortune".

When the defeated Meccans had returned from Bedr, Abu Sofian swore to eat no food cooked in oil till he had avenged the leaders of Quraish. In April 624, he left with between a hundred and two hundred men, killed two or three men and burned two houses on the southern fringe of Medina and returned hastily to Mecca. The Muslims gave chase but failed to overtake him. To lighten their animals, the Meccans threw away some dried porridge they were carrying as rations, with the result that the affair came to be known as the "Porridge Raid".

In May 624, the Apostle led a raid of about two hundred riders against the nomadic tribes of Ghatafan and Beni Sulaim. Some five hundred camels were discovered, grazing at a distance from the tribal camp and were driven off by the Muslims. This affair was called the Al Kidr raid.

Living with another Jewish tribe, Beni al Nadheer, was an Arab by the name of Kaab ibn al Ashraf of the tribe of Tai. Kaab's father had married a Jewess of Beni al Nadheer and her son was now living with his mother's people. Kaab was a poet and had composed a lament on the leaders of Quraish killed at Bedr. He had subsequently visited Mecca, where he was believed to have consulted the Meccans on measures to be taken against the Muslims. According to Ibn Ishaq, the Apostle had exclaimed "Who will rid me of Ibn al Ashraf?"

A certain Helper, Muhammad ibn Maslama, had replied that he would kill him if the Prophet wished. "Do so if you can," the Messenger of God replied. "We shall have to tell lies," said the would-be assassin, and the Prophet authorised him to lie if it were necessary.

Muhammad ibn Maslama secured the services of a foster-brother of Kaab called Silkán, who was a Muslim. This man, who was also a poet, visited Kaab and the foster-brothers spent a pleasant evening together reciting poetry. Suffice it to say that, after dark, Kaab was decoyed out of doors and was murdered by Muhammad ibn Maslama, Silkan and two accomplices. This incident occurred in July 624.

The following paragraph is taken verbatim from Ibn Ishaq. "The Apostle said 'Kill any Jew who falls into your power.' Thereupon Muhaiyisa ibn Masood leaped upon Ibn Sunaina, a Jewish merchant . . . and killed him . . . His elder brother beat him, saying 'Did you kill him when much of the fat on your belly comes from his wealth?'

But Muhaiyisa replied, 'Had the one who told me to kill him'
ordered me to kill you, my brother, I would have cut off your head'."

*   *   *

In June 624, the Apostle with four hundred and fifty men set out
to raid Ghatafan. The tribes, however, received warning and moved
away. The Muslims returned without fighting. This expedition was
known as the raid of Dhu Amr.

In August 624, Muhammad again set out with three hundred
riders to raid Beni Sulaim. Reaching a place called Bahran, east of
Medina, and finding no one, the party returned to Medina.

The season for the departure of the annual Meccan caravan
to Syria had now arrived. We have already noted that a great part of
the wealth of Quraish was gained in two great annual caravans, the
one to the Yemen and the other to Syria. As far as can now be
ascertained, the risk of the capture of these caravans had, before the
rise of Islam, been very small. Doubtless all the tribes along the
caravan routes assisted in the trade, provided guides and escorts and
were paid the recognised dues. Bedouin raids against one another
were well regulated "sporting events" and did not normally inter-
fere with commerce. This system was still in force in Arabia at the
beginning of the present century.

The opinion often expressed by Western writers that Arabia at the
time of Muhammad was in a perpetual, chaotic bloodbath with no
holds barred, is completely erroneous. Carefully balanced and universally recognised systems governed both the hostilities between the
tribes and also the relationship between the tribes and the merchants.
Century after century, these systems were only disturbed by two
phenomena. Of these the first was the intervention of a dynasty, such
as the Himyarites or Beni Ghassan, who tried to impose their authority over many tribes by ruthless methods. The second phenomenon
which broke up the well-balanced merchant-and-tribe system was a
religious movement.

If the comparative bloodlessness of tribal raiding be doubted, it
will suffice to notice the tribal raids referred to in the present narrative, in which scarcely any casualties are mentioned. For no profound moral, social or racial differences were involved in tribal wars.
To make away with the camels or sheep of another tribe was an
exhilarating experience like a hard game of polo or football. But it

was not worth while for many men to be killed or wounded in order to secure a few camels, which might be lost next week to other raiders.

The battles fought by the Muslims, however, were in an entirely different category. For the Muslims lived in a state of exaltation, believing that God had delegated them to fight and to kill His enemies. Whereas the normal bedouin raid might result in one or two killed, a total of some seventy or eighty persons had been killed at Bedr.

In the same manner, the Muslim blockade of Mecca by intercepting the Quraish caravans was an entirely new and original form of hostilities. Caravans were periodically robbed in Arabia, but the attackers were normally outlaws or bandits, as in the case of King Naaman's caravan, which caused the Sacrilegious War.[5] The interception of caravans as a means of bringing political pressure was unknown.

It is, therefore, a misconception to say that Muhammad was a man of his times and used the popular methods in vogue among the bloodthirsty Arabs. The reverse is the case. The Prophet's methods were original and had little in common with bedouin war, though princely dynasties had at times fought battles of a somewhat similar kind.

Since Bedr, the livelihood of Mecca was in jeopardy. After anxious consultations, it was decided to send the Syrian caravan through Nejed and not up the Red Sea coast. Ibn Ishaq states that it went "by the Iraq route". It is not clear whether they meant to go right across Arabia to the Euphrates or merely to make a wide detour to the east of Medina. The Persians were, at this time, in occupation of Iraq, Syria and Palestine, so there were no imperial frontiers to cross. Quraish hired bedouin guides to lead them by this deviation.

With the usual inefficiency which resulted from the absence of leadership in Quraish, full information concerning their plans reached Medina. The Muslims, on the other hand, were becoming more efficient. It will be remembered that, before Bedr, information of the intentions of the Muslims reached Abu Sofian before he left Syria. On the present occasion, however, Quraish seem to have been ignorant of the Muslim plan to intercept them.

The Apostle's adopted son, Zaid ibn Haritha, was put in command of a force of one hundred riders, detailed to intercept the caravan, which was surprised and captured at the well of Qarda in Nejed. The plunder proved extremely rich, for a great part of the caravan had been laden with silver. One account estimates the loot at a hundred thousand dirhems.

*   *   *

After Bedr, the surviving leaders of Quraish had called upon the Meccans to contribute to a fund the object of which was to raise such a military force as would destroy Muhammad and the Muslims once and for all. The fund appears to have been well subscribed, the merchants doubtless appreciating that the caravan-raiding activities of the Muslims threatened entirely to ruin business.

It will be remembered that Beni Kinana, who lived on the coastal plain, had a tradition of tribal co-operation with Quraish. Messengers were accordingly sent to urge the tribe to support the Meccans in the forthcoming operations against Muhammad and his followers. As usual, the assistance of the poets was obtained to stir up the generous feelings of Beni Kinana.

Abu Sofian ibn Harb, who had been in charge of the caravan in the Bedr campaign, had become the most prominent man of Quraish since the death of so many former leaders at Bedr. He was consequently given command of the expedition. He belonged to the descendants of Umaiya, which, with Beni Makhzoom, included the majority of the richest business men in Mecca.[6]

In January 625, the expedition left Mecca for Medina. It consisted of approximately three thousand men, partly of Quraish and a number of clients and mercenaries of theirs, and partly of Beni Kinana. As the area south of the oasis was confined and mountainous, the Meccan force passed west of Medina and its settlements and bivouacked at Ainain or the Two Springs on an open plain north of Medina, at the foot of a rocky outcrop called Mount Uhud.

The Quraish force arrived below Mount Uhud on a Wednesday. They remained there resting on Thursday, turning their camels and horses out to graze in the green crops on the open plain north of Medina. The arrival of so large a force, three times as numerous as that which the Meccans had brought to Bedr, caused no little consternation among the Muslims, and Thursday was spent in anxious consultations. The Apostle felt inclined to defend the town,

[6] Genealogical tree, p. 63.

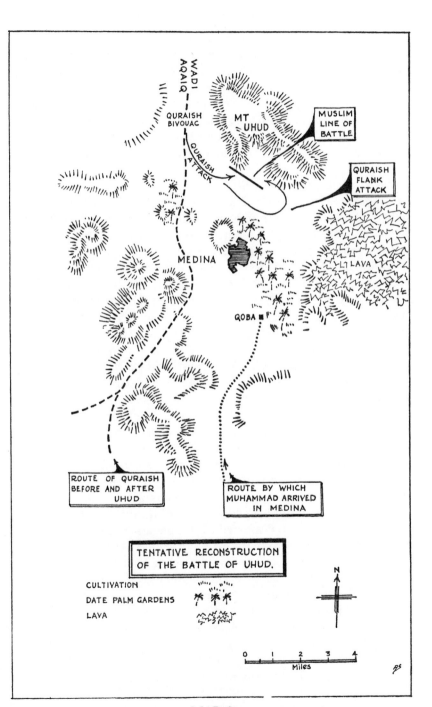

TENTATIVE RECONSTRUCTION
OF THE BATTLE OF UHUD.

CULTIVATION
DATE PALM GARDENS
LAVA

N

0   1   2   3   4
Miles

MAP 9

without venturing into the open country. All the tribal groups in the oasis lived in their own settlements, the houses of which were closely joined together, making each into a little fortress.

Abdulla ibn Ubay, always anxious to avoid bloodshed, strongly supported the Prophet's plan to remain behind walls. The Arabs, armed with lances, swords, bows and arrows, possessed no weapon capable of attacking buildings, as we have already seen in the case of the Muslim attack on Beni Qainuqa. Moreover, they had no system of supplies and thus would probably run out of food before they had besieged Medina for many days.

Unfortunately, however, Muhammad had attributed the victory at Bedr to a miracle. God had been on the side of the Muslims and had sent his angels to fight for them. If divine assistance were available, any discrepancy of numbers would be negligible. Many of the younger or more fanatical believers clamoured to be led out at once to confront the enemies of God in open battle. But Abdulla ibn Ubay continued to recommend a defensive policy. "O Messenger of God," he said, "remain in Medina, do not go out to them. We have never gone out to fight an enemy but we have met with disaster, and no one has ever attacked us without being defeated. If they stay where they are, they will soon be in difficulties, and if they come in to attack us, the men will fight them and the women and children will throw rocks on to them from the walls."

The debate seems to have lasted all day on Thursday and on Friday until midday, when the Apostle led the prayers in the mosque. On emerging from the mosque, he was again surrounded by the young men, clamouring to be led out to battle. As a result, Muhammad went into his house and put on his armour. This incident is of very great interest in the study of the Prophet's character. The idea that he was a strong, fierce ruthless character—or "a captain of banditti" as Margoliouth says—is disproved. He appears rather as hesitant, finding it difficult to make up his mind. Some Muslims may resent such a suggestion but others claim it as an additional proof of his mission. When he acted on a revelation, they say, he was always right, but when he acted without a revelation, he often made mistakes. His human weakness can be regarded as additional evidence in support of the view that his staggering successes must be attributed to divine support.

The description of the Battle of Uhud given in Chapter III of the Qoran, however, does not say that the Apostle first wanted to stay in the town but gave way to popular clamour. Yet, if this did actually occur, it would perhaps have been mentioned, as it would have exonerated the Prophet from having made an error of judgement and would have laid the blame on the unruly conduct of his young supporters. As the Apostle's original unwillingness is mentioned by later historians but not in the contemporary Qoranic account, it may have been an afterthought by his over-enthusiastic admirers, to clear him from the charge of having caused the subsequent defeat.

On this Friday morning, when Muhammad emerged from his house in his armour, the fickle crowd had changed its mind. "We were wrong to oppose your plan to stay in the town," they said. "If you wish to remain in the city, we will not oppose you." But the Apostle, who had suffered thirty-six hours of vacillation, had now made up his mind. "It is not meet that a prophet who has donned his armour should put it off again without fighting," he said. Collecting his followers, he set out with about a thousand men.

When the force had travelled a short distance, the Apostle saw another body of men, following behind the Muslims, and asked who they were. He was told that they were Jews, allies of Abdulla ibn Ubay. "It is not right," he said, "to invoke the aid of polytheists[7] to fight other polytheists." The Jews were accordingly told to go back. The Muslims then camped for the night at a spot called Shaikhain. The enemy had seen the Muslims coming and brought in their horses and camels, which had been grazing in the crops.

The next morning the Muslims resumed their advance until they came in sight of the enemy. At this point, Abdulla ibn Ubay turned back with three hundred men. "He refused my advice and followed that of young men who have no experience," he said. Probably Abdulla, who was already jealous of Muhammad, was piqued by the rejection of his advice to stand on the defensive in the town. Perhaps also he feared that Quraish would win the battle and would then occupy the town. He accordingly wished to keep his men intact, in order to be able to defend his own settlement.

The defection of Abdulla ibn Ubay and his three hundred followers left the Messenger of God with only seven hundred men, to face Quraish with about three thousand.

The Apostle then asked for a guide to conduct him to a position facing the enemy. As the enemy had been sighted the evening before,

---

[7] This is the word used by Waqidi. It does not seem reasonable to call the Jews polytheists.

the continued need for a guide is remarkable. No attempt was made to deliver a surprise attack. On the contrary, emerging into the open opposite the Quraish bivouac, the Muslims halted. The Messenger of God then proceeded to draw up his men in order of battle.

The Muslims were about seven hundred strong but without horses. Only one hundred of them had breastplates and helmets. Quraish, on the other hand, are alleged by the Muslim historians to have had seven hundred men in coats of mail and two hundred horsemen. To deal with the mounted Meccans, Muhammad placed fifty archers on the Muslim flank, with orders to repulse any turning movement by the enemy's horsemen and on no account to leave their allotted position. The Apostle then himself donned two coats of mail and gave his standard to Musaab ibn Umair, the first missionary whom he had sent to Yathrib. Musaab was of the descendants of Abdul Dar, whose hereditary right it was to carry the standard of Quraish,[8] a point showing that the Apostle had not entirely discarded tribal tradition.

The Messenger of God then brandished a sword and cried, "Who will take this sword and use it as it should be used?" Tradition alleges that both Umar ibn al Khattab and Muhammad's cousin, Zubair ibn al Awwam, volunteered but were rejected. The Apostle handed it to one Abu Dujána, telling him to smite the enemy with it until it bent in his hand. Strutting up and down between the two armies, Abu Dujana recited in a loud voice:

> I'm the man who took the sword
> When "use it right" was the Prophet's word
> For the sake of God, of all the Lord,
> Who doth to all their food afford.

It was the custom of the Arabs to take women into battle,[9] their duty being to sing, to recite poetry and to inflame the courage of the combatants. Abu Sofian had brought with him his wife Hind, the daughter of Utba ibn Rabia, who had been killed in single combat at Bedr by Hamza, the Apostle's uncle. The mother of Musaab ibn Umair was also with Quraish, and another son of hers was fighting for the idolaters, though Musaab was carrying Muhammad's standard, a further example of how Islam had divided families.

[8] Page 66.
[9] In Central Arabia, this practice was only discontinued at the beginning of the twentieth century.

Hind was intent on avenging the death of her father by killing Hamza ibn Abdul Muttalib.[10] For this purpose, she had hired an Abyssinian slave called Wahshi, who was promised his freedom if he succeeded. He was famous as a javelin thrower, a skill apparently especially cultivated by the Abyssinians.

In the Quraish ranks, as among the Muslims, the standard was entrusted to the clan of Abdul Dar. The day before the battle, Abu Sofian had addressed the men of Abdul Dar. "O Beni Abdul Dar," he said. "You bore our standard at Bedr and you know what happened. Either defend our standard successfully this time, or else we will take it and save you the trouble." "Are we to surrender the standard to you?" they answered indignantly. "You will see tomorrow how we fight, when the battle is joined."

As the two sides drew near to one another, the women of Quraish formed up behind the fighting line singing:

> Daughters of Tariq fair are we,
> Advance—we'll give our kisses free,
> Our perfumed beds will ready be.
> But we'll desert you if you flee;
> Our love for braver men will be.

The two lines drew up opposite one another. Talha ibn Abdul Uzza, of Abdul Dar, burning with resentment at the taunts of Abu Sofian and bearing the standard of Quraish, stepped out before the line and challenged any Muslim to single combat. Ali ran forward and slew him with a single slash of his sword, the Quraish standard falling to the ground. From the Muslim line rose a great shout, *Allahu akbar*, God is most Great.

But Abdul Dar were on their mettle that morning. Scarcely had Talha fallen than his brother Othman stepped forward, raised the standard and repeated the challenge. This time the formidable Hamza, the Apostle's uncle, strode out between the lines and after a brief exchange of swordplay, Othman too was cut down and the standard fell once more. Three more men of Abdul Dar stepped out one after the other to meet their death and the standard again fell in the dust.

At this stage the Muslim line ran forward and fell upon the enemy with the same fury as had brought them victory at Bedr. Abu

[10] Genealogical tree, p. 120.

Dujana, wielding the Apostle's sword, burst right through the centre of the Quraish line until he scattered the women singing behind it. A negro slave of Abdul Dar snatched the Quraish banner and raised it aloft once more, but the Muslims fell upon him, slashing off both his hands. Still clasping the blood-drenched banner to his chest, he fell forward hacked to pieces with swords cuts crying, "O God, have I now done my duty?"—an incident illustrating the devotion of African slaves to the Arab clan to which they belonged.

Meanwhile Hamza, towering above the combatants, was swinging his sword right and left, cutting down unbelievers. Shortly before the fighting became general, Hind, the daughter of Utba ibn Rabia, had seen Wahshi, the Abyssinian slave, pass by and had called to him, "Come on, O father of blackness, satisfy our longing for revenge."

Wahshi himself tells us what ensued. "By God," he used to say afterwards, "I was watching Hamza while he was killing man after man with his sword, sparing no one . . . I made towards him, hiding behind bushes and rocks in order to get near to him. I poised my javelin until I was sure of my aim and then threw it. It entered the lower part of his body and came out between his legs. He staggered forward and collapsed. I recovered my javelin and returned to the bivouac, as I had no further job to perform. When we returned to Mecca, I was freed from slavery."

In spite of the death of Hamza, however, the day seemed to be won. The Muslims were pressing on, wild with the excitement of victory, and some of the unbelievers began to take to their heels. At this moment, most of the fifty archers, posted by the Apostle on the flank to keep the horsemen at bay, left their position to join the advancing swordsmen and to share in the plunder.

It so happened that the two hundred Quraish horsemen were commanded by Khalid ibn al Waleed and Amr ibn al Aasi,[11] both of whom were subsequently to become great conquerors for Islam. They quickly noticed the departure of the archers, leaving the flank of the Muslim line exposed. The two hundred horsemen swung round the flank and charged the rear of the advancing Muslim line. Here they came upon the Prophet himself and a few men with him, who had been following behind the Muslim advance. Sweeping over them without recognising Muhammad, the horsemen attacked the Muslims from the rear.

[11] Another report says they were commanded by Safwan, the son of Umaiya ibn Khalaf, who had been killed by Bilal after Bedr.

A swordsman by the name of Ibn Qamia, of Beni Kinana, attacked Musaab ibn Umair, who was carrying the Prophet's standard in the front rank and cut him down with a single slash from his sword. Mistaking Musaab for the Messenger of God, Ibn Qamia waved his sword wildly above his head shouting, "Muhammad is dead! I have killed Muhammad!" Alarmed by this cry and attacked from behind by the Quraish horsemen, the Muslims, a minute previously advancing in triumph, now broke and fled in confusion.

The standard of Quraish had lain in the dust since the death of the African slave who had given his life to defend it. Now a brave girl of Abdul Dar, Amra, the daughter of Alqama, pulled it from the grasp of the dead negro and raised it once more aloft, and the men of Quraish rallied round it. The Meccans returned to the attack, while many of the Muslims ran for cover to the rocky slopes of Uhud.

Seized with sudden panic, they hurried past the Apostle and the little group surrounding him, perhaps without even seeing them. As his defeated followers raced by him, Muhammad cried passionately, "Where are you going? Come back, I am the Messenger of God." But no one took any notice.

Dr. Montgomery Watt[12] suggests that this panic on the part of the Muslims may have been due to the increase in their numbers since Bedr. When Islam meant only poverty and persecution, those who were willing to fight for it must have been sincere. But when Islam began to mean loot, many men who were only partly sincere were willing to join.

Hearing the cry that Muhammad was dead, Anees ibn al Nadhr, one of the Muslims, called to the fugitives who were running past, "Why are we still alive? Come, let us die, as the Messenger of God has died." Turning back, he ran, sword in hand, into the advancing Meccans, slashing right and left till he fell covered with wounds.

Meanwhile, the enemy was closing in on the bewildered little group surrounding the Apostle. Arrows and stones from slings rained upon them. A stone struck Muhammad in the face, knocking out one of his teeth. A sword-cut on his head forced his helmet down over his eyes, while blood ran down his face. "Who will sell his life for me?" he called and five Helpers rallied to his side. His cousin Talha warded off another sword-cut from his head with his hand, which was to remain maimed for the rest of his life.

The Prophet had fallen to the ground, covered with blood. But

[12] W. Montgomery Watt, *Muhammad at Medina.*

meanwhile the Meccans had not recognised him and a few Muslims rallied round him. The energetic Ali appeared and the faithful Abu Bekr. Talha raised him from the ground and, supporting him between them, the little group of devoted followers, half-running and half-walking, hurried up the rocky slopes of Mount Uhud and concealed themselves in a hollow. Ali fetched some water to wash the Apostle's face. "How shall a people prosper who have thus treated their Prophet when he called them to their Lord?" said the Messenger of God.

The battle was over. Many of the Muslims had fled from the field and were no longer to be seen. A scattered remnant, including the Apostle's little group, were clinging to the rocky slopes of Mount Uhud. Hind, the wife of Abu Sofian, the vindictive daughter of Utba ibn Rabia, was busy mutilating the dead bodies of the Muslims on the plain below, where the victorious Quraish were wandering about. Finding the body of Hamza, Hind cut out the liver and tried to chew it, but spat it out. Her attempt was a relic of animism many thousands of years old, according to which those who ate the liver of some great hero inherited his courage.

Abu Sofian, standing opposite the place where the Muslims were sheltering called up to them, "Victory in war is like a bucket in a well, going alternately up and down. Today is in exchange for Bedr. Show thy strength, O Hubal."[13] The Apostle told Umar ibn al Khattab to call back, "Our dead are in paradise, yours in hell-fire." At this Abu Sofian shouted to Umar to come down and talk to him. At the Apostle's order, Umar went down and confronted him. "I adjure you by God, Umar," said the Meccan leader, "have we killed Muhammad?" "By God, you have not," replied Umar, stoutly. "He can hear you speaking."

Turning away, Abu Sofian called back once more, "Some of your dead are mutilated. I did not order it. We will meet again next year at Bedr." Quraish, having stripped the dead of their weapons, moved away to their bivouac and began to saddle their camels and horses.

NOTABLE DATES

Birth of Muhammad	570
Commencement of Preaching	613
Migration to Medina	June 622

[13] Hubal was the male idol in the Kaaba.

Battle of Bedr	March 624
Assassination of Asma bint Merwan	March 624
Exile of Beni Qainuqa	April 624
Abu Sofian's Porridge Raid	April 624
Raid of Dhu Amr	June 624
Murder of Kaab ibn al Ashraf	July 624
Bahran Raid	August 624
Capture of Quraish caravan at Qarda	September 624
Battle of Uhud	March 625

PERSONALITIES

Muslims—Emigrants

Abu Bekr
Umar ibn al Khattab
Ali ibn abi Talib
Hamza ibn Abdul Muttalib, Muhammad's uncle
Zaid ibn Haritha, Muhammad's adopted son
Zubair ibn al Awwam, Muhammad's cousin
Talha ibn Ubaidullah
Musaab ibn Umair, killed at Uhud

Muslims—Helpers

Saad ibn Ubada, a chief of the Khazraj
Saad ibn Muadh, a chief of the Aus
Abdulla ibn Ubay of the Khazraj, "the Hypocrite"
Muhammad ibn Maslama, killer of Kaab ibn al Ashraf

XI

Raids and Rules for the Muslim Community

Fierce will be the anger of God against those who caused blood to flow from the face of the Prophet.

BUKHARI, The True Traditions

We will rejoice in thy salvation, and in the name of our God will we set up our banners . . . Some trust in chariots and some in horses, but we will remember the name of the Lord. They are brought down and fallen, but we are risen and stand upright.

Psalm XX, 5 to 8

Do not mourn and grieve. You will have the upper hand if you are believers . . . O you who believe, if you obey unbelievers, you will be put to flight and suffer loss. But God is your ruler and he is the best giver of victory.

Qoran III, 138, 148, 149

The messenger of God sent some men of the Helpers under Abdulla ibn Atiq to kill the Jew Abu Rafi. This Abu Rafi was doing injury to the Messenger of God and was assisting his enemies.

BUKHARI, The True Traditions

ON the morning of the Battle of Uhud, the Muslims had drawn up their line with their backs to Mount Uhud, with the result that Quraish now stood between them and the oasis. If the Meccans had, after their victory, marched on Medina, they could probably have come to terms with Abdulla ibn Ubay and with the Jews, and perhaps have brought the war to a successful conclusion.

Alternatively, they could have climbed Mount Uhud at the cost of a few casualties and possibly killed the Messenger of God and the little group of devoted followers who had remained with him. When Abu Sofian had asked Umar ibn al Khattab if Muhammad were dead, he had replied, "No, by God. He can hear you speaking." But it never occurred to Abu Sofian to take advantage of this dangerous breach of security.

To us, so utterly ruthless and cruel in our wars, such methods of conducting operations seem almost incredible. But we have already seen that the Arab tribes did not wage war in order to exterminate their enemies. Except for an unknown number of Beni Kinana, and a few other tribal elements, the combatants at Uhud were admittedly not nomads. Quraish were merchants and peace was essential to their business. But the bedouins were the professional war-makers, and something of their spirit also clung to the townspeople's ideas of war.

But if the Arabs did not normally wage war in order to achieve final victory, their relentless pursuit of blood revenge made their wars at times ferocious. At Bedr, the Meccans had lost between forty-nine and seventy killed to about fourteen Muslims. At Uhud, the proportions were almost exactly reversed, seventy-four Muslims being killed, "which, if not victory, was yet revenge".[1] To the ordinary Arab of the seventh century, blood revenge was more important than final victory. Thus the rank and file of the Meccans may well have felt satisfied that their dead had been avenged and the object of the campaign achieved. Abu Sofian's remark, "This is in exchange for Bedr", seems to give voice to this attitude.

[1] John Milton, *Paradise Lost.*

Of course, it is possible that they realised that (as we shall see later) they would not be able to take the villages of the oasis, especially as Abdulla ibn Ubay had not taken part in the battle and was ready to defend the town. This factor, if in reality it occurred to Quraish, would be somewhat ironical. Abdulla ibn Ubay, by deserting the Muslims before the battle and preparing to defend the town had actually saved the Muslims, who would have been lost if Quraish had occupied the oasis.

From their eyrie on Mount Uhud, the Muslims could see Quraish packing up their bivouac and mounting their camels. The Messenger of God appreciated the danger to Medina and sent Ali to follow the Meccans at a distance. After a short absence, he returned shouting that they had by-passed Medina and taken the track leading back to Mecca.

The Muslims then came down from their hiding-places, sore and stiff from their wounds, to seek their relatives among the dead. The Apostle found the mutilated body of Hamza and swore in his anger that he would mutilate thirty Quraish in revenge. But later, when his indignation had subsided, he abandoned the idea of retaliation and forbade the Muslims to mutilate the bodies of their enemies in future battles.

Seventy-four Muslims had been killed, of whom between sixty and seventy had been Helpers and only four or five Emigrants. Only some twenty-two polytheists had lost their lives. The Apostle prayed over the Muslim dead before their burial.

Meanwhile a number of Muslim women had arrived and were busily engaged in dressing the wounds of the injured, staunching the flow of blood and giving them water to drink. At this moment, the Apostle's aunt Safiya, the sister of Hamza, of whose death she had heard, also arrived on the field. She was the mother of Zubair ibn al Awwam, one of the little group of the faithful who had saved the Apostle's life.

Muhammad sent her son, Zubair, to turn her back, hoping to spare her the spectacle of the mangled body of her brother. But she answered, "I know that his body has been mutilated, but God has reconciled me to what has happened. I will be quiet and patient, if God wills." Coming up silently, she prayed over her brother's corpse, saying, "We belong to God and to God we return". Then the Muslims completed the burial of their dead on the field of battle, and returned wearily to Medina.

The next day, the Messenger of God sent a crier round the settlements, ordering all who had been present at the battle to ride with him in pursuit of the enemy. They halted some fifty miles from Medina at Hamrat al Asad,[2] and camp fires were lighted over a wide area to give the impression of a large force. Muhammad had wisely ordered this march for reasons of morale, to raise the spirits of his followers and to convey to Quraish the impression that the Muslims were still undaunted.

When, however, Quraish halted at the end of their first day's march, they consulted together and began to regret that they had not exterminated the Muslims when they had the opportunity. Voices were raised demanding that the force return to Medina and complete their victory. Fortunately a bedouin of the tribe of Khuzaa overtook the Meccans at this moment, coming from Medina and having seen Muhammad's little party on the way. Abu Sofian called him over and asked him the news.

Khuzaa were on friendly terms with the Apostle, although most of them were still idolaters. The tribesmen, consequently, informed the Quraish leaders that Muhammad was pursuing them with a large force, the members of which were burning with zeal to avenge the deaths of their comrades at Uhud. As a result, the Meccans decided to continue their homeward journey. Small coincidences sometimes seem to decide great and even world-shaking events. If this bedouin had reported the real state of the Muslims, Abu Sofian might have turned back, overwhelmed Muhammad's party and killed the Prophet himself.

The fact that the victory of Bedr had been attributed to the direct assistance of God and the intervention of the angels, made it all the more difficult to explain the defeat of Uhud. The explanation was given in a long revelation, now incorporated in Chapter III of the Qoran, verses 120 to 199.

A summary of the relevant points seems to be contained in the following extracts from this lengthy revelation.

Verse 139. "If you have suffered injury, the enemy has also suffered in the same way. We cause days like this to occur to all people, in order that God may know who are believers and that He may take martyrs from among you, and that He may purge the believers ... Did you think that you could enter paradise before God knows which of you are really striving in His service and patiently

[2] Map 6, p. 174.

enduring affliction? You were longing for death before you met it, but now indeed you have seen it and looked upon it.

"Muhammad is nothing but a messenger and before him other messengers have died, so if he dies or is killed, will you turn back in your tracks? (Apparently a reference to the fact that many Muslims ran away when they heard the cry that the Apostle had been killed.)

"And certainly God made good to you his promise when you slew them with his permission, until you behaved shamefully and disputed over the affair and disobeyed, after that He had shown you that which you wanted . . . Then He turned you back from them and brought disaster upon you but now He has forgiven you . . .

"You ran off without waiting for anyone, leaving the Apostle behind you, calling after you . . ."

Then follows a reference to those who had recommended that the Muslims remain in their houses and defend the settlements, instead of going out to battle. These, presumably Abdulla ibn Ubay and his supporters, were now saying, "Did we have any say in the plan which led to defeat? If we had had any say, we should not have been killed. Say: If you had been in your houses, those of whom it was written that they should die would have gone to the slaughter . . .

"As for those of you who fled on the day when the two armies met, it was the devil who caused them to slip."

The length of this revelation, of which only a few brief extracts are quoted, seems to underline the precarious nature of the situation after the disaster. In brief, the argument was that God had allowed the Muslims to be defeated in order to test them, and to show which of them were faithful and patient. The devil had decoyed some of them into running away, but God had now forgiven them. Let them learn the lesson but, in other respects, everything could now continue as before.

*   *   *

Meanwhile, the quarrel between the Muslims and Quraish was spreading to the surrounding tribes. The Messenger of God had already won the friendship of Juhaina and Khuzaa.[3] We have seen some of Beni Kinana fighting on the Meccan side at Uhud. Two months after Uhud, in May 625, a number of tribesmen from the country between Mecca and Medina came to the Prophet, asking

[3] Map 7, p. 176.

him to send some of his companions to instruct them in his religion. Muhammad accepted the invitation and sent with them six Muslims who could read and write.

The party proceeded until they reached a watering place called Al Raji, about thirty miles from Mecca. Here they were ambushed by the Beni Lihyan clan of the tribe of Hudhail. Of the six Muslims three died fighting and three were taken prisoners, one of whom, however, was killed trying to escape. The two survivors, Khubaib ibn Adi and Zaid ibn al Dathinna, both Helpers, were sold by Hudhail to Quraish.

Khubaib was bought by the family of Al Harith ibn Aamir ibn Nofal, whom Khubaib had killed at Bedr. He was taken to a site outside the sacred area of Mecca to be killed. He requested permission to make a prayer of two prostrations before his execution, permission for which was granted. He thereby established a tradition according to which Muslims in the future would customarily make a prayer of two prostrations before being put to death.

His devotions completed, he was bound with ropes to a wooden cross, for the Romans had crucified with nails, but the Arabs did so with ropes. When the cross was raised in position, the victim suddenly cried in a loud voice, "O God, reckon all those present today and slay them one by one; let none of them escape!" Abu Sofian was present with his son Muawiya, then still a boy. Nearly forty years later, Muawiya was to become Khalif of the Muslim world and the most powerful ruler on earth. He used to recall how his father, Abu Sofian, suddenly threw him violently to the ground, in order that Khubaib's curse should pass harmlessly over him.

The son of Al Harith whom Khubaib had killed, a child called Utba, was then brought forward to take blood revenge for his father. He was too young to kill his victim unaided, but a spear was placed in his hands while a man stood beside him, his hands placed over the hands of the boy. They then walked up to Khubaib on his cross and jabbed him with the spear until he died.

Zaid, the other prisoner, was simply decapitated, in revenge for Umaiya ibn Khalaf, who had been killed at Bedr by Bilal, the negro.[4] Zaid was perhaps treated more mercifully than Khubaib, because he had not been himself the killer. The Prophet, however, had laid down that all Muslims paid blood money as one family. Zaid was, therefore, killed to expiate Umaiya, although he had not killed him.

[4] Page 187.

The cold-blooded brutality of these killings illustrates once more the extraordinary contrast between the easy-going and often chivalrous warfare of the Arabs and the brutalities of their blood-feuds. Abu Sofian talks familiarly with Umar ibn al Khattab on the battlefield of Uhud, for neither had killed a relative of the other. But Abu Sofian's wife, Hind, the daughter of Utba ibn Rabia, mutilates the dead body of Hamza, who had killed her father. In the same way, a child was made to stab Khubaib until he died, to avenge the death of his father.

In revenge for the treachery of the tribe of Hudhail, who ambushed the Muslim party at Al Raji, the Apostle sent an assassin to murder Sofian ibn Khalid, the Hudhaili chief. Sofian was surprised and killed while riding with his wives to a new camping ground, in May or June 625.

The Prophet also sent two men to assassinate Abu Sofian in Mecca, one being a Meccan and the other a Helper. The Meccan was recognised in the streets of the town, a hue and cry was started and he had some difficulty in making good his escape, killing one of his pursuers. On his way back to Medina, he killed two more men, one of them in his sleep, merely because they were idolaters. He took a third man prisoner and brought him to the Messenger of God, who praised the Meccan for his devotion.

The question of the assassinations carried out at the orders of the Apostle has aroused widespread controversy. Western writers have either denounced these murders as political terrorism, or defended them as being the custom of the seventh century in Arabia. Neither of these viewpoints seems to be entirely adequate.

It does not appear that political assassinations of this kind were the custom of Arabia. It is true that many men died a violent death but this was almost always due to one of two causes—either a sudden, violent burst of passion, or a chance encounter in battle.

In either case, a blood-feud was liable to result, reducing the life of the killer and of his relatives to an endless nightmare of anxiety. The horrors of the blood-feud were, of course, designed to make assassinations unattractive. In all the voluminous accounts of the Prophet's life, there does not seem to be any mention of anyone else sending assassins to murder anyone. Two men are alleged to have said that they would kill Muhammad but to have lost their nerve. We have seen how the tribal fear of blood-feuds prevented the use of violence, while the Apostle was still living in Mecca.

It is surely remarkable also that, when Muhammad was in Medina and was destroying the commercial prosperity of Mecca, Quraish are not reported as sending assassins to kill him, though he sent them to murder Abu Sofian. His enemies were doubtless not deterred by moral scruples, but by fear of a tribal blood-feud. For, although Muhammad was an enemy, there were many relatives of his in Mecca who might have thought it a duty to avenge his death. It may also be noted in passing that Ibn Qamia, who claimed to have killed the Apostle at Uhud, was not of Quraish but of Beni Kinana. Tribal feeling was far less strong concerning the killing of a man of another tribe than it was in the case of a fellow-clansman. The Apostle, therefore, showed some courage in risking a blood-feud by employing assassination, particularly against Quraish.

The second point of interest is that the majority of the victims were poets and satirists. The Hudhail chief, Sofian ibn Khalid, is the only tribesman killed in retaliation for the murder of Muslims. No attempt was made to assassinate Abdulla ibn Ubay, who was a professed Muslim.

All the persons murdered were active opponents of the Islamic movement, not personal rivals of the Apostle. This point is of particular interest in the case of the Jews, for the Messenger of God also laid down that Jews and Christians, unlike idolaters, were not to be coerced into becoming Muslims. In fact, after the exile or the execution of the members of the three Jewish tribes, a number of Jews still remained in Medina and continued to do business. Thus it may be argued that the exile or persecution of the Jewish tribes was not due to hatred of their religion, but to the fact that they persisted in casting doubts on the mission of the Apostle by trying to catch him out in his Old Testament quotations.

It may be admitted, however, that the assassinations have ever since exercised an unhappy influence on Islamic society. Political murders have always been tragically numerous in Muslim countries.

*   *   *

The incident at Al Raji was followed soon afterwards by an even more disastrous reverse. In May or June 625, a tribal chief from Nejed, called Abu Bará, visited the Apostle. He was an old man, head of a clan called Beni Aamir ibn Saasaa, a branch of the Hawazin. Abu Bara professed his willingness to become a Muslim, if his tribe could also be converted. He accordingly asked the Messenger of God to send some Muslims to Nejed to instruct the tribe.

Muhammad was doubtful of the advisability of doing so, in view of the fate of the six men who had been sent to Al Raji. But Abu Bara promised to take them under his protection and to guarantee their safety. As a result, forty camelmen were sent, according to Ibn Ishaq, though Tabari gives the number as seventy, and Waqidi mentions both versions.

The party halted at a well called Bir Maoona,[5] some fifty miles south-east of Medina, where they were attacked by Beni Sulaim, apparently instigated by one Aamir ibn al Tufail, the nephew of Abu Bara. The Muslims fought on until all were killed. Two of the men, however, had taken the camels out grazing while their comrades rested at the well, and had thus not been present at the fight. When they returned, they saw the ground strewn with their dead and large numbers of Beni Sulaim close by. One of the two expressed the view that, as they had not been seen, they should slip away and take the news to the Messenger of God. But the other, saying that he could not bring himself to survive his comrades, charged the enemy alone and was hacked to pieces.

One of those killed at Bir Maoona was Aamir ibn Fuhaira, the freedman of Abu Bekr, who had accompanied the Apostle on his flight from Mecca.

One Muslim escaped from the massacre of Bir Maoona and, on his way back to Medina, met two men of the tribe of Abu Bara and Aamir ibn al Tufail. The two men, coming from Medina, were unaware of the incident at Bir Maoona and were thus not particularly on their guard. The Muslim succeeded in killing them both while they were resting, in revenge for the Muslims killed.

The Apostle of God, however, disapproved of his action. Abu Bara and his tribe, Beni Aamir, were friendly to the Muslims and had asked for missionaries. It is true that Abu Bara's nephew, Aamir ibn al Tufail, had disapproved of his uncle's action, but he had been unable to secure the support of the tribe. He had accordingly instigated Beni Sulaim to kill the Muslims. The blood-feud does not take account of such vague offences as instigation or suggestion. Beni Sulaim had killed the Muslims and thus the blood-feud was against them.

Perhaps also, and apparently wisely, the Apostle did not wish to

[5] Map 6, p. 174.

alienate Beni Aamir, who seemed to be about to adopt Islam. He accordingly agreed to pay blood money for their two men killed.

*　　*　　*

The Muslims had suffered three successive reverses in four months —Uhud, Al Raji and Bir Maoona. There is no sign, at least in the official histories, that the Apostle was discouraged by these setbacks nor that there was any considerable number of desertions from the Muslim ranks. Nevertheless, it is possible that Muhammad realised that a victory was now very desirable, if not in order to encourage the Muslims, at least to impress the idolaters with the fact that the Muslims were still to be feared. There seems to be no doubt that Quraish propaganda, following the Battle of Uhud, had created among the tribes the impression that the Muslim movement was petering out and would soon come to an end.

Having agreed to pay blood-money for the two men of Beni Aamir, the Apostle began to raise the necessary cash. Down to this very day, a man who finds himself in the unfortunate situation of having to pay blood-money asks his friends to contribute towards the large sum which he has to collect. With this pretext, the Messenger of God, accompanied by a small deputation, which included Abu Bekr, Umar and Ali, called at the settlement of the Jewish tribe of Beni al Nadheer to invite their financial assistance. He was cordially received by Beni al Nadheer, who immediately agreed to contribute.

According to Ibn Ishaq, the Jews hastily consulted together, saying that they would never again get such an opportunity to murder Muhammad, who was sitting on the ground in the open air, with his back against the wall of the house. A certain Amr ibn Jahash is alleged to have volunteered to go up on the roof and drop a rock on his head from above. One version seems to suggest that the Muslims overheard the plotters. Ibn Ishaq states that a message reached the Apostle from heaven, apprising him of his danger. He accordingly rose and walked away into the gardens, telling his companions to wait where they were until he returned. No sooner, however, was he out of sight than he hastened back to Medina. Collecting his followers, he told them that Beni al Nadheer had tried to murder him and that he had decided to make war on them.

The Jews shut themselves up in their fortified village, which was besieged by the Muslims. Abdulla ibn Ubay and his supporters are alleged to have sent messages to Beni al Nadheer urging them to resist and promising their support. Beni al Nadheer were cultivators and their settlement was surrounded by many exceptionally fine gardens of date palms, which the Messenger of God ordered to be cut down. Beni al Nadheer called from the flat roofs of their houses, "O Muhammad, you yourself have forbidden wanton destruction. Why then are you cutting down our date palms?"

It does indeed appear surprising that the Apostle should give such an order, for he must already have foreseen that these gardens would add greatly to the wealth of the Muslims. Perhaps he feared that Abdulla ibn Ubay might really come to the assistance of the Jews, and was accordingly anxious to bring the operation to a speedy conclusion. Any criticism on the subject of cutting down the date palms was rejected by Chapter LIX, verse 5, of the Qoran, revealed at the time and which says, "Whatever palm tree you cut down or leave standing up, it is by permission of God, that He might shame the evildoers."

At last, in September 625, after a seige of two or three weeks, Beni al Nadheer agreed to surrender on condition that they be allowed to emigrate to Syria, taking with them all such possessions as they could load on their camels Their armour, however, was excluded and they were obliged to surrender it all to the Muslims.

Chapter LIX of the Qoran says that it was God "who drove out the unbelievers, the People of the Book, from their houses on the first banishment. You[6] did not think that they would go out. They thought that their forts would defend them against God. But God came at them from a direction which they did not expect."

Some of Beni al Nadheer are alleged to have even pulled out the lintels over the doors of their houses and carried them away to Syria. Two of their chief men, Sallam ibn abi al Huqaiq and Huyai ibn Akhtab, settled in Kheibar, where we shall meet them again.

Presumably as some kind of act of defiance, they left the oasis gaily dressed, to the music of pipes and tambourines and the singing of beautiful girls. Two of the Jews professed conversion to Islam and stayed behind, retaining possession of all their property.

The whole affair of Beni al Nadheer passed without any fighting or bloodshed. This enabled the Messenger of God to take over all their property and to divide it as he wished. In war, only one-fifth of the booty was allotted to the treasury, the remaining four-fifths being

[6] God is speaking to the Apostle.

distributed amongst the men who fought. But when there was no fighting, all the proceeds went to the Apostle, to distribute as he thought best.

Only two Helpers received a share. The remainder was divided among the Emigrants from Mecca who, although they had arrived destitute in Medina, were now rapidly growing rich.

* * *

It will be remembered that, after Uhud, Abu Sofian had called to the remnants of the Muslims that he would meet them again the following year at Bedr for a return battle. The Messenger of God decided to accept the challenge and, in April 626, a Muslim force moved down to Bedr. Abu Sofian remembered the rendezvous and is said likewise to have collected a war-party and left Mecca.

But halfway to Bedr, he decided to turn back, for reasons which are not clear to us. He is alleged to have made the excuse that the grazing was poor owing to lack of rain, and that the horses and camels were consequently in too weak a condition for a campaign. It is true that to this day in Arabia, riding animals are rarely fed but rely almost entirely on natural grazing. As a result, it does actually occur that, in years of bad rainfall, horses and camels are incapable of undertaking a journey. Whether or not the lack of grazing was the real reason for Quraish failing to carry out their own challenge cannot now be known.

Undoubtedly, however, the fact that the Muslims went to Bedr and that Quraish failed to appear produced a considerable moral effect. After Uhud, acts of hostility against the Muslims by the local tribes had emphasised the general belief that Quraish were winning the war. Now the Muslims camped defiantly for eight days at Bedr with fifteen hundred men, but Quraish failed to answer the challenge. It was noticed that, in spite of Uhud and other reverses, the Apostle had gone to Bedr in 626 with twice as many men as he had the year before at Uhud. Obviously Islam was still growing.

Meanwhile, Sallam ibn abi al Huqaiq, nicknamed Abu Rafi, one of the chiefs of Beni al Nadheer, had not migrated to Syria but had settled with the Jewish community at Kheibar.[7] In May 626, the Apostle sent a small party of Muslims, who succeeded in assassinating him in his bed.[8]

[7] Map 5, p. 157.
[8] Waqidi places the assassination of Sallam in May 626. Ibn Ishaq dates it in 627, after the extermination of Beni Quraidha. See Chapter XII.

In May or June 626, the Apostle of God set out with a party to raid Ghatafan. The Muslims reached a place called Dhat al Riqa,[9] which seems to have been some sixty miles north-east of Mecca. Here a strong party of Ghatafan was encountered but no fighting took place. Both sides were afraid of the other and they withdrew in different directions. It appears to have been on this occasion that the Prophet introduced the Prayer of Fear, which was to become a regular part of Muslim ritual. One half of the force prayed at a time, while the other stood with their weapons in their hands facing the enemy.

Attention may here be drawn to the frequent occasions on which Muslim raiders during these years encountered a bedouin enemy, but then passed on without fighting, particularly if the Messenger of God were himself present. This occurred so often that it seems to afford us a further insight into his character as a man who disliked battles. Where there was a chance of contacting the enemy, he preferred to talk but, if this were impossible, he merely withdrew. Possibly also, in so far as the believers were concerned, there may have been an unwillingness to fight where the Apostle was present, owing to a reluctance to expose him to danger. It was obvious that his death might result in the collapse of the whole movement.

It is, however, important to notice that this easy-going way of avoiding a confrontation which might result in heavy casualties was the normal bedouin way of fighting one another. The poverty of our vocabulary, which causes us to apply the word "war" to bedouin raiding and to the mass butcheries of modern civilisation, gives rise to many misunderstandings. Western writers have at times denounced Arab nomads as cowards, because, when raiding parties met, they did not shoot one another to pieces till all were dead. The answer is that such was not the object of the operation. The tribes normally bore no hate to one another and their raids were little more than a manly sport.

But if the Muslims avoided casualties when raiding bedouins, this was not so when they were confronted by Quraish. Bedr and Uhud, though insignificant in the numbers of the combatants, were pitched battles in comparison with the bedouin type of raiding. The reason was, of course, that neither Quraish nor the Muslims were fighting for sport, but for power, one of the strongest human incentives to ruthlessness. The Muslims were also fighting for religion, another profoundly emotional incentive.

[9] Map 6, p. 174.

These two simultaneous, but entirely distinct, types of warfare were obvious on the occasion of the Wahhabi outburst in the 1920's. The Wahhabis were religious revivalists, who endeavoured to reproduce the fervour of the first Muslims. Their wars, which resulted in a great deal of bloodshed in Arabia, took place simultaneously with inter-tribal raiding between the bedouins unconverted to Wahhabism, who still maintained the old, "sporting" method of fighting. The two methods of "war", practised close to one another at the same time, reproduced in the twentieth century almost exactly the situation which had existed during the life of the Apostle.

*   *   *

Ibn Ishaq has preserved for us, in connection with the raid of Dhat al Riqa, a piece of seventh-century dialogue, which seems to bear the natural freshness of truth. A certain Jabir ibn Abdulla tells the story.

"I went out with the Apostle on the raid of Dhat al Riqa of Nakhl on a feeble old camel of mine. On the way back, the company kept going on ahead while I dropped farther behind until the Apostle rode up to me and asked me what the trouble was. I told him that my camel was keeping me back and he told me to make it kneel. I did so and the Apostle made his camel to kneel and said, 'Give me this stick you are holding' . . . He took it and prodded the beast a few times. Then he told me to remount and off we went. By Him who sent him with the truth, my old camel kept up with the rapid pace of his camel.

"As we were talking, the Apostle asked me if I would sell him my camel. I said that I would give it to him but he insisted on buying it, so I asked him to make me an offer. He said he would give me a dirhem.[10] I refused and said that would be cheating me. Then he offered two dirhems and I still refused and the Apostle went on raising his offer until it amounted to an ounce of gold. When I asked him if he was really satisfied, he said that he was and I said that the camel was his.

"Then he asked me if I were married; then was she a virgin or a woman previously married? I told him she had been married before and he said, 'No young girl so that you could sport together!' I told him that my father had been killed at Uhud, leaving seven daughters, and I had married a motherly woman who could look after them

[10] The Apostle was obviously in playful mood. A dirhem was a few shillings.

efficiently. He said, 'You have done well, if God will. Had we come to Sirar, we would order camels to be slaughtered and stay there for the day and she would hear about us and shake the dust off her cushions.' I said, 'But, by God, we have no cushions!' He said, 'But you will have. When you return, behave wisely.'

"When we got to Sirar,[11] the Apostle ordered camels to be slaughtered and we stayed there for the day. At night the Apostle went home and so did we. I told my wife the news and what the Apostle had said to me. She said, 'Look alive and do what he tells you.' In the morning, I led the camel away and made it kneel at the Apostle's door. Then I sat in the mosque near by. He came out and saw it and asked what it was and I was summoned to him. He said, 'O son of my brother, take away your camel for it is yours,' and he called Bilal[12] and told him to give me an ounce of gold. He did so and added a little more. By God, it continued to thrive with me."

This little narrative illustrates the kind familiarity which bound the Muslims to the Prophet, and the generous patronage which he bestowed on the poorer members of his community.

The fact that the Messenger of God ordered a lunchtime halt just outside Medina to allow the wives of the raiders to "shake the dust off their cushions" emphasises his consideration for family life. Both Bukhari and Muslim report Muhammad as saying that men who have been away a long time should not arrive home during the night. Opportunity should be given for news of their impending return to precede them, "to allow the woman whose husband has been away to clean herself" and to comb her hair.

The Apostle himself, incidentally, was always scrupulously clean in his clothing and person. In some ways, he was even fastidious. He was disgusted to see how food adhered to long moustaches. He kept his cut very short, as pious Muslims do to this day. He was fond of perfume but hated strong smells and would never touch food flavoured with onions or garlic.

In another tradition, Muslim states that when the Apostle returned from a journey, he was met by the children of his household. Abdulla, the son of Jaafar ibn abi Talib, is reported as saying: "When the Messenger of God arrived after a journey, he was met by the children of his household. Once when he arrived after a journey, I was the first to meet him and he lifted me in front of him (on his camel).

---

[11] About three miles from Medina.

[12] Bilal will be remembered as the freed African slave, who used to give the call to prayer.

Then one of Fatima's two sons was brought along and he sat him behind him, and we entered Medina, three on one camel."[13]

Another tradition reported by both Bukhari and Muslim emphasises the Prophet's attachment to family life. "Travel," he is alleged to have said, "is a piece of punishment which deprives a man of his sleep, food and drink, so when he accomplishes his purpose wherever he has gone, he should hasten back to his family."

*　　*　　*

In August or September 626, the Messenger of God led a force of about a thousand men northwards, ostensibly to raid the oasis of Dumat al Jandal,[14] the modern Jauf. Once again, he returned to Medina without fighting. The reason for this expedition, as for that before it to Dhat al Riqa, may perhaps be attributed to the fact that Quraish were trying to organise a large expedition to attack Medina and, for this purpose, were seeking an alliance with Ghatafan. The Jew Sallam, who had been murdered in Kheibar, had also been accused of having visited Ghatafan, in order to persuade them to join this anti-Muslim alliance.

Thus both the assassination of Sallam, the expedition to Dhat al Riqa and that allegedly directed against Duma—we do not know how far it went—were probably all demonstrations of force, intended to deter the nomadic tribes from joining the league which Quraish were seeking to organise.

*　　*　　*

Western scholars have often drawn attention to the remarkable change in the contents of the Apostle's revelations in Medina, as compared with the early chapters of the Qoran which had been revealed in Mecca.

There was something noble and inspiring in some of the short but powerful early chapters revealed in Mecca, when the Apostle was suffering ridicule and persecution.

> Say: God is One.
> God the Eternal.
> He begets not neither is He begotten:
> None is equal to Him.[15]

[13] Mishkat al Masabih.　　[14] Map 10, p. 279.　　[15] Qoran, Chapter CXII.

Say: I take refuge in the Lord of men,
The King of men,
The God of men,
From the evil whisperings of the devil,
Who whispers in the hearts of men,
From jinns and men.[16]

Say: I take refuge in the Lord of the Universe,
From the evil of that which He created,
And from the evil of darkness when it falls;
From the evil of those who undermine faith,
And from the evil of the envious when he envies.[17]

The catastrophe!
What is the catastrophe?
What will make you understand the catastrophe?
The day on which men shall be scattered like moths.
And the mountains like dead leaves or wool.[18]

After the Migration to Medina, however, the Apostle of God became involved in politics, then in war and finally in administration. Take for example the following excerpts from Chapter IV, revealed in Medina.

"Give to orphans their property, and do not substitute worthless articles for their valuables.

"If you fear that you cannot fulfil your obligations to orphans, marry such women as seem good to you, two or three or four; but if you are afraid that you cannot act justly between your wives, then marry only one, or such slave women as you own . . .

"Men shall have a portion of what their parents and relatives leave (when they die) and women shall also have a fixed portion. The male shall have the equal of the portion of two females. But if there are more than two daughters, they shall have two-thirds of the property left by the deceased . . ." and so on for many pages.

The contrast between Muhammad in Mecca and Muhammad in Medina touches upon one of the great problems of religion. On the one hand, we see the preaching of a saint or a prophet, intensely living, inspiring, passionate and vivid. On the other, the rigid codes

---

[16] Qoran, Chapter CXIV.   [17] Qoran, Chapter CXIII.
[18] Qoran, Chapter CI, verses 1 to 5.

of morals, and the rules and ritual of an established "church". It is easy to condemn formal, organised religion, and to praise the inspiring message of the saint. The law kills, says St. Paul, but the Spirit gives life.

The fallacy lies in the weakness of men. While the prophet is with them, his followers may be inspired with his spirit, but after his death the whole movement tends to evaporate unless it has been embodied in laws and ritual. Even in such a case, the laws and the ritual eventually kill the spirit. Yet the tradition is retained by such an organisation, allowing revivals of the true Spirit to occur from time to time. If Muhammad had not laid down innumerable laws and regulations, his message might not have outlasted the death of his companions.

The establishment of Islam was indeed facilitated by the fact that it was not opposed by a hierarchy of priests, backed by an established code of laws, dogma and ritual. Arab idolatry had no priesthood to defend it. The attachment of the Arabs to Al Lat, Al Uzza and Hubal was perhaps little more than that of English people to Tudor cottages or parish churches. They are connected in our minds with the "good old days".

The opposition of the leaders of Quraish may have been largely political. A man who claimed to receive direct instructions from God on the subject of day to day events must inevitably himself become the ruler of the state. If this was in reality their motive, everything which happened after the arrival of the Apostle in Medina must have confirmed their fears. It is not to be assumed that the Apostle decided consciously to abandon contemplation for the regulation of mundane affairs. Yet the revelations which he received, in Mecca so passionate and overwhelming, seemed in Medina to become increasingly, though perhaps unconsciously, the result of reason and thought.

As, however, the Muslim community increased in numbers, everything was lacking. Money, land, houses, animals, weapons, food— all the necessities of life had to be provided for the little group which he had created and which looked to him for everything. Day after day, the Prophet found it increasingly difficult to defend his own privacy, much more to find leisure for solitary contemplation. If he had refused the busy round of daily duties, the whole movement might have collapsed.

These developments were radically to affect the whole future of

Islam. When the Messenger of God died, his successor's only ambition was to follow exactly in his footsteps. Muhammad had been, at one and the same time, prophet, statesman, legislator and military commander. This fact set an enduring pattern for all Muslim states, which have, for thirteen centuries, been nearly always ruled by one man, combining, in theory at least, all the above functions.

Such a ruler need not be a hereditary prince but should be the best candidate available. He should give himself no airs or graces, be only the first citizen not the haughty monarch and he should be freely accessible to all his subjects.

NOTABLE DATES

Birth of Muhammad	570
Migration to Medina	622
Battle of Bedr	March 624
Battle of Uhud	March 625
Incident at Al Raji	May 625
Massacre of Muslims at Bir Maoona	June 625
Siege and Exile of Beni al Nadheer	August to September 625
Unopposed occupation of Bedr	March 626
Dhat al Riqa raid	June 626
"Dumat al Jandal" raid (which never reached there)	August 626

PERSONALITIES

Khubaib ibn Adi
Zaid ibn al Dathinna   } Martyrs killed by Quraish

Bilal, the Apostle's *muedhdhin*

Sofian ibn Khalid, chief of Beni Lahyan of Hudhail, assassinated

Sallam ibn abi al Huqaiq
Huyai ibn Akhtab   } Chiefs of Beni al Nadheer

XII

The Ditch

O woman! lovely woman! nature made thee
To temper man; we had been brutes without you.
THOMAS OTWAY

I must have women. There is nothing unbends the mind like
them.
JOHN GAY

O you who believe, it is not permitted to you to inherit women
against their will. And do not coerce them and take back what
you have given them . . . And deal kindly with them.
Qoran IV, v. 19

Not long ago, many people, especially members of the Church,
felt qualified to judge others and to tell them . . . how to act.
Today we feel deeply the arrogance of this attitude.
PAUL TILLICH, *The Eternal Now*

You have accounted yourselves happy on being environed with
a great ditch from all the world beside.
OLIVER CROMWELL, *Speeches to Parliament*

There is one certain means by which I can be sure never to see
my country's ruin—I will die in the last ditch.
WILLIAM OF ORANGE

XII

BEFORE proceeding with our chronological narrative, it is necessary to refer to certain developments in the Apostle's family life which have since given rise to considerable discussion. The first, in passing, is his marriage to Hafsa, the daughter of Umar ibn al Khattab. Her husband had been killed at Bedr and her father offered her to the Prophet, who married her. She was a woman of violent temper like her father and was to cause the Apostle of God a good deal of trouble. Abu Bekr and Umar were the two principal lieutenants of Muhammad. He had already married Aisha, the daughter of Abu Bekr, and his marriage to the daughter of Umar may perhaps be ascribed to his desire to bind his two principal assistants more closely to himself. Hafsa, however, though a widow, was still quite young, being only seventeen at the time of her marriage to the Apostle.

After his wedding to Hafsa, Muhammad's fourth bride was Zainab bint Khuzaima, whose husband had been killed at Uhud. She had a reputation for her charities to the poor. Not long afterwards, perhaps in January 626, the Prophet was married to Umm Salama. She had been with her husband one of the early emigrants to Abyssinia. Her husband had died of wounds received at Uhud.

A marriage which has given rise to more controversy was that of the Messenger of God to his cousin, Zainab bint Jahash. It will be recollected that the Apostle, before his call, had adopted a slave boy, Zaid ibn Haritha, as his son.[1] Zaid had, since his adoption, formed part of the family together with Ali, and had been known as Zaid ibn Muhammad. Having been a slave, Zaid had first been married to a freedwoman but subsequently married Zainab, the Prophet's own cousin. Zaid enjoyed a high measure of the confidence of the Apostle and, as we have seen, had been appointed commander of the force which had captured the caravan of Quraish at Qarda in Nejed.[2]

It seems to have been at this period, possibly in 626, after Uhud, that the Messenger of God desired to marry Zainab, the wife of his adopted son, Zaid. The latter, who presumably was not greatly attached to her, divorced her, and she was married to Muhammad.

[1] Page 83.   [2] Page 201.

The two bases of criticism used by his adversaries were, firstly the fact that, before Islam, adopted sons were considered to be the sons of their adopted fathers, on the same terms as their natural sons. The Apostle had adopted Zaid in the Kaaba of Mecca in the Days of Ignorance before his call.

Secondly, before Islam, when a man died, his wives became the property of his son. The Apostle himself had prohibited this practice, saying that it was disgraceful for a man to marry his late father's wives.[3] The critics of the marriage of Muhammad to Zainab claimed that the Prophet had virtually broken his own law by marrying his son's wife, though in fact the prohibition seems to have been directed against the marriage of a son to his father's wife. The incident, however, was terminated by a revelation which laid down that adopted sons were not to be regarded as on the same basis as natural sons. As a result, adoption has never since been legally recognised by Islam.

The revelation which authorised the marriage of Zainab to the Apostle blames the latter for his hesitation in marrying her, out of fear of men, whereas he should only have considered God's will, whether or not it entailed the criticism of human beings. Chapter XXXIII, verse 37, of the Qoran refers to this affair, Zaid being actually mentioned by name.

"And when you said to him to whom God had shown favour and to whom you had done kindness,[4] 'Keep your wife to yourself and seek protection from God,'[5] you hid in your heart what God desired to expose and you were afraid of what people would say. But it is God, not other men, who has a right to be feared. But when Zaid had finished with her, We[6] married her to you, in order that the believers should not in the future be in a dilemma regarding the wives of their adopted sons, if the latter finished with them, and may the command of God by fufilled."

There appears to be a tradition that Zainab, who is said to have been remarkable for her piety, hesitated to marry Muhammad until this revelation came down.

[3] The man's own mother was, of course, excluded from this practice.

[4] Muhammad had manumitted Zaid from slavery.

[5] The implication seems to be that Zaid had told the Apostle that he was not happy with Zainab, but that Muhammad had told him not to divorce her for fear of scandal. Maulana Muhammad Ali, in his commentary on the Qoran, alleges that Zainab resented her marriage to Zaid, because he had once been a slave.

[6] The speaker is God, as throughout the Qoran.

Chapter IV of the Qoran had limited the number of the wives of a believer to four. The Apostle, however, had now exceeded this number, but Chapter XXXIII of the Qoran specifically authorised him to do so. Verse 50 reads as follows:

"O Prophet! We have made lawful to you your wives to whom you have given their dowries and those whom your right hand possesses[7] ... and a believing woman, if she gave herself to the Prophet and the Prophet desired to marry her—this is a privilege for you alone, not for the other believers."

When the revelation came down, ordering Muhammad to marry Zainab, Aisha, who alone ventured to speak to him in a frivolous tone, is alleged to have remarked, "Your Lord certainly seems anxious to gratify your desires."

The question of the marriages of the Messenger of God has aroused intense discussion and heated resentments into which we need not enter. It is, however, worthy of note that of all his wives, only Aisha was a virgin when he married her. Zainab bint Jahash was a divorced wife and all the rest were widows, some of them, it would seem, not particularly attractive. Moreover, the Apostle had married Khadija when he was twenty-five and she was a widow considerably older than he was. He had remained completely faithful to her for twenty-four years until her death.

As we have seen, the Apostle's numerous marriages are sanctioned by the Qoran, Chapter XXXIII, verse 50, which is normally interpreted as authorising him to marry more than the statutory four wives, the privilege being limited to himself, and not for other believers.

This may perhaps be a suitable place in which to give the list of the wives, although, at the stage of his life which we have now reached, he had not yet married them all.

1. Khadija bint Khuwailid married Muhammad in 595, when she is alleged to have been about forty years old. She remained his only wife until she died in 619.
2. Sauda bint Zamaa of Quraish. She was a widow, perhaps some thirty years old, when she married the Apostle in 619.
3. Aisha bint abi Bekr. She married Muhammad in 623 and was his only virgin wife.
4. Hafsa bint Umar ibn al Khattab. She was a young widow when she married Muhammad in 625.

[7] That is, slaves.

5. Zainab bint Khuzaima, of Beni Aamir (Ghatafan). She was already twice a widow and married the Apostle in 625, but died a few months later.

6. Umm Salama (her name was Hind). She was of Beni Makhzoom, Quraish, the widow of a Muslim. She was perhaps aged twenty-nine or thirty.

7. Zainab bint Jahash, a cousin of Muhammad. She married the Apostle after being divorced by his adopted son, Zaid ibn Haritha.

8. Raihana bint Amr, a Jewess of Beni Quraidha, captured when the tribe surrendered in 627.

9. Juwairiya, daughter of the chief of Beni Mustaliq of Khuzaa. Captured in the raid on Beni Mustaliq in January 628.[8]

10. Umm Habeeba bint abi Sofian. She had been with her husband in Abyssinia. When he died, she came back to Arabia and married the Apostle on his return from Kheibar in 628.

11. Safiya bint Huyai ibn al Akhtab. Wife of Kinana ibn abi al Huqaiq, Jewish leader of Kheibar, killed by the Muslims. She was converted from Judaism to Islam.

12. Maimoona bint al Harith, the sister-in-law of Abbas. She married the Apostle in 629, on the occasion of his pilgrimage to Mecca.[9]

13. Mary, the Egyptian slave girl, who was sent to the Apostle as gift by the "ruler" of Egypt.[10]

It is not desired here to enter into a moral discussion on this subject. A few points may, however, be noted in passing. The first of these is that the Apostle greatly enjoyed female company. This need not mean the same thing as sensuality. He himself admitted this feeling. The saying attributed to him is probably genuine, "I like women and perfume better than anything else, but the apple of my eye is prayer." The connection of his love of women with prayer seems to prove that it never occurred to him that his fondness for female company could be anything but innocent.

But he was no advocate of promiscuous love. He used to praise God that, when a young man before his mission, he had never had immoral relations with a woman. After his mission, it was said that he would not even touch the hand of a woman who was not his wife. The great majority of his marriages took place after he was fifty-five.

[8] Page 263 below.   [9] Page 286 below.   [10] Page 302 below.

It is noticeable that nearly all his wives were widows, may of them middle-aged. It would seem as if he enjoyed the company of mature, sensible women rather than that of young girls. It has been suggested that his many marriages were due to his desire to have a son, but, had this been the case, younger women would have afforded him a better hope of an heir.

Others have supposed that he married many women for political reasons, to form bridges by which he could conciliate his opponents, or bind his friends more closely to himself. The daughter of Abu Sofian might come under the first head, while those of Abu Bekr and Umar might cement their loyalty to the Apostle, but most of the others are not susceptible of such an explanation. Others have thought it possible that he married so many widows of deceased Muslims in order to provide for them and their orphaned children. The seventy Muslims killed at Uhud left many women and children behind them.

It is noticeable that the Apostle, when a young man, had six children by Khadija, yet he had no children by the twelve women who followed her, except for a son by Mary, the Egyptian concubine. Most of his wives, though not in their first youth, were capable of bearing children. In Medina, Muhammad had less and less leisure time and must often have been mentally and physically exhausted, especially as he was in his fifties and latterly over sixty. These are not the circumstances under which men are interested in the indulgence of extreme sexuality.

The assumption that he was a sensualist because he had eleven wives when he died at the age of sixty-two is therefore not absolutely a foregone conclusion, as many have assumed. This is particularly so in view of the fact that he had only one wife until he was fifty.

The minds of men and women are different and complementary, as well as their bodies. Is it possible that, when he grew old and came home exhausted in the evening, he found relaxation in female society, quite apart from physical attraction? It must be remembered that, in the Western countries today, men are constantly engaged in talking to women throughout most of the day without any physical contact. Under the system in vogue in Medina, however, this was not the case. A man could not mix freely with the wives and daughters of other men. Under such circumstances, he might enjoy the society of several women, without being physically a sensualist.

Perhaps we may summarise the discussion by saying that the

Messenger of God enjoyed the company of women. He considered it an innocent pleasure for which he praised God. He was always kind and considerate towards his wives, who gave him this enjoyment.

*   *   *

It is not possible to discover a uniform procedure in Arabia before Islam, on the subject of whether or not women were allowed to reject suitors. Nor, for that matter, is custom identical in this respect in the different Muslim countries, even today. In general, the customs of Arabia are perhaps slightly more generous than in some Muslim countries. Variations in different specific cases often seem to depend on the personalities concerned. A dominating father forced his daughter to marry the man he chose, a more lenient father allowed her to accept or reject a suitor.

In general, it may be said that young girls were often married at eight or ten years old, when, probably, the husband was chosen for them. Widows and divorced women, however, frequently remarried as they felt inclined. The Prophet seems to have considered that a girl had the right to refuse a suitor. When a man wished to marry one of his daughters, he consulted the girl. If she said no, the suitor was rejected. The woman did not so much have the right of selection as that of rejection, if she did not like the man concerned. A system of this kind is still followed in most tribes.

We have, however, already seen that Khadija herself made a proposal of marriage to Muhammad. It is true that she was obliged subsequently to obtain the consent of her uncle, but it cannot be denied that it was she who took the initiative.

It is all too easy to say, as many Western writers do, "the seventh century Arabs were a crude and brutal race, who treated their women as chattels". Such a conclusion, moreover, gives the writer a pleasant sense of superiority. Examples can be quoted to support this view. But when we examine all aspects of the subject with complete objectivity, we realise that this explanation is not enough. We find the endless stories and poems of romantic courtship. We find women riding across the desert alone, taking part in public debates and poetical contests and fighting in battles. In many anecdotes, we find women rebuking their husbands or offering them advice in forcible language, and we realise that the subject is one of considerable complexity.

In general, it may be said that the Apostle normally took the side of the woman when disputes arose.

* * *

It was two years after Uhud before Quraish succeeded in preparing another large force in the hope of putting an end to the activities of the Muslims, whose blockade had ruined the commercial prosperity of their town.

The Muslim historians allege that the expedition was partly the result of propaganda carried out by the Jews. They cite particularly the names of Sallam ibn abi al Huqaiq[11] and Huyai ibn Akhtab, both of Beni al Nadheer, who, as we have seen, had not followed the bulk of their tribesmen in migrating to Syria. These and other Jewish leaders are alleged to have visited Quraish in Mecca, suggesting a grand alliance against the Muslims. Having obtained the consent of the Meccan chiefs, the Jews are said to have approached the bedouin tribe of Ghatafan and persuaded them to co-operate.

The object of the operation was to take Medina, which should have been done two years before, immediately after the Battle of Uhud, if Quraish had been more efficient.

Quraish succeeded in raising a force of ten thousand men against which the Apostle could muster only three thousand. The Meccans themselves had four thousand men, which included Quraish and their clients and allies, and a contingent of Beni Kinana. Ghatafan were the most numerous bedouin tribe, having perhaps two thousand or more. Beni Sulaim are alleged to have brought some seven hundred men, and there was also a party from Beni Asad. The figures are only approximate and may be greatly exaggerated.

One of the most fervent converts in Medina was a man called Sulman. He was the son of a Persian landowner, who had been converted as a boy to Christianity, and had passed some years in Syria in religious studies, as the pupil of various Christian anchorites. His Christian teacher having died, he is alleged to have set out for the Hejaz, where he had heard of the appearance of a new prophet. Seized and sold as a slave to a Jew of Medina, he had earned enough money, assisted by Muhammad, to buy his own freedom, after which he had become a devoted Muslim.

[11] Sallam had already been assassinated by the Muslims for these activities, as mentioned in the previous chapter.

The news of the imminent advance of a large force of Meccans and bedouins renewed among the Muslims the anxious discussions which had preceded Uhud. Should they sally out and accept battle in the open or fortify themselves in their houses?

Sulman had grown up in the highly cultured and up-to-date Kingdom of Persia and had subsequently spent many years in the equally civilised country of Syria. He had doubtless heard about, and perhaps witnessed, the wars between Persia and the Byzantine Empire, which had been raging for many years. Tradition attributes to Sulman the suggestion that Medina could be more easily defended if its fortifications were strengthened by a ditch. It is not clear where the ditch was to be dug or how the defences were designed. There seems to be a suggestion that it was used to fill a gap, where the walls and houses were not continuous.

In any case, Sulman's plan was adopted, and the Apostle set the example by himself marking out the alignment of the trench and commencing work with spade and pickaxe. The Muslims rallied round and, as there was little time left, worked frantically in relays, under the encouragement of the Messenger of God. As they had done when building the first mosque, the Prophet chanted as he worked, while his followers, dusty and sweating, digging and carrying away the earth, joined in the responses. The Apostle sang:

> Let Paradise, O Lord, our guerden be.
> Helpers and Emigrants look for help to Thee.

To which the men responded with the refrain:

> To God's Apostle we have pledged our faith,
> To fight his foes and not to flee from death.

The false Muslims or "hypocrites", however, worked slackly and stole away without permission when the Apostle was not looking. The great majority toiled diligently and asked his permission if they found themselves obliged for a short time to leave the work. According to Ibn Ishaq, Chapter XXIV, verse 62, of the Qoran refers to this situation.

"They only are believers in God and in His Apostle who, when engaged on important work, do not go away without asking permission. Those who ask permission of thee, they are those who believe in God and in His Apostle. So if they ask thy permission for some affair of theirs, give leave to them as you see fit, and ask God's pardon for them. Do not treat the Apostle's call to you as you would a request from one of you to another. God knows those who steal away. Let those beware who disobey his order, lest trouble overtake them and a painful punishment."

The trench was scarcely finished on 31st March, 627, when the enemy began to arrive. Quraish were accompanied by their own paid guards and by their allies of Beni Kinana. Then Ghatafan appeared and settled themselves north of the oasis on the track leading to Uhud. The Messenger of God thereupon gave orders that the women and children be placed in the buildings and forts. He and the three thousand Muslims bivouacked immediately behind the trench facing the enemy, presumably north of the town.

No sooner had the besiegers established themselves round Medina than Huyai ibn Akhtab, the Jewish chief of Beni al Nadheer, arrived at the village of Beni Quraidha, the only Jewish tribe left in Medina, who apparently lived in a separate settlement at the south of the oasis. The chief of Beni Quraidha had sworn friendship with the Apostle and for some time resisted the blandishments of Huyai ibn Akhtab, but eventually he agreed to break his agreement with Muhammad.

Having heard reports of Huyai's visit to Beni Quraidha, the Apostle sent Saad ibn Muadh, the chief of the Aus, and Saad ibn Ubada, the head of the Khazraj, to call on Beni Quraidha. According to Ibn Ishaq, the Jews abused them saying, "Who is the Apostle of God? We have no agreement with Muhammad."

Meanwhile, morale in Medina was weakening and the false Muslims began to whisper that Muhammad had promised that God would give them victory but that now their lives, their families and their children were in imminent danger.

Mention has already been made of the fact that the Arab tribes regarded war as an endemic and natural feature of human life. Perpetual peace would have had for them no conceivable attraction. But one of the reasons why this state of affairs seemed to them not only endurable but desirable, was because they regarded war as a means of gaining honour and plunder, rather than of destroying their enemies.

This casual and sporting attitude to inter-tribal hostilities constituted an obstacle to the development of military science, which is the study of outwitting, surprising and defeating the enemy and ultimately encompassing his utter destruction. But, to the Arab tribes, surprising the enemy by the use of new methods or secret weapons would have brought no honour but rather the reverse. A fair, open fight was their ideal.

Historically it is fascinating to remember that, in the hundred years after the death of the Messenger of God, these Arab tribes conquered Egypt, all North Africa, Spain and the southern half of France. Subsequently expelled from France, they were to remain in Spain for nearly eight centuries, a period as long as that from Richard Coeur de Lion to our own times.

During these eight centuries, they established in Spain and France, and thence in England, their conception of war as a means of gaining honour rather than of destroying their enemies. As Shakespeare makes Henry V say:

> By Jove, I am not covetous for gold;
> Nor care I who doth feed upon my cost;
> It yearns me not if men my garments wear;
> Such outward things dwell not in my desires:
> But if it be a sin to covet honour,
> I am the most offending soul alive.[12]

With the return of classical ideas at the Renaissance, war in the West gradually became "rationalised" once more, the only object being the destruction of the enemy, by fair means or foul. This everincreasing ruthlessness has now brought us to a point where the human race is threatened with self-extirpation.

Men, however, rarely analyse the environment in which they find themselves, or trace the origins of their institutions. As a result, the armies of Western Europe clung for centuries to the Arab idea of war as a glorious and chivalrous contest. Yet at the same time, the desire to win at all costs continued to grow. These two views of war were, in reality, incompatible.

Owing to a residual attachment to the idea of military honour, the armies of the West repeatedly opposed the progress of lethal weapons. Officers were always to be found who favoured the bow and arrow

[12] Shakespeare, *King Henry V*, Act IV, scene iii. The whole speech is in bedouin style.

rather than firearms and who denounced as dishonourable the use of artillery! Generals still hankered for the days of cavalry charges, sword in hand, preceded and followed by the exchange of courteous messages between the rival commanders. Arab warfare was inefficient, but it gave us the idea of chivalry, which immensely enriched our Western civilisation.

*   *   *

It seems normally to have been accepted by Western writers that Quraish were so completely surprised at the appearance of a trench that they gave up their plan to attack the town. At the same time, however, it appears that the trench only closed one gap, the remainder of the perimeter being occupied by houses. No attempt whatever was made to attack these. It seems, therefore, to be nearer the truth to say that Quraish had come on the assumption that the Muslims would come out and fight, as they had done at Uhud. Perhaps, even without the trench, they had no plan to attack the town and its houses. It also seems relevant to recall the advice of Abdulla ibn Ubay Uhud. "If we stay in our homes, they will be unable to do us any harm," he had said. His views now were proved to have been correct.

Men whose only weapons were lances, swords and bows and arrows could be stopped short by the simplest masonry wall. Even if the allies had crossed the ditch, they would still have been obliged to assault the buildings. I have personally found myself, with a party of men armed only with rifles, confronted by a masonry fort in the desert and have been completely unable to find any way to capture it.

The Muslim historians, however, were perhaps unwilling to allow that the chief "hypocrite", Abdulla ibn Ubay, had all along known best. They could not, therefore, admit that the enemy had failed because they could not assault buildings, as Abdulla had said. They consequently emphasised that it was the Prophet's ditch which defeated the enemy.

Another important consideration is the fact that Quraish had brought—between them and their bedouin allies—no less than six hundred horsemen. It was the horsemen who had won the victory at Uhud. With so large a mounted force, they doubtless felt assured of victory, if only the Muslims would accept an open battle.

The Muslims and the polytheists spent nearly a month facing one another across the trench without fighting, except for an occasional flight of arrows. The Apostle of God, however, was in profound anxiety, for the whole responsibility rested on him. Being, as we have seen, by inclination a politician and a diplomat, he thought anxiously of some way of ending the deadlock without a battle. Accordingly he sent a messenger to the chiefs of Ghatafan, offering them as a bribe one-third of the date crop of Medina, if they would break with Quraish and return to their homes. The two tribal shaikhs, who were doubtless bored with a war which promised neither loot nor excitement, agreed to the proposal.

The Apostle of God then sent for the shaikhs of the Aus and the Khazraj, Saad ibn Muadh and Saad ibn Ubada, and told them of his plan. As has already been explained, the Muslims differentiated sharply between the revelations sent down to the Prophet, which they believed to be the exact words of God, and Muhammad's own human ideas, which were far from infallible. "Is this an order from God, which we are bound to obey," they enquired, "or is it just an idea of yours, to which you want our consent?" "It is something which I am doing for your sake," replied Muhammad. "I am distressed to see the Arabs all collected round you, and I wish to save you by causing them to disperse."

"When we and all these people were idolaters," replied Saad ibn Muadh, "they never could wrest a single date from us by force. Are we to hand over our property to them now, when God has guided us to Islam? We most certainly will not!" "Have it as you will," said the Apostle mildly, and the siege continued. This is one of several occasions on which we see the Apostle himself leaning to compromise, but obliged to fight it out by the intransigence of his followers.

It is possible, indeed probable, that the leaders of Quraish soon learned that their allies, Ghatafan, had been engaged in secret negotiations with the Messenger of God, with a view to the conclusion of a private peace. In this case, the negotiations would have served a valuable purpose by breeding suspicion between the allies, resulting in the ultimate break-up of the confederation.

One day a party of four Quraish horsemen actually crossed the ditch at a narrow place and took up their stand in front of the Muslims. Their leader, Amr ibn Abid Wudd, called out a personal challenge to any man in the Muslim camp. The challenge was repeated three times, together with the taunt, "Where is the paradise to which you say you go when you are killed, if you are afraid to fight me now?"

Eventually the Apostle gave permission to Ali to accept the

challenge. He walked towards Amr, who was on horseback. "How can I fight you when you are on a horse?" he shouted "Dismount and let us fight on equal terms." So Amr dismounted, driving his horse away by slapping it on the rump with the flat of his sword. The two men advanced upon one another, then, crouching low, began to circle slowly round one another, each watching his opponent for an opportunity. Soon their agile footwork raised a cloud of dust obscuring them from view. Then the dust drifted away, to reveal Amr lying dead and Ali wiping the blood off his sword, on his victim's clothes. The Muslims raised a shout, *Allahu akbar*, God is most Great, and the other three horsemen galloped back across the trench.

While cantering up, his long lance in his hand, to join in the skirmish, the chief of the Aus, Saad ibn Muadh, was wounded in the forearm by an arrow. We shall hear more of this wound.

A man called Nuaim ibn Masood, of Ghatafan, had been converted to Islam and had joined the Apostle of God in Medina. The Quraish leaders seem to have urged the Beni Quraidha Jews to make a diversion from the south against the Muslims. There was some talk of Quraish giving hostages to Beni Quraidha, as a surety that they would not march away and leave the Jews exposed to the Prophet's reprisals.

Nuaim is alleged to have gone to Quraish and warned them that Beni Quraidha proposed to hand over their hostages to the Apostle, as a means of making their peace with him. Then he went to the Jews, and advised them not to do anything unless they received hostages, as Quraish proposed to betray them. By this means distrust was sown between Quraish and Beni Quraidha. Ibn Ishaq alleges that it was the Apostle who thought of this plan and sent Nuaim to execute it.

As has been previously explained, the Arabs in the seventh century (and the bedouins even today) did not feed their horses and camels, but relied solely on natural grazing. A large concentration of animals could not long remain stationary in one place, as all the grazing within reach would soon be eaten up. It would then be necessary to move elsewhere. Only such persons as have lived with Arab nomads can appreciate the fact that the greater part of their thoughts at all times are occupied with the state of the grazing and the condition of their animals. Quraish and their bedouin allies had now been camped for nearly a month outside Medina, all the grazing had been eaten and their camels and horses were beginning to die.

Professor Margoliouth is contemptuous of the besiegers of Medina, whom he blames, not only for incapacity, but for physical cowardice. Such a charge can only be made with considerable reservations, for these same men, only seven years later, were to embark on a career of conquest unprecedented in the history of the world, and which was to carry them to Central France in the West and to the borders of China in the East.

Moreover, it must be remembered that, when the Muslims had declared war on the Jews of Beni Qainuqa and Beni al Nadheer, they had made no attempt to assault their houses, although they were three or four times as numerous as the defenders. On the contrary, they too had been content merely to blockade them. This fact seems further to confirm that buildings could not be captured with the weapons which the Arabs possessed.

If there were any difference in the fighting performance of the two sides, it was in the sphere of morale rather than in that of physical courage. Quraish were waging a negative and, therefore, an uninspiring war. They did not want changes introduced into their way of life. The Muslims, on the other hand, were fired by the positive conviction that God had entrusted to them the task of reforming the world. It was in the spirit which inspired them that the two sides differed.

If we admit that buildings were assault-proof against the weapons which the seventh century Arabs possessed, it seems safe to assume that the whole basis of the Quraish advance on Medina was the assumption that the Muslims would come out and fight, as they had done at Uhud. Once they realised that this was not going to happen, there was nothing left for Quraish to do but to go home.

The immediate cause of the abandonment of the siege is alleged to have been a violent gale which raged one night, accompanied by torrents of cold rain, blowing down the tents, scattering the camp fires and sending the cooking pots bowling away across the desert. It is possible also that this cold wind killed some of the horses and camels, already thin and weak from lack of grazing.

No sooner was the storm over than Abu Sofian summoned Quraish to a council, at which he announced his intention of going home. Indeed, according to a Muslim spy who was present, he was in such a hurry to leave that he mounted his camel while one of its legs was still hobbled.

Another consideration impelling Quraish to abandon the siege

was perhaps the fact that the season of the annual pilgrimage to
Mecca was only a month away. As we have already seen, the month
before the pilgrimage was occupied by the public fairs at which a
great deal of profitable business was conducted. The leaders of Quraish
may well have been unwilling to sacrifice both the financial profits of
the fairs and the religious prestige which they gained by supervising
the pagan pilgrimage.

As soon as Quraish began to move, their bedouin allies vanished
into the desert. The siege of Medina was at an end. The spy who had
watched them go reported back to Muhammad the next morning,
while he was saying the dawn prayer wrapped against the cold in a
cloak belonging to one of his wives. Sending orders for the evacua-
tion of the trench, he returned to his house and took off his armour.

*   *   *

At noon the same day, however, when the Apostle of God was
going to the mosque for the midday prayer, he met the Archangel
Gabriel wearing an embroidered turban and riding on a mule the
saddle of which was covered with brocade. He asked the Apostle
whether he had stopped fighting, to which Muhammad replied in
the affirmative. But Gabriel replied that the angels had not yet laid
down their arms. "God commands you, O Muhammad", he said, "to
go to Beni Quraidha. I am going there myself," and he cantered away.

The Apostle immediately issued orders that no one was to pray
the afternoon prayer until he reached the settlement of Beni
Quraidha. Before he arrived there, the Apostle passed a number of
his followers and asked them if anyone had passed on before him.
"We saw Dahiya ibn Khalifa," they replied, "riding a white mule
with a piece of brocade over his saddle." But the Messenger of God
answered, "That was Gabriel, who has been sent to Beni Quraidha
to shake their forts."

We have seen that Huyai ibn Akhtab, the chief of the Beni al
Nadheer Jews, had proposed to Quraish and to Ghatafan the plan to
attack Medina, and had urged Beni Quraidha to join in against the
Muslims. When the allies raised the siege and marched away, he had
entered the Beni Quraidha village. "O Jews," he is reported as
saying, "you see what has happened to us. I now put before your
three possible courses of action. Firstly, we can accept this man as a
prophet, and then your lives, your property, your women and your

children will be safe." Beni Quraidha replied that they would never abandon their religion. "In that case," continued Huyai, "let us kill our women and children and go out and fight Muhammad, sword in hand, with no encumbrances." "How could we kill these poor creatures?" they cried. "What would be the use of life without them?"

"Tonight is the eve of the Sabbath," Huyai then suggested. "The third course is that we sally out tonight and surprise Muhammad and his companions. Thinking that we never fight on the Sabbath, they may well have relaxed their vigilance." "Are we to profane the Sabbath?" cried the assembled Jews in horror. "Not a single man of you since the day you were born has ever resolved to do what he knows ought to be done, and stuck to it," cried Huyai bitterly.

Soon afterwards, the Jews sent to the Apostle of God asking him to send them a man of the Aus called Abu Lubaba, for Beni Quraidha had previously been allies of the Aus. When he came to them, he was deeply moved at their miserable state, the women and children all weeping and crying out. "O Abu Lubaba," they asked him, "do you advise us to submit to Muhammad?" According to his own account, he said "Yes", but at the same moment he drew his right forefinger across his throat, signifying that they would all be massacred. "Scarcely had I done so," he used to tell afterwards, "than I suddenly realised that I had been false to God and his Apostle."

Turning suddenly on his heel, he hurried back to the mosque, avoiding the Prophet on the way, and tied himself up to a pillar. "If he had come straight to me," Muhammad commented, "I would have asked God to forgive him. But as he has behaved in this way, I will not release him until God forgives him." The Messenger of God was sleeping that night with his wife, Umm Salama, who used to recount the incident after his death. "At dawn," she used to say, "I heard the Apostle laugh and I said to him, 'What are you laughing at?' He replied that God had forgiven Abu Lubaba."

"Can I give him the good news?" she asked excitedly, for the Prophet's house was built against the side of the mosque, where Abu Lubaba had tied himself up. When she received permission to do so, she ran to the door which opened on to the courtyard of the mosque and cried out, "O Abu Lubaba, rejoice, for God has forgiven you." (This was before the Apostle gave the order for the veiling of women.) A number of men who were in the mosque hastened up to release him but he refused to allow them, saying, "No, not until the Apostle releases me with his own hand."

The next morning Beni Quraidha surrendered after a siege of twenty-five days. It will be remembered that when the Beni Qainuqa Jews had done the same, the shaikh of the Khazraj, Abdulla ibn Ubay, had persuaded the Apostle to spare their lives, for they had been allies of the Khazraj. Beni Quraidha, on the other hand, had been allies of the Aus. As soon, therefore, as they surrendered, the Aus cried out to the Messenger of God asking for the same treatment as had been given to Beni Qainuqa, the allies of the Khazraj. "Would you be satisfied, O men of the Aus," said the Apostle, "if one of you pronounce judgement on them?"

It will be remembered that Saad ibn Muadh, the Aus chief, had been wounded in the arm by an arrow at the trench. His wound had turned septic and now he was dying. Muhammad sent for him and he came riding on a donkey, supported on both sides by his relatives. "Deal kindly with your friends," his men whispered to him, "for the Apostle has made you their judge."

"The time has come for Saad, in the cause of God, to disregard the censure of men," he replied, feeling the nearness of his own death. The Apostle and all the Muslims then pledged themselves to abide by whatever he decided.

"I give judgement," he answered, "that the men be killed, their property divided and the women and children be made captives."

"You have given the judgement of God, who is above the Seven Heavens," said the Apostle, in confirmation of the sentence.

Trenches were dug during the night near the main market of Medina. In the morning, the Jews were led out in small batches, their hands tied behind them, and made to kneel down beside the trench. Their heads were then cut off and their bodies pushed into the trench. Before execution, they were offered conversion to Islam but few took advantage of the offer.

The life of an Arab called Thabit ibn Qais had once been saved by a man of Beni Quraidha, before the appearance of Islam. Thabit now went to the Apostle and secured his agreement to spare the life of his former rescuer, together with his family and his property. But when Thabit hastened to tell his friend that he had secured his pardon, the Jew refused to live. "I prefer to go with my people," he said, "and I cannot wait to join my loved ones." When Abu Bekr heard his words about joining his loved ones, "Yes," he commented grimly, "he will join them in hell for ever and ever."

Between seven and eight hundred men are believed to have been put to death. Some of the women and children were taken to Nejed and sold as slaves, the money thus gained being used to buy weapons and horses for the Muslims. One of the women, Raihana bint Amr, became a member of the Apostle's household.

Part of Chapter XXXIII of the Qoran, from which a few relevant extracts are here given, is believed to refer to the Quraish siege of Medina.

> Verse 9. O you who believe, remember the blessing of God upon you when the troops came against you. We sent a wind against them and invisible troops and God saw all your actions.

The suggestion seems here to be that the gale of wind was caused by an angelic attack.

> Verse 25. God drove back the unbelievers in their rage and they gained no advantage and God was a sufficient defence for the believers, so that they did not have to fight for God was Mighty and Glorious. And He brought low those of the People of the Book[13] who supported them from their forts, some of whom you killed and some you made captives.

*   *   *

The end of the operations of the seige of Medina was followed by new regulations regarding women. The wives of the Prophet are enjoined to remain in their houses and not to flaunt their jewelry in public. Men who spoke to them were to do so only from behind a veil and, when they did appear in public, the women were to wear cloaks covering up their dresses and their ornaments. These rules, originally directed at the Prophet's wives, were subsequently assumed to be applicable to all Muslim women.

Debate has waxed hot as to whether the Prophet caused an improvement or a deterioration in the status of women. Financially he assisted them by laying down for them the exact shares to which they were entitled in the inheritance of their parents. Previously the sons alone had inherited. Muhammad had also forbidden the burial alive

[13] People of the Book in this instance refers to the Jews, whose book was the Old Testament.

of girl babies and marriage by his sons of the wives of a deceased father.

Qoran, Chapter IV, verse 32, lays down that women who work have the right to keep their earnings. "Men shall have the benefit of what they earn and women shall have the benefit of what they earn." Verse 35 of the same Chapter directs that, in the event of a serious matrimonial dispute, arbitrators be appointed, one for him and one for her, and that they do their best to effect a reconciliation. On the other hand, the Messenger of God stated firmly that the father was the head of the family, that he had the right to strike an insubordinate wife (though not severely) and that good women would be obedient.

The restrictions which he imposed on women were inspired by his ideas regarding morality, not by any hardness, contempt or lack of sympathy for women. On the contrary, he was endlessly advocating kindness and consideration for them. But, although he sanctioned polygamy, he was strongly opposed to extra-marital sexual familiarities. As we have seen, he married thirteen wives, or concubines, but he would not even touch the hand of a woman who was not his wife.

He believed that free social relations between men and women outside the family, and the exposure of parts of the female body to the eyes of men, would lead to sexual immorality. He accordingly imposed on women restrictions regarding their clothing and their movements, while, at the same time, securing their rights and urging their male relatives to treat them with sympathy and kindness.

The severe measures of veiling and confinement which some people in the West attribute to Islam were not, however, introduced by the Apostle but appeared some two centuries later under Persian influence.

NOTABLE DATES

Migration to Medina	622
Battle of Uhud	625
Siege of Medina	March–April 627
Extermination of Beni Quraidha	April 627

PERSONALITIES

The Apostle's Family
Ali ibn abi Talib
Zaid ibn Haritha

The Apostle's Wives in 627

Sauda, daughter of Zamaa

Aisha, daughter of Abu Bekr

Hafsa, daughter of Umar

Zainab, daughter of Khuzaima, died soon after her marriage to Muhammad

Hind Umm Salama, widow of Abu Salama

Zainab, divorced wife of Zaid ibn Haritha

Raihana, daughter of Amr of Beni Quraidha

Muslims

Sulman the Persian, designer of the Ditch

Abdulla ibn Ubay, "the Hypocrite"

Saad ibn Muadh, chief of the Aus. Condemner of Beni Quraidha. He died of his wound soon afterwards

Saad ibn Ubada, the chief of the Khazraj

Nuaim ibn Masood, of Ghatafan, the Apostle's spy

Abu Lubaba, who warned Beni Quraidha of their fate

Jewish Leaders

Sallam ibn abi al Huqaiq, chief of Beni al Nadheer, assassinated in Kheibar

Huyai ibn Akhtab, of Beni al Nadheer, executed with Beni Quraidha

Idolaters

Abu Sofian, commander of the forces of Quraish at the Siege of Medina

XIII

Hudaibiya

The struggle with Mecca, after the unsuccessful siege of the "war of the ditch", moved into a new and surprising phase with the episode of Hudaibiya, which shows us a pliant, opportunist Muhammad, open to negotiation and compromise . . . At the edge of the sacred ground of Mecca, the Prophet halted his armed advance and stooped to bargain with his enemies, to the astonishment and discomfiture of his own companions . . . This episode will serve to give the measure of the Prophet's tactical ability, of the absolute obedience he was able to command from his followers, and of the situation, by now seriously weakened, of the Quraysh.

FRANCESCO GABRIELI, *Muhammad and the Conquests of Islam*

Let us make an honourable retreat.

WILLIAM SHAKESPEARE, *As You Like It*

We triumph without glory when we conquer without danger.

PIERRE CORNEILLE

XIII

ENGROSSED in the narrative of events which mark the Apostle's career, we have omitted hitherto to refer to a number of edicts, prohibitions and reforms, which he introduced during the early years in Medina. In some cases, the dates of promulgation of the reforms in question are doubtful, though their nature is known.

The Arabs had, before Islam, been regular consumers of alcohol. The pre-Islamic poets praise the virtues of wine, though drunkenness was deprecated by the pagan Arabs. Their ever-present feeling for human dignity made them critical of the drunkard. Some drank their wine diluted with water or added honey to it.[1]

The complete prohibition of intoxicants was announced by the Messenger of God in Medina, either before or after the Battle of Uhud. That doughty champion of the Muslims on the battlefield, the Apostle's uncle, Hamza, is said to have been a heavy drinker. Perhaps his death at Uhud facilitated the prohibition of alcohol.

Chapter V of the Qoran, verse 90, says: "O you who believe! Wine and intoxicants and gambling and the arrow game are unclean devil's work. Keep clear of them that you may meet with success."

Chapter II, verse 219: "They ask you concerning wine and games of chance. Say: There is great sin in them and profits for men. But their evil is greater than their utility."

The prohibition against alcohol was ultimately largely successful but never completely so. We read of wine-drinking parties among some of the heroes of the first Muslim conquests only a few years after the death of the Prophet. In Damascus, wine was regularly consumed at the court of the Umaiyid khalifs. Some *modus vivendi* was perhaps reached, the drinkers taking their pleasure without too much ostentation, in return for which the pious abstained from public denunciation. Even today, while many Muslims drink, the vast majority do not and have never done so. In most Muslim countries, no alcohol is served at public functions. The arrow game, in which a bundle of arrows was thrown on the ground, success depending on the way in which they fell, was a form of gambling.

[1] Compare Goldziher, *Muslim Studies.*

Rules concerning diet were generally similar to those in force among Jews. Pigs' flesh was forbidden, as was that of animals which had died or been strangled. Animals were to be slaughtered by cutting the throat and allowing the blood to flow out. Sacrifices offered to idols were forbidden as food.

Chapter II, verse 278, prohibits usury. "O you who believe! Fear God, and give up what remains to you of your profits from usury. But if you refuse to do so, be warned of war against you by God and by His Messenger. But if you repent, your capital will remain yours. Do not oppress others, and you will not be oppressed . . .

"Guard against the day when you will return to God. Then every soul shall be paid what it has earned."

The Arabs have always been a commercial people. Unlike so many empires built through military conquests, the great Arab empires which came into being after the Apostle's death never became proud militarists, despising merchants. As we have seen, the Prophet came of a business family and was himself for many years engaged in commerce. The terms used in the Qoranic passage just quoted—your capital will remain yours—every soul shall be paid what it has earned—are commercial expressions.

We have also seen that almost every person in Mecca, even some women also, invested their money in the annual caravans to the Yemen and Syria, and received their shares in the profits. The Apostle never condemned such investments. Presumably the prohibition was directed against professional money-lenders, who took no share in commercial enterprise but demanded extortionate rates of interest for a loan. Whereas the prohibition against alcohol has been largely successful, the prohibition against usury has been easier to elude.

Before proceeding further, it may be well to explain that Muslims claim that the Apostle set practicable standards of moral conduct. To quote a modern Muslim writer,[2] "He does not say, 'Love your enemy' . . . he says, 'Inflict on him as much injury as he has inflicted on you (but not more); and if you forgive him, God will reward you.'"

He did not ask men to give up their wealth, but sought the best of both worlds. Qoran, Chapter II, verse 201, has, "There are some among them who say: O our Lord, give us good things in this world and good things in the next world and save us from the punishment of the fire.

[2] Muhammad Hamidullah, *Le Prophète de l'Islam.*

"They shall receive their share of what they have earned and God is swift to reckon up the account."[3] Yet although he said that God would give prosperity in this world to believers, he did not approve of great wealth and never acquired any himself.

To a considerable extent, this middle-of-the-way morality may be said to have been achieved. Both circumstances and human nature vary so immensely that generalisations can only be applied with great care. We can, however, notice that this Muslim ideal does not envisage the complete and heroic self-donation, the absolute selflessness, which has been the ideal of many Christian saints. Nor does Islam, as a whole, seem to have adopted the Christian thesis of perfection through suffering. After the death of the Apostle, however, Muslim mystics were in fact to appear who did aim at complete self-donation. Muhammad, on the other hand, disapproved of extreme asceticism.

Nevertheless, it can be said that, on the whole, the majority of Muslims are honest, moral, simple and believing worshippers of a Single and Almighty God. Yet, before we can evaluate such a claim, we must allow also for the fact that the greater part of the Muslim population of the world today is living in agricultural communities where the local conditions tend to make them hardworking and simple-minded. As a result, differences between the morality and the steadfastness of West Europeans and Central Asians cannot be attributed solely to differences between Christianity and Islam. The morality of the West has been corroded by a long period of wealth, ease, city life and power. During the golden age of the Arab Empire, the Muslims showed the same signs of moral laxity as are visible today in Europe.

*   *   *

The failure of their great attack on Medina had seriously depressed the morale of Quraish. Muhammad's star seemed to be continuously in the ascendant. A number of people commenced to whisper that perhaps he really was a prophet, while others, indifferent to his religious claims, nevertheless began to envisage his ultimate victory and to contemplate changing sides while there was still time.

It was the settled policy of the Apostle and of the early Muslims never to allow an injury to pass unavenged. The murder of Sallam

[3] Note the commercial phraseology once again.

ibn abi al Huqaiq had been an example of this principle. It will be remembered that, two years before, after the Battle of Uhud, the clan of Beni Lihyan of the Hudhail tribe had invited the Messenger of God to send a party of missionaries to teach them Islam, but that when six men had been sent, they had been ambushed. Four had been killed while Zaid and Khubaib had been sold to the Meccans to be sacrificed as blood revenge for their relatives killed at Bedr.

In October, 627, six months after the extermination of Beni Quraidha, the Apostle decided to raid Beni Lihyan to punish them for their treachery. It may almost be said that intelligence is the key to success in bedouin raiding. Every desert Arab is continually on the alert for information. Their camps are so scattered and their great flocks so unwieldy that defence against an unexpected raid is almost impossible. Hence their constant cross-questioning of every traveller or passer-by, in the hope of obtaining prior information of the raiding preparations of their enemies.

Quraish, as we have seen, were primarily merchants, not raiders, and the early attempts of the Muslims to carry out raids had been almost invariably abortive. Now, however, they were gaining experience. Moreover, many bedouins had now become Muslims and the Prophet was well provided with advisers and desert guides.

In order to allay any apprehensions on the part of his intended victims, the Apostle set out from Medina northwards, announcing his intention to raid Syria. When the force reached a point some twenty miles north-west of the oasis, however, it swung round to the left and headed southwards to where Beni Lihyan were camped near Usfan.[4] Nevertheless, even these precautions were inadequate, the enemy received news of the raid and retired to the tops of the mountains where they prepared to defend themselves vigorously. Having failed to achieve surprise, the party returned to Medina without fighting.

Only a few days after the return of the abortive raid on Beni Lihyan, probably in November 627, the Apostle's own flocks of camels, while out grazing north of Medina, were driven off by a party of Ghatafan. It is firstly interesting to note that Muhammad, who had emigrated penniless from Mecca, now owned flocks of camels. His newly acquired wealth, however, was not devoted to raising his own standard of comfort, but to the promotion of the cause which he had at heart.

[4] Map 6, p. 174.

The Ghatafan raiders killed the herdsman of the Apostle's camels and carried off his wife. It so happened that a Muslim bedouin called Salama ibn al Akwa was in the area that morning, accompanied by another man who was a slave of Quraish. Topping a pass in the hills, he suddenly saw the Ghatafan raiders below him, riding about, rounding up and driving off the Apostle's herds. Sending the slave back posthaste to give the alarm, Ibn al Akwa alone ran after the raiders, whose escape was, of course, hampered by the slower pace of the herds which they were driving.

Closing up fearlessly to within two hundred yards of the raiders, he shot the arrows from his quiver at them, crying at the same time, "I am Ibn al Akwa! Take that from me!" Some of the horsemen turned and rode after him, whereupon he dodged behind the shrubs, shooting at them, and then scrambled away up a rocky slope, where the horses could not follow. The raiders were, of course, principally anxious to get away with the camels before a rescue party could overtake them from Medina. Having pursued Salama for a short distance, they turned to rejoin their comrades. Thereupon he also turned again and ran after them, shooting his arrows and shouting in stentorian tones, "I'm the son of Al Akwa! Here's another present from me!"

Meanwhile, the messenger had returned to Medina and given the alarm and a party of six horsemen set out in pursuit at a wild gallop, while the Apostle gathered a larger force to follow them. One of the horsemen, outstripping his fellows, by-passed the raiders and the looted camels and pulled up in front of them, trying to stop their escape, but the raiders rode him down and killed him. The remainder of the horsemen overtook the raiders from the rear and galloped into them with lance and sword. The son of the shaikh of Ghatafan was killed. Ukasha, a famous Muslim warrior, overtook two men riding on the same camel and ran them both through together with his lance.

The raiders, most of whom were mounted on camels, were thrown into confusion by the horsemen and abandoned some of the camels but made good their escape with the remainder. When the Apostle arrived with a large force, the enemy was already too far ahead for it to be possible to overtake him. The Messenger of God stopped at a well called Dhu Qarad, and ordered that camels be slaughtered and roasted, and the Muslims enjoyed a good meal before returning to Medina. The affair accordingly became known as the Day of Dhu Qarad. Such, from time immemorial, have been the excitements of desert life. I have myself, in the 1920's, been present at skirmishes exactly similar, except that rifles had replaced bows and arrows. Fortunately the rifles were mostly used from horseback at a gallop, with the result that the casualties were no more numerous than those inflicted by the bows and arrows.

In the confusion of the raiders' retreat, the wife of the dead herdsman had made her escape, clinging to the back of one of the camels. She went to the Apostle and told him of her adventures and of how she had eluded the enemy and returned alone. Then she concluded, "It was this camel which carried me to safety. I vowed to God that I would slaughter her to Him, if He enabled me to escape on her back." The Apostle smiled kindly and said, "You would repay her badly, if you slaughtered her, when God by her means has enabled you to escape! Anyhow a vow to sacrifice something which does not belong to you is not valid, for she is one of my camels. So leave her alone and God bless you!"

This little incident is, in passing, another example of the freedom and resourcefulness of Arab women.

*   *   *

In December 627, or perhaps in January 628, the Apostle of God received a report that Beni Mustaliq, a clan of Khuzaa, were preparing to raid the Muslims. He decided to forestall them, set out with a raiding party and encountered them at Al Muraisi,[5] near the seashore. After a short skirmish, in which the bedouins were surprised and several of them killed, the Muslims were victorious and captured a number of women and children and other property belonging to the tribe. The Muslims then halted on the wells to rest.[6] Some of the Mustaliq women appear to have been raped, an action presumably justified by the rule that unbelieving women taken prisoners in war could be used as concubines.

While the animals were being watered, a bedouin servant of Umar quarrelled with a man who was an ally of the Khazraj, each trying to water his camels before the other. They came to blows, and

[5] Map 6, p. 174.
[6] Having, on several occasions, drawn attention to the similarity of desert raiding in the seventh and early twentieth centuries, I may add here that the practice of taking prisoners has long ago been abandoned, possibly from a time soon after the Prophet's death. I never heard of a case of rape by raiders in my time.

Umar's servant called out, "Help, O Emigrants!" While the ally of Khazraj shouted, "To me, O Helpers!" For a tense moment, the Muslims of Mecca glared at their co-religionists of Medina.

Abdulla ibn Ubay, the former accepted chief of Medina, was furious. To a group of his own people, he is alleged to have said angrily, referring to the Meccans, "They dispute our priority, they outnumber us in our own town. Nothing fits us and these Quraish vagabonds better than the old saying, 'Feed a dog and it will devour you'. By God, when we return to Medina, the stronger will drive out the weaker."

A boy who heard this outburst of ill temper on the part of Ibn Ubay went and told the Apostle. Umar, who was standing by, immediately advised him to send someone to murder Abdulla ibn Ubay. But the Messenger of God was less hasty. "What if men should then say that Muhammad kills his own companions?" he asked. But a number of Helpers who overheard these remarks, and who still seem to have retained their respect and loyalty for their old chief, said, soothingly, "This boy was probably mistaken and did not report Abdulla's words correctly."

To avoid further quarrels, the Apostle gave orders to march although it was noon and the heat was almost unbearable. He kept the force on the move all day, the following night and the next day until the sun grew hot. When the word was eventually given for the midday halt, the men, completely exhausted, fell asleep as soon as they sat down on the ground.

One of the Beni Mustaliq prisoners was Juwairiya, the daughter of their chief. She went up to Muhammad to ask his aid on her behalf, saying that her father would pay her ransom. According to Ibn Ishaq, whe was "a most beautiful woman who captivated every man who saw her". When she addressed him, the Prophet replied, "Would you like something better than that? I will pay your ransom and marry you myself", a proposal to which she consented. As soon as the Muslims heard that the Apostle had married Juwairiya, and that Beni Mustaliq had thus become his relatives by marriage, they all released their prisoners, amounting, it was said, to a hundred families of women and children. If Ibn Ishaq had not laid such emphasis on her beauty, we might have concluded that this was a purely political marriage, for it won over Beni Mustaliq to Islam more successfully than a battle.

A few women used often to accompany these early Muslim raids, making themselves useful by preparing meals and by attending to the wounded in the event of a battle. When on an expedition outside Medina, the Messenger of God also normally took one of his wives with him. In the Beni Mustaliq raid, he had been accompanied by Aisha, the daughter of Abu Bekr. When the returning raiding party neared Medina, a halt was made in the evening and the men slept for the first part of the night. The march was resumed before dawn, while it was still dark. Before getting into her litter, Aisha walked a little way away in the dark for a certain purpose. When she returned to her camel, she noticed that she had lost a string of beads which had been round her neck and she went back in the dark to look for it.

When on the march, Aisha sat in her curtained litter, while a man led the camel by its halter. Imagining her to be inside the litter, the man had come and led the camel away with the remainder of the convoy. Aisha, having finally found her beads, returned to mount her camel, only to find that the whole party had moved off, and that she was alone in the desert. Imagining, according to her own account, that her absence would soon be noticed and that someone would come back for her, she wrapped herself in her cloak and lay down.

A young man called Safwan had been a member of the raiding party but had straggled behind the main body, and was now following the tracks of his comrades, returning to Medina. He presently came riding along when, to his amazement, he saw the Prophet's wife, alone in mid-desert. Making his camel kneel down, he told her to mount, while himself averting his gaze until she had settled herself in the saddle and arranged her clothing. He then took the head-rope of the camel and walked on ahead, leading it behind him.

It was already broad daylight when Aisha and her escort overtook the main body, the men of which saw with astonishment the arrival of the Apostle's young wife, alone with a young man. The ensuing scandal rocked Medina. The false Muslims shook their heads while other women, jealous of the Apostle's dearest wife, gave free rein to their gossip. Even the Messenger of God was suspicious and allowed Aisha to leave his house and go to stay with her father, Abu Bekr.

The Apostle of God held a consultation with the two young men of his household, Ali and Zaid ibn Haritha. Zaid defended Aisha's reputation, saying that all the gossip was mere idle lies. But Ali said, "Women are plentiful, and you can easily replace Aisha with another,

Ask her slave girl. She may tell you the truth." When the slave girl came, Ali hit her, saying, "Mind you tell the Apostle the truth." But with charming simplicity the maid replied, "I know only good of her. The only fault I have to find is that when I was kneading dough to make bread, I asked her to watch it for a minute, but she fell asleep and her pet lamb ate it all!"

Later the Messenger of God called on Abu Bekr and a painful scene ensued between him and Aisha and her father and mother. Muhammad called upon Aisha to confess if she had done wrong, for God accepted the repentance of sinners. But Aisha, in floods of tears, insisted that she had nothing to confess. At this moment, the Apostle felt the approach of a revelation. He lay down and was covered with a cloak, while a leather cushion was put under his head. Abu Bekr and his wife sat in tense anxiety, fearing that the Prophet might receive a revelation confirming the immoral charges directed against their daughter.

At last the Apostle of God stirred and sat up. He was perspiring profusely and began to mop the sweat which was running down his face. Then he looked up and said, "Good news, Aisha! God has sent down word that you are innocent." He then gave orders for three men, who were alleged to have circulated the scandal, each to be flogged with eighty lashes, one of them being the Apostle's chief poet, Hassan ibn Thabit.

Chapter XXIV of the Qoran, from verse 11 onwards, is believed to be the revelation which came down on this occasion.

"Surely they who brought out this lie are a party from among you . . . Every man of them shall have what wickedness he has deserved, and he among them who took the lead will suffer a terrible punishment.[7] If the believers who heard it, both men and women, had been well meaning, they would have said, 'This is an obvious lie. Why did they not bring four witnesses[8] of it? But since they brought no witnesses, they themselves are liars before God!'"

Aisha thereupon returned joyfully to the Apostle's family.

*   *   *

Early in 628, the Messenger of God dreamed that he had performed the pilgrimage to Mecca unopposed. He immediately

---

[7] Some believe the reference to be to Abdulla ibn Ubay, others to the poet, Hassan ibn Thabit.

[8] Henceforward, in Islam, a charge of adultery always required four eye-witnesses.

announced his intention of doing so and called upon his followers to accompany him.

Then, as now, there were two distinct types of pilgrimage to Mecca. The *haj*, or greater pilgrimage, could only be performed on a specified day of the year but *Omra*, the lesser pilgrimage, could be carried out at any time. It was this lesser pilgrimage which the Apostle now proposed to perform. It was Dhu al Qaada, the month preceding that of the greater pilgrimage. Both months, however, were months of truce according to the old dispensation, with the result that Quraish had in theory no right to oppose the Muslims by force.

Many of the Emigrants and Helpers prepared to accompany the Prophet but the greater part of the bedouins, even those who had professed Islam, hung back, presumably not wishing to become involved in battle. In an attempt to convince the Meccans of his peaceful intentions the Apostle of God himself donned the conventional garb of a pilgrim. He also brought with him seventy camels as sacrificial victims, hung with garlands as was the custom in such cases. The numbers of the Muslims accompanying the Messenger of God are variously reported as seven hundred or, more probably, fourteen hundred. Moreover, they are alleged to have been armed only with swords, as a further proof that they did not mean to fight. In any case, their strength would have been unequal to a pitched battle with Quraish.

Some western writers have nevertheless suggested that the Apostle did really intend to seize Mecca on this occasion. In weighing the possibility of this interpretation, we must remember the inability of the Meccans to attack the buildings of Medina. In the same manner, the Muslims themselves had been unable to capture by assault even the little Jewish settlements in their oasis. The same considerations would apply to any attempt to assault Mecca. The Prophet, as we have constantly seen, was no brutal fighter, ready to suffer heavy casualties to smash his way to victory. His only hope of taking Mecca was by winning over Quraish to his side. It appears possible also that contemporary standards of honour forbade an armed attack on buildings, in which women and children might be taking refuge.

When the Muslims reached Usfan, they received a report that Quraish had moved out to meet them, swearing that neither Muhammad nor his supporters would enter Mecca. A screen of horsemen covering their front was deployed only eight miles south of Usfan. The Messenger of God, realising that his men were not strong enough to fight, yet unwilling so easily to run back, asked for a guide to lead him round the flank of the Quraish position.

A local bedouin was found who conducted the convoy through narrow passes in the rocky hills until they emerged on open ground at Hudaibiya,[9] some eight miles west-north-west of Mecca. Here the Apostle gave orders to bivouac and the camels drank from a water-hole in the bed of a valley.

A leading man of Khuzaa, Budail ibn Waraqa, came to the Apostle to ask him his intentions. He was told that the Muslims had not come to fight but to make a pilgrimage to the Kaaba. These Khuzaa tribesmen, who lived on the coastal plain, were friendly to the Prophet, though many of them were still polytheists. Budail rode into Mecca and reported Muhammad's words to Quraish. "He may or may not want war," they replied, "but, by God, he is not going to enter Mecca against our will."

Quraish then sent a man called Hulais of Beni Kinana, to see what was happening. Seeing the apparently peaceful aspect of the Muslims and the seventy camels with their garlands, dressed for sacrifice, he returned to the Meccans and told them that these were genuine pilgrims. "Sit down, Hulais," they said contemptuously, "you are only a bedouin and don't understand anything."

Hulais was annoyed at this snub. He seems to have been the commander of the mercenaries, who guarded the caravans of Quraish. "It was not for this that we Beni Kinana made an alliance with you men of Quraish," he replied angrily. "Is a man who comes to honour God's house to be kept out by you?" "O keep quiet, Hulais," they answered. "We only want time to negotiate acceptable terms."

Quraish then sent a man, a resident of Mecca, of the tribe of Thaqeef, to see the Apostle. Sitting on the ground facing him, he said: "O Muhammad, have you collected a mixed crowd of people and brought them now to your own country to destroy your own people? Quraish are determined to fight and have sworn that you will never enter Mecca by force. If it comes to fighting, I can see you deserted by this motley crowd." "You can suck the breasts of Al Lat!" exclaimed Abu Bekr, rather coarsely, "we should never desert him."

[9] Map 6, p. 174.

In this scrap of dialogue, we see once again the echo of the profound revolution which the Prophet was attempting to introduce. The man of Thaqeef could not conceive any loyalty which would stand the strain of battle or disaster, except family loyalty. As Muhammad's supporters were of many different tribes, he imagined that a severe trial would produce disintegration.

The Messenger of God replied that he had not come to fight but to pay his respect to the Kaaba, the House of God. The Thaqafi thereupon remounted and returned to Mecca. Reporting on his mission to the leaders of Quraish, he said, "I have visited Chosroes, King of Persia, at his court, the Roman Caesar in Constantinople and the Negus of Abyssinia in his country, but never have I seen a king treated by his subjects with the veneration which Muhammad receives from his companions. I believe that these people will never forsake him for any reason whatsoever. So you can decide what to do on that assumption."

It is one of the principal difficulties facing the would-be historian that he is unable to conceive the extraordinary power and magnetism of great men whom he cannot see in the flesh. The triumphs of Alexander, Jenghis Khan or Napoleon Bonaparte can be analysed from the political, economic or military angle, but we can never know what quality each of these men possessed which made thousands of their fellow-men willing, even anxious, to die for them.

The Thaqafi's report to the Meccan leaders had been no exaggeration. Although the Apostle himself emphasised that he was only a man, his followers now accorded him a veneration almost amounting to deification. When his hair was cut, people scrambled for bits of it and preserved them as sacred relics. The parings of his fingernails were treasured with the same veneration as Christians accorded to the bones of mediaeval saints. After his death, many Muslims kept bits of his hair, which they asked should be buried with them at their deaths.

When the Prophet washed, enthusiastic devotees struggled to obtain the dirty water and to drink it. Even if he spat, records Ibn Ishaq, his companions ran to collect his spittle. The faithful had to be admonished not to crowd too closely round the Apostle when he appeared in public, but to allow room for people to breathe.

Yet he never, with all this veneration, agreed to wear a silk robe, or jewels or cloth of gold. When his wives complained that, now that money was available, their lives might be made a little more comfortable, they met with a severe rebuke.

* * *

After the departure of the Thaqafi, the Messenger of God sent Othman ibn Affan to negotiate with Quraish in Mecca. Othman was the most suitable go-between, because he was of the Beni Umaiya and a second cousin of Abu Sofian himself. With family loyalties so strong in Mecca, Othman would be safe, even if he came as Muhammad's messenger.

Quraish listened to what he had to say, and then told him that, if he wished, he could make the prescribed circumambulations round the Kaaba. They then decided to detain him in Mecca until they had decided what course of action to adopt.

As Mecca was only eight miles away, Othman had been expected to return in a few hours and his lengthening absence, with no word of explanation, caused the Muslims great anxiety. Then a rumour was circulated that Othman had been killed. If Quraish had really killed Othman, a cousin of Abu Sofian, in spite of their devotion to family loyalties, then indeed it was evident that they intended to stop at nothing.

In fact, the Meccans had at this moment their last opportunity to destroy Islam and Muhammad once and for all. The Apostle's idea of a pilgrimage had placed him at the mercy of his enemies, bivouacked as he was outside Mecca with only a small force, armed with nothing but swords. If Quraish had been led by a single, determined commander, they could have seized this priceless opportunity to end the struggle in a few hours. But, as had been proved after Uhud, the Quraish leaders were incapable of swift, determined action.

Nevertheless, the tension and anxiety among the Muslims at Hudaibiya were acute. The Prophet himself seems to have thought that a battle, with the odds against the Muslims, was inpending at any moment. He consequently called upon all those present to renew their oath of loyalty. Standing with his back to one of those thorny acacia trees which are to be seen here and there in these arid, rockstrewn mountains, he invited every man to come and swear. The Muslims filed past him one by one, each in turn giving him his hand and pledging his faith, as seven years before the pilgrims from Yathrib had done at the second Aqaba. The atmosphere was tense and all were keyed to the highest pitch of readiness for sacrifice. Only one man, according to Ibn Ishaq, dodged the oath by hiding behind his camel.

The exact wording of the oath is in doubt. It is conceivable that the Apostle had no intention of fighting and had already decided to make concessions, but feared that his more passionate followers would insist on a battle. We have seen on previous occasions that the Prophet was often more conciliatory than his followers. If this were the case, he may have asked for an oath of loyalty to ensure that they would not rebel against his orders.

The anxieties endured by the Muslims at Hudaibiya are empha-sised by the way in which those days of suspense remained etched on their memories. Many years after, when the Muslim armies had already built up a great empire, when veteran comrades spoke of the early days, the deepest respect was always shown to the men who had fought at Bedr and to those who had taken the oath at Hudaibiya—the two most tense crises of the rise of Islam.

Suddenly a camel-rider appeared, coming from the direction of Mecca. When he drew near, he was seen to be Suhail ibn Amr, a man known for his diplomatic gifts and his persuasive manner. "They want to make peace, seeing that they have sent this man," exclaimed the Apostle with intense relief. We have already met Suhail, a prisoner in the Apostle's house after Bedr, his hands tied behind his back.[10]

After a long discussion, terms of peace were concluded, and it was decided to draw up a formal document. The fiery Umar, however, who is always represented as advocating violence, drew Abu Bekr aside and said to him angrily, "Is he not the Apostle of God, are we not Muslims and are they not polytheists? Then why should we agree to a humiliating compromise?" "Do what he says," replied the dedicated Abu Bekr, who always defended everything done by Muhammad. "I bear witness that he is the Messenger of God."

Umar, however, was not satisfied and went to ask the Prophet the same question. "I am God's slave and his messenger," said Muhammad gently. "I will not go against His commandments and He will not allow me to be the loser."

Ali was then ordered to write the draft agreement. The Apostle began to dictate, "This is what Muhammad, the Apostle of God, has agreed with Suhail ibn Amr . . ." But Suhail interrupted, "If I

[10] Page 188.

witnessed that you were the Apostle of God, I would not have fought against you. Write your name and the name of your father." The Apostle turned patiently to Ali and said, "Write, 'This is what Muhammad the son of Abdulla agreed with Suhail the son of Amr'."

The terms laid down that a truce was established between the two sides for ten years, during which all men could move about in safety.

Secondly, if anyone from Mecca went over to Muhammad the Muslims would be obliged to send him back, but if any of Muhammad's people deserted him and returned to Mecca, they would not be forced to go back to Medina.

Thirdly, any tribes who wished to enter into an agreement with Muhammad were entitled to do so, while such tribes as so desired were free to make an alliance with Quraish. Under these circumstances, the tribes concerned would be deemed to be covered by the ten-year truce.

Fourthly, the Muslims were now to return to Medina but the following year they would be free to make an Omra pilgrimage to the Kaaba, remain three days in Mecca and then withdraw. The Muslims were, on that occasion, to be armed only with swords.

*　　*　　*

The Muslims were plunged into the most profound depression and bewilderment by these terms. It will be remembered that the ostensible reason for the whole operation had been the Apostle's dream that he was performing the pilgrimage unopposed. Believing this dream to have been sent by God, they had confidently expected it to happen.

Now the terms of the agreement seemed to them to spell complete victory for Quraish. Ten years of peace would enable the Meccans to re-establish their caravan trade to its former prosperity. The Apostle was already fifty-eight years old, and was unlikely to live for another ten years. The paragraph which stipulated that Meccans who wished to join Muhammad were to be handed back, while any of his followers who deserted to Mecca need not be returned, seemed particularly humiliating.

As if to rub salt into the wound, while the document was being signed, Abu Jandal, the young son of Suhail ibn Amr, arrived from Mecca, hobbling along as best he could with fetters on his legs. He wished to become a Muslim and had been put in chains by his family but had escaped. When Suhail saw his son, he went up to him and struck him in the face. Attention has already been drawn to the fact that many of the Muslim converts were young men, whose fathers were fighting for Quraish.

"Muhammad," cried Suhail, "our agreement was concluded before this man came to join you." The Apostle admitted the truth of this claim, and Suhail seized his son by the collar and began to drag him away. "Am I to be sent back to the polytheists that they may entice me away from my religion, O fellow Muslims?" shrieked the young man. The humiliating sight of a Muslim being forcibly dragged away to be imprisoned for his religion was almost more than the men could bear. "O Abu Jandal," intervened the Apostle of God, "be patient and God will find a way out."

As the youth was led away, Umar walked a few paces beside him and whispered in his ear, "They are only polytheists. The blood of one of them is but the blood of a dog." At the same time he held out the hilt of his sword. "I was hoping that he would snatch my sword and kill his father," Umar used to say afterwards when narrating the incident. But Abu Jandal found his own way out of his trouble, as we shall see in the next chapter.

NOTABLE DATES

The Siege of Medina	March–April 627
Extermination of Beni Quraidha	April 627
Beni Lihyan raid	October 627
Ghatafan raid on the Apostle's camels	October or November 627
Beni Mustaliq raid	December 627 or January 628
Truce of Hudaibiya	March 628

PERSONALITIES

Muslims

Othman ibn Affan, the Prophet's emissary to Quraish

Women

Aisha, daughter of Abu Bekr, victim of the scandal of the Beni Mustaliq raid

Juwairiya, daughter of the Beni Mustaliq chief, married to
the Apostle of God

Idolaters

Budail ibn Waraqa, a shaikh of Khuzaa
Suhail ibn Amr, negotiator on behalf of Mecca, of the Truce
of Hudaibiya
Abu Jandal ibn Suhail, his son

XIV

Kheibar and Mota

Mahomet's conciliatory diplomacy recorded a new success which put an end to complaints. He diverted the martial ardour of his people against the Kheibar Jews.

EMILE DERMENGHEM, *The Life of Mahomet*

Welcome, Paradise, so near,
Sweet and cool to drink its cheer.
Greeks will soon have much to fear
Infidels, of descent unclear,
When we meet their necks I'll shear.

JAAFAR IBN ABI TALIB [on the way to
Mota, where he was killed]

The Messenger of God was asked who was the most deserving of men. He replied, "It is the believer who fights in the way of God, expending himself and his goods."

BUKHARI, *The True Traditions*

XIV

NO sooner had Suhail ibn Amr left for Mecca, dragging his unwilling son, than the Apostle gave orders for the slaughter of the sacrificial camels and for the men to shave their heads. These were parts of the ritual of pilgrimage, which should have been performed in Mecca. But as Mecca was unattainable, they did the best they could at Hudaibiya. The whole party then loaded up their possessions and set out for Medina in a state of gloomy depression.

Halfway back to Medina, Chapter XLVIII of the Qoran was revealed. It began with the unexpected declaration,

"We have indeed given you a manifest victory."

Verse 10 is believed to refer to the oath taken beneath the tree at Hudaibiya.

"Those who swear allegiance to you most certainly swear allegiance to God—God's hand is over their hands. He who breaks his oath, breaks it to his own harm and he who fulfils his pledge will receive from God a great reward."

Verse 11 goes on to blame the tribes for not having accompanied the Apostle on the expedition to Hudaibiya.

"Those of the tribes who stayed behind will say to you, 'Our flocks and our families kept us busy, so ask pardon of God on our behalf'. They say things with their tongues which are not the same as the thoughts of their hearts."

Verse 12 even accuses the tribes of secret hostility to the Apostle.

"The fact is that you thought that the Apostle and the believers would never return to their homes and this possibility was pleasing to your hearts, and you thought evil thoughts."

Verse 18 returns once more to the oath.

"Surely God was pleased with the believers when they swore allegiance to you beneath the tree."

A number of commentators have pointed out (being wise after the event) that the peace of Hudaibiya actually benefited the Muslims more than a military victory. The believers who were present completely failed to realise this possibility and regarded the whole affair as a humiliating defeat. In practice, however, peace and security enabled the unbelievers to mix freely with the Muslims, with the result that conversions actually increased greatly in number.

Whether the Messenger of God fully realised that this would happen cannot now be known, but it is probable that something of the kind was in his mind. We have frequently seen that he was not a man of war and that he disliked fighting. But he had come to realise as a result of experience, that he was an extremely persuasive proselytiser. Would not free conditions of peace and security afford him a clearer field for making conversions than was obtainable in war time?

These questions make it appear doubtful whether the war against Quraish and the capture of their caravans had not been a mistake from the very beginning. The message of Islam produced so deep an effect on the minds of the polytheistic Arabs that they might well have been more rapidly converted by preaching alone, if fighting had not kindled their tribal loyalties and inspired their desire for revenge. For loyalty to family and clan was probably much stronger than any feeling for the Meccan pantheon.

*　　　*　　　*

When the Apostle arrived back in Medina, a young man called Abu Baseer came to him. He had escaped from Mecca in order to become a Muslim. Hot on his tracks, however, were two Meccans with a letter to the Prophet asking for his return under the Hudaibiya agreement. The Apostle was obliged to hand him over to the escort. Seven miles south of Medina, however, the prisoner turned on his guards, killing one while the other ran away. He then returned to Medina. "What a man!" exclaimed the Prophet. "If there had been some companions with him he would have started a war!"

Abu Baseer went off alone to the Wadi al Ais, west of Medina. The Apostle's enigmatic remark was interpreted by a number of young men detained by their relatives in Mecca to mean that he wished that Abu Baseer had had more men. One after another, would-be Muslims began to slip away from Mecca, but they did not

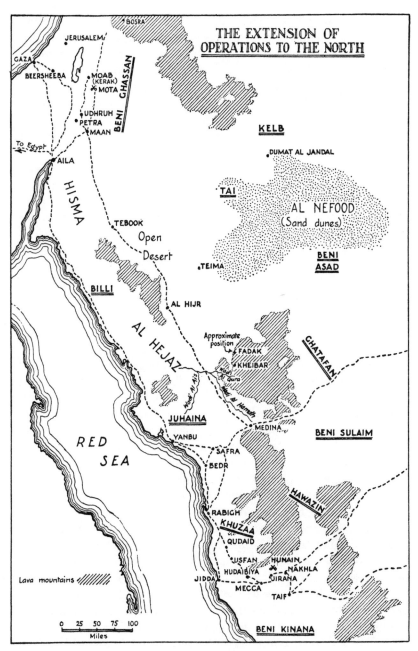

THE EXTENSION OF
OPERATIONS TO THE NORTH

BOSRA

JERUSALEM

GAZA

BEERSHEEBA

MOAB
(KERAK)
MOTA

BENI GHASSAN

KELB

UDHRUH
PETRA
MAAN

To Egypt

DUMAT AL JANDAL

AILA

HISMA

TAI

AL NEFOOD
(Sand dunes)

TEBOOK

Open
Desert

TEIMA

BENI
ASAD

BILLI

AL HIJR

AL HEJAZ

Approximate
position
FADAK

KHEIBAR

GHATAFAN

Wadi
Al Qura

Wadi Al Hamdh

JUHAINA

YANBU

MEDINA

BENI SULAIM

RED
SEA

SAFRA

BEDR

HAWAZIN

RABIGH

KHUZAA

QUDAID

USFAN
HUDAIBIYA
JIDDA

HUNAIN
NAKHLA
JIRANA

Lava mountains

MECCA

TAIF

0 25 50 75 100
Miles

BENI KINANA

MAP 10

go to the Apostle. They joined Abu Baseer in the Wadi al Ais. Soon he had collected a gang of seventy and proceeded to cut the Quraish caravan route to Syria. Eventually the Meccan leaders wrote to the Messenger of God, begging him to accept these Muslim converts in Medina and stop them from robbing Meccan merchants!

A number of women also escaped from Mecca and came to the Apostle of God. When, however, their relatives quoted the agreement of Hudaibiya to ask for their extradition, Chapter LX of the Qoran came down.

Verse 10 says, "O you who believe, if believing women come to you who have emigrated, examine them. God knows best about their belief. If you discover that they are believers, do not return them to the heathen. For they are no longer lawful wives for the heathen nor the heathen lawful husbands for them. So send the husbands whatever they spent on them,[1] after which it will not be a crime for you to marry them." As a result, the Apostle informed the Meccans that the extradition clause in the Hudaibiya agreement did not apply to women.

*   *   *

After his return from Hudaibiya, the Messenger of God stayed for only about ten weeks in Medina. Then, in September 628, he announced his intention to attack Kheibar, an oasis seventy-five miles north of Medina, which was also inhabited by Jews. These Kheibar Jews, like those of Medina, seem to have been completely Arab in their names, their customs and their language. It would seem probable that they too were ethnically Arabs, converted by Jewish missionaries, perhaps some centuries earlier.

Anticipating valuable booty from the expedition, many eager volunteers came forward in answer to the Prophet's summons. Some accounts state that the Apostle would only accept men who had been at Hudaibiya. Waqidi, however, says that he sent a crier round Medina to announce that persons whose only object was plunder would not be allowed to join the force. Whatever were the exact words used, it appears that the attack on Kheibar was looked upon as compensation for the disappointments of Hudaibiya. In passing, it is interesting to note that there were still Jews in Medina as Waqidi reports their sympathy with their co-religionists in Kheibar.

[1] Their marriage dowries.

When the Muslim raiders topped the last pass through the mountains and looked down on the green oasis with its gardens of palm trees, the Apostle halted and prayed in a loud voice: "O God, we ask Thee for the good of this village and the good of its people and the good of what is in it, and we take refuge in Thee from its evil and the evil that is in it." Then he said, "Forward, with God's blessing".

The people of Kheibar, like those of Medina, made their living by agriculture, particularly from date palms. Even today, the tribes have a saying, "To take dates for sale to the people of Kheibar", which means the same as our expression, "To carry coals to Newcastle". Kheibar was said to be the richest oasis in the Hejaz. As in Medina, each clan had its own separate settlement and fort. This situation enabled the Muslims to attack one fort after another. These fortified homesteads were doubtless adequate to keep night marauders at bay, but they were insufficient to repel a regular attack. Moreover, according to Waqidi, a number of Jews came over to the Muslims. Among others, a Jew informed the Apostle of the existence of a mangonel[2] in one of the forts. When this fort was taken, the mangonel was erected and used against the other castles.

The Jews of Kheibar did not normally take part in the tribal wars of the Arabs but relied on their neutrality and on the protection of their bedouin allies, chief of whom were Ghatafan. It will be remembered that it was these Jews who had persuaded Ghatafan to join Quraish in the siege of Medina.

On the present occasion, the chief of Ghatafan, Uyaina ibn Hisn, answered the appeal of his Jewish allies for help and manned some of their forts. But after a few days, the tribesmen heard that their own homes were in danger. (Waqidi says they heard a voice from heaven or from the earth warning them.) As a result, they left Kheibar and hastened home.

Kheibar offered a more vigorous resistance than the Jews of Medina. A number of Jewish warriors came out of the forts and defied the Muslims to meet them in single combat. This seems to be the only occasion on which Jewish champions challenged the Muslims.

The length of the operations resulted in a serious shortage of food among the Muslims. One day, however, they captured a flock of twenty donkeys, which the men joyfully slaughtered and cut up. Fires were hastily lighted and rows of cooking pots were soon boiling

[2] The mangonel was the siege artillery of the time. A long pole which, when bent backwards and released, threw rocks at the walls of a fort.

with fragrant stew. At this moment, however, the Apostle happened to pass by and asked what was being cooked. On hearing that it was donkey meat, he called Bilal the Negro, and ordered him to cry throughout the bivouac that donkey meat was forbidden. Within a minute all the pots were overturned and the Muslims remained without their dinner.

By contrast, however, the Prophet permitted the slaughter of horses, which enabled some of the men to enjoy a solid meal. Horses were, as we have seen, both extremely rare and very highly prized in war, so few men were willing to use them as food. Soon afterwards, however, one of the forts captured was found to be well stocked with barley, dates, oil and honey. Thereafter adequate rations were available in the Muslim bivouac.

For a long time, none of the numerous forts surrendered without fighting. The average period necessary to attack and capture each one appears to have been about three days. Nevertheless, there could only be one end to such a contest, for the different clans, isolated each in its own little fortress, were unable to assist one another. The whole force of the Muslims was able to attack and capture each fort in turn. On one occasion, an arrow shot from the walls of a tower passed through the Apostle's clothing without wounding him.

At length only three forts were left, but these appeared to be the strongest yet encountered. When they had been besieged for fourteen days, they asked for terms. Kinana ibn abi al Huqaiq, the surviving Jewish leader, was the grandson of the chief, Sallam ibn abi al Huqaiq, who had previously been assassinated by the Muslims. Receiving safe conduct, he emerged from his fort and came to the Messenger of God and agreed that the Jews would surrender all their possessions to him, in return for their lives.

Weapons, clothing and foodstuffs were handed over in large quantities but Kinana denied the existence of treasure in the form of silver or gold, claiming that all their capital had been expended in preparing for the war. However, a cousin of Kinana told the Apostle to search in some ruined buildings. Guided by the Jewish informer, the Muslims discovered some of the buried treasure. The Prophet, thereupon, gave orders that Kinana be tortured and finally executed.

One of the women captured in the settlement was Safiya, daughter of that Huyai ibn Akhtab who had been executed with Beni Quraidha. She was married to Kinana ibn abi al Huqaiq. Her father, her brother and now her husband, had been killed by the Muslims. She and another woman were led out of one of the captured forts to where the Apostle was waiting. He chose Safiya for himself, throwing his cloak over her shoulders to show that he had taken her. She agreed to profess Islam and the Prophet married her shortly afterwards in a tent in the oasis.

A few days later, the Apostle found Safiya in tears. When he asked her the reason, she replied that his other wives mocked her, calling her Jewess. The Messenger of God was angry. "Tell me if they are unkind to you again," he said, "for Aaron was my father, and Moses my uncle," acknowledging once again his debt to the "religion of Abraham".

When the fighting was over, a Jewess called Zainab invited the Apostle to dinner. It is said that she had enquired what portion of a roast sheep he liked best and had been told that it was the shoulder. She accordingly slaughtered and roasted a lamb, inserting a dose of poison in the shoulder. The Messenger of God took a mouthful of meat from the shoulder but spat it out before swallowing it, saying that he believed it to be poisoned.

He called for Zainab, who readily admitted the accusation. She excused herself by saying, "You know what you have done to my people. I said to myself that if you were just a tribal chief, we should get rid of you, but that if you were a prophet you would know what I had done." According to Ibn Ishaq, the Apostle gave her a free pardon.

A man from Medina, who was sitting beside him, swallowed a mouthful of the meat and died shortly afterwards. When Muhammad himself died three years later, he attributed the agonies of his last illness to the Jewess's poison, thereby winning for himself the title of martyr, as having been killed by an unbeliever.

When all was settled, the Jews came to the Apostle and asked him if they could continue to cultivate their lands if they paid half the annual produce to the Muslims. He agreed to their proposal, on condition that the Muslims retained the right to expel them at will. In fact, the Prophet would have been unable to spare Muslims to settle in Kheibar.

Meanwhile, the people of Fadak, who were also Jews, having sent a messenger to the Apostle to negotiate with him, he agreed to the same terms for them as for Kheibar. The agreement with Fadak was extremely favourable to the Prophet. As there had been no fighting, the rank and file were not entitled to a share of the plunder. All the booty, therefore, became the property of the treasury. This meant that the Apostle himself disposed of it as he thought best.

A number of orders issued while the Kheibar operation was in progress subsequently became part of the Muslim code.

To take women from a defeated enemy and use them as slaves or concubines was already permitted. At Kheibar, however, it was ordained that such women, if they were pregnant when captured, were not to be used as concubines until after they had given birth.

A problem which constantly demanded active supervision was the prevention of the Muslims from keeping portions of the booty which they had themselves taken, instead of handing it in to the common stock to be equally divided between the whole force. At Kheibar, a new form of such dodging drew a prohibition. Some men, it appeared, would capture an animal, ride it themselves until it was exhausted and then hand it into the common pool. Or they would take a garment from an enemy, wear it until it was threadbare and then surrender it.

The spoils of Kheibar proved to be the richest which God had as yet bestowed upon the believers. Moreover, the oasis was in future to pay half its annual produce to the Muslims, thereby giving them a permanent income. Hitherto the usual plunder of war had consisted of clothing, weapons, camels or money.

The booty taken in the campaign was divided between the men who had taken the oath at Hudaibiya, all but one of whom had accompanied the Apostle to Kheibar. This procedure seems to confirm that one motive at least of the expedition against Kheibar was to compensate the men who had been disappointed by the result of Hudaibiya. The booty of Kheibar was divided into one thousand and eight hundred shares between one thousand and four hundred men. Two hundred of the one thousand four hundred were horsemen, who received three shares, one for themselves and two for the horse. The fact that at Kheibar the Muslims had two hundred horses gives some idea of the improvement in their resources. At Uhud they had only one horse. Sixteen Muslims achieved the happiness of martyrdom at Kheibar.

On completion of the division of the spoils of Kheibar, the Apostle went on and took Wadi al Qura, a smaller oasis near by, also inhabited by Jews.

*   *   *

A number of the early Muslims, who had emigrated from Mecca to Abyssinia in 615 to escape persecution, had settled down in that country. The Apostle had sent a messenger to the Negus asking him to facilitate their return. A party of sixteen men, some of whom had wives and children with them, accepted the invitation, crossed the Red Sea in two Abyssinian vessels and joined the Messenger of God while he was besieging Kheibar. They had been in Abyssinia for thirteen years. Seven men had died in Africa and a further thirty-four ultimately returned to Arabia. Many of these had children born to them in Abyssinia by their Arab wives, who had accompanied them. There does not seem to be any record of any of them marrying Abyssinians. The most notable of those who returned from Abyssinia and joined the Apostle in Kheibar was Jaafar ibn abi Talib, the brother of Ali.[3]

One of the women who returned at this time was a daughter of Abu Sofian, the leader of the idolaters in Mecca. Her husband had died in Abyssinia and she returned as a widow. On her arrival, she was married to the Prophet. If it be true that the Negus sent a handsome dowry with her, it must be assumed that Muhammad's messenger to the Negus carried a proposal of marriage with him and that Umm Habeeba came back with the avowed object of marrying the Apostle.

* * *

In February 629, the year after the signature of the truce of Hudaibiya, the Messenger of God set out to accomplish the lesser pilgrimage, according to the terms of the agreement. Estimates of the number of Muslims who accompanied him vary from twelve hundred to two thousand—not many more than he had had at Hudaibiya. Presumably the nomadic tribes, though some were his allies and others had accepted Islam, still held back from an expedition which might give rise to a battle against Quraish

According to the terms of the Hudaibiya agreement, the people of Mecca evacuated the town and camped on the surrounding mountains from which they could observe all that occurred in the valley below. Whether this action was taken to avoid clashes in the town or, on the contrary, because the leaders of Quraish feared that the Meccans would fraternise with the enemy, is not recorded.

At dawn, from their camps and bivouacs on the surrounding hills,

[3] Genealogical tree, p. 120.

the people of Mecca saw a column of dust rising into the air above the valley to the north through which passed the track coming from Medina. At length, the head of the Muslim convoy came into sight. The Apostle himself was in the lead, riding a camel and surrounded by a group of his intimate companions, including Ali, Abu Bekr and Umar ibn al Khattab. Sixty decorated camels prepared for sacrifice accompanied the party. Behind the Messenger of God and his principal supporters, a great cloud of dust marked the advance of his followers.

Ever since the Apostle had migrated to Medina seven years earlier, his uncle Abbas had remained in Mecca. We have seen that he had been taken prisoner at Bedr fighting for the polytheists, and the Prophet had obliged him to pay his ransom. It is alleged that, before Uhud, he had sent a secret message to his nephew, warning him of the intentions of Quraish. In other words, he appears to have shown some skill in simultaneously running with the hare and hunting with the hounds.

Other accounts, however, depict him as a Muslim convert, who had remained in Mecca to assist the interests of his brother's son. A hundred and twenty years later, the descendants of Abbas were to become the world's greatest emperors by usurping power over the vast Arab Empire, which by then extended from Spain and Morocco to the borders of China. Most of the early Muslim historians whose work survives to this day lived when the descendants of Abbas were in power, and when to accuse him of having been an intriguer would have been dangerous.

However that may be, the probabilities are that Abbas had hitherto been an idolater, but that at this stage he decided that his nephew was going to win. He accordingly did not withdraw with the other leaders of Quraish to the mountains, but welcomed his nephew cordially and informed him that he had prepared a bride for him. She was a widow by the name of Maimoona, the sister of Abbas's own wife. It seems likely that it was on this occasion that Abbas professed Islam and only thereafter did he act as Muhammad's secret agent in Mecca.

Entering the town, the Apostle went straight to the Kaaba, touched the black stone and made the seven ritual circumambulations of the temple.

When the Messenger of God had been three days in Mecca, a message came to him from the leaders of Quraish, reminding him that, according to the agreement of Hudaibiya, he was only to remain three days in the town. They now warned him curtly that the time was up and that he could get out. Muhammad replied, apparently in a conciliatory tone, "What harm would it do you if you were to allow me to stay until I could give a wedding party to which you could all come." But the emissary of the Meccan leaders answered rudely, "We don't want your food, so get out of this." As the Hudaibiya agreement had been specific concerning the right of the Muslims to remain only three days in Mecca, the Apostle was obliged to give the order for the return march to Medina.

While the set-back suffered at Hudaibiya a year before had seemed to the Muslims at the time to be a disastrous defeat, it now gradually began to appear that the idea of a Muslim pilgrimage to Mecca had been a stroke of genius. Perhaps Hudaibiya had been premature and for a few days the Muslims had exposed themselves to a devastating military disaster. But the Meccan leaders possessed neither the unity, the authority, nor the determination to seize a fleeting military opportunity.

The pilgrimage of the year 629 was, however, a long step forward towards the ultimate triumph of the Muslims. To begin with, much of the opposition to the Prophet in Mecca had been due to the belief that his new religion would discredit the Kaaba and do great injury to the interests of Quraish, as the guardians of that venerated shrine. Moreover, there was the fact that the local fairs at the time of the pilgrimages enabled the merchants of the town to do profitable business. By himself coming on pilgrimage, kissing the black stone and performing the seven traditional circuits of the Kaaba, the Apostle had shown that his religion did not foreshadow any reduction in the sanctity of Mecca.

As we have already seen, what might be called the rehabilitation of Mecca had already begun when, after his breach with the Jews, the Apostle had changed the *Qibla*, or direction of prayer, from Jerusalem to Mecca. The explanation given had been to the effect that the Kaaba had been built by Abraham. The well of Zemzem, in the courtyard of the Kaaba, was the spring which the Archangel Gabriel opened for Hagar and her son Ishmael, who were dying of thirst in the desert.[4] Ishmael had assisted the Patriarch Abraham in building the Kaaba.[5]

[4] Genesis XXI, 16 to 19.

[5] The selection of Abraham as the alleged founder of Islam is interesting, for the patriarch was traditionally the common ancestor of Jews and Arabs. Though venerated by Jews and Christians, he had himself been neither a Jew nor a Christian by religion.

The change of attitude towards Mecca which had followed the refusal of the Jews to join the new faith had paved the way for a complete change in the relationship between Muhammad and the Meccans. The importance of this revolution had been obscured by the hatreds roused by Bedr, Uhud and the siege of Medina. But once a truce was negotiated at Hudaibiya, the new relationship gradually permeated the minds of the Meccans, especially when the Muslim pilgrimage of 629 gave them an ocular demonstration of the respect which the Apostle entertained for the Kaaba and the ancient ritual.

After the gradual realisation of this changed relationship, the Meccans slowly became aware of a second factor. Muhammad was held in profound veneration by his followers, whose wealth and power were constantly expanding. He now not only held Medina, but the oases of Kheibar, Wadi al Qura and Fadak and their revenues. Two hundred horsemen, as many as the Meccans could raise, had accompanied the Apostle on his pilgrimage. If he were on the way to become a powerful king, would it not be better to invite him to make Mecca the capital of his empire and to employ his cousins of Quraish in positions of authority?

We must not, however, analyse the motives of the Meccans in a modern spirit, on the basis of financial or political interest alone. The principal leaders of Quraish may have been swayed by such motives but the bulk of the population were less materialistic. The religion which the Apostle was preaching was far superior to their own superstitions. Moreover, the Arabs, though endlessly insubordinate to authority, are firm hero-worshippers, when they find a man whom they consider worthy of respect. We have already seen what charm Muhammad could deploy to win men.

*   *   *

One of the most striking examples of the swing of popular opinion at this time was the arrival of Khalid ibn al Waleed, Amr ibn al Aasi and Othman ibn Talha in Medina. Khalid was the nephew of Maimoona, the Prophet's latest bride. Perhaps her influential connections made her a desirable match, rather than her personal attractions, for she was by no means young. Khalid and Amr had been responsible for the victory of Quraish at Uhud, by leading the mounted charge round the left flank and on to the rear of the believers. Both were to become great military commanders for the Muslims.

Othman ibn Talha was not so gifted as his two companions but he was the hereditary custodian of the keys of the Kaaba. The desertion of three such prominent men must have deeply impressed the Meccans.

* * *

In September 629, six months after the pilgrimage, the first clash occurred between the Muslims and the outside world. The Messenger of God had sent a letter to one of the princes of Beni Ghassan, who appears to have been the governor of Bosra[6] in Syria. It is not clear whether the person in question received the letter or, if he did so, what reply he gave. It appears, however, that the messenger was set upon and killed on his way home, some say by the local tribes, others by order of another member of Beni Ghassan. We have already seen that the dynasty had lost its supreme position as kings of eastern Syria, but that different members of the family had remained as local chiefs or governors in various districts. The murder of Muhammad's emissary must have occurred in what is now the state of Jordan.

The murder of an envoy, who comes peaceably bearing a letter, has always been regarded as a gross affront. The Apostle decided on a punitive expedition and a force of three thousand men was organised in Medina. It is possible that he visualised the operation as a mere raid on the tribes who had murdered his emissary, a purpose for which three thousand men would normally have been ample.

The Prophet's "son", Zaid ibn Haritha, was placed in command.[7] Jaafar ibn abi Talib, the brother of Ali, recently returned from Abyssinia, was named second-in-command, with the duty of taking charge if Zaid were killed. Abdulla ibn Rawáha, a Helper of Medina, was nominated third.

The force moved out of Medina, accompanied by the Messenger of God himself, on the first day's journey. Then, after long and in some cases tearful farewells, they tore themselves away from their fellow-Muslims and set their faces to the north.

In Arabia it was virtually impossible to keep secret the departure

---

[6] Sixty-five miles south of Damascus.

[7] It will be remembered that Zaid had been considered to be the Apostle's adopted son, prior to the incident of his divorce of his wife, Zainab.

of three thousand men on a raid. It must be remembered that no such thing as an army existed, nor was there anything in the nature of an establishment of officers or other ranks. In the simple communities of Arabia, every man was automatically a fighter.

When the chief of a tribe, or in this case the Apostle, ordered a raid, the word had to be passed round to all the men of the community. Each man had to provide himself with a horse or camel, or arrange to share a camel with a friend or relative, for a camel could carry two. Every man had also to provide himself with food for the campaign, for there was no organisation for the transport and issue of rations. Each man would also require a good water-skin, perhaps two, and his weapons, sword, lance, and bow and arrows. All this kept the whole community in a bustle of activity, speculation and rumour for a considerable time, perhaps two or three weeks. During this period, casual travellers, merchants or bedouins inevitably carried news of the preparations to the intended victims.

This process occurred in the present instance and the people and tribes of eastern Syria received ample notice of what was afoot. It is probable that Beni Ghassan organised the local tribes of what is now Jordan to enable them to resist. The rendezvous seems to have been in the neighbourhood of the modern town of Kerak, still at that time called by the local Arabs, Maab, the biblical Moab.

The campaign was to end in a disastrous defeat for the Muslims, to account for which Ibn Ishaq gives the enemy a hundred thousand Greek troops and another hundred thousand Arab tribesmen. Such numbers are impossible in such a terrain, where water is scarce even for a small raiding party. The bulk of the enemy probably consisted of four or five thousand Arab tribesmen, perhaps stiffened by a regiment of soldiers or local auxiliaries.

When they reached Maan,[8] the Muslims heard of the forces assembled around Kerak for their reception. They halted for two days in Maan to decide on what course to pursue. The majority were in favour of remaining in Maan and reporting back to the Apostle in Medina, telling him of the enemy preparations and asking for his orders. The distance to Medina, however, was nearly six hundred miles. For a camel-rider to make such a journey and return, allowing a few days for discussions in Medina and the drafting of a reply, might take more than a month.

The Muslims, however, could have remained in the vicinity for

[8] Map 10, p. 279.

several weeks, moving about here and there for fresh grazing. They might even have conquered the tribes between Maan and Teima and obliged them to swear allegiance. If the enemy had moved south of Maan, their effectiveness would have been greatly reduced by desert conditions and no Byzantine troops could have accompanied them. Thus a battle south of Maan would probably have been won by the Muslims.

It was Abdulla ibn Rawaha, the Helper, who turned the scale in favour of an immediate advance. Abdulla was a passionate enthusiast, and a devoted follower of the Apostle. "O men," he cried, "you seem now to be afraid of the one thing which you came out to seek—martyrdom. We are not fighting the enemy in our own strength or with numbers of men, but with the religion of God. Only two prospects confront us, victory or martyrdom, and both are equally glorious!" Stirred by these inspiring words, the Muslims unanimously voted for an immediate advance against the enemy.

The first contact was apparently made on the ridge of the mountains east of Moab. After a skirmish, the Muslims withdrew a few miles to a village called Mota, which still exists under the same name. The withdrawal was probably due to the fact that the ridge of these stony hills was intersected by narrow gorges and broken ground, whereas Mota is on a small open plain, large enough to allow the deployment of several thousand men.

The Arab battles of those days, as we have seen, were chivalrous contests in which the two sides drew up opposite one another. The sole task of the commander was to be the first in the fight, either by stepping forward and challenging the enemy to single combat, or by leading the charge, carrying the war banner. As no reserves were held back and no tactical manoeuvres were envisaged, the commander had nothing to do but to set an example of heroism.

In accordance with these principles, Zaid ibn Haritha took the war banner, which the Prophet with his own hands had entrusted to him, and charged straight into the enemy's ranks. He fell in the mêlée, pierced by their spears, the white banner falling to the ground. Jaafar ibn abi Talib was close behind and, snatching up the banner, raised it once more crying, "Paradise, O Muslims, Paradise" The enemy closed in round the heroic Jaafar. Tradition relates that when both his hands were cut off holding the staff of the banner, he still kept it erect by clasping it between his two stumps until he also, covered with wounds, received a mortal thrust from a Byzantine soldier.

The next in seniority was the Helper, Abdulla ibn Rawaha. One tradition later alleged that Abdulla hesitated for a moment before he rushed into the fight. Ibn Ishaq makes him recite a poem at this moment of decision.

> I swear, O soul, that thou shalt face this
> battle,
> You must now fight and to this honour rise.
> 'Midst shouts and din and dying men's deadly
> rattle;
> What? Falter at the gates of Paradise?

Looking around him, he saw the Muslim ranks already in confusion. He dismounted from his horse and a cousin came up to him with a piece of meat saying. "Have something to eat to keep your strength up." He ate a few mouthfuls, then threw the rest away. "Are you still alive?" he is said to have asked himself, and, snatching up the banner, he ran into the thick of the fight and fell covered with wounds.

The Muslims were now in considerable disorder and began to fall back. The newly converted Khalid ibn al Waleed, one of the best war leaders of Quraish, who had led the flank attack at Uhud, was fighting in the ranks. Perhaps a less passionate Muslim than Zaid or Jaafar, he was a more experienced commander than either. Seeing the battle to be irretrievably lost, he rallied the remnant of the Muslims and succeeded in withdrawing them from the field.

Such is the dramatic official account of the Battle of Mota. The extraordinary fact is, however, that, having been stirred by this heroic story, we find that Ibn Ishaq reports only eight Muslims to have been killed. The biggest casualty list reported by any historian is fourteen dead, out of an army of three thousand. Were the Muslims in fact, seized by panic at the sight of the enemy, including perhaps a few Byzantine soldiers? Did the historians attempt to gloss over something disgraceful by concentrating on the heroism of the three leaders, all of whom were killed?

The point is of interest because, a few years later, the Muslims were again and again to defeat the regular and highly trained armies of Byzantium.

The theory that Mota was in reality a disgraceful episode receives some support from the fact that, when the defeated Muslim column returned to Medina, the people threw dirt at them and shouted, "You runaways, you fled in the way of God!" If Mota had been a heroic incident, why were the men pelted with dirt when they got home?

The Apostle was obliged to intervene to rescue his own warriors. "No, they are not runaways but come-agains, if God wills," he cried, with that kind paternalism with which he won so many hearts. Going to Jaafar's house, he hugged and kissed his children with tears in his eyes. Then he went to the house of his "son", Zaid ibn Haritha, whose little daughter rushed weeping into his arms, making the Apostle himself burst into tears.

In the mosque next morning, Muhammad announced that he had seen the martyrs of Mota, reclining on rich couches in the gardens of Paradise. He particularly mentioned Jaafar, the son of Abu Talib, who had appeared to him in the guise of an angel, with two wings stained a deep red with the blood of maryrdom. Ever since the Apostle's vision, Jaafar has been called, in Muslim tradition, Jaafar al Tayyár, Jaafar the Flyer.

*   *   *

We have already seen that the Messenger of God claimed that it was his mission to restore the religion of Abraham. He had hoped for Jewish support in this task and had declared Jerusalem to be the Holy City towards which prayer should be made. He used many Old Testament stories to illustrate his theses and adopted Prayer, Fasting and Alms as the cornerstones of his religious rites, as the Jews had done. Many of the revelations which he received were couched in a style similar to passages in the Old Testament. The rules which he promulgated on the subject of food were similar to those observed by the Jews.

After the migration to Medina, however, the Apostle changed a number of these rules, notably those concerned with praying towards Jerusalem, Sabbath observance and the annual fast, in order to make them differ from Jewish practice. The separation between the Muslims and the Jews, however, was not due to divergences over religious dogma. Except only for the rejection of Muhammad as the Messiah, Judaism closely resembled Islam. The breach was due to the fact that the Jews of Medina insisted on pouring ridicule on the Prophet and on trying to make him and his message appear to be absurd. The messenger of God virtually eliminated the Jews of Medina, because their activities were doing injury to his mission.

Once he had established unquestioned authority over the Hejaz, however, he did not persecute them, and Jews continued to live in the area unmolested until they were evicted by Umar, after the Apostle's death. It is interesting to note that, once the Jews ceased to be a danger to the survival of Islam, the two faiths once again became allies against Christianity and were to remain so until the rise of Zionism in the twentieth century. It is interesting to speculate whether the time-honoured friendship between Judaism and Islam is to be attributed more to political causes or to the basic similarity of their faiths.

*   *   *

The early history of the relationship between Islam and Christianity is, in some ways, the opposite of that between the Muslims and the Jews. There were no powerful communities of Christians in the Hejaz to clash with the Muslims. Moreover, the Apostle, on his early trips to Syria, seems to have come in contact with Christian monks and hermits and to have been impressed by them.

Even in a comparatively late Medina revelation, we find, "Certainly you will find that the bitterest enemies of the believers are the Jews and the polytheists: and you will find that the nearest in their affection for the believers are those who said, 'We are Christians'. This is because there are among them priests and monks and because they are not arrogant."

No rivalry for power occurred between Christians and Muslims during the Prophet's lifetime, unless we consider Mota as such. The criticisms directed by Muhammad against Christians were related to dogma, not to power politics. When we consider the attacks launched by him against Christian dogma, they seem to be largely due to misunderstanding.

The first point to note is that Syria was a hotbed of sects, factions, intrigues, and rivalries. The Greek Orthodox, the official Byzantine church, delighted in hair-splitting dogmatic arguments, dear to the subtle intellects of Greeks, but giving rise to bitter schisms. The population of the cities and of the sea coast were predominantly Greek, whether in race or in culture.

The rural population was principally of an earlier and less intellectual ethnic origin. The Greek subtleties were too much for them and they tended to reject Byzantine dogma. This did not, however, mean that they adhered to the simple message of the Sermon on the Mount. Far from it. The Christianity of the rural and tribal Syrians was intermixed with legend, magic and ancient superstitions left over by paganism.

Many references to Christianity in the Qoran seem to refer to the superstitions of the Syrian "heretics", who were nearer to the Arabs in their mental background than were the Greeks. The heretics of Syria and Egypt produced a number of "gospels" and legends, consisting largely of superstition and magic. There are several references in the Qoran to the legends contained in these apocryphal gospels, suggesting that the Prophet's knowledge of Christianity may have been derived from some such sources.

The most commonly quoted examples of this nature are, firstly, the statement that Mary was brought up in the Temple in Jerusalem, where she was fed by angels. This tradition was to be found in the "Protevangelium of James the Less", an apocryphal work, and also in certain apocryphal gospels produced in Egypt. The Qoran also states that Christ spoke in his cradle, apparently a Coptic legend told in the apocryphal "Gospel of the Infancy". Yet another example is the reference to Christ, as a child, having made birds of clay and having breathed into them, whereupon they became live birds and flew away. This legend appears in the apocryphal "Gospel of Thomas the Israelite".

The Apostle of God also taught that Christ was not crucified, but that someone resembling Him suffered. This was an old Christian heresy. As early as A.D. 120 a Gnostic called Basilides began to teach that it was Simon of Cyrene who was crucified. In later centuries, a Christian sect called the Docetists held a variety of views of a somewhat similar nature. The Julianists were another Christian sect who denied the Crucifixion.

Perhaps the aspect of these misunderstandings which has been most discussed is that of the Trinity. Muhammad seems to have believed that Christians considered the Trinity to be Mary, Jesus and God. Once again, we find that there were Christian sects who carried the worship of Mary to so extreme a degree that such an impression might well be produced on an outsider.

Similarly, the Prophet objected to the expression "the Son of

God", asking how God can give birth to a son. The use of the terms "Father and Son" were in fact technical expressions, intended to establish that the Spirit which was in Christ was the Divine Spirit. But Qoran IV, 171, says:

"Jesus the Messiah, the Son of Mary, was a Messenger of God, His word which he placed in Mary, and His Spirit."

Muhammad also believed in the Virgin Birth.

In brief, the Prophet was confused by the hotchpotch of conflicting sects, ancient legends and subtle technical terms, of which popular Syrian Christianity in the seventh century largely consisted. Yet, as is always the case, the loud-voiced controversies of nominal Christians had not been able entirely to obliterate the true spirit of saintliness, cultivated rather by humble hermits and anchorites rather than by the sectarian controversialists. It was this true spirit of sainthood to which Muhammad had paid tribute, when he said that the Christians were the nearest in their affection because they were not arrogant.

It will be recollected that, when the first Muslim refugees had migrated from Mecca to Abyssinia, the Prophet had told the emigrants that the Abyssinian government, being Christian, was a just one. When the Muslims, summoned before the Emperor of Abyssinia, explained the tenets of Islam, the emperor is alleged to have exclaimed that this was Christianity. It is sad to realise that, starting so near to one another, Christians and Muslims were, for many centuries to be bitter rivals.

NOTABLE DATES

The Emigration to Medina	622
Battle of Bedr	624
Battle of Uhud	24th March 625
Siege of Medina	March–April 627
Truce of Hudaibiya	March 628
Conquest of Kheibar	September 628
Muslim pilgrimage to Mecca	February 629
Battle of Mota	September 629

PERSONALITIES

Muslims

Abu Baseer, the young Muslim convert who held up caravans in the Wadi al Ais

Zaid ibn Haritha
Jaafar ibn abi Talib   } Killed at Mota
Abdulla ibn Rawaha

Abbas ibn Abdul Muttalib, the Apostle's uncle

Jewish Leaders

Sallam ibn abi al Huqaiq, nicknamed Abu Rafi, assassinated by the Muslims

Huyai ibn al Akhtab of Beni Nadheer, executed with Beni Quraidha

Kinana ibn abi al Huqaiq, leader in Kheibar, executed by the Muslims

Pagan Arabs

Uyaina ibn Hisn, chief of Ghatafan, ally of the Jews of Kheibar

Khalid ibn al Waleed
Amr ibn al Aasi   } Leaders of Quraish who came
Othman ibn Talha   over to Muhammad in 629

Women

Safiya, a Jewess, wife of Kinana ibn abi al Huqaiq, leader in Kheibar. Married Muhammad after the execution of Kinana

Zainab, a Jewess of Kheibar, who tried to poison the Apostle

Umm Habeeba, widowed daughter of Abu Sofian, married the Apostle in 628

Maimoona, sister-in-law of Abbas, married the Apostle on the pilgrimage to Mecca in 629

XV

The Capture of Mecca

The conduct of Mahomet on the conquest of Mecca, was marked by singular magnanimity and moderation. It was indeed for his own interest to forgive the past, and to cast all its slights and injuries into oblivion. But it did not the less require a large and generous heart to do this.

SIR WILLIAM MUIR, *The Life of Mahomet*

On the day of the capture of Mecca the Prophet entered the town. Three hundred and sixty idols were ranged in the temple. He touched them one after the other with a cane which he was holding in his hand, repeating, "Truth has come, Falsehood will cease to exist."

BUKHARI, *The True Traditions*

XV

MOST historians have accepted the tradition that, after the return from Hudaibiya in March 628, the Apostle sent messengers to the kings and princes of surrounding territories, summoning them to accept Islam. The rulers to whom the messages were sent are alleged to have been the Byzantine Emperor, the King of Persia, the Ruler of Egypt, the Emperor of Abyssinia, and a number of local princes on the verge of Arabia.

The first point to be noticed in this connection is that the Byzantine Empire was at war with Persia from 602 to 628. In 610, the Persians had captured Antioch, in 614 Jerusalem and, in 616, they occupied Egypt and Asia Minor. The whole of Syria, Palestine, Egypt and Asia Minor were held by the Persians until 628. In February of that year, Chosroes Parwiz was assassinated and the Persian Empire collapsed.

Ibn Saad[1] alleges that all the Apostle's messengers were sent out after Hudaibiya in May 628, before the expedition to Kheibar. This would have been three months after the assassination of Chosroes, when the Persian Empire was in chaos. One tradition alleges that the Byzantine Emperor Heraclius received his letter in Jerusalem. In fact, however, Heraclius did not visit Jerusalem to restore the True Cross to its place[2] until March 630. Heraclius is alleged to have sent for Abu Sofian, who happened to be in Syria, to ask him about Muhammad but, as we shall see, Abu Sofian in March 630 was in Mecca.

In fact, however, we know that the Apostle was steadily but cautiously widening his field of operations. He began by suppressing opposition in Medina and making agreements with tribes just outside the oasis, like Juhaina and Khuzaa. Then he extended his field to Beni Sulaim, Kheibar and Ghatafan and later, as we shall see, to Teima, Aila and Duma. With considerable skill, he used the threat of armed force to win political victories, but he always preferred diplomacy to arms.

Beni Ghassan, as we have seen, had in 581 lost their position of "kings" under the Byzantine Empire, but members of the family

---

[1] Ibn Saad, *Al Tabaqat al Kabira.*   [2] It had been carried off by the Persians.

302 THE LIFE AND TIMES OF MUHAMMAD

continued to be the tribal lords of various areas of eastern and southern Syria. It is more than likely that the Apostle, after extending his influence to Duma, sent letters to the chiefs of Beni Ghassan. In other known cases of his early dealings with Christian rulers, however, he offered political alliance but did not insist on their conversion to Islam. We may, perhaps, surmise that the Messenger of God exchanged communications with more than one prince of Beni Ghassan. We have already noted that the murder of one of these envoys led to the Battle of Mota.

It is quite probable that the Apostle corresponded with the Negus of Abyssinia on several occasions. In fact, it was possibly immediately after Hudaibiya that he wrote to him to ask for the return of the Muslim Emigrants and the despatch of Umm Habeeba, whom he wished to marry. This may have been the communication to which Ibn Saad refers. It is, however, unlikely that the Prophet demanded the conversion of the Negus, who had always been extremely friendly, and who seems to have believed Islam to be some kind of Christian sect.

The story of the emissary to the King of Persia was probably incorrect. We know, however, that the Prophet did correspond with the Persian governor of the Yemen, and possibly also with the governor of Bahrain. These communications may have been exaggerated into a correspondence with the Great King himself.

A difficult problem, however, is presented by the letter to the ruler of Egypt, who is alleged to have replied to the Apostle's communication and to have sent a white riding mule and two Coptic slave girls as a present to Muhammad. One of these girls, a Christian called Mary, became a concubine of the Prophet and bore him a son called Ibrahim.

The other girl was given by Muhammad to the poet Hassan ibn Thabit. Hassan was an unpleasant person, whose poems were often obscene. He had joined in spreading the scandal about Aisha, after the Beni Mustaliq raid,[3] and had incurred the Apostle's wrath. A short time afterwards, however, a reconciliation ensued and was sealed by the gift of the second Egyptian slave girl to Hassan, who made her his concubine. This would seem to place the arrival of the girls from Egypt in about January or February 627. At this time, however, the Persians were still in occupation of Egypt. The Arabs call this "ruler of Egypt" *Al Muqawqis*, possibly a corruption of a

[3] Page 265.

Greek word, but it is impossible to identify the dignitary in question. Scholars differ in their opinions as to whether the Messenger of God foresaw that the Arabs would conquer many lands and establish a great empire, or whether he visualised Islam as being the religion of Arabia. There is no reference to the question in the Qoran, unless it be Chapter XVI, verse 84, which reads, "On the day when we will send a witness from every nation, then no permission will be given to unbelievers". The meaning is not clear.

* * *

It will be remembered that, in the Hudaibiya truce, a clause had been included authorising both sides to make treaties with any tribes which desired to join them. When such agreements were concluded, the tribes concerned would be considered as being covered by the terms of the ten-year truce. On this basis, Quraish had made a treaty with Beni Kinana, while the Apostle had done the same with Khuzaa.

It so happened that, before the return of the defeated raiders from Mota, a portion of Khuzaa had camped at Al Wateer, a well of theirs just outside Mecca. A clan of Beni Kinana, known as Beni Bekr, seized the opportunity to attack them and to kill one of their men, in fulfilment of an old blood-feud. Further desultory fighting ensued, in which, according to Ibn Ishaq, some men of Quraish secretly assisted Beni Kinana against Khuzaa. The statement, which is remarkably vague, may have been added to the story in order to prove that Quraish themselves had infringed the ten-year truce.

Budail ibn Waraqa, the principal chief of Khuzaa, the same who had come to Muhammad at Hudaibiya, rode forthwith to the Apostle of God in Medina. Pointing out that both Khuzaa and Beni Kinana were covered by the ten-year agreement, Budail claimed that the truce had been violated by Quraish.

As has already been indicated, the rather unexpected result of the Hudaibiya agreement and the Muslim pilgrimage a year later had been a marked swing in public opinion in Mecca in favour of Muhammad. It is possible that the Prophet himself was ill content at the prospect of having to wait ten years before he could march on Mecca, which now seemed as ready as a ripe plum to fall into his lap. He may consequently have welcomed the opportunity Beni Kinana had supplied, enabling him to break the truce.

Having lodged his complaint, Budail ibn Waraqa, the Khuzaa chief, was returning to Mecca where he had a town house, when at Usfan he met Abu Sofian. The Quraish leader, alarmed at the possibility of a resumption of hostilities, was hastening to Muhammad to explain away the incident and to ask for the continuance of the truce. The precipitancy of his departure for Medina revealed the depth of his anxiety.

Although, from Bedr to the siege of Medina, Abu Sofian had been the leader of Quraish against the Muslims, his name after that seems to fade. He is not mentioned in the negotiations over Hudaibiya. More extreme elements from the clans of Abid Shems and Makhzoom seem to have come to the front.

It will be recollected that Umm Habeeba, a daughter of Abu Sofian, had gone to Abyssinia as the wife of one of the early Muslim refugees who had fled there. Her husband had died in Africa and the Apostle had written to the Negus asking him to send her to Medina to be his bride. Umm Habeeba was now one of the Prophet's wives and Abu Sofian was his father-in-law.

Abu Sofian thought that his wisest course would be first to visit his daughter and to solicit her intervention with her husband on his behalf. The result, however, fell short of his hopes. Entering his daughter's apartment, he prepared to sit down on a carpet which was unrolled on the floor.[4] Before he could do so, his daughter pulled it away, then rolled it up and put it on one side. "My dear daughter," the old man is said to have exclaimed, "I hardly know if you think that carpet is too good for me or that I am too good for the carpet." "It is the Apostle's carpet," she replied sharply, "and you are a dirty polytheist." "By God," replied her father, "your manners have not improved since you left home", and he walked out of the room.

This amusing anecdote leaves us with a number of guesses. The Apostle may often have married women in order to employ them as bridges to establish relationship between himself and their families. He took the trouble to write to the Emperor of Abyssinia to send him Umm Habeeba to be his bride. If his object had been merely to acquire another woman, there must have been hundreds of more attractive brides available in Arabia. Possibly he sent for Umm Habeeba as a bridge to establish relations with Abu Sofian who, he had noticed, was now adopting a more conciliatory attitude.

Soon afterwards, he was to make use of Abu Sofian. Did he think

[4] The Arabs, of course, sat on carpets and cushions on the floor, not on chairs.

that he would be more pliable if he had first been a little humiliated? Was Umm Habeeba rude to her father on instructions from Muhammad?

Thus repulsed by his daughter, Abu Sofian decided that a direct approach might be more dignified and greeted the Apostle in the street. Muhammad, however, walked straight past him without answering. He next begged Abu Bekr to intercede for him but the old man refused to act as a go-between. Having been likewise rudely repulsed by Umar, he visited Ali to ask his help. Ali was in his house with his wife Fatima, the Prophet's daughter. Their little son, Hasan, was crawling about the floor.

Abu Sofian made a pathetic appeal to Ali to intercede with the Apostle to allow him an interview but he replied that, if Muhammad had made up his mind about something, it was useless to intercede with him. Eventually, foiled in all his attempts, the leader of once proud Quraish mounted his camel and set off for Mecca with an anxious heart.

Such, at least, is the official Muslim tradition. It is possible, however, that Abu Sofian actually came to a secret agreement with Muhammad on this occasion. Alarmed at the prospect of street fighting in Mecca, he may well have undertaken to go on ahead and persuade the Meccans not to resist the Muslim occupation of their town.

This possibility seems to be strengthened by the fact that, no sooner had Abu Sofian left, than the Apostle gave orders for all to prepare for the march on Mecca. Ten thousand men are said to have answered his call. When we remember that, only two years before, he had been followed to Hudaibiya by only one thousand four hundred Muslims, the extent of the revolution in his favour in those two years can be readily appreciated.

The expedition set out on 1st January, 630. As it was Ramadhan, the month of fasting, the whole force abstained from food and drink from dawn to sunset while on the march. In fact, persons who are travelling or men engaged in a holy war are exempt from the obligation to fast in Ramadhan, on condition that they make up the lost days on another occasion. The Apostle and the Muslims, however, broke their fast when they reached Al Qudaid, seventy-five miles from Mecca. After the departure from Medina, the Muslims were joined by between seven hundred and a thousand men of Beni Sulaim, a tribe which had till then remained hostile.

The Apostle's astute uncle Abbas had hitherto, as we have seen, remained with the polytheists in Mecca, though keeping a foot in both camps by periodically sending information to Medina. He now, however, decided that the long contest was over and, taking his family with him, he set out openly to join the victor. He met the advancing Muslims at Al Juhfa, seventy miles north of Mecca.

According to Abbas' own account, he was worried over the fate of Quraish if the Muslims should capture Mecca by force. He accordingly, having made his own position secure by joining the advancing Muslims, rode on in front of them in the hope of finding a messenger whom he could send to the Meccans to urge them to sue for peace. Apparently after dark, he suddenly encountered Abu Sofian. According to the Muslim historians, Abbas told Abu Sofian that the Muslims were advancing in overwhelming strength. "If the Apostle takes you," he said, "he will cut off your head. Get up behind me on this mule, so that I can take you to him and ask him to protect you."

So, once again, says the official version. But if Abu Sofian was already in agreement with the Prophet, it seems more probable that Abbas went to meet him at a prearranged rendezvous. The key to these possible distortions of the historical facts is not far to seek. Twenty-nine years after the death of the Apostle, the descendants of Abu Sofian became the khalifs of the Muslim world which they ruled for eighty-nine years. At the end of this period, they were overthrown by the descendants of Abbas. It was under the rule of the family of Abbas that most of the historians wrote. They were, therefore, tempted, if not obliged, to glorify the part played by Abbas in the first years of Islam and to minimise the rôle of Abu Sofian. In all these incidents, therefore, they may have striven to attribute the key rôle to Abbas even if, in fact, it was Abu Sofian who brought Mecca over to the side of Muhammad.

Returning once more to the official version, we are told that Abu Sofian mounted behind Abbas on his mule—a white one belonging to the Apostle himself—and he and Abbas rode into the Muslim bivouac. As they passed each camp fire they were challenged but, when the men recognised Abbas and the Apostle's mule they allowed them to pass without asking who the man was who was riding pillion.

The Apostle, who must have felt the most intense elation at the abject humiliation of his former enemy, behaved with calm suavity. "Take him away now," he said to Abbas, "and bring him back in the morning."

Next day, when Abu Sofian was brought once again to the Apostle's tent, the latter said to him, "Isn't it time for you to admit that there is no god but God?" The old man is supposed to have replied, "If there had been any other god, he might have helped me." "Isn't it time also for you to recognise that I am the Messenger of God?" Muhammad continued. "As far as that is concerned, I still have my doubts," Abu Sofian is said to have replied stoutly.

Abbas subsequently claimed that he intervened at this stage to say to Abu Sofian, "Testify that there is no god but God and that Muhammad is the Messenger of God, or else your head will be cut off." Other accounts attribute these words to Umar. The argument was unanswerable, whoever used it, and Abu Sofian duly recited the Muslim confession. Once again, however, this account may be an adjustment of the facts, intended to glorify Abbas and to depreciate Abu Sofian whose descendants, the Umaiyids, had been driven from the throne by the Abbasids.

The discussion then turned to the forthcoming Muslim occupation of Mecca. It was agreed that Abu Sofian should ride on ahead and convey the terms of surrender. If no opposition were offered, the Apostle agreed that all persons who took refuge in the house of Abu Sofian would be safe. Persons who remained within their own houses and locked their doors would also go unharmed—the equivalent of the modern curfew used in some countries at times of civil disturbances. Finally, all persons who collected in the courtyard of the Kaaba would remain uninjured.

Abu Sofian then received permission to return to Mecca and announce these terms to the public. Before he did so, however, the Apostle whispered to Abbas to ride out with him and to delay him on a spur of the hills which overlooked the valley up which the Muslims were about to pass, in order yet further to impress him. The whole force thus filed past the Meccan leader. The tribal contingents passed on in front, each with its own war banner. At the rear of the column rode the Apostle himself, surrounded by the Emigrants and the Helpers, every one of whom was clad in breast- and backplate and steel helmet. "By God," Abu Sofian remarked drily to Abbas, "your little nephew has become a man of power."

Abu Sofian then rode on ahead and entered Mecca, where he proclaimed at the top of his voice to the assembled people: "O Quraish, Muhammad has come with a force which you cannot resist." His wife, Hind, the daughter of Utba ibn Rabia—she who had chewed the liver of Hamza at Uhud—jumped up beside him, screaming, "Don't take any notice of this fat old fool! A nice protector of his people he is!" (In addition to his other anxieties, Abu Sofian must have had a trying time at home with this shrewish female.)

"Don't let this woman deceive you," repeated the old leader. "You cannot resist the force which has come. He who enters Abu Sofian's house will be safe. He who locks himself into his own house and he who gathers in the courtyard of the Kaaba will be safe also." So the people dispersed to take refuge in their own houses or round the Kaaba.

On reaching Dhu Towa, just outside Mecca, the Apostle drew rein and, bowing his head, gave praise and thanks to God who had given him victory over his enemies. He then divided his force into four columns. His cousin, Al Zubair ibn al Awwam, was given the left-hand column, which was to enter Mecca from the north-east. Next came Saad ibn Ubada, the chief of the Khazraj. As the latter rode off, he is alleged to have recited some lines of poetry to the effect that this day was to be a day of war, in which no quarter would be granted. Umar is said to have heard him and hastened to tell the Apostle, who immediately replaced him by Ali. The Messenger of God himself with the Helpers and the Emigrants advanced directly on Mecca.

The fourth column was commanded by Khalid ibn al Waleed, the victor of Uhud, who had extricated the defeated Muslims from the field of Mota. He was told to enter Mecca from the south-west. This column was to meet with some resistance from extremists under Ikrima, the son of Abu Jahal, but the enemy was quickly overcome at the cost of some twelve casualties.

The Apostle had given orders that no force was to be used except in self-defence. A short list, however, was prepared of persons who were, if caught, to be killed instantly. Those included in this ban were two men who had come to Medina and professed Islam but had subsequently returned to Mecca and apostasised. One of them, Abdulla ibn Saad, had actually been employed in Medina as a clerk to take down the Prophet's revelations. When, however, he returned to Mecca, he had declared them to be all a hoax. In any case, Muhammad always pronounced the severest sentences on apostates. In spite of this, however, Abdulla ibn Saad was pardoned when he gave himself up. Less worthy victims were a pair of professional singing-girls, who had apparently given some kind of satirical show at the Apostle's expense. He was always particularly resentful of ridicule.

Another man excluded from the amnesty were a certain Huwairith, who had insulted the Apostle in early Meccan days, and had struck his daughter Zainab. Yet another was Suhail ibn Amr, the man who had negotiated the truce of Hudaibiya, and had refused to insert the phrase "Muhammad, the Apostle of God" in the preamble. Orders were likewise given for the immediate execution of Ikrima, the son of Abu Jahal, who had followed in his father's footsteps as a leader of the opposition to Islam. Abu Jahal, the chief of the Beni Makhzoom clan of Quraish, was, it will be rembered, killed at Bedr.

The Prophet's tent was pitched on an eminence to the north-west of the town, from which he could oversee the progress of his columns. Before the sun was high, Mecca had been occupied and all was quiet. The Apostle then mounted his camel and rode into the town to the public square in which the Kaaba was situated. He performed the seven ritual circuits of the House of God, mounted on his camel, touching the black stone with his stick each time he passed it. He then prayed the midday prayer in the courtyard of the Kaaba.

There are said to have been three hundred and sixty idols in and around the Kaaba. These the Apostle now ordered to be thrown down and smashed, and their remains to be burned.

He then summoned Othman ibn Talha of the clan of Abdul Dar, who were the hereditary guardians of the key of the Kaaba.[5] Othman ibn Talha, it will be recollected, had been converted with Khalid ibn al Waleed and Amr ibn al Aasi. Othman now brought the key and opened the door and the Apostle entered the small cubical building. It is alleged that there were paintings on the walls, including pictures of Mary and of Jesus. According to an old tradition, Muhammad ordered that all the paintings be erased except those depicting Jesus and His Mother.

The Apostle then emerged from the door of the Kaaba and addressed the people who had assembled. Ibn Ishaq reports the following extracts from his statement:

"There is no god but God alone. He has no partner. He has fulfilled His promise and has helped His servant, putting to flight those who were leagued against him. All hereditary authority or claims of blood or property are abolished, except the hereditary guardianship

[5] Page 66.

of the Kaaba and the right to water the pilgrims . . . O Quraish, God has abolished the pride of paganism and its veneration of ancestors. Man is descended from Adam and Adam was created from the dust." Then he recited to them verse 13, of Chapter XLIX of the Qoran:

"O people! I created you male and female, and I made you into nations and tribes, that you may know one another. Surely the most honourable of you in God's sight is the most pious."

Then he looked up at them and said, "O Quraish, what do you think that I am about to do with you?" Some replied, "You are our noble brother." "Go now," the Apostle concluded, "you are all free."

All the people of Mecca were gathered to swear allegiance to the Messenger of God. The men filed past one by one each giving him his hand and promising to obey God and His Apostle. When the men had finished, the women of Mecca were summoned. Hind, the daughter of Utba, though she was on the list of those proscribed, veiled her face and mingled with the crowd.

The Messenger of God then addressed the assembled women. He began by saying that he wished them to promise not to associate anything with God.[6] Hind, the daughter of Utba, called out from the crowd that he had not asked the men to promise that. This formidable woman, whose life was now in real danger, apparently could not keep quiet. In the course of the ensuing argument, the Apostle recognised his heckler. "Are you Hind, the daughter of Utba?" he asked. "Yes," she said, "I am Hind. I ask you to forgive what is passed." "This is a day on which the past is forgotten," said Muhammad quietly. "God has forgiven you."

Continuing his address, he enjoined the women not to kill their children, referring presumably to the practice of female infanticide already mentioned. "We brought up our children when they were little and you killed them on the day of Bedr when they had grown up," interjected the irrepressible Hind.

The Apostle then asked the women to swear to obey his orders, and instructed Umar to accept their oaths by striking hands. He himself would never touch the hand of a woman, unless she were one of his wives or his daughters.

These exchanges, and many other passing incidents which we

---

[6] Islam has always laid especial emphasis on the Unity of God. The pagans of Arabia were denounced not as idolaters, but as "associators". While admitting the existence of one supreme God, they "associated" with Him their own local deities.

have already related, illustrate once more the active and open part played by women in Arabian society in the seventh century. It is true that the Prophet imposed some restrictions on their free activities. There are in the Muslim traditions many accounts of incidents related by women in which they describe how they were paying visits or talking to their male friends, when this or that occurred. But each such narrative is concluded with the comment, "This was before the Apostle received the revelation about veiling." Nevertheless, the restrictions imposed by the Apostle were relatively slight—less perhaps than those social rules which existed in Victorian society. Only a few years after the death of Muhammad, for example, Aisha, his favourite wife, took part in a battle, riding on her own camel.

One point to which, curiously enough, hostile critics rarely seem to refer is the Apostle's description of paradise. Every believer, he said, when he reaches the eternal gardens will be greeted by two black-eyed maidens, infinitely beautiful and eternally young. But if their husbands are to be joined to the houris, there is no explanation as to what will become of Muslim women, to whom also paradise is promised.

The basic difference between the attitudes of Islam and the modern West is perhaps not so much one of equality between the sexes as of differentiation. Men and women are entirely different, a fact which enables them to work together perfectly in pairs. It is surely as ridiculous to suggest that women are not "equal" to men, because they have fewer members of parliament or admirals of the fleet, as to claim that men are not equal to women because they are less skilful as dressmakers or baby-sitters.

In brief, the theoretical attitude of Islam to women is that their rôle in life is different from that of men. It is true that women, owing to their physical weakness, have often been oppressed by men, but the general Western conception of the position of women in Muslim society is grossly distorted.

*   *   *

The peaceful capture of Mecca, the supreme triumph of the Apostle's career, provides a suitable opportunity to summarise his methods. The first fact to notice is that he enjoyed no unbroken career of military victories. His defeats were as many as his successes.

Uhud cancelled out Bedr. Hudaibiya, an apparent military failure, was barely atoned for by Kheibar, while Mota was a shattering defeat. By contrast, after the Apostle's death, the Muslims won a dazzling succession of victories, not over Quraish or Ghatafan, but over Byzantium and Persia.

There can be no doubt that Muhammad's ultimate triumph was not due to his military success but to his personality. Nowadays we perhaps attach too much importance to the need of a strong man as a leader. Muhammad was not a naturally strong man, but he had the rare gift of inspiring intense devotion. We scarcely ever read of him as issuing dictatorial orders or as punishing those who disobeyed. He frequently asked the advice of his principal subordinates and often (where, of course, no revelation was involved) he submitted to their opinions.

Such a system provided the only way permanently to win the loyalty of the old Arabs of Arabia, who vehemently resisted autocratic orders but readily gave their all in answer to an appeal for help. This quality, which still persists in the Central Arabians, has to some extent affected the Syrians and the Iraqis also. Easily moved by an emotional appeal, they show an unexpected perseverance in their resistance to arbitrary force. Goldziher,[7] discussing Muhammad's prohibition of alcohol, has diagnosed this peculiarity of the old Arabs. "The Arab," he writes, "was not to be deterred from his pleasures by imprisonment. Indeed it is characteristic of these people that he gladly gives up wine voluntarily but remains defiant in the face of threatened punishment."

Another factor of considerable importance is that the Muslim historians whose biographies of the Prophet have come down to us lived in a luxurious and sophisticated society, a hundred and fifty or more years after the events which they recorded.

In most cases, they were not even descended from the inhabitants of Arabia, while many of them were Persians, Greeks, Egyptians or Spaniards in origin, Arabicised only in education and culture.

By the time that these "Arab" historians wrote their extremely learned works, the Arabian tribes, the raw material of Islam, were already alienated from the Muslim imperial government in Baghdad and were looked upon as turbulent bandits. Later Western historians can scarcely be blamed for following the "Arab" historians. The

[7] Goldziher, *Muslim Studies*.

belief that the peoples of the Hejaz in the seventh century were lawless murderers, deprived of all moral qualitites, would naturally lead to the conclusion that Muhammad can only have won their allegiance by bribery or bloodshed. A prophet who indulged in camel thieving would doubtless be considered a worthy character by Arab tribesmen, sneers Professor Margoliouth.

My only excuse for writing this book is that I lived for years in the ragged tents of Arab nomads. In doing so, I discovered that, in spite of their unkempt appearance, these men are deeply susceptible to a purely spiritual call. When I read that the tribesmen, when addressed by the Prophet, "wept till their beards were wet", I know that this is not a poetic exaggeration. I have seen these men shed tears over a purely altruistic appeal. Once we appreciate that the Arab tribesman was sensitive to spiritual influences, the way is open for us to realise that the Prophet's ministry which won them over may well have been spiritual and altruistic, rather than based on fear and greed.

Yet we have already seen that the Apostle preached the best of both worlds, riches in this world and bliss in paradise. And we found that a modern Muslim protagonist claimed that this method was more practical than the heroic self-abandonment of the Gospels. Would it be wrong to wonder whether the Prophet himself did not sometimes underestimate the capacity of his converts for self-immolation? He opposed asceticism and recommended moderation but innumerable multitudes of Muslims since then have joyously abandoned everything to live in poverty and suffering.

Whatever we may think of his spiritual mission, we can readily admit that the Messenger of God had an instinctive touch in politics and in diplomacy. We have seen how often he preferred to avoid a battle and to engage the potential enemy in a conversation, which often resulted in his conversion. It was his political genius alone which conceived the idea of winning the Meccans to his side by himself performing a pilgrimage.

Yet we may also notice that many of his generous, charming and equalitarian ways were not peculiar to himself but were an integral part of Abrabian character and custom. The picture of the little daughter of Zaid ibn Haritha, flying to his arms in a flood of tears, is an extremely endearing one. But nearly all Arabs love children.

Then again, there is much that is attractive in Muhammad's

kindly humour, his little jokes with his friends and his family, the giving of nicknames to his intimates and his warm equalitarianism. Yet all these qualities are typical of the Central Arabian way of life. The traditional structure of Arabian society is patriarchal, the chief being as it were, the grandfather. The significance of this system is that the chief man did not belong to an "upper class", but was the blood relation of his followers. This background produced a system which resulted in respect for authority combined with social equality. It was a system more human and less cold-blooded than government by an impersonal bureaucracy.

*   *   *

Yet with all his kindliness, the Apostle could be ruthless, according to our ideas. The execution of seven hundred men of Beni Quraidha, for example, could be matched in the annals of Arabian princes, but not in tribal wars. I believe that Dr. Montgomery Watt is quite wrong in saying that, in tribal war, nothing was barred. On the contrary, killings in tribal wars were never wholesale and casualties were normally light in any one encounter. As wars between tribes were endemic, no one would have been left alive if massacres had been of frequent occurrence. I believe that it can be said with confidence that tribal battles were governed by rules and that massacres of one tribe by another were virtually unknown. From the earliest period, long before Islam, down to our own times, massacre seems only to have been used either by rulers in search of power or in the name of religion, but never in tribal conflicts.

The massacre of Beni Quraidha appears, indeed, difficult to explain. We have seen that the Apostle always preferred diplomacy to fighting. His clemency and generosity on the occasion of his capture of Mecca were quite remarkable. The readiness with which he freely forgave his bitterest enemies, when they fell into his hands, was extraordinary.

Perhaps we can summarise his policy, after this long digression, by saying that he probably endeavoured to be all things to all men. To those susceptible to a spiritual appeal, he employed a religious approach. The worldly he bribed or threatened, with the traitor or the apostate he was normally ruthless, but even they were often forgiven.

NOTABLE DATES

PERSONALITIES

Muslims

Ali
Abu Bekr } The Apostle's closest friends
Umar

Saad ibn Ubada, chief of the Khazraj
Khalid ibn al Waleed } Distinguished war leaders of
Amr ibn al Aasi } Quraish
Othman ibn Talha, custodian of the Kaaba
Abbas ibn Abdul Muttalib } Latter-day converts
Abu Sofian }

Foreign Potentates

Heraclius, the Byzantine Emperor
Chosroes Parwiz, King of Persia
The Negus of Abyssinia
The "Muqawqis" of Egypt

Women

Mary, the Coptic concubine
Hind, the daughter of Utba, wife of Abu Sofian

XVI

The Day of Hunain

A people that jeoparded their lives unto the death in the high places of the field.

Judges V, 18

All this assembly shall know that the Lord saveth not with sword or spear: for the battle is the Lord's, and He will give you into our hands.

I Samuel XVII, 47

God certainly gave you victory on many fields and on the Day of Hunain, when your great numbers made you pleased with yourselves; but they did not avail you and the wide world became too strait for you; then you turned and fled.

Qoran IX, 25

Al Bará used to say, when he was asked if he ran away on the Day of Hunain: "The Prophet did not run away. The Hawazin were shooting their arrows. Then the Prophet called out, 'I am the Prophet, not an impostor. I am the son of Abdul Muttalib.'"

BUKHARI, *The True Traditions*

ALTHOUGH a list of persons proscribed, whom it was legitimate to kill, had been drawn up before the capture of Mecca, only four seem actually to have been executed. Ikrima, the son of one of Muhammad's bitterest enemies, Abu Jahal, escaped to the Yemen, but his wife went to the Apostle and secured a free pardon for him. This gallant woman then set out on the long and precarious journey to the Yemen, found her husband and brought him back to Mecca. Three years later, he was to command an army of Muslims in war.

Safwan, the son of that Umaiya ibn Khalaf who was killed at Bedr,[1] escaped from Mecca to Jidda, where he intended to take ship to go overseas. But a friend of his interceded for him with the Apostle, who agreed to pardon him. The friend overtook Safwan just as he was about to embark and brought him back to Muhammad.

The Messenger of God won universal respect by his generosity and clemency on the day of his triumph. There were still many people living in the town who had been his bitter opponents and who had covered him with ridicule and abuse during the early days of his mission.

The occupation of Mecca was followed by an outburst of iconoclasm. Many Meccan families had private gods or images, which they kept in their houses or carried about with them. A call for their destruction was widely obeyed, whether from fear or because their devotees were convinced by the Muslim capture of Mecca that their old gods were indeed powerless to defend them.

Emissaries were also sent to the surrounding tribes to urge them to destroy their local gods and pagan shrines. One such party was commanded by Khalid ibn al Waleed, the victor of Uhud and the man who had extricated the Muslims from the defeat of Mota. Khalid was a highly successful fighter but a headstrong, violent and bloodthirsty man. He was sent to the Beni Jadheema clan of Beni Kinana, on the coastal plain south-west of Mecca.

By a tragic coincidence, these Beni Jadheema had killed Khalid's uncle many years before, when he was returning from a business trip

---

[1] Page 187. He was killed at the instigation of Bilal.

to the Yemen. The Apostle, who was probably unaware that Khalid had a private feud with the people he was sent to convert, had told him to avoid bloodshed. When he reached Beni Jadheema, Khalid told them to lay down their arms as the war was over and everyone had now accepted Islam. When they had done so, however, he suddenly seized a number of the men, tied their hands behind their backs and gave orders that they be beheaded, as satisfaction for the murder of his uncle.

An Arab horseman who was with Khalid's force subsequently told how a young man of Beni Jadheema, his hands tied, asked him to allow him to speak to some women who were standing a little way apart. The Muslim agreed and led the prisoner across to the women. "Goodbye, Hubaisha," the youth said to a girl among them, "my life is at an end now." But she cried passionately, "No, no, may your life be prolonged for many years to come." The prisoner was led back and immediately decapitated. As he fell, the girl broke away from the group of women and ran to him. Bending over him, she covered him with kisses, refusing to let go of his body until they killed her also.

The Apostle was genuinely horrified when he heard of Khalid's action. Standing in the courtyard of the Kaaba, he raised his hands above his head and cried aloud, "O God, I am innocent before Thee of what Khalid has done." Ali was sent immediately with a large sum of cash to pay blood-money for all who had been killed, and generous compensation for any losses of property.

Khalid was also sent to destroy the shrine of Al Uzza at Nakhla, some forty miles north-east of Mecca. The guardians of the goddess were men of Beni Sulaim. When her custodian heard of the approach of the Muslims, he hung his sword round the neck of the idol, urging her to defend herself and kill Khalid if he approached her. Thereupon he climbed to the top of a neighbouring hill, where he sat down to observe the progress of events. Al Uzza proved unequal to the challenge. Khalid arrived and smashed her into small fragments.

*　　*　　*

When the Hawazin heard that the Muslims had taken Mecca, some of them decided to fight. A certain Málik ibn Auf, chief of the clan of Beni Nasr, was the moving spirit of this resistance. Several other clans of Hawazin, however, remained aloof, although the tribe of Thaqeef, which included the people of Taif, agreed to join in.

One of those present at the gathering of these tribes was Duraid ibn al Simma, whom we met as a raider when he was a young man, many years before.[2] The Hawazin chief, Malik ibn Auf, decided that the tribe should gather for war, accompanied by their flocks and their families. The object of this action, which has been used by Arab nomads on great occasions down to the beginning of the present century, is to encourage the men to fight more fiercely. If their wives and families and all their worldly possessions risk capture by the enemy, the warriors are thought less likely to accept defeat.

Duraid ibn al Simma, now so old that he had to be carried in a litter, vigorously opposed this plan. He pointed out that only some of the clans of Hawazin were present and consequently that the tribesmen would be outnumbered. If the risk of a pitched battle must be accepted, he said, then meet the enemy on horseback, after sending your flocks and your families to some high mountain where they will be safe. But Malik ibn Auf, apparently a young man, was fiery and headstrong. "You are an old fool who is senile," he shouted. "I will not do what you say. Follow me, O Hawazin, or I shall fall on my own sword and kill myself."

The Apostle, who had now learned the value of intelligence in war, had sent a bedouin to mingle with Hawazin. He remained in their midst for several days and then returned with a full report. Doubtless Muhammad thought that, having collected so large a force for the occupation of Mecca, the occasion presented an extremely valuable opportunity to teach these tribes a lesson. If Malik ibn Auf had been a wiser man, he would have waited until the Messenger of God returned to Medina and dispersed the force which he had collected, and which it would have been difficult to mobilise again quickly.

As it was, the Apostle decided to deal with Hawazin immediately. Probably at the end of January or the beginning of February 630, he left Mecca for the east, after a stay of only about two weeks in the town. He is alleged to have had with him the ten thousand men with whom he had taken Mecca and an additional two thousand newly converted Meccans. As against these twelve thousand, Hawazin could only put four thousand men in the field.

At dawn on the second or third day out, the Muslims were early

[2] Page 30.

on the move, and descended a sloping valley which was a tributary of the Wadi Hunain.[3] The floor of this valley was bare of vegetation, while it was shut in on both sides between bare, rocky hills, cut up by small valleys and ravines. Hawazin had moved up during the night and had hidden in the broken hills on either side.

As the Muslims poured down the valley in the twilight of dawn, men suddenly sprang out from the hills on both sides and charged down on to the unsuspecting crowd. Although the enemy was known to be near, there seem to have been no scouts, no advanced guard and no flank guards. The leading contingents of the Muslims panicked and fled back wildly up the valley towards the pass by which they had previously entered it, throwing into complete confusion those behind them who were still coming forward.

The Apostle and his immediate companions were at first caught up by the rout and swept away. But they succeeded in reaching the foot of the hills on one side of the valley, thereby allowing the stream of fugitives to pass by in front of them. Here they clung to the base of the mountains, the Prophet himself, Abu Bekr, Umar, Ali, Abbas and Usama, the son of Zaid ibn Haritha, who had been killed at Mota. "Where are you going men?" shouted Muhammad. "Rally here to me. I am the Apostle of God. O citizens of Medina! O Helpers! O men of the pledge of the tree."[4] Old Abu Sofian, who was in personal attendance on the Prophet, was secretly delighted at the scene. "Nothing can now stop their flight but the sea," he whispered gleefully to a fellow Meccan.

In the lead of Hawazin, now in wild pursuit of the fleeing Muslims, rode a man on a camel carrying a black flag and armed with a lance with which he thrust the flying Muslims through their backs as he overtook them. Ali galloped after the man and, coming up behind him unnoticed, hamstrung his camel, so that he and it fell headlong. Before he could rise, a man of Medina jumped on him and killed him.

At least half the Muslim force may well have been new converts or men who merely wished to be on the winning side. The two thousand Meccans, whose town had only been captured two weeks before, may have intentionally encouraged the panic. One man, whose father had been killed on the side of the polytheists at Uhud, thought the opportunity a good one to obtain his revenge by killing the Apostle. He pushed his way forward to reach him but was unable to

[3] Map 6, page 174.   [4] Referring to the oath taken at Hudaibiya. Page 269.

THE DAY OF HUNAIN

do so. In any case, as Muhammad was completely dressed in armour, it would not have been easy to murder him.

The Prophet was seated upon his white mule, while his uncle Abbas (according to his own account) was standing by its side. He told Abbas to shout at the top of his voice "O Helpers! O comrades of the acacia tree!" Abbas's voice began to be effective, and cries of, "Here we are!" were heard from here and there. Many men, however, were carried away by their camels and horses, which bolted in the confusion and refused to obey the rein.

Gradually more men were added to the Apostle's immediate escort. "To me, Helpers!" he kept shouting, and then, "To me, Khazraj", thinking perhaps that the old tribal names would stir deeper emotion than his artificial nicknames. The men who had rallied to the Messenger of God beneath the mountain now began to fight their way forward, cutting into the flank of the bedouins who were following the Muslims and compelling them to stand and fight. Although Muhammad himself never fought if he could avoid it, he seems to have remained cool in moments of crisis. Standing up in his stirrups on his white mule, the better to observe what was happening. "Now the oven is hot," he exclaimed.

Behind the group surrounding the Apostle sat a woman, Umm Sulaim, the wife of one of the Muslims. She carried a knife in her hand, while she held her husband's camel. "What are you going to do with that knife?" her husband asked her. "If an idolater should come near me, I will rip him open with it," replied this amiable young lady, who was in an advanced state of pregnancy. It was said that her husband, Abu Talha, killed twenty polytheists that day, so they were obviously a well-matched couple.

The panic had now been checked and the fugitives began to return. The three-to-one numerical superiority which the Muslims enjoyed commenced to tell and Hawazin were first brought to a halt and then driven back, until finally they broke and fled. Considering the disparity in numbers and the superiority of the Emigrants and the Helpers in armour, with which they were now well supplied, Thaqeef and Hawazin had certainly caused the Muslims a great deal of trouble. Seventy men of Thaqeef were killed standing round their war banner, which their chief, Uthman ibn Abdulla, died to protect.

At one stage not quite clear, Beni Sulaim put in a mounted charge, which swept Hawazin from the field. Beni Sulaim had only announced their conversion three weeks earlier, when the Apostle set out for Mecca. But whether they were genuine Muslims or not, they were doubtless veterans in tribal battles.

The Day of Hunain is referred to in the Qoran, Chapter IX, verse 25.

"Certainly God gave you victory on many fields and on the Day of Hunain when your great numbers gratified you and made you proud but availed you nothing. Then the very earth, in spite of its extent, seemed too small to provide a refuge for you when you turned your backs in flight. Then God sent down confidence on His Messenger and on the believers, and he sent down His soldiers, though you did not see them. They drove back the heathen and such is the reward of the unbelievers."

It will be seen that, in this passage, the repulse of the idolaters is attributed to angelic intervention.

*   *   *

It will be remembered that Muhammad, when a baby, had been brought up by a wet nurse of the Beni Saad tribe. These Beni Saad were a clan of Hawazin. A party of Muslims now brought in a group of Beni Saad prisoners with whom was an old woman. She told her captors that she was Shima, the foster-sister of the Apostle, but the men laughed at her and pushed her roughly along, telling her not to talk rubbish.

When, however, they reached the bivouac, she made the same claim to Muhammad himself. He asked whether she had any proof of her identity. In answer she pulled her smock down over her skinny old shoulder and pointed to a tiny white scar. "That was where you bit me one day when I was carrying you back to the tent on my hip," she said, looking indulgently at her former unruly charge.

With that charming paternalism which he knew so well how to use, he spread his cloak on the ground for her to sit on, and talked kindly to her of the days of their infancy. He offered her a comfortable home with love and honour, if she wished to end her days in his household. But she preferred to return to her ragged desert tent with her own people. Before allowing her to go, the Apostle loaded her with gifts. According to Ibn Ishaq, he also gave her a slave and a slave girl, who married one another and whose descendants were still living with Beni Saad a hundred years later.

*   *   *

Some of the men of Thaqeef retired from Hunain to Taif, a town which belonged to their tribe. They appear to have been men of some courage and determination, for we are told that their chiefs at this very time were absent in the Yemen, where they had gone to buy siege artillery, probably consisting of mangonels, and to receive training in its use.

It will be remembered that the Persians had held the Yemen from the year 574 onwards,[5] and doubtless kept there a garrison of regular troops with a siege train of artillery. Persian control of the Yemen had petered out during the course of the long war against Byzantium from 602 to 628, but the remains of the troops and of their heavy weapons were never evacuated. Possibly the chiefs of Thaqeef hoped to acquire some of these Persian weapons, to help them to defend their town.

In 619, the Apostle had visited Taif, hoping to find there the sanctuary which was ultimately provided by Medina, but had been harshly treated. The men of Taif having joined Hawazin at Hunain, the Messenger of God determined to seek his revenge. He marched on the town, to which he laid siege, but he found the gates and walls too strong for men armed only with lances, swords and arrows. There was much to be done elsewhere and, after fifteen or twenty days, he abandoned the attempt to capture the town.

Taif was principally famous for its gardens and its vineyards. Being situated in the mountains, it enjoyed a cool summer and was able to grow the fruits which belong to a temperate climate. Before raising the siege, the Messenger of God gave orders for these gardens to be destroyed. Twelve Muslims are alleged to have been killed by arrows from the walls of Taif, a number which suggests that no serious fighting took place.

*   *   *

After withdrawing from Taif, the Apostle halted at Jirana on the track leading back to Mecca. Here the immense plunder captured from Hawazin had been collected. Duraid ibn al Simma had been killed at Hunain. The old man was decapitated, while lying helpless in his litter. As his attacker's first sword-cut only wounded him, the old warrior is said to have advised his assailant how to strike at the nape of the neck, a stroke, he claimed, which always proved fatal.

[5] Page 51.

But though Duraid was dead, his advice to the Hawazin chief, Malik ibn Auf, was proved to have been correct. If Malik had attacked the Muslims, after depositing his wives and flocks in a place of safety, he could now have withdrawn with the tribe into the desert to await further developments. But after his defeat at Hunain, all the families and the flocks of Hawazin had been captured by the Muslims and were now rounded up in a vast concentration at Jirana.

The fact that Beni Saad, the clan to which Muhammad's foster-parents had belonged, formed part of Hawazin, offered an opening for negotiation. Some of Beni Saad approached him, saying, "O Apostle of God, the women who suckled you and who looked after you as an infant are in this concentration camp. Have pity on the poor people who have suffered this catastrophe." The Messenger of God replied, "Which are dearest to you? Your children and your wives, or your flocks and herds?" "Give us back our wives and our children," they answered.

The Apostle replied that, as far as he himself or his immediate relatives were concerned, the women and children would be released. He then told them to wait until he had prayed the noon prayer with the men. All the Muslims would then be present. At that moment, he explained to them, they should stand up and call out, 'We ask the Apostle's intercession with the Muslims, and the Muslims' intercession with the Apostle, to release our wives and our children."

The Hawazin delegation carefully executed the Apostle's instructions. The Emigrants and the Helpers immediately said that their share of the spoil was at the Prophet's disposal. The tribesmen, however, many of whom had not seriously adopted Islam, were less enthusiastic. The Fuzara and Beni Temeem said no. The chief of Beni Sulaim likewise refused to abandon his share, but the rank and file of the tribe shouted, "Not so! What is ours belongs to the Apostle." The Apostle intervened at this stage, saying, "Whoever insists on his right to a share of the prisoners should release them now and I will compensate him with six camels to every man from the next booty we take." As a result of this promise, all agreed to release the women and children.

The incident is of interest as showing the "democratic" political methods used by the Apostle. He told the delegation to appeal to the general assembly of Muslims, using his own influence on the side of humanity and moderation. But, although he was venerated as a superman by his devoted followers, he did not issue an order.

The Apostle used the Hawazin deputation to send a message to their chief, Malik ibn Auf, who, after his defeat at Hunain, had taken refuge with Thaqeef in Taif. The message promised that, if Malik came to Muhammad and professed Islam, he would receive back his family and property and, in addition, a present of a hundred camels from the Prophet himself. Malik readily accepted the offer, slipped out of Taif without telling his allies and rode to the Apostle at Jirana. Thus, a month after his defeat, he was richer than before. To show his gratitude, if not his constancy, he collected those clans of Hawazin who professed themselves ready to become Muslims, and declared war on Thaqeef, his allies of yesterday.

While the Apostle had been engaged in the matter of the release of the Hawazin women and children, the Muslims had been impatiently awaiting the moment when the captured herds of camels and flocks of sheep would be divided among them. When he moved away after completing the arrangements for the return of the families, a crowd of men followed and surrounded him crying, "O Apostle, divide the spoil of camels and sheep among us." They pressed upon him so closely that his cloak was torn from his back and trampled under foot. At length he gained some respite by leaning his back against a tree. "Give me back my cloak," he cried, laughing. "By God, if I had as many sheep as the trees on the coastal plain, I would give them all to you."

It so happened that, in 1929, I was myself, on two occasions, in a position to distribute captured herds to large crowds of bedouin tribesmen. To me, then, this little pen-picture from Ibn Ishaq is a pure jewel of realistic description. It exactly depicts the tribesmen of Central Arabia, as I have known them, although the scenes described took place more than thirteen centuries ago. In a few lines, it epitomises the tribesmen's greedy clamour for loot, combined with their free, humorous and familiar attitude to their leaders, which they somehow combine with a spirit of veneration and affection for a chief whom they admire and love. For they succeed in maintaining, on the one hand, a constant state of anarchy and half-rebellion and, on the other, an equalitarian respect for a popular leader.

When the Prophet came to distribute the camels, he gave the largest gifts to some of his bitterest enemies. Abu Sofian received a hundred camels and his son, Muawiya, another hundred. Suhail ibn Amr and Safwan ibn Umaiya, both of whose names had been on the short list of persons to be killed wherever found, but who had since been pardoned,[6] were given a hundred camels each likewise. Chiefs of Ghatafan and Beni Temeem, recent and doubtful converts, received the same generous gifts. But, for some reason, Abbás ibn Mirdás, the chief of Beni Sulaim, received only a trivial share of ten camels, although the tribe was said to have carried out a decisive mounted charge at Hunain.

Abbas ibn Mirdas, however, was a noted poet and immediately recited some biting verses, complaining of the manner in which the plunder had been distributed. When the Apostle heard the poem, he said to his intimates, "Get rid of this fellow and stop his mouth by gifts from me." So they called Abbas ibn Mirdas and gave him more and more camels until he expressed himself satisfied.

These details teach us endless aspects of the mentality of the people of Central Arabia.[7] Abbas ibn Mirdas was indignant from jealousy, rather than from greed, for other chiefs had received more than he, and had thus been treated with more honour. The Apostle, in this moment of supreme triumph and power, did not become arrogant or dictatorial. He tried to please everybody, and when one recipient of his generosity expressed himself dissatisfied, he did not lose his temper—he ordered that the gift be increased until the complainant was happy.

Not everyone, however, was satisfied with the manner in which the loot had been divided. The Helpers of Medina were among those who had been most bitterly disappointed, for it was chiefly they who had rallied to the Apostle during the first panic at Hunain and had thereby made the victory possible. Now, in the distribution of the plunder, they had received nothing. The camels had been distributed as bribes to win over the Prophet's enemies.

Saad ibn Ubada, the chief of the Khazraj, went to the Messenger of God to tell him of the resentment which the Helpers were expressing. "How do you yourself feel on this question, Saad?" asked Muhammad. "I feel with my people," answered the chief grimly. "Then collect them together and I will speak to them," said the Apostle. When Saad ibn Ubada had collected all the men of Medina, Muhammad addressed them.

[6] Page 319.
[7] At the risk of wearying the reader, I must repeat here the caution that the word Arab is used today of a great number of mixed peoples from Morocco to the Sudan and Iraq. Many of these people do not show any of the characteristics here outlined. I refer to the people of Arabia proper, most of whom are now in Saudi Arabia.

"O Helpers," he began, "what is this that I hear of you? Do you think ill of me in your hearts? Did I not come to you when you were erring and God guided you; poor and God made you rich; enemies and God softened your hearts? Why don't you answer me, O Helpers?" They replied, "How shall we answer you? Kindness and generosity belong to God and His Apostle."

"Had you so wished," the Prophet continued, "you could have said 'You came to us discredited, and we believed in you; deserted and we helped you; a fugitive and we took you in; poor and we comforted you.' In saying this, you would have spoken the truth. Are you disturbed in your minds because of the good things of this life, by which I win over a people that they may become Muslims, while I entrust you to your reliance upon God? Are you not satisfied that other men should take away flocks and herds, while you take the Apostle of God back with you to Medina? If all men went one way and the Helpers the other, I should take the way of the Helpers. May God have mercy on the Helpers, their sons and their sons' sons."[8] Such was the magnetism of the Apostle's personality that the men of Medina burts into tears "and wept until their beards were wet".

From the camp at Jirana, the Messenger of God rode into Mecca and performed the lesser pilgrimage. Thence he returned to Medina, which was now his home. He left a governor in charge of Mecca and a teacher to instruct the people in the Muslim religion and to recite the Qoran to them. The remainder of the plunder, which had not been distributed, followed him to Medina. He made his triumphant entry into the oasis on 16th March, 630.

NOTABLE DATES

Truce of Hudaibiya	March 628
Muslim Pilgrimage to Mecca	February 629
Battle of Mota	September 629
Capture of Mecca	January 630
Battle of Hunain	1st February 630
Siege of Taif	February–March 630
Return of Muhammad to Medina	16th March 630

[8] Ibn Ishaq.

PERSONALITIES

Muslims

Abu Bekr
Umar ibn al Khattab
Ali ibn abi Talib   } The Apostle's staff at
Abbas ibn Abdul Muttalib   Hunain
Usama ibn Zaid ibn Haritha
Abu Sofian ibn Harb

Muawiya ibn abi Sofian
Suhail ibn Amr   } Meccan opponents pardoned
Safwan ibn Umaiya   by Muhammad
Ikrima ibn abi Jahal

Khalid ibn al Waleed   War leader

Tribal Chiefs

Malik ibn Auf, chief of Hawazin defeated at Hunain
Abbas ibn Mirdas, chief of Beni Sulaim

Women

Shima, Muhammad's foster-sister

XVII

Tebook to Taif

Looking around them, and seeing no enemy remain—the Romans even having retired and left them alone in their deserts, the followers of the Prophet began to sell their arms, saying, "The wars for religion are now ended."

SIR WILLAIM MUIR, Life of Mahomet

Surely God has bought from the believers their persons and their possessions in return for which they will have Paradise. They fight in the way of God, they kill and are killed. This is faithfully promised in the Torah, the Gospel and the Qoran. And who is more faithful to his pledges than God? Rejoice together therefore in the sale which you have made.

Qoran IX, 111

Say: Nothing will happen to us, other than what God has decreed for us. He is our Lord. Let the believers rely on Him.

Qoran IX, 51, revealed on occasion of the Tebook expedition

XVII

IT will be remembered that the ruler of Egypt had sent Mary, a Christian slave girl, as a present to Muhammad, who had made her his concubine. She had born him a son, whom he called Ibrahim, doubtless after the patriarch, whose religion was the model for Islam. In March 630, however, when the Apostle returned to Medina, Ibrahim died at the age of one year. The Apostle had been devoted to the child and his death must have been a deep sorrow to him.

The loss of their son drew Muhammad and Mary closer to one another in their bereavement with the result that Hafsa, the somewhat irascible daughter of Umar, grew jealous. She was supported by Aisha and something of a domestic turmoil ensued. Peace, however, was ultimately restored.

The Messenger of God remained seven months in Medina after his return from Mecca. In September or October 630, he gave orders to prepare for an expedition to the Byzantine frontier. The weather in the Hejaz was still oppressively hot, water and grazing were scarce, and the movements of a large force would be extremely difficult. Perhaps also memories of the disaster at Mota deprived many men of the wish to face the Byzantines again.

It is not plain from the surviving accounts why the Apostle of God insisted on carrying out the expedition at this unfavourable season, when a delay of two months would have introduced easier conditions. It is true that a merchant is said to have come from the north and reported that a large Byzantine force had assembled at Tebook.[1]

This suggestion seems to be extremely improbable. Tebook itself was divided by two hundred miles of desert from the nearest Byzantine garrison and it would have been quite impossible for a force of Byzantine regular troops to reach Tebook in the late summer, or indeed at any time of year. Even if by "Byzantines", the Arab tribes of the area are intended, the same difficulties would have confronted them as were experienced by the Muslims—lack of water or grazing at the end of the summer.

[1] Tebook is pronounced as in fluke or Luke, not as in the English word "book". Map 10, page 279.

The unwillingness of the ordinary poor Arab to embark on a military operation at this season was not due solely to dislike of the exhaustion and the discomforts involved, which would not have daunted the bedouins, though it might have deterred the oasis dwellers of Medina. The Arabs, however, owned their own camels and horses, an extremely valuable part of their property. An arduous march at this time of year might well cause many of the camels or the horses to collapse and die of exhaustion, a serious loss to the owners.

The people of Medina, moreover, lived to a considerable extent on the produce of their date palms and October was the season for picking the date crop. It is possible that the Prophet himself, who with his closest advisers came of a merchant family, might at first not have made enough allowance for his followers, who lived by farming or stockbreeding. But it is curious that he insisted on leaving at this difficult season, when the proposal was greeted by so many protests. As we have seen, he was usually accessible, democratic and ready to listen to suggestions.

Perhaps many of the men called up excused themselves on the grounds that their riding camels were in poor condition, for the Apostle called upon the richer Muslims to assist in the preparations by supplying riding camels, or their purchase price in money. Othman ibn Affan, his son-in-law, a rich member of the Abid Shems branch of Quraish, gained special merit by his generous contribution. According to Ibn Hisham, the Apostle exclaimed, "O God, be pleased with Othman, for I am pleased with him." Abdulla ibn Ubay is alleged once again to have expressed his sympathy with those who complained of the unsuitability of the season for campaigning.

The Messenger of God ordered a camp to be pitched at Farewell Pass, a defile just north of Medina, where expeditions commonly assembled before starting for Syria. Thereupon, according to Ibn Ishaq, Abdulla ibn Ubay pitched a camp below him on the edge of the oasis. The object of this manœuvre is not obvious. Perhaps significant, however, is his observation that the camp of Ibn Ubay was the larger of the two. When the Apostle set out, Abdulla ibn Ubay returned home.

The difficulties encountered in the organisation of the expedition were the subject of a revelation, now embodied in Chapter IX of the Qoran.

Verse 38 begins: "O you who believe, what is the matter with you, when you are told to go forth in the way of God, that you make such heavy weather about starting? Are you satisfied with this earthly life rather than with the life to come? The good things of this life are but trivial in comparison with the life to come.

"If you will not go forth, God will punish you with a painful punishment and He will exchange you for another people and you will not do Him any harm . . .

"So go forth, both light and heavy, and fight with your goods and with your own selves in the way of God. If it had been an objective near by or a short journey, they would have followed you,[2] but the distance seemed to them too great. And they will swear to you, 'By God, we would certainly have gone with you if we had been able'."

Eventually the expedition set out. Further murmuring, however, was caused by the fact that the Prophet left behind the redoubtable Ali, who was the principal Muslim champion in single combats. Ali in fact was anxious to go, but the Apostle would not allow him to do so.

A hundred and eighty miles north of Medina, the raiders passed the ruins of Al Hijr.[3] This place, like Petra, had been inhabited in an earlier age by a partly troglodyte people. It seems probable that they placed their houses against the face of the sandstone cliffs, so that one or two rooms were built with walls of stone and mortar. They then dug into the cliff behind, so that another room or two were actually excavated into the rock. These inside rooms would be completely protected from the weather, cool in summer and warm and dry in winter. With the passage of time, the built-up part of the house would fall down and disappear leaving the back room looking like a rectangular cave cut in the cliff.

The large and more spectacular monuments of this nature, still to be seen at Petra and Al Hijr, were apparently temples and tombs. Arab tradition before Islam included many stories relating to the tribe of Thamood, who were alleged to have lived in the caves at Al Hijr. This tribe seems indeed to have existed, for it is mentioned in an inscription of Sargon, King of Assyria, in 715 B.C. In classical times, the name also appears in Ptolemy and Pliny.

According to the Qoran, God sent a Prophet by the name of Salih to warn Thamood to turn to Him. The poorer and weaker

[2] God is speaking to the Apostle.   [3] Also called Medain Salih.

members of the tribe obeyed the summons and turned to God but the richer and prouder tribesmen mocked him and persecuted him. He accordingly warned them of impending divine punishment and they were in fact exterminated by a cataclysm called in the Qoran an earthquake and a thunderbolt. In actual fact, a high but now extinct, range of volcanoes does overhang the ruins of Al Hijr on the west, and it is more than likely that Arab tradition was in this case correct, and that the settlement was destroyed by streams of lava from the volcanoes.

During the early years of his mission in Mecca, the Apostle saw in the story of the Prophet Salih, and the persecution and mockery which he suffered at the hands of Thamood, a parallel to his own rejection by the proud and wealthy clans of Quraish. The story is several times referred to in the Qoranic chapters revealed in Mecca, but when the Apostle became powerful and successful he probably ceased to compare himself with the Prophet Salih.

In Chapter VII, Verse 73, the Qoran says: "And to Thamood We[4] sent their brother Salih, who said to them, 'O people, worship God for there is no other god but He'." The same words are attributed to the Prophet Salih as were used by Muhammad himself.

The Apostle was deeply moved on this expedition to Tebook to see the ruined habitations of Thamood, of which he had so often spoken. The men began to draw water from a well but the Prophet prohibited its use for drinking or for ablutions. He believed the place to be haunted and forbade any of them to leave the camp singly. The following morning the men complained that they had no water, not having been allowed to draw from the well. Thereupon the Apostle prayed, and a heavy rainstorm supplied all the water which was required.

The story of the Prophet Salih and his mission to Thamood is of considerable interest, if it be true that he preached monotheism. The Qoran also mentions Hood[5] as having preached to the tribe of Ad, the location of which is uncertain, though it is believed to have lived in south Arabia.

Another monotheist predecessor of Muhammad is alleged to have been the Prophet Shuaib, whose mission was to Midian, a name associated with the northern Hejaz or Southern Trans-Jordan. The tomb of Shuaib, is still shown in a valley west of Amman. Lot is also mentioned with these early monotheists and is alleged to have

---

[4] As usual, God is speaking.   [5] Hood is pronounced as in food.

preached to the people of Sodom, who drove him out. Sodom was subsequently destroyed by an earthquake in the same way as Thamood.

In the case of all four of these prophets, their message is stated in the Qoran to have been accepted by the poor and humble but rejected by the rich and arrogant members of the tribe, as had occurred to Muhammad himself. Whether these ancient Arab prophets, lost in the mists of antiquity, represented early attempts to preach monotheism in Arabia, it is impossible to say.

*   *   *

At this stage of the journey, the Apostle's riding camel strayed away when out grazing and for a time was lost. One of the men was heard to remark, "Does Muhammad claim to be a prophet and to receive revelations from God and yet he does not know where his camel is?" We read also of the Apostle sending his confidential companions to mingle with the men round the camp-fires and to listen to their conversation. Thus the suspicion and malaise which had marked the departure of the expedition from Medina seems still to have persisted.

It is unlikely that this trouble resulted from any deterioration in the devotion of the convinced Muslims to the Apostle. It is more probable that it was caused by the rapid expansion which followed success. The rise of Islam depended almost entirely on the personality of Muhammad. As long as the believers consisted of less than two thousand men, most of them townsmen or villagers of Mecca or Medina, every man could be intimately known to the leader and could come under his personal influence. But when the number of professed Muslims exceeded ten thousand, the personal touch was lost.

Doubtless many now professed Islam because it was the easiest thing to do. Indeed, the wheel had turned full circle and it became increasingly dangerous to admit to being an idolater. Most of the neighbouring bedouin tribes, moreover, had now declared themselves Muslims. The bedouin tribe was in general a closely-knit community, distinct from the oasis dwellers in outlook and in way of life. Many tribes had become Muslims *en bloc*, as the result of a visit of their chief to the Apostle. Their resulting "conversion" was more in the nature of a political agreement than a genuine religious change.

Most of the tribesmen who were now declared to be Muslims had probably never seen the Apostle and had little idea of what their new faith involved.

*   *   *

The Muslim expedition halted at Tebook. The "governor" of Aila,[6] Yohanna ibn Ruba, came to Tebook to pay his respects and concluded an agreement with the Messenger of God. The people of Aila were Christians and Yohanna was probably their chief, not a Byzantine official. He agreed to pay a poll-tax in return for an undertaking that the people of Aila would be protected by the Muslims. They seem to have been a mercantile community, for the protection promised by Muhammad specifically included their caravans and their ships.

This agreement was subsequently to become the precedent everywhere used in countries conquered by the Muslims. No pressure was exerted on the Jews or the Christians to change their religion. They were declared to be under Muslim protection as soon as they agreed to pay the poll-tax. The Christian inhabitants of Jerba and Udhruh, some eighty miles north of Aila, likewise agreed to pay tax to ensure their own safety. Udhruh had once been the station of the Fourth Roman Legion and the ruins of their cantonment are still visible today. This territory was universally admitted to be under Byzantine suzerainty.

The Apostle then summoned Khalid ibn al Waleed and sent him with a detachment to Dumat al Jandal.[7] The ruler of Duma was a Christian Arab by the name of Ukaidir ibn Abdul Malik, of the ancient dynasty of Kinda. Ukaidir and his brother were out hunting oryx, which have always been numerous in the area until exterminated in recent years by the introduction of firearms. The hunting party was surprised by Khalid, who captured Ukaidir and killed his brother. Khalid never could carry out any mission without killing somebody.

The prince himself was taken prisoner. He is said to have been wearing a magnificent gown of brocade, heavily embroidered with gold lace, which scarcely seems the right garment for hunting in the desert. Whether, however, Khalid stripped the gown from his back

---

[6] The modern port of Aqaba. Map 10, page 279.

[7] Duma is mentioned in Isaiah XXI, 11. Its modern name is Jauf. Map 10, page 279.

or found it in his castle is immaterial. He sent it to the Apostle by a special messenger, in advance of his own return. The simple Arabs were amazed at the splendour of the garment, which they felt between their fingers and gazed at admiringly. "Do you admire this material?" asked the Messenger of God. "By Him in whose hand my life rests, the napkins used by Saad ibn Muadh[8] in paradise are better than this stuff."

Khalid brought Ukaidir to the Apostle as a prisoner of war. Muhammad talked with him and eventually concluded an agreement with him, according to which he consented to pay poll-tax for the people of Duma and to enter under the protection of the Muslims. The Prophet does not appear to have pressed him to change his religion. Ukaidir's court robe and his Christian faith perhaps suggest that he had visited Constantinople, but the Byzantines were too weak and too distant to afford him any protection now. Perhaps Khalid resented the leniency with which his prisoner was treated for, after the Apostle's death, he revisited Duma, killed Ukaidir and sacked the oasis.

The Muslims remained only ten days in Tebook and then returned to Medina. It will be remembered that, in the early days in Medina, raiding parties led by the Apostle himself rarely engaged in fighting. More often, the Prophet met and conversed with the tribal chiefs encountered and came to an agreement with them. The expedition to Tebook was another example of the same technique, though on a larger scale.

Under this system, the armed raiding parties which accompanied the Apostle on his expeditions were in reality little more than escorts to enhance his importance and to provide for his safety. The tacit threat conveyed by these military deomonstrations persuaded the local chiefs to come in. When they did so, they were exposed to the persuasiveness of the Apostle's talk, the real weapon which so rapidly extended his influence and that of the Muslim faith.

The name of "raids" was retained for these military expeditions, possibly to attract as many men as possible to them in the hopes of plunder. As we have seen, a part at least of the men who accompanied the Tebook expedition were by no means sincere Muslims. We may guess also that the reluctance of some of the false Muslims to

[8] Saad ibn Muadh, it will be remembered, was the chief of the Aus, who gave the verdict for the execution of the men of Beni Quraidha, and who died of a wound received at the siege of Medina.

accompany this particular party was due to the fact that they were beginning to realise that "raids" led by the Apostle in person rarely
resulted in much loot.

I have myself been a witness of similar situations in the 1920's,
when raiding was still common in Arabia and when Ibn Saud
himself periodically led armies composed of several thousand men
from different tribes. The bedouins greatly preferred a small tribal
raid, where they were their own masters and had a chance to seize and
dispose of any plunder they could take. They were half-hearted in joining Ibn Saud's larger operations, which had a political object, and which
produced a negligible amount of loot for the individual tribesman.

*   *   *

Before the Apostle set out for Tebook, a party of men of one of the
oasis groups in Medina had come to him and told him that they had
built a mosque "for the sick and the needy and for nights of bad
weather", and asked him to inaugurate it by coming there to pray
for them. He replied, however, that he was about to set out on the
expedition and that, if God willed, when he returned, he would
come and pray in their new mosque. The incident, at this stage,
appears perfectly normal.

On the return of the expedition, however, the Prophet ordered a
halt some five miles before reaching Medina. From this place, he
sent a party to burn down and completely to destroy the new mosque.
The Apostle's emissaries duly executed his orders, the mosque was
burnt down, and the people who were in it ran away.

The explanations of this incident are to the effect that the new
mosque was built near the Prophet's first mosque in Qoba, with a
view to drawing away its congregation. Alternatively it is alleged
that the builders of it were adherents of Abu Aamir, the Monk,[9] a
monotheist, who had rejected the leadership of Muhammad. Abu
Aamir had meanwhile migrated to Constantinople, whence he is
supposed to have sent a message to Medina, stating that he was coming with a Byzantine army to conquer Medina and ordering his
adherents to build a mosque for him. Perhaps the rumour of a
Byzantine army concentrating in the north had been connected
with the alleged threat of Abu Aamir.

The story in this form seems sufficiently ridiculous. The Byzantine

[9] Page 170.

Empire was in weakness and confusion after twenty-six years of war with Persia. It enjoyed so little prestige even in southern Jordan, that its subjects in Aila, Jerba and Udhruh, more than five hundred miles north of Medina, had placed themselves under the protection of Islam. Even at the very height of its power, the Roman Empire itself had never succeeded in subjecting the Hejaz. In any case, for Abu Aamir and the Byzantines to reach Medina would require months if not years of preparation, of none of which there was the least sign.

Possibly later Muslim commentators were as much in the dark as we are regarding the reasons for the destruction of this mosque. A charge that its builders had been instigated to do so "by a foreign imperialist power" would provide a plausible explanation and has, in this twentieth century, a decidedly familiar ring. *Plus ça change, plus c'est la même chose.*[10]

The association of the name of Abu Aamir with the builders of the new mosque *might* possibly suggest that they were monotheists who, however, were not prepared to admit the claims of Muhammad to divine revelation.

Chapter IX of the Qoran, which has already been quoted in regard to the reluctance of certain persons to go on the Tebook raid, goes on to deal with the incident of the mosque.

"As for the first believers, the Emigrants and the Helpers, and those who followed them in good works, God is well pleased with them and they with Him . . .

"But as for the nomadic tribesmen who are around you, they are false Muslims, as also the people of Medina are persistent in their hypocrisy. You do not know them but We[11] know them."

Verse 107 continues: "And those who built a mosque to cause harm and unbelief and to cause dissension between the believers . . ."

As Muslims, at the time, were already marking out mosques in other places, there must obviously have been some especial objection to this one.

*　　*　　*

On his return to Medina, three sincere Muslims came to the Apostle and confessed that they had not gone on the Tebook expedition. In punishment, he issued orders that no one was to speak to the three

---

[10] The more things change, the more do they turn out to be the same as before.
[11] God is speaking.

men. Such, it appears, was his power that no one, not even the members of their own families, would address a word to them. After forty days, an additional order was issued, telling them to separate from their wives and to send the women back to their parents, though without divorcing them.

On the fiftieth day of the boycott, the Apostle prayed the dawn prayer in the mosque. When prayers were over, he turned to a group of men beside him and told them that God had forgiven the three offenders. Immediately their friends dashed out to bear them the good news. Three men galloped off at full speed to find them, while others shouted at the tops of their voices, "Good news, Kaab ibn Malik!" "Good news, Hilal ibn abi Umaiya!"

Kaab ibn Malik, a well known poet, has described what happened. "Then I set off to find the Apostle," he used to say, when telling the story. "Men met me by the way, told me the good news and congratulated me on God having forgiven me. When I saluted the Apostle, his face shone with joy. 'This is the best day of your life. Congratulations on the good news,' he said to me. 'From you or from God?' I asked. 'From God, of course,' he replied. When he told anyone good news, his face used to shine like the moon . . . I sat before him, and told him that, as an act of penitence, I would give away my property to God and His Apostle."

It seemed to me worth while to tell this story in full, to show the extraordinary power wielded by the Messenger of God and the simple faith of the first Muslims.

The long revelation in Chapter IX of the Qoran, which deals with all the unfortunate misunderstandings connected with the Tebook raid, refers to the three who were punished by the boycott in verses 117 and 118.

"God has truly accepted the Prophet and the Emigrants and the Helpers who followed him in the time of hardship, when the hearts of some of them nearly deviated . . .

"And to the three whose case was postponed until the world seemed to them too narrow to hold them, and their own souls were straitened within them. Then they knew that there was no refuge from God but in Him. Then He forgave them in order that they might repent."

*   *   *

After his return to Medina, in December 630 the Apostle received an emissary from Taif, who came to treat for an agreement. As a result of his conversations with Muhammad, he himself accepted Islam sincerely. Returning to Taif, he addressed the people from a window on the first floor of his house. But they shot at him and killed him, though he had previously been extremely popular with the people, who had chosen him as their representative to negotiate a peace.

A few months later, however, the tribe of Thaqeef, to which most of the people of Taif belonged, decided that they could not indefinitely oppose the triumphant extension of Islam. Most of the surrounding desert tribes had now declared themselves Muslims and took pleasure in driving off the flocks and plundering the caravans of the people of Taif, activities additionally gratifying when they could be carried out in the name of God. Eventually a new delegation, this time consisting of six members, one from each clan, was sent to negotiate in Medina.

The Messenger of God caused a tent to be pitched for them near the mosque. They explained that they had come to tender their submission and to accept Islam, on condition that the Apostle give them a document guaranteeing the safety of their people, their lands and their livestock. A difficulty arose, however, over the request put forward by the delegates that, although they would accept Islam, they be allowed to retain their goddess, Al Lat, for a period of three years. When the Apostle refused their request, they tried to bargain for two years, one year, six months or even one month.

Eventually the Apostle of God sent Abu Sofian with them to destroy the statue of Al Lat, a remarkable and perhaps wise choice, for Abu Sofian had, only a few months before, been a persevering idolater. The delegation also requested that they be exempted from saying prayers, which involved bows and prostrations which seemed to them undignified. But the Prophet replied that there was no good in a religion which had no prayers. The delegates were consequently obliged to yield this point also, but, in return, they obtained the document guaranteeing the security of their lives and their property.

When, however, the Messenger of God chose a man of Taif to teach his fellow-citizens how to pray, he secretly enjoined him to keep the prayers short. "You should measure men by their weakest members," he said. "For there are among them old and young, sick and infirm." Muhammad was always reasonable in his demands on human nature. He strenuously opposed asceticism and self-inflicted hardships, though all these features were to appear after his death. "God has not ordered us to destroy ourselves," he would say. Yet even so, five prayers a day and fasting for a month in Ramadhan were no easy discipline.

Al Jáhiz[12] tells how once a Muslim was praising a pious friend for his fasting when a bedouin interrupted him. "This man seems to believe", the tribesman exclaimed, "that God will have no mercy on him unless he tortures himself in this way." Most bedouins, according to our standards of diet, were half-starved anyhow, without additional imposed fasts.

The delegation travelled back to Taif in some trepidation, in view of the fate which had overtaken the first delegate on his return to the town. Abu Sofian firmly refused to have anything to do with the destruction of the idol and decided to stay on a property he owned outside the town. However, a Muslim called Al Mughira ibn Shuba, a native of Taif who had previously accepted Islam in Medina, went up to Al Lat and struck her with an axe. Next the gold, jewels and necklaces with which she was adorned and the treasure buried in the ground beneath her, were collected and removed. The statue[13] of the goddess was then smashed to pieces. There was, this time, no armed resistance, though the women of Taif collected, dishevelled and bare-headed, to weep for the loss of their protectress, basely abandoned by their cowardly men.

*   *   *

When the first pilgrimage season came round after the Muslim occupation of Mecca, the Apostle sent Abu Bekr to supervise the ceremonies. After he had left Medina for Mecca, however, the Apostle received a new revelation, which was written out and sent after Abu Bekr, by the hand of Ali. The pilgrimage took place according to the ancient ritual, those taking part being a mixture of Muslims and polytheists. When the pilgrims were gathered at Mina, in the course of the normal ceremonies, Ali read out the new revelation to the assembled crowds.

In brief, it declared that idolaters were to be allowed a period of

---

[12] Al Jáhiz, *Bayan* (quoted by Goldziher).

[13] The term statue is perhaps deceptive, for she seems to have been little more than a slab of white stone.

four months' grace, after which the Muslims would declare war on them. The Apostle accordingly announced that, after a period of four months, he was free of all responsibility towards idolaters, who would be attacked, killed and plundered wherever met. An exception was made, however, in the case of such idolatrous communities as had a past agreement with the Apostle, pledging them security for a certain specified time. Such agreements would be respected by the Muslims until the expiry of the period stated.

A second innovation introduced in this new revelation was that in future only Muslims were to be permitted to perform the pilgrimage. Idolaters would no longer be allowed to visit the shrine where their idols had, until a year before, reigned supreme. The circumambulation of the Kaaba by men in a state of nakedness was also forbidden.

These new orders are contained in the opening verses of Chapter IX of the Qoran. The later part of this chapter deals with the Tebook expedition. The verses of the chapter are therefore not in the chronological order of the events.

Chapter IX, verse 1, begins: "An exemption from responsibility from God and from His Apostle towards the polytheists with whom you have entered into agreements.

"Go freely about the earth for four months and know that you cannot wear God out and that God will bring shame on unbelievers.

"An announcement from God and from His Messenger to the people on the day of the great pilgrimage. God is clear of liability towards the polytheists and so is His Messenger. If you repent, it will be better for you. If you turn back, you cannot exhaust God. So give the unbelievers warning of a painful punishment . . .

"So when the forbidden months[14] are passed, kill the polytheists wherever you find them. Seize them, lay siege to them, and lay ambushes for them. But if they repent and say their prayers and pay the poor tax, release them and let them go free."

The new orders applied only to idolaters—not to Jews or Christians against whom force was not to be used.

* * *

Abdulla ibn Ubay died in February 631. On his deathbed, he sent a message to the Apostle of God, begging him to attend his funeral and

[14] This refers to the four months' grace allowed to idolaters to repent.

to pray over his grave. In spite of the remonstrances of the vindictive Umar, Muhammad complied with the dying man's last request.

Abdulla remains a somewhat puzzling character. He was probably jealous of the Apostle, who had replaced him as chief of his home town. He did not fight with enthusiasm for Islam, but then he did not like fighting. Before Islam, in the war between the Aus and the Khazraj, he had not fought for his own tribe.

If he was as hostile as the historians pretend, it is curious that the Prophet did not have him assassinated, as he did several lesser men. Indeed, tradition relates that his own son offered to murder him but that the Apostle refused. Was this because he was not so bad as the historians make out or because he continued to be liked and respected by the people of Medina, in spite of his "hypocrisy"?

NOTABLE DATES

The Migration to Medina	622
Battle of Bedr	624
Battle of Uhud	625
Siege of Medina (The Ditch)	627
Truce of Hudaibiya	628
Occupation of Mecca	630
Death of the Apostle's son Ibrahim	March 630
Expedition to Tebook	September–October 630
The first Muslim pilgrimage	
Ultimatum to all remaining idolaters	February 631

PERSONALITIES

Muslims

Othman ibn Affan, the Apostle's son-in-law, who gave funds to equip the Tebook expedition

Khalid ibn al Waleed, the bloodthirsty Commander

Abdulla ibn Ubay, "the Hypocrite"

Ibrahim, the Apostle's son

Non-Muslims

Ukaidir ibn Abdul Malik, Christian Prince of Duma

Abu Aamir the Monk, the hostile monotheist

Yohanna ibn Ruba, Prince of Aila

Women

Mary, the Egyptian Christian concubine. Mother of the Apostle's son, Ibrahim

XVIII

Completion and Farewell

Lay injunctions on women kindly . . . You have taken them only as a trust from God . . . know that every Muslim is a Muslim's brother, and that all the Muslims are brethren.

IBN ISHAQ, *Muhammad's Farewell Sermon*

Of all the wonders that I yet have heard,
It seems to me most strange, that men should fear;
Seeing that death, a necessary end,
Will come when it will come.

WILLIAM SHAKESPEARE, *Julius Caesar*

No great man lives in vain,
The history of the world is but the biography of great men.

THOMAS CARLYLE, *On Heroes and Hero-Worship*

Farewell! A long farewell, to all my greatness!
This is the state of man.

WILLIAM SHAKESPEARE, *King Henry VIII*

Even so we in like manner, as soon as we were born, began to draw to our end.

The Wisdom of Solomon V, 13

XVIII

IT will be remembered[1] that the primitive Arabs originally made use of lunar months, the simplest form of calendar among an uneducated people, because the phases of the moon are plainly visible in the sky. Twelve lunar months, however, are approximately eleven days short of the solar year of three hundred and sixty-five days. Thus a year of twelve lunar months moves round the calendar. A month which at one time falls in summer, moves gradually into spring, then into winter and so on.

The Apostle's great-great-great-grandfather, the famous Qusai, had introduced an intercalary month to make the lunar year fit in with the solar year. Every third year, the lunar year had thirteen months. The object of this was to ensure that the pilgrimage always came at the same time of the year. Unfortunately Qusai's intercalary month was not quite accurate enough, but it was a gallant attempt.

In 631, at the time which we have now reached, the Messenger of God received a revelation forbidding the intercalation of the thirteenth lunar month.

Chapter IX, verse 37, reads: "The intercalation of an extra month is only greater unbelief, whereby unbelievers go astray, making it legal one year and sacred the next year, that they may agree in the number of months which God has made sacred. Thereby they make open that which God has made sacred. Their evil deeds seem good to them, for God does not guide an unbelieving people."

Ever since this prohibition, the lunar year, which is observed for Muslim religious feasts, including the month of fasting and the date of the pilgrimage, loses about eleven days a year as compared to the solar calendar. The significance of the prohibition is difficult for us today to understand.

*   *   *

When the news was spread by the returning pilgrims that the Apostle had declared war to the knife on all polytheists, the remaining tribes were alarmed. There could be no doubt that many tribes

[1] Page 64.

would be ready to join him if he announced a campaign against any community which still practised the old religion. Such tribesmen might well be but half-hearted Muslims, but nobody disliked a raid, which might bring a chance of loot.

Moreover, it must again be emphasised that the idolatry of the Arabs was outworn and, in any case, commanded no great enthusiasm. The fact that the Muslims had everywhere smashed up figures of Al Lat, Al Uzza and other local gods, and had not, as a result, met with divine retribution, proved to many men that the old gods were indeed powerless. Where, therefore, further resistance might result in a devastating war at great odds, the most reasonable course seemed to be to ride to Medina and make peace.

The year 631 has, therefore, been called the Year of Deputations. From all over Arabia, representative parties of Arabs arrived in Medina to meet the Messenger of God, to accept Islam and to make peace. We are, of course, inclined to think that conversions due to fear or greed are of no value, but historically this is not the case. The actual man who changes his religion from fear is probably insincere. But when he has done so, his children can be brought up in the new faith. By the time the third or fourth generation is reached, the original method of conversion is forgotten and the descendants of the original false converts have become whole-hearted believers.

This result was to ensue in the case of the Arabs, whom the Apostle had so often denounced as hypocrites. The fact that they were indeed time-servers was proved immediately after the Prophet's death, when almost all the Arab tribes rebelled and had to be conquered by force. But the second, third, and fourth generations of the false Muslims were to conquer a great part of the civilised world with a passionate enthusiasm which could not be resisted.

The Apostle only required a professed convert to repeat the formula, "There is no god but God and Muhammad is the Messenger of God". This done, the neophyte was immediately accepted as a Muslim on terms of equality with his brother-Muslims and no questions were asked. Of the insincerity of these professions the companions of the Apostle often complained. A Muslim might, sword in hand, be pursuing a fleeing polytheist and about to slash off his head, when the fugitive would shout, "There is no god but God, and Muhammad is the Messenger of God". The Muslim would be obliged immediately to sheath his sword and welcome his brother in the faith.

To pronounce a dozen words seemed deceptively easy. But, although the convert was asked no questions, the apostate was instantly killed. The new convert, though perhaps insincere, found himself caught in a trap. From then onwards, any suspicion of backsliding might mean death.

*   *   *

The account of the arrival of a deputation from the large tribe of Beni Temeem[2] from central Nejed presents certain typical, and even amusing features. One or two chiefs of the tribe had already become Muslims and had been with the Apostle at the capture of Mecca and on the Day of Hunain, but this time they had brought a large deputation from the leaders of the tribe. Bedouins have always been equalitarian, frank and outspoken. In our own times, I have often heard them addressing as "O man" an important government official to whom his subordinates spoke as "Your Excellency". The desert has been justly compared to the sea, and bedouins have loud, gruff voices like sea-captains.

The large group of Beni Temeem visitors arrived in the Apostle's mosque in Medina, still an open space with mud-brick buildings around it and a canopy overhead formed by the waving date palms. Not seeing anyone to receive them, they shouted outside the Prophet's house, which formed one side of the courtyard of the mosque, "Come out, O Muhammad, and talk to us". This loud and unceremonious shout annoyed the Apostle, who was accustomed to more deferential treatment, as it has annoyed most of the important people who have come in contact with Arab nomads for the last thirteen centuries. Nevertheless, the Apostle came out to them and greeted them.

They challenged him to a contest in poetry and oratory, which he was courteous enough to accept, though he himself disliked poetry and viewed the glorification of the deeds of ancestors as little more than heathenism. The respect and affection felt by the old Arabs for their ancestors was not quite a religion, but was a deep and genuine emotion, like the patriotic pride felt by modern Europeans or Americans in the past histories of their countries. The vehemence with which the Messenger of God denounced the glorification of ancestral heroism seems to indicate that he sensed that its emotional appeal was indeed a rival to religion.

[2] Beni Temeen still exist in the same area, chiefly in the oases. Map 7, page 176.

Beni Temeem opened the contest with a speech declaring the power and wealth of their tribe, which entitled its chiefs to claim equality in rank with the kings and princes of the world. The Apostle called up a man of the Khazraj, a Helper of Medina, to reply to this speech. This he did by praising God for His bounty to men and for the fact that He had chosen the Apostle and had revealed to him His book, the Qoran. The first of creatures to answer the call of the Apostle had been the men of Medina, who came forward as God's Helpers. They were ready to continue fighting unceasingly in the cause of God.

The speeches over, Beni Temeem asked permission for their poets to recite. The Apostle sent hastily for his principal poetical champion, Hassan ibn Thabit, to answer the visitors, and a number of compositions were exchanged between the two parties. When the poets had exhausted their rhymes, Al Aqra ibn Hábis of Beni Temeem stood up and said, "By the life of my father, this man has some ready helpers. His orator and his poets are better than ours and their voices are more melodious." The visitors accepted Islam and departed for their homes with valuable gifts presented to them by the Apostle.

Their pride, their boastfulness, their addiction to poetry and their rough egalitarianism are as typical of the Nejed tribesmen of today as of the seventh century. Presumably they felt it somewhat beneath their dignity simply to make their submission, especially to a mere townsman, who belonged to a race of shopkeepers. Thus the pretence of a contest, followed by the recognition of the superiority of the Apostle's poet, and their own pretence of a deliberate weighing in the balance of whether or not to come to an agreement, made the process more dignified. The practice of making presents to visiting chiefs when they take their leave is thousands of years old and is still followed by Ibn Saud to this day.

Thus the visit ended successfully and Beni Temeem joined the ranks of the Muslims. Nevertheless, the rough manners of the tribesmen left a slightly unpleasant taste, if Ibn Ishaq and Tabari are right in saying that Chapter XLIX, verses 1 to 5, came down from God in reference to this incident.

"O you who believe, do not push yourselves forward in the presence of God and His Apostle . . .

"O you who believe, do not raise your voices above the voice of the Prophet and do not speak to him in a loud voice as you speak to one another . . .

"Surely those who lower their voices in the presence of God's Apostle are those whose hearts God has proved and who will be in His keeping and will receive His forgiveness and a great reward.

"Surely those who call to you[3] when you are in your private apartments are mostly people who do not understand. If they had waited patiently until you came out to them, it would have been better for them and God is forgiving and merciful."

*   *   *

The deputations followed one another in rapid succession, as if Medina had been the capital of a great empire. Two men came to the Apostle in order to assassinate him, but they lost their nerve at the last moment. One man required Muhammad to swear an oath in his presence that he really was a messenger of God and, declaring himself satisfied when he did so, went away and converted his whole tribe.

A deputation is said to have come from Beni Haneefa, accompanied by a certain Musailima, who was later himself to claim to be a messenger from God. According to one account, when he returned to the tribe in eastern Nejed, he wrote a letter to Muhammad.

"From Musailima, the Apostle of God, to Muhammad, the Apostle of God. Let us divide the earth between us, half to me and half to you." The Prophet is alleged to have replied, "From Muhammad, the Apostle of God, to Musailima, the liar. The earth is the Lord's. He causes such of His servants to inherit it as He pleases."

Immediately after the death of Muhammad, Musailima and Beni Haneefa rejected Islam and hard fighting and heavy casualties were necessary before they were again reduced to subjection. We know little about Musailima, the only surviving records being the writings of Muslims, who refer to him briefly with hatred and contempt.

A more welcome visitor was a chief of the tribe of Tai, called Zaid al Khail, or Zaid of the Horses. As his name indicated, he was a famous champon on horseback. Zaid and the majority of his party conversed at length with the Apostle and eventually accepted Islam. After their departure, Muhammad is alleged to have said, "Whenever I have met an Arab whom I have previously heard praised in the highest terms, I have always found him to be below the estimate which I had heard of him. The only exception was Zaid of the Horses. He exceeded all that I had heard of him." One member of Zaid's

[3] God is speaking to the Apostle.

party, however, had remained obdurate. After the interview with the Messenger of God, he said, "I see here a man who wishes to gain ascendancy over all people, but nobody shall rule over me but myself." Here spoke the genuine voice of the anarchic love of freedom of the desert.

Zaid of the Horses died almost immediately after his visit to Medina, and thus this famous knight did not share in the great Arab conquests which were to begin three years later. His tribe, Tai, however, played a distinguished part. The Apostle attached great importance to omens conveyed by names and frequently changed names in order to make theme more auspicious. On this occasion, he was not happy about the sobriquet Zaid al Khail and changed it to Zaid al Khair—Zaid of Goodness instead of Zaid of the Horses.

On another occasion, on the campaign of Bedr, the Apostle had passed through a valley called Narrow Valley. The omen was unfavourable, so he ordered the name to be changed to Easy Valley. The custom survived in Muslim Arabia. Many places are to be found called Al Tayyiba, the Good, or Tayyib Ism, Good Name, the original appellation of which conveyed some unpleasant idea. I once accompanied King Abdulla of Jordan on a visit to a rural area. He enquired the name of a certain ravine and was told that it was called *Wadi al Yabis*, or Dry Valley. He immediately ordered its name to be changed to the Well-Watered Valley, *Wadi al Rayan.*

Mention has already been made of Hatim, the chief of Tai,[4] whose name has long been proverbial for his generosity. Hatim was dead at the time of which we are writing, but his son, Adi, was a Christian and had moved to Syria to avoid the Muslims. On the advice of his sister, however, he visited Medina and greeted the Apostle in his mosque. The latter invited him to his house but, on the way, was accosted by an old woman. The Prophet stood patiently without interrupting her, until she had confided in him all her troubles. The two then entered Muhammad's house. The Apostle offered his visitor a quilt to sit on, while he himself sat on the bare ground. These signs of humility so impressed Adi that he agreed to become a Muslim.

Another aristocratic deputation came from the tribe of Kinda, who had formerly been one of the princely dynasties of Arabia. The extension of Islam had hitherto been limited to the Hejaz and to

[4] Page 32. Map 7, page 176.

neighbouring Nejed, but had not apparently penetrated the Yemen or Hadhramaut, distant countries, mountainous and difficult of approach. Possibly in April 631, deputations came from Zubaid, who lived on the Red Sea coast. Soon they were followed by Beni Bajeela, whose country lay in the mountains of the interior of the Yemen. After the return of the expedition from Tebook, a messenger had arrived with a letter from the sons of Abid Kulal and other princes of the once famous and glorious dynasty of Himyar.

The Apostle wrote them a long and detailed letter in reply, setting out the exact scale of taxation which they would have to pay on their lands and cattle, if they wished to join the Muslim community. They would also be obliged to fight those tribes which were still idolaters, a task perhaps more congenial than the payment of taxes.

So skilful was the Apostle's diplomacy, or so quarrelsome were the Yemenites, that the chiefs who came to Medina returned home and attacked their idolatrous neighbours. By this means, a large part of the Yemen was won for Islam, although no army was ever sent there by Muhammad.

We have seen[5] that there had long been communities of Christians and Jews in the Yemen and in Najran.[6] The following extract from the Apostle's letter to the Himyarite princes is therefore of interest.

"If a Jew or a Christian becomes a Muslim, he is a believer with the same rights and obligations as the other Muslims. Those, however, who hold fast to their religion, whether Jews or Christians, are not to be obliged to change it. They must pay the poll-tax, one dinar for every adult, male or female, slave or free, or its equivalent in goods. He who pays this tax to God and His Apostle has his security guaranteed by God and His Apostle, but he who withholds the tax, is the enemy of God and His Apostle."

The Prophet sent a party of Muslims to the Himyarite princes, under the leadership of Muadh ibn Jabal, to collect the taxes and bring the proceeds to Medina. He warned the people of the Yemen not to send the tax collectors back unsatisfied. To Muadh ibn Jabal, however, he is said to have given instructions to deal gently and not harshly with the new converts. We need not conclude that the Apostle was insistent upon the payment of taxes from financial motives alone. In Arabia, the payment of a tax has always been

[5] Page 49.   [6] Map 3, page 47.

looked upon as the sign of political subjection. The taxes were thus the seal of submission to God and His Messenger.

*   *   *

The arrival of so many deputations in Medina has struck certain Western historians as an extraordinary tribute to the power achieved by the Apostle. It did, of course, signify that his reputation had spread to the furthest bounds of Arabia. The fact, however, that most of the tribes rebelled as soon as Muhammad was dead, proves that their respect was accorded to him personally, rather than to his religion.

In practice, however, deputations have been an ancient custom of the Arab nomads from time immemorial. First of all, we must remember that the basic loyalty of the bedouins was to the tribe alone. As we have seen, "rulers" periodically rose above the tribal level and, by military methods, imposed their rule—more or less— on many different tribes. Such princes were often cruel, ruthless and treacherous, because they were in search of power over other men. Tribes did not seek to subjugate other tribes, and, as a result, their endless wars were sporting rather than ruthless.

To a tribe, however, a ruler was a constant danger and it was the duty of the chiefs to ward off the menace by diplomacy. This was normally accomplished by a deputation of chiefs, who went to visit the would-be ruler. The latter would welcome his visitors with pleasure, for they represented armed men who could be won to support him, or who could weaken him by giving their allegiance to a rival. The prince would therefore greet the deputation, invite the leaders to dinner with him, entertain them for several days with cordiality and dismiss them with gifts and with handsome suits of clothes. The visitors would ride home dressed as gaily as peacocks, thereby spreading the fame of the prince's generosity.

The tribes, however, would feel no more loyalty for the ruler than most Americans, British or French people feel for the United Nations, a purely political organisation, above the national loyalty which commands their emotions.

For the tribal chiefs, these visits were valuable occasions, for the acquisition of gifts of money, horses or camels and handsome clothing, which enhanced their prestige when they reached home. The value of the gifts was carefully graded according to the importance of the chief and the power of his tribe, and a leader who received an inferior present was offended in his honour. We have seen the indignation of Abbas ibn Mirdas of Beni Sulaim, when he received only ten camels after Hunain.[7]

* * *

It is noteworthy that the simple faith first expounded by the Apostle in Meccan days had now acquired a legal and a ritual code. At the first pledge of Aqaba, the converts were told to worship the One God alone and not to associate with Him any minor spirits or deities; not to steal, commit fornication or kill their children; they were not to slander their neighbours nor disobey the Apostle in what was right. Those who fulfilled these pledges were promised admission to Paradise.

Now, however, the instructions given to converts in the Yemen were long and detailed. They were to be taught the ritual and the obligations of the greater and the lesser pilgrimage. In the event of disputes, their cases were not to be decided, as hitherto, by ancient tribal custom but by Muslim law. Those who continued to follow tribal custom were to be smitten with the sword. In performing their ablutions before prayer, they were to wash their faces, their hands up to the elbow and their feet up to the ankle, and so on.

The obligation to pay taxes was elaborated for irrigated land, land watered by rain or by bucket or water-lift, and the rates of taxation on camels, sheep and cows were carefully regulated. Islam had become a government, an administration and a way of life, laying down in ever greater detail every action in the daily routine of the Muslim.

* * *

When the pilgrimage season of 632 came round the Messenger of God decided to direct the ceremonies himself. He set out from Medina on 20th February, 632, surrounded by an immense crowd of the faithful, some on foot and some mounted on camels, extending as far as the eye could see in every direction.

Muhammad's last pilgrimage, which he celebrated on 9th March, 632, carried an immense significance. Everything he did on this

[7] Page 328.

historic occasion was subsequently embodied in the ritual which is followed to this day. The historians record the sermon which the ageing Apostle is said to have delivered to the assembled pilgrims. Among various points emphasised are alleged to have been a prohibition of usury, but a confirmation of the rights of private property. All blood-feuds dating from the period of idolatry were abolished. The twelve lunar months were to be used and intercalary months were forbidden. Women were to be kindly treated, for husbands held their wives in trust from God. Every Muslim was the brother of every other Muslim. Pride of ancestry was wicked and was abolished.

At the end of his sermon, he asked those present, "Have I not told you what to do and completed my mission?" The men replied in a loud voice, "Yes, by God, you have". The Apostle raised his eyes to heaven and cried, "O God, bear witness".

Every detail of the ceremonies was indicated by the Prophet, as he went through them, the ritual throwing of stones at the devil at Muzdalifa, the slaughtering of the sacrificial victims at Mina, the circumambulation of the Kaaba and the wearing of the special pilgrim dress. At length, he dismissed the pilgrims, and set out on the return journey to Medina. He was never to see Mecca again. His pilgrimage has ever since been referred to in Muslim history as the Pilgrimage of Farewell.

*   *   *

In May 632, after the Farewell Pilgrimage, the Apostle called for a levy of men for an expedition to Syria. An interesting and significant feature of this expedition is the fact that Usama, the son of Zaid ibn Haritha, was appointed as commander, although he was only twenty years old and had no experience of command. His father, Zaid ibn Haritha, had been killed on the Day of Mota. Thus, once again, we see the reappearance of the motive of private revenge. It was the right of this young man to avenge his father's defeat and death.

In spite of the fact that this was a familiar Arab pattern, the appointment provoked a good deal of criticism, especially among the more experienced veterans, who found themselves placed under the command of a beardless boy. The Arab historians are virtually silent on the outcome of this expedition. Ibn Ishaq has a brief note to the

effect that they took some prisoners from a port, presumably on the
Red Sea.

*   *   *

Fatima, the Apostle's surviving daughter, had been married to Ali
and had given birth to two sons, Hasan and Husain. To these, his
only male descendants, the Prophet was profoundly devoted. He
was never happier than when he was playing with them. When he
prostrated himself in prayer, they would climb on his back and he,
with no sign of impatience, would put them quietly down and continue
his devotions. Although his own descendants were limited to these
two little boys, his house was often filled with little relations or cousins.
He loved children and he always enjoyed playing with them.

The last two years of his life, especially after the fall of Mecca and
the defeat of Hawazin at Hunain, were one endless round of obligations. There were frequent delegations to be received, each requiring
long discussions, explanations of the Muslim religion, and legal and
financial orders.

There were many minor legal and administrative problems to
settle, his decisions in which were passed down in Muslim tradition
and became unchanging laws for hundreds of millions of persons,
for centuries to come. Although most of these incidents did not
necessitate revelations and were not, therefore, recorded in the
Qoran, many passed into the Traditions of the Prophet and acquired
the force of law.

His kindness to women, children and slaves even extended to
animals. He forbade men to hit horses or donkeys on the head, or to
cut off their manes and tails.

He greeted all his visitors with kindness and usually with smiles.
He was even known at times to play little practical jokes on his
intimates. Although he smiled frequently, he never laughed loudly,
but this may have been, then as now, a universal Arab quality. The
loud roar of laughter with the mouth wide open, as practised by
Europeans, is considered by the Arabs undignified.

*   *   *

One night in June 632, the Apostle called to one of his freedmen
and told him that God had ordered him to go to the cemetery and

pray for the dead. Accompanied by this man, he went out until he stood among the graves, whereupon he addressed the dead.

> "Peace be unto you, O people of the graves. Happy are you, for you are much better off than men here. Dissensions have come like waves of darkness, one after another, the last being worse than the first."

When he had prayed, he called his freedman and returned to his house. The next morning, he felt a violent headache. He tried to visit his wives, going to each in her separate room, but he collapsed in Maimoona's apartment. His wives gathered round, and he obtained their permission for him to be nursed through this illness in Aisha's room.[8]

Men had been slow to complete their preparations and join Usama's raid, already mentioned, owing to their resentment at his appointment. The Apostle, however, was strong enough to perform the ceremony of presenting Usama with the war-banner for his expedition, a ritual first introduced by Qusai.[9]

Then he bound a scarf tightly round his head to ease the throbbing pain of his headache and struggled into the mosque for prayers. The departure of Usama's expedition was delayed in view of the serious state of the Prophet's health. He suffered a burning fever, to find relief from which he ordered his wives to bring in a tub in which he sat, while they poured cold water over him until he cried, "Enough, enough!"[10]

Unable any longer to lead the public prayers, he gave orders for Abu Bekr to take his place. On one occasion, Abu Bekr happening to be absent, Umar ibn al Khattab stood up to lead the prayers. But the Apostle, recognising his voice, for Aisha's room opened directly on to the mosque, called out from his bed, "No, No! Only Abu Bekr." Presumably he was afraid of rivalry between Abu Bekr and Umar after his death and wished to emphasise that he regarded Abu Bekr as the senior.

On another occasion, he said, "O Emigrants, behave kindly to the Helpers, for other men increase but they cannot grow more numerous. They have been my continual support and comfort. So treat their good men well and forgive those who are remiss."[11]

---

[8] Normally he visited each of his wives in strict rotation.   [9] Page 64.
[10] Ibn Ishaq.   [11] Ibn Ishaq.

Some of his wives collected together with some other women and decided to force him to take medicine. His uncle Abbas was present and offered to help, but the women seem to have succeeded in forcing it down. The Apostle asked why they had done so, and they said, "We were afraid you might get pleurisy". But he replied that God would not afflict him with so diabolical a disease. He then gave an order, according to Ibn Ishaq, that all the women were to be made to take their own medicine!

In fact, in the light of modern knowledge, it seems probable that the Apostle died of pneumonia. He perhaps caught a chill when praying after midnight in the graveyard, for the next morning he had a headache and thereafter his fever increased continually. On the tenth day of his illness, the fever was at its highest, he was partly unconscious and his body was racked with pain. Then the following morning, when Abu Bekr was leading the dawn prayer, the door of Aisha's room suddenly opened and the Apostle appeared smiling in the courtyard of the mosque. He motioned with his hand for the prayers to continue and himself sat down on the ground to rest.

When the prayers were over, Abu Bekr came to him, saying happily, "O Apostle of God, I see that today you enjoy the favour and goodness of God, as we all wish". Thinking that Muhammad had recovered, he asked leave to visit his family, who lived in a settlement on the other side of the oasis.

The Apostle then returned to his bed and lay down with his head on Aisha's breast. He cleaned his teeth energetically and then lay back again. The morning was getting hot and he lay still. Suddenly Aisha noticed that his head had grown heavy. "Lord, grant me pardon," he said. His eyes grew fixed. She seemed to hear him say, "The most Exalted Companion is of Paradise". The Prophet of the Arabs had gone to meet his Lord.

Aisha gently put down his head, then scrambled to her feet, weeping and beating her breast.

*   *   *

Abu Bekr had gone to see his family and would be away all day. Umar was the nearest leader of the community but, when told that the Messenger of God was dead, he protested violently, "The disloyal will say that the Apostle is dead," he said excitedly, "but, by God, he is not dead. He has gone to God, as Moses went to see

God, and was hidden from the people for forty days, returning to them after they said he was dead. By God, the Apostle will return as Moses returned, and he will cut off the hands and the feet of those who have said he was dead."

Meanwhile, Abu Bekr had heard the news and had hurried back to the mosque, where Umar was still excitedly haranguing the crowd. Abu Bekr slipped by silently, pushed open the door and entered Aisha's room, where the body lay covered by an embroidered cloak of Yemeni work. Lifting the corner of the cloak, he kissed the dead man's face saying, "You are dearer to me than my father and mother. You have tasted death as God decreed." Replacing the cloak he went out again into the crowded courtyard.

Umar was still excitedly addressing the crowd. "Gently, Umar, keep quiet," Abu Bekr said, but Umar was too excited to listen. Abu Bekr accordingly moved a few paces away and called to the people, whereupon they left Umar and came to him.

"O men," he said quietly, "if anyone worships Muhammad, let him know now that Muhammad is dead. But if anyone worships God, let him know that God is alive and immortal for ever." Then he recited Chapter III, verse 143, of the Qoran.

"And Muhammad is only a messenger and the apostles before him have died. If he died or were killed, would you turn back in your tracks? Whoever turns back in his tracks, will not do any injury to God but God will reward those who give thanks to him."

NOTABLE DATES

Birth of Muhammad	570
The First Call	610
The Commencement of Preaching	613
The Emigration to Abyssinia	615
The Boycott of Beni Hashim	617–620
Death of Khadija	619
The First Pledge of Aqaba (The Pledge of Women)	621
The Second Pledge of Aqaba	622
The Migration to Medina	622
Battle of Bedr	624
Battle of Uhud	625
Siege of Medina (The Ditch)	627

PERSONALITIES

Muslims   The Prophet's Family

Muhammad, the Messenger of God
Ali ibn abi Talib } Zaid ibn Haritha } Young men in his house
Hasan } Husain } His grandsons, sons of Ali and Fatima
Fatima, Muhammad's daughter, married to Ali
Khadija, Muhammad's first wife, mother of Fatima
Aisha, daughter of Abu Bekr, his favourite wife
Hamza } Abbas } Muhammad's uncles

Muslims

Abu Bekr, Muhammad's close friend and first successor
Umar ibn al Khattab, his second successor
Saad ibn abi Waqqas } Zubair ibn al Awwam } Othman ibn Affan } Talha ibn Ubaidullah } Early Quraish converts
Saad ibn Muadh, chief of the Aus
Saad ibn Ubada, chief of the Khazraj
Khalid ibn al Waleed } Amr ibn al Aasi } Converts, later to become great commanders
Abdulla ibn Ubay, of the Khazraj, "the Hypocrite"

Leaders of Quraish

Abu Sofian ibn Harb, who led the caravan past Bedr
Utba ibn Rabia ⎱
Abu Jahal ⎰ Killed at Bedr
Abu Lahab, Muhammad's wicked uncle

Bedouins

Uyaina ibn Hisn, chief of Ghatafan
Abbas ibn Mirdas, chief of Beni Sulaim
Budail ibn Waraqa, chief of Khuzaa
Malik ibn Auf, chief of Hawazin
Musailima "the Liar", the prophet of Beni Haneefa

Jews

Sallam ibn abi al Huqaiq, chief of Beni al Nadheer
Huyai ibn Akhtab, executed with Beni Quraidha
Kinana ibn abi al Huqaiq, executed at Khaibar

Rulers

Heraclius, Byzantine Emperor
Chosroes Parwiz, King of Persia

Arab Dynasties before Islam

The Himyarites in the Yemen
Beni Ghassan in East Syria
The Lakhmids of Hira
The Kinda of Hadhramaut, then of Nejed

XIX

The Conquests

Of all the lands comparable to Arabia in size, and of all the peoples approaching the Arabs in historical interest and importance, no country and no nationality has received so little consideration and study in modern times as have Arabia and the Arabs . . .

In medieval times Arabia gave birth to a people who conquered most of the then civilised world . . . Around the name of the Arabs gleams that halo which belongs to the world-conquerors. Within a century after their rise this people became the masters of an empire extending from the shores of the Atlantic Ocean to the confines of China.

PHILIP K. HITTI, *History of the Arabs*

> Mine honour is my life; both grow in one;
> Take honour from me and my life is done.
> WILLIAM SHAKESPEARE, *King Richard II*

NO sooner was it known that the Messenger of God had died than the men of Medina assembled to elect Saad ibn Ubada of the Khazraj as his successor. The rivalry between the Meccan Emigrants and the original inhabitants of Medina, which had lain dormant as long as the Apostle was alive, suddenly flared up once more. The now old and somewhat frail Abu Bekr fearlessly faced the assembly, insisting that only a man of Quraish would be acceptable to all the Arabs. With the support of the Meccans and of a few bedouins who were present, he was himself elected to be the Prophet's successor or khalif. The crisis passed but, for a short time, the little Islamic community had been on the brink of civil strife.

No sooner had this disaster been averted than news came that the great majority of the tribes of Arabia had renounced Islam and refused to pay the Poor Tax. The ensuing twelve months were spent in a series of bitter battles, far more bloody than any which had taken place in the lifetime of the Messenger of God. The principal Muslim commander was Khalid ibn al Waleed, the former victor of Uhud. A year after the death of Muhammad, all the tribes of Arabia had been reduced to submission, not by preaching or by diplomacy, but by sheer military force. This universal rebellion is known in Arab history as the Apostasy.

But the Arabs, from time immemorial, had passed their time in fighting one another, not, it is true, with any particular object but just as a way of life. Muslims, however, were forbidden to fight one another. How could all these martial tribesmen be compelled for ever to live at peace?

The Messenger of God himself, by sending the expedition which had been defeated at Mota, had suggested the answer. In the winter of 633–634, three Arab columns from Medina invaded Palestine and Syria. Meanwhile, the tribes of eastern Arabia, alienated from Persia since the abolition of the Lakhmid dynasty of Hira, moved up to the Euphrates and seized Hira.

On 26th August, 636, the Byzantines were completely defeated at the Battle of the Yarmouk and all Syria was occupied up to the Taurus. In February 637, the Persian army was destroyed at Qadasiya, a few miles south of Hira, and all Iraq was occupied, including Ctesiphon, the capital of Persia, on the Tigris south of the present site of Baghdad.

In 640, Egypt was invaded and the Byzantines once more defeated. The occupation of Egypt was completed in September 642. The Persian army, in the same year, was destroyed at Nehawand and the Persian Empire ceased to exist.

*   *   *

We have seen how diligently the Messenger of God had attempted to destroy tribal loyalties, which appeared to him destructive of the solidarity of Islam. A year after his death, however, when the Apostasy had been suppressed, all Arabia became Muslim. The Arabs were no longer confronted by rival loyalties to Islam or to the tribes, for all the tribes were themselves Muslim. As a result, Islam did not destroy the tribes but absorbed them into itself. A man, thenceforward, could be a good Muslim and also be loyal to his tribe, just as a Frenchman, an Englishman or an American can be loyal to his country and also be a Christian.

The internal feuds of Quraish, however, were far more dangerous. We have seen how, during the Prophet's lifetime, the descendants of Abid Shems[1] had been the bitterest opponents of Islam and of the Apostle's family, the descendants of Hashim. In 656, Ali ibn abi Talib, the Apostle's cousin, was elected khalif, but Muawiya, the son of Abu Sofian of the clan of Abid Shems, who happened to be governor of Syria at the time, refused to recognise him. Five years of civil war resulted between Muawiya, the son of Abu Sofian, based on Damascus, and Ali ibn abi Talib, of Beni Hashim, based on Kufa.

In 661, Ali was assassinated, and Muawiya became sole khalif and established the Umaiyid[2] dynasty, which ruled the Muslim world for ninety years, from 661 to 750. Husain, the grandson of the Messenger of God, was brutally killed by the Umaiyids at Kerbela in Iraq, on 10th October, 680. The feud between the Umaiyids and Beni Hashim split the Muslim world down to our own times. Those who supported the claims of Ali ibn abi Talib and his descendants to the khalifate became known as the Shia, and constituted a sect spiritually divided from their fellow-Muslims.

*   *   *

[1] Genealogical tree, page 120.
[2] Genealogical tree, page 120. Umaiya was the son of Abid Shems.

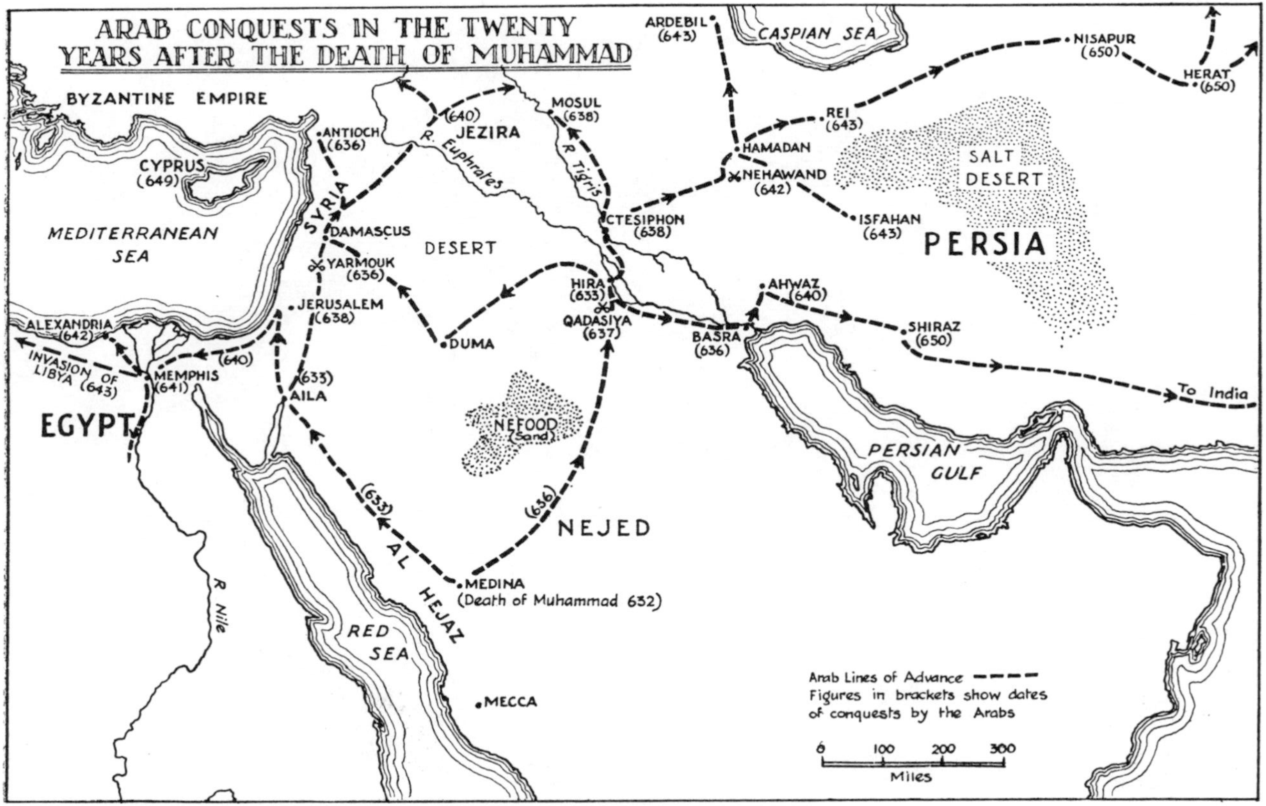
ARAB CONQUESTS IN THE TWENTY YEARS AFTER THE DEATH OF MUHAMMAD
BYZANTINE EMPIRE
CYPRUS (649)
MEDITERRANEAN SEA
ALEXANDRIA (642)
INVASION OF LIBYA (643)
MEMPHIS (641)
(640)
EGYPT
R Nile
RED SEA
ANTIOCH (636)
SYRIA
DAMASCUS
YARMOUK (636)
JERUSALEM (638)
(633)
AILA
(633)
AL HEJAZ
MEDINA
(Death of Muhammad 632)
MECCA
(640)
JEZIRA
R. Euphrates
DESERT
DUMA
NEFOOD (Sand)
(636)
NEJED
MOSUL (638)
R Tigris
CTESIPHON (638)
HIRA (633)
QADASIYA (637)
BASRA (636)
AHWAZ (640)
SHIRAZ (650)
To India
PERSIAN GULF
ARDEBIL (643)
CASPIAN SEA
HAMADAN
NEHAWAND (642)
REI (643)
ISFAHAN (643)
SALT DESERT
PERSIA
NISAPUR (650)
HERAT (650)
Arab Lines of Advance
Figures in brackets show dates of conquests by the Arabs
0 100 200 300
Miles

MAP 11

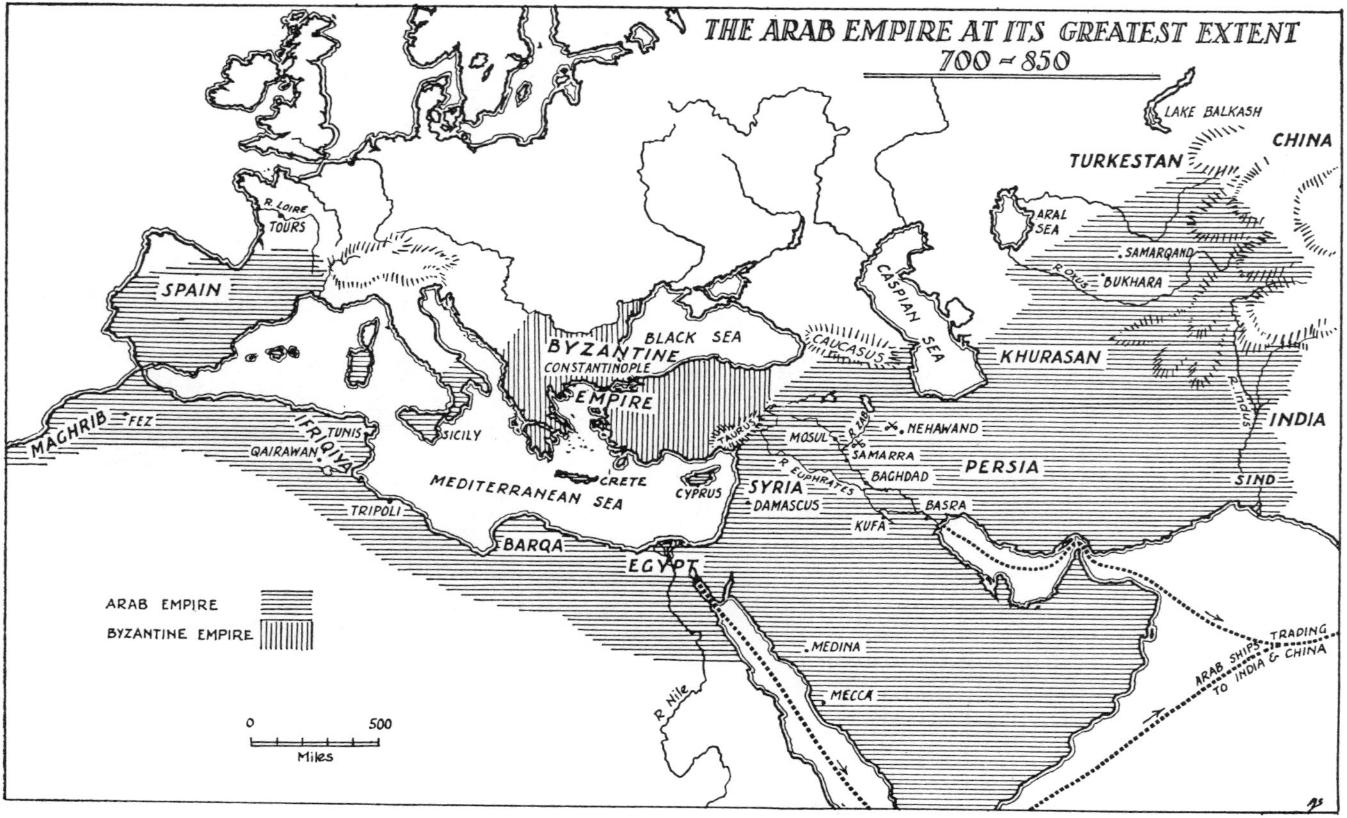

THE ARAB EMPIRE AT ITS GREATEST EXTENT
700 – 850

CHINA

LAKE BALKASH

TURKESTAN

ARAL
SEA

SAMARQAND
OXUS
BUKHARA

KHURASAN

INDIA

Indus

SIND

CASPIAN SEA

NEHAWAND
MOSUL
SAMARRA
BAGHDAD
R. EUPHRATES
KUFA
BASRA

PERSIA

CAUCASUS
MTS.

DAMASCUS
SYRIA

BLACK SEA

BYZANTINE
EMPIRE
CONSTANTINOPLE

CYPRUS

CRETE

MEDITERRANEAN SEA

SICILY

R. ROME
TOURS

SPAIN

MAGHRIB
FEZ

TUNIS
QAIRAWAN
IFRIQIYA
TRIPOLI

BARQA

EGYPT

NILE

MEDINA

MECCA

ARAB SHIPS TO CHINA
TRADING
TO INDIA & CHINA

MILES
0   500

ARAB EMPIRE

BYZANTINE EMPIRE

MAP 12

Under the Umaiyids, from 661 to 750, the Muslims conquered the greater part of the known civilised world if we exclude China. By 712, the Arabs had reached the frontier of China north of Tibet, and had occupied what is now West Pakistan. They reached their maximum expansion to the West in 732, when they were defeated at Tours, in Central France, only 250 miles from Dover.

The Arab expansion, from a tangle of mutually hostile nomadic tribes in a remote desert to the world's greatest empire,[3] is one of the most astonishing and dramatic incidents in world history.

The Arab Empire reached its greatest territorial extent in 732, exactly a hundred years after the death of the Messenger of God. In 1750, the descendants of Abbas, the Prophet's uncle, rose in revolt and overthrew the Umaiyids, the descendants of Abu Sofian. Thereafter the Abbasid dynasty ruled the Muslim Empire. Abandoning Damascus, the Umaiyid capital, the Abbasids built Baghdad as the seat of their government.

The change of dynasty produced two principal results. Firstly, Iraq had always been part of Persia, while Damascus had belonged for a thousand years to the Graeco-Roman world. The transfer of the Muslim capital from Syria to Baghdad resulted in the orientalisation of Islam. Secondly, the Abbasids had, to a considerable extent, succeeded in overthrowing the Umaiyids with the support of the Muslims of Persia. When, therefore, their power was firmly established, they gave many important posts to Persians. During the Umaiyid period, the Arabs had been the rulers of the empire. Thereafter, the empire became an international Muslim state.

The empire had been conquered by the Arabs, commanded by the Umaiyids. After 750, there were no more great conquests. The empire was on the defensive and began to shrink. But if the Abbasids were less successful than the Umaiyids as conquerors, their period of power, from 750 to 861, witnessed an extraordinary florescence of wealth, culture and science.

During the one hundred and ten years of active Abbasid rule, Baghdad was the wealthiest and the most luxurious city in the world. This was the period when Europe had relapsed into a state of semi-barbarism, and which is contemptuously dismissed in two or three paragraphs in our history books as *The Dark Ages*. They were dark only for Europe but, in the Muslim world, they were brilliantly illuminated.

[3] The Arab Empire was about half as big again as that of Rome.

Arab civilisation was, of course, built on the ancient cultures of Greece, Rome and Persia. The works of the Greek philosophers and physicians were translated into Arabic and incorporated into Arab culture. But, in every field of learning, the Muslims added to and improved the culture which they inherited.

Medical schools were extremely active in Baghdad in the ninth century under the Abbasid Khalifs. Medical students underwent four years of training, at the end of which they were obliged to pass their final examinations before they were allowed to practise. Arabic textbooks on medicine and ophthalmology were standard works in European universities until the sixteenth century.

Arab astronomers measured the circumference of the earth with surprising accuracy, eight hundred years before Europe recognised that the world was not flat.

Their most outstanding contribution to human knowledge, however, was in the field of mathematics. It was they who introduced to the Western world the use of zero and with it our modern system of writing numbers in tens, hundreds, thousands and so on. All modern mathematics is founded on this discovery. The clumsy Roman system of writing numerals had, until then, been a bar to progress in mathematics.

The Arabs also invented algebra, trigonometry, logarithms and trigonometrical ratios, sine and cosine, tangent and cotangent. "This brings us far beyond the point reached by the Greeks and really opens up the era of modern science."[4] All this learning was widely diffused among the people in the Muslim countries. For example, in Baghdad in the ninth century there were hundreds of bookshops. This general diffusion of learning was made possible by the fact that the Arabs introduced the manufacture of paper, which reached Europe ultimately from the Arabs in Spain and Sicily. At a time when even peasants and farmers could read and write in Muslim Spain, kings, princes and dukes in Christian Europe were mostly illiterate.

The Arab Empire enjoyed naval command of the Mediterranean and of the Indian Ocean. Their commercial vessels plied to Indonesia and the Far East. In Canton, China, Arab business men had a reservation, just as Europeans had in the nineteenth century in Shanghai. At a time when European rulers kept their financial reserves in the form of sacks of coins, the Arabs had a well developed

[4] Carra de Vaux in *The Legacy of Islam.*

banking system. Their business men could cash cheques in Canton on their bank accounts in Baghdad.

From the seventh century to the eleventh, the Arab Empire enjoyed a virtual monopoly of industry. Northern and Western Europe was a purely agricultural area without overseas trade. It produced its own food and rough clothing and little else. In the Muslim world, textiles were probably the most prosperous and efficient branch of industry. The Arab Empire was the world's greatest producer of silk fabrics. Cotton goods, embroideries, carpets, satin, velvet, muslin (from Mosul), damask (from Damascus) were produced on a great scale. Carpets were used in profusion, though this luxury did not reach Europe until several centuries later.

Other industries were weapons, inlaid gold and silver work, glazed coloured tiles, pottery, lustre and glass. Architecture was a field of artistic activity in which the Arabs, combining the styles of East and West with many original features, produced some of the most beautiful buildings the world has ever seen.

Arabic culture continued the old bedouin tradition by treating poetry as the queen of the arts. It was from them that rhymed verse was introduced to Europe. The classical Greek and Latin poets never discovered the art and beauty of rhyme.

It would be wearisome to prolong the catalogue. Suffice it to say that for five centuries after Muhammad, the Muslims dominated the world both culturally and militarily as completely as Europe and America have done for the last two hundred and fifty years.

*   *   *

"But how," we may well ask, "was this rich and brilliant culture produced by the illiterate Prophet of Arabia and his primitive tribesmen?" Limitation of space will allow only a brief analysis of the process.

The tribes of Central Arabia, in the seventh century, were principally dedicated to war. The Messenger of God did not share this predilection. As we have seen, he was basically a religious enthusiast with a magnetic personality which won over to his side great numbers of men and women, if he had the opportunity to talk to them. Although he found himself from time to time involved in fighting, he owed his greatest successes to speech and persuasion. Militarily, his followers were far more successful after his death than when he was alive and in command.

Many Western scholars who, although deeply learned, had never lived with the Arabian tribes, have accepted the idea that the bedouins were bloodthirsty ruffians, inspired solely by greed for loot. The inevitable conclusion was that the Prophet won them to his cause by the prospect of plunder. I cannot personally subscribe to this view. I have found the Arabians to be extremely open to a spiritual or an emotional appeal, and I believe that it was by such an appeal that they were converted to Islam.

Like all great religious movements, however, the enthusiasm roused by the Apostle gradually cooled after his death. Fifty years later, the rulers of the empire founded by his followers were worldly power-politicians, though the simpler believers maintained their enthusiasm rather longer. But if we find examples of greed or of frivolity in Umaiyid or Abbasid times, we are not thereby justified in concluding that the men of Bedr or of Hudaibiya were inspired by lust for plunder.

The course of Arab history may, therefore, be analysed somewhat as follows:

The appeal which the Prophet made to the people of Arabia was principally a spiritual one, which aroused genuine emotional enthusiasm. The presence of Muhammad was, however, rather an obstacle than a help in military operations.

After the Apostle's death, the enthusiasm which he had aroused was still at white heat, but the removal of his authority allowed the Arabians to fight in their own way. The successes they achieved seem almost miraculous, in complete contrast with the varying military failures and successes during the life of the Prophet. Unpaid, untrained and unorganised, the tribes of Arabia exterminated the Empire of Persia and crippled that of Byzantium, in the fifty years following the death of Muhammad. This period of Enthusiastic Conquest may be said to end with the death of Muawiya in 680.

After 680, two fundamental changes occurred:

(a) Religious enthusiasm cooled. The conquests were to continue for another fifty years but this was largely the result of the momentum already gained. After 732, a hundred years after the Apostle's death, conquests virtually ceased, but, by this time, the empire was so vast that it had no foreign rival. It remained the world's greatest power until it fell apart from internal degeneration.

(b) The second fundamental change which appeared after 680 was the fact that the supply of Arabian tribesmen ran out. This is an extremely important point, almost entirely neglected by modern Western scholars.

The opinion sometimes expressed that, after the conquests of Syria, Iraq and Egypt, Arabs poured into those countries and settled there, is, I believe, completely erroneous. The point requires careful elucidation.

Firstly, the population of the Arabian Peninsula today is far less than that of the tiny Nile delta alone. In the seventh century Egypt was prosperous and densely populated. Central Arabia was peopled by constantly warring tribes. It is probable, therefore, that, in the seventh century, the population of Central Arabia was even smaller than it is now in comparison with that of Egypt.

Syria and Iraq were also civilised and well populated Roman and Persian provinces. The combined populations of these countries greatly exceeded that of all Arabia. How then were the Arabs able to "pour into" these countries, transforming them into "Arab" countries? And if the Arabs poured in and occupied these countries, what became of the original inhabitants, for the Arab conquests were marked by no massacres or evictions of the previous populations?

Moreover, to modern scholars in the West, nomadism may seem an extremely dirty and uncomfortable way of life. Obviously, it is argued, the conquering Arabians would eagerly seize the opportunity to abandon their ragged tents and to move into the palaces and the mansions of Roman Syria? But, in practice, nomads do not react that way. Many different governments, by education, training, force or legislation, have attempted to suppress nomadism and have met with obstinate opposition. Several bedouin tribes mentioned in the Apostle's life history, Juhaina for example, are still today nomadic in the same area as in the seventh century.

There is something attractive to basic human nature in life in entirely natural surroundings, in great open spaces far from city crowds. There is an endless attraction in movement, in sleeping every night in a different place, in the open air fire, the new, virgin camp site, the sunrise and the sunset. These longings persist, even in our city dwellers, who spend their holidays on walking tours, or camping, in caravans, or on a coach tour of Europe.

The intoxication of the military conquests of Syria, Iraq and Egypt did not inspire the bedouins with a desire to settle down to lives of bourgeois respectability in Damascus or in Egypt. On the contrary, it taught them an even more glorious form of nomadism than they knew before—the ever advancing frontier of military conquests. A few tribesmen, who had good government employment, remained in the cities, but the great majority moved on, to find fresh fields to conquer in East Persia, North Africa or Spain.

Thereafter the tribesmen of Arabia divided into two distinct categories. The first group continued to lead the wave of conquests—to North Africa, Spain, Turkestan or India. The remainder returned to their native deserts in Arabia. Very few settled down in Syria, Palestine or Egypt as cultivators. In these countries, the Arab conquests produced little or no change in the ethnic composition of the inhabitants.

But, although they did not themselves become Syrians or Egyptians, the Arab nomads had, by their military victories, acquired an extraordinary prestige. Every conquered nation aspired to the name of Arab. The Apostle himself had provided a way by which the conquered peoples could escape from the shame of their defeat. Anyone who repeated the formula "There is no god but God and Muhammad is the Messenger of God" became thereby a Muslim and the legal and social equal of the proud Arab conquerors. Many escaped from the shame of subjection to their primitive tribal conquerors by professing Islam and claiming to be Arabs. Documents dated within a hundred years of the death of the Prophet still exist in which the words Muslim and Arab are used interchangeably and without any ethnic significance.

It is interesting to note that the early Muslim conquests in the age of enthusiasm were effected by bedouins, fighting in tribes and using the same tactics as in their old Arabian wars. But, in the period from 700 onwards in Syria, and later under the Abbasids in Baghdad, the "Arab" armies consisted of regular troops, organised and trained on the lines of the professional Byzantine military forces. The personnel of these armies were not the descendants of the original Arabian conquerors, but of the indigenous peoples of these countries.

The same factors apply in our consideration of the brilliant intellectual achievements of the great age of the Abbasids of Baghdad. "Arab" culture was Muslim and its language was Arabic. But the artists, the historians, the philosophers and the mathematicians of the Golden Age were not the descendants of the bedouins of Arabia. They were new and brilliant races produced by the fusion of innumerable ethnic groups, who had come together to enjoy the splendid civilisation of the khalifs. Turks, Greeks, Persians, Armenians, Berbers and Goths, Italians and Vandals, Indians and Caucasians were alike drawn in to build up the new nations of the Muslim world.

Whether we call the Abbasid Golden Age "Arab" or not is immaterial. But if we wish to understand it, we must appreciate the complexities of the ethnic patterns of Middle Eastern countries. Yet we need not experience such great difficulty in grasping the idea of new, mixed ethnic groupings, for we have one of the greatest examples before our eyes. The people of the United States speak English and most of their customs are of British origin, yet, in fact, their ethnic composition is so mixed as really to constitute a new nation.

In a sense, however, the situation in America is less complicated than that in the Muslim countries. While it is true that large unassimilated groups of Germans, Italians, Greeks or other stocks are still to be found in the United States, yet, when these become finally integrated, the resulting compound will geographically probably be fairly evenly distributed. Yet in the so-called Arab countries this is not the case. The Syrians, the Egyptians and the Algerians (let us say) are "Arabicised", though they have little Arabian blood in their make-up—but neither are they like one another. Each of these distinct nations is still living in its original country.

* * *

Although the original people of Arabia had faded out of most of the imperial scene a hundred years after the Apostle's death, yet the bedouins left behind them a heritage entirely peculiar to themselves, that is to say, chivalrous warfare. The fact that the Arab tribes continued to move on with the leading wave of conquest is proved by the appearance of chivalrous warfare in countries as far apart as Afghanistan and Spain. Here, at the furthest outposts of empire, the first Arab conquerors came to a standstill. We have seen how they bequeathed to Western Europe their ideas of chivalry—ideas which never gained acceptance in Syria, Egypt or Iraq.

* * *

In the tenth century, the Arab Empire was split in half by the recrudescence of the ancient feuds of Quraish. A new Arab dynasty, claiming descent from Ali ibn abi Talib, seized power in Egypt in 973, and declared war to the knife against the Abbasids of Baghdad, themselves already in decadence.

In 1055, the Seljuq Turks, wild nomads from Central Asia, occupied Baghdad. In 1087, the Crusaders arrived in Syria, In 1250, the Mamlooks, also Turks, seized power in Egypt. Finally, in 1517, the Ottoman Turks conquered Syria and Egypt, and later Iraq and Algeria.

The first rise of the Arabs to world power was inspired, it will be remembered, from two distinct sources. The first and the highest of these was the religious teaching of the Messenger of God. But the rapid dissemination of the new faith from Spain to China was achieved by the fighting spirit of the tribes. The spearhead of the tribes finished up in Spain, Morocco or Afghanistan, while those who stayed behind retired once more into the deserts of Arabia.

Islam, however, absorbed all her conquerors. Cut off from the Arabs of the peninsula, she took the Ottomans into her fold. The Turks became simple, brave and dedicated Muslims, but they lacked the chivalrous gallantry of the Arabian tribes or the intellectual culture of the Syrians, the Persians, the Iraqis or the Egyptians.

A CHRONOLOGY OF THE MUSLIM EMPIRES

Death of the Messenger of God	632
Rule of the first four khalifs in Medina— Abu Bekr, Umar ibn al Khattab, Othman ibn Affan and Ali ibn abi Talib	632–661
Umaiyid Dynasty of Damascus (the family of Abu Sofian)	661–750
Abbasid dynasty of Baghdad (the Abbasids remained in Baghdad till 1258, but largely as figureheads)	750–861
Fatimid dynasty in Egypt (These claimed to be descendants of Ali. The name Fatimid refers to Fatima, the Prophet's daughter)	973–1171
Conquest of Baghdad by the Seljuq Turks	1055
The Crusades	1098–1291
Conquest of Syria and Egypt by the Ottoman Turks	1517
Evacuation of the Arabic-speaking countries by the Ottoman Turks	1918

XX

The Expansion of Islam as a Religion

The golden age of the Saracens was the twelve years, A.D. 632 to 644, comprised in the reigns of Abu Bekr and Umar. This was a period of uninterrupted harmony and external conquest. Once granting the principle of aggressive conquest, there is comparatively little to condemn in the conduct of the conquerors . . . These men, so terrible in battle, are eminently mild in victory.

E. A. FREEMAN, *Conquests of the Saracens*

When the Messenger of God appointed a commander, he said, "When you meet the polytheists, summon them to three things. Firstly, summon them to Islam and, if they agree, refrain from them. Secondly, demand the poll tax from them and, if they agree, refrain from them. If they refuse both these, seek God's help and fight them."

Mishkat al Masabih

The mysticisms of Islam and Christianity have many points of contact. By mysticism, perhaps, will be first bridged the wide gap which separates Islam from Christendom.

VON KREMER, quoted by Claud Field, *Mystics and Saints of Islam*

Why should it be impossible that beyond reason there should be a further plane, on which appear things which do not appear on the plane of the intelligence? . . . Beware of making the ultimate perfection stop at thyself!

MUHAMMAD AL GHAZZALI, *Mishkat al Anwar*

XX

IN an age so deeply influenced by material science and mathe-
matical precision, we tend to feel that every effect must have a
cause. The two can then be associated, the problem solved and
satisfactorily recorded, placed in the relevant file and relegated to a
suitable cupboard.

Unfortunately, however, few, if any, of the great human movements
of history can be attributed to a single cause. Human life is infinitely
complicated, and it is rarely possible to reach a final result amid the
many contributory or conflicting influences at work. When, therefore, we are asked what was the cause of the rapid religious expansion
of Islam after the death of the Apostle, to cite one or two causes would
be a deceptive over-simplification. Yet the question is so frequently
asked that some attempt must be made to answer it.

We may perhaps begin by dividing the subject into two parts—
firstly, the conversion of Arabia and, secondly, the spread of the new
religion to other non-Arab countries.

*   *   *

We have already seen that a large number of persons, perhaps
some ten thousand or more, were completely convinced by
Muhammad's preaching. Most of these dedicated enthusiasts were
people of Mecca or Medina or the tribes in the immediate vicinity.
But the more distant tribes were but little affected and many of
them regarded the Messenger of God as a potential ruler, similar to
the Himyarites, the Lakhmids or Beni Ghassan.

When the Apostle began to grow powerful, deputations of tribal
chiefs visited him, professed allegiance and received gifts in return.
This was a purely political manœuvre, which had been employed in
Arabia since before the dawn of history. The fact that most of the
tribes regarded him as a political figure is shown by the tribal revolt
which broke out over most of the peninsula immediately after his
death. We are, therefore, probably right in assuming that the first
cause of the success of Islam in the Arabian peninsula was the ability
of the Prophet to inspire almost unlimited devotion in persons with
whom he came in close contact.

The second reason for the rapid spread of Islam in Arabia was the shallowness and inadequacy of the paganism of the Arabs, who indeed attached but little importance to their old religion. Arab idolatry had no priests to defend it, no hierarchy and indeed no organisation whatever. The increasing familiarity of the merchant classes with their Christian, Jewish and Zoroastrian neighbours had already begun to suggest to them the ridiculous nature of their own religion. Not one Arab sacrificed himself as a martyr to defend Al Lat, Al Uzza or Manat.

But if the Arabs were readily persuaded of the inadequacy of their pagan goddesses, they were intensely tenacious of their ancient customs. Indeed, it was their conception of *muruwwa*, the gallantry of the Arab knight, rather than their pagan religion, which had provided the emotional, and perhaps even the spiritual, background of their lives. At first, the Messenger of God had seen these customs as his principal enemies and had bitterly combated Arab chivalry, pride of ancestors, tribal loyalty and poetry.

But after his death, the Arabs reached a *modus vivendi* with Islam. The new monotheism was manifestly so far superior to the idols of the Kaaba that no reasonable man could argue the point. Indeed, they had never really fought to defend the idols. It was the attempt to change their ancient and romantic customs which had roused their indignation. But once all the tribes had accepted Islam, there was no longer any conflict between religion and loyalty to a tribe which was itself Muslim.

Thenceforward there was no reason why Islam should oppose the "Arab virtues". On the subject of revenge, the Messenger of God, as we have seen, had not told the Muslims to love their enemies. He had said that they were entitled to revenge themselves upon them but that, if they forgave them, their action would be pleasing to God. Thus the Arabs were able to continue their old customs regarding revenge also. The third reason for the rapid conversion of the Arabians was therefore that, after the Apostasy, all the tribes accepted Islam and the former conflict between religion and tribal loyalty disappeared.

Fourthly, as soon as war commenced against Byzantium and Persia, all the objections to Islam disappeared. It was no longer necessary to live in peace and to deny the virtues of bravery, hospitality, and poetry. On the contrary, wars against non-Muslims were more inspiring, more romantic and more lucrative than the tribal wars of the past. Moreover, to a people whose only religion had previously been so uninspiring, the belief in a single Almighty God, who ruled the whole earth, produced a deep emotional reaction. In addition, this Glorious and Omnipotent God had chosen *them* to conquer the world for Him. We can readily see how this staggering new conception could electrify the souls of these simple people.

The tribes of Arabia only became completely united in this new outlook after the death of the Messenger of God. It may, indeed, have been this factor which made the Arabs always victorious after his death. At Bedr, Uhud and Hunain, they had been Arabs fighting against Arabs, largely, it appeared, in support of a religion which wished to abolish the romantic and ancient way of life to which they were all devoted. But once all the Arabs were Muslims pitted against Greeks or Persians, the situation was reversed. Fighting was "the way of God" and the virtues of Arab knighthood could be used in the service of religion.

The fifth reason for the rapid spread of Islam in Arabia after Muhammad's death was that there is nothing which succeeds like success. Simple and primitive peoples expect God to reward his faithful servants in this life. This idea appears frequently in the Old Testament—the Children of Israel expected Jehovah to give them victory. The Messenger of God believed that the faithful would be rewarded in this world and in the next.

At a more sophisticated stage, religious people realise that this in practice does not happen. The saints in Heaven are described as "they which came out of great tribulation".[1] "We glory in tribulations", writes St. Paul.[2] The bedouins of Arabia were more simple minded. They were confident that God would give wealth, success and power to those whom He had chosen. Thus the staggering victories which they won over the Byzantines and the Persians served to reinforce the belief that God must really be fighting on their side.

A sixth reason for the rapid success of Islam in Arabia was its perfect suitability to the people and the age. It was essentially an Arabian religion. The Qoran was revealed in Arabic, which must therefore, they thought, be the language used by God Himself in Heaven. The people of Arabia had, and still have, simple straightforward minds, contrasting vividly with the subtle intellectuality of the Greeks, the Syrians and other peoples of the eastern shores of the Mediterranean. Islam resembles Judaism in its bold and simple

[1] Revelation VII, 14.   [2] Romans V, 3.

outlines—a single Almighty and Glorious God, infinitely great rewards in paradise for the faithful and punishment in hell for the wicked.

It is noticeable that Islam spread most rapidly to the east and the west, between the parallels of latitude of 15° and 35° north of the equator. This area covers the long belt of deserts which, from Morocco to Pakistan, divides the temperate from the tropical zone. Perhaps deserts tend to produce men with simple and straightforward minds. The Berbers of Africa accepted Islam with enthusiasm, though they do not appear to have been ethnically related to the Arabs and though they bitterly resisted Arab rule.

We have seen that the peoples of Arabia at this time were by no means firmly wedded to their paganism, but were ripe for a higher and a more spiritual faith. But the principal monotheism offered to them was Greek Christianity, not the simple faith of the Sermon on the Mount. Greek Christianity in the seventh century was torn by bitter intellectual disputes regarding definitions of the Incarnation. These furious arguments provoked bitter hatreds and were completely incomprehensible to the simple minded Arabs. The Christian ideals of love, joy and peace were conspicuous by their absence.

While, therefore, the Arabs were anxious for a higher religion, they found little to attract them in the Christianity of the Byzantines. Judaism, a simple monotheism, they found more congenial and we have seen that the Messenger of God at one stage hoped to join forces with the Jews. The petty vanity of the Judaistic tribes of Medina, however, caused the disappointment of his hopes. They failed to seize the opportunity to convert the Arabs to their faith but preferred to show their superior cleverness by catching out the Prophet in his talk.

Foiled in their search for a congenial monotheism, the Arabs produced one of their own, founded on both its predecessors, but with a native Arab flavour which quickly ensured its success throughout the peninsula.

*　　*　　*

It may perhaps be admitted that the reasons given above provide a logical explanation of the rapid spread of Islam in the Arabian peninsula. But how are we to account for its acceptance by so many peoples who were completely foreign to the Arabs? This question becomes all the more pertinent in the cases of countries which boasted cultures thousands of years old and which already practised monotheistic religions.

It was a common belief in the Christian nations of the West that Islam was propagated by the sword. Such a statement, however, can only be accepted with many reservations. It was probably nearest to being true in Arabia itself, where we have seen that the Apostasy, the tribal revolt following the death of Muhammad, was suppressed by sheer armed force. A few months later, however, the outbreak of war against Byzantium and Persia caused these internal stresses to be forgotten in the universal enthusiasm for war against foreigners.

The rapid conquests of Syria, Egypt and Palestine have already been sketched in the previous chapter. The most interesting aspect of these conquests, however, is that they were not followed by the compulsory conversion of the conquered. The Messenger of God, as we have already seen, had not advocated the compulsory conversion of Jews or Christians. The Jews of Medina had been killed or driven out because, as cohesive tribes, they had opposed the Prophet's mission. In other words, their opposition had been political rather than religious. After their final destruction individual Jews had remained in Medina in business. No pressure was brought to bear on them to change their religion once they had ceased to oppose the activities of the Apostle.

As far as Christians were concerned, the Messenger of God had concluded treaties with the Christians of Najran, with the Christian tribes of southern Jordan, with the people of Aila (the modern Aqaba) and with the Prince of Duma.

There are several passages in the Qoran which state that the duty of the Prophet is only to warn, not to coerce. "Summon them to the faith and walk steadfastly as you have been ordered.[3] Do not follow their vain desires but say: 'I trust in the books which God has sent down' . . . God is our Lord and your Lord. Our actions are ours and your actions are yours. Let there be no disputation between us and you. God will bring us together and to Him we shall all return."[4]

If this verse refers to Christians and Jews (which is not certain), it shows a remarkable degree of toleration.

Or again, Qoran XXIV, verse 54, says, "If you obey him, you will be guided aright. No responsibility rests on the Apostle except to deliver a clear message." This passage seems to indicate that the Prophet's only duty was to preach, not to use force.

[3] God is speaking to the Apostle.   [4] Qoran XLII, verse 15.

If we admit that Qoranic verses can be quoted both advocating and prohibiting the use of force, we can turn to the actions of the Muslim conquerors for enlightenment. When ordering the invasion of Syria, two years after the Prophet's death, Abu Bekr gave the following instructions: "Be just. Do not break faith . . . Do not kill children, old men or women. Do not cut down fruit trees. If you come across men in monasteries, leave them in peace."[5]

The terms offered to conquered peoples were commonly, "Islam, tribute or the sword", but not, as far as I am aware (except in Arabia), "Islam or the sword." This formula, used when summoning an enemy to surrender, is worthy of further analysis. First, let us remember that enemies who became converted were immediately admitted to the ranks of the conquerors on a basis of equality. These were terms of quite exceptional generosity. It is rare indeed in history to find examples of a conquering race which immediately, on the very field of battle, accepts the defeated enemy as equals. In practice, it did not always happen quite completely. The Arabs, intoxicated with victory, were at times a little socially supercilious towards lesser breeds. But it is something that such was the genuine official policy.

The key to the leniency of the Arab conquests, however, lies in the second choice offered to the defeated—tribute. It has already been indicated, in connection with the payment of the poor tax by the Arab tribes, that submission to taxation, however light, has always been regarded in Arabia as an admission of political subjection. Thus the imposition of a poll-tax on Jews and Christians was largely a political gesture, signifying Muslim superiority.

Rates and currencies varied in different places and at different times with the result that it is difficult to express the poll-tax in terms of modern money. In general, it may be estimated at perhaps two pounds or five dollars for every man. But even if it were estimated at five or ten times those amounts, it would not have been unduly onerous.[6] It was normally collected from men only, and paupers and monks[7] were exempt.

In return for this small payment, moreover, the Jews and the Christians were exempt from military service, which applied only to

[5] Tabari, quoted by T. W. Arnold in *The Preaching of Islam* (slightly abridged).

[6] The financial burden of the poll-tax appears even lighter when we remember that Jews and Christians were exempt from the poor tax which Muslims had to pay.

[7] The frequent mention of monks and monasteries for preferential treatment may have been the result of the impression made on the Apostle by the Christian hermits during his early visits to Syria.

Muslims. As the price of such exemption, the poll-tax was probably a profitable bargain. The corollary of exemption from military service was Muslim protection. When Khalid ibn al Waleed accepted the surrender of the towns on the Euphrates, he wrote, "If we protect you, then poll-tax is due to us; but if we do not, then it is not due."[8]

In fact, the Muslims took the duty of protection very seriously. In 635, they captured Damascus and occupied the greater part of Syria unopposed, collecting poll-tax from the Christian inhabitants. The following year, the arrival of a new Byzantine army compelled the Arabs to evacuate Syria. Before doing so, however, Abu Ubaida, the Muslim commander, ordered that all sums collected in poll-tax be repaid. It had been collected, he said, in return for protection but the Arabs were unable any longer to give protection to the Syrians.[9]

A number of the nomadic tribes of the Syrian desert had adopted Christianity before the appearance of Islam. When the Muslims invaded Syria and Iraq, these Arab Christian tribes, being similar to the invaders in their language and way of life, sometimes fought on the side of the Muslims. When such Christians joined the invading armies, they were exempted from poll-tax but were not compelled to change their religion. This slightly confused thinking on the difference between Arabs and Muslims is revealed in the case of Taghlib, an Arab tribe on the upper Euphrates. These people remained Christians and were at first ordered to pay poll-tax, but were subsequently excused on the grounds that they were Arabs.

Curiously enough, during the reign of the Umaiyid Khalifs in Damascus from 661 to 750, the Arabs actually discouraged conversions to Islam. The treasury relied largely on the poll-tax to balance the budget. But Muslims were not liable to pay it. Thus any rapid increase of conversions threatened the stability of the financial system. When unbelievers persisted in becoming Muslims, local tax collectors were instructed to continue collecting poll-tax from them, in spite of their conversion!

In fact, the poll-tax ultimately proved the strongest incentive to conversion, though not because of the financial burden involved. The payment of a tax was regarded as a sign of political subjection. The Arabs were kind and tolerant towards the conquered races,

[8] Tabari.

[9] Abu Yusuf, quoted by T. W. Arnold. I cannot remember any other occasion in history when a government returned taxes already collected, on the grounds that it had failed in its obligations.

protected them and their possessions and employed them in clerical and technical appointments.

But there was never any doubt as to who was in control. The oath of a Muslim was preferred to that of a man of any other religion. All executive posts (*not* clerical or administrative) in the government and the army were held by Muslims. A Muslim could marry a Christian woman but a Christian could not take a Muslim to wife, and the same social inequality permeated the whole of society. Christians and Jews were not persecuted and were often richer than the Muslims, but they suffered from an atmosphere of slight social inferiority.

The mere repetition of the Muslim formula—"There is no god but God and Muhammad is His Messenger"—automatically and instantaneously removed this handicap. Thenceforward they could lord it as the equals of the conquerors, marry Arab women and aspire to the highest rank in the army and in the government. As already mentioned, increasing numbers of the conquered peoples were unable to resist the temptation, even when, after their conversion, they were still required to pay poll-tax.

*　　*　　*

We are thus obliged to admit that, in the early Arab conquests, Jews and Christians were not compelled by the sword to become Muslims, nor indeed did they do so. For many generations after the conquest, the majority of Syrians retained the Christian faith. Indeed, the Lebanese have continued to do so until the present day.

Not only so, but Jews and Christians were permitted to observe their own laws, which were applied by their own judges. According to Muslim ideas, law arose from religion. Their own laws were derived from the Qoran and the Traditions. If, therefore, Jews and Christians were not to be obliged to become Muslims, it followed that they should not be compelled to observe Muslim laws. Each religion should follow the laws prescribed by its own faith.

But even if the Arabs did not oblige conquered peoples to become Muslims, why, it may be asked, did they, as invaders meet with no opposition from the Jews and the Christians of Syria and Egypt?

The first cause was probably the narrow-minded policy of the Byzantine Orthodox Church. The Syrians had been Hellenised for a thousand years and many of the city-dwellers were undoubtedly of Greek or partly-Greek origin. Syria has always been a home of many sects, secret societies and political parties. The Syrians of the seventh century were no exception and they vigorously supported the various heresies of the Monophysites, the Nestorians, the Jacobites and others. The Byzantines demanded conformity with the Orthodox Church and actively persecuted the Christian dissenters.

The Muslim invaders were indifferent to Greek theological niceties and promised equal toleration for all Christians. Thus the many non-Orthodox Christian Syrians received from the Muslims that impartial religious toleration which they had sought in vain from the Byzantines. Under the Arab khalifs, the Syrian Christians flourished, many of them holding high positions at court, chiefly in clerical posts or as doctors of medicine. Syrian Christian support of the Muslims was, in the words of T. W. Arnold, "a revolt against the empty theological polemics" of the Greeks.

It is true that, in the early years of the conquest when the Muslims were still enthusiastic, they sometimes endeavoured to convert the Christians by argument. The greatest attraction of Islam, at any rate to the uneducated, was its simplicity as opposed to the hair-splitting theology of the Orthodox Church.

The Egyptians were converted to Islam much more quickly than the Syrians. They had become Christians with equal facility at the beginning of the fourth century. They have always been a quiet and orderly people, submissive to authority, whereas the Syrians have always been factious.

Meanwhile, intermixture with the Christians of Syria commenced to influence Islam. The first Muslims were simple souls with scarcely any interest in theology. It was their arguments with the Christians which obliged them to study the subject, and eventually to produce an intellectual theology and philosophy of their own.

Islam also became affected in many other ways as it spread to non-Arab peoples. In Syria, Christian modes of thought seeped unperceived into the mentality of the Muslims. To most Europeans, Islam appears a hard, cruel, savage faith, typified by the hawk-nosed Muslim fanatic, a drawn scimitar in his hand, and the Crescent banner fluttering above his head. This image has perhaps been reinforced in the last twenty years by the bombastic threats of Levantine politicians, principally Egyptians, about exterminating Israel.

It is only those who live for several years in a Muslim country and who speak the language fluently, who discover that Muslims are often kind and gentle people. The equalitarian nature of their society, their geniality and helpfulness to their neighbours, the tender-hearted compassion shown by their women and their passionate love of children make them a very lovable community.

It may be added, however, that the indigenous Christian communities who live among them show the same qualities. Are we to conclude that these qualities are peculiar to the peoples of the Middle East, irrespective of religion? Can we claim that the Christians of Syria and Egypt brought these qualities with them when they were converted from Christianity to Islam? Once again, all human movements are far too complicated to be attributed to one cause.

That much Christian thought permeated Islam cannot be denied. One example must suffice. Bukhari has a tradition that "the Prophet is reported to have said, 'God says I have prepared for My righteous servants what no eye has seen and no ear has heard, and what the heart of man has never conceived'."

I Corinthians II, verse 9, reads as follows: "Eye hath not seen, nor ear heard, neither have entered into the heart of man, the things which God hath prepared for them that love Him." Bukhari was a careful writer and I do not wish for one moment to accuse him of conscious plagiarism. I imagine that this verse, written by St. Paul eight hundred years before Bukhari published his great book, had become incorporated in the thought-pattern of Syria and was unwittingly transferred to the Messenger of God.

Innumerable other such influences doubtless interpenetrated the two religions. The austerity of Islam, for example, was doubtless responsible for the iconoclastic movement in Constantinople and the abolition of images. Thus while, on the superficial level of politics, Christianity and Islam often appeared to be bitter enemies, beneath the surface their roots were often intertwined.[10]

Islam also became affected in many other ways as it spread to non-Arab peoples. The Messenger of God, for example, had deprecated asceticism, yet asceticism appeared even in his lifetime and among his intimate Arab companions. It was to become greatly extended and reinforced when it reached other races.

A mystic may perhaps be defined as a person who seeks, by renouncing the world, to obtain direct spiritual communion with God, culminating ultimately, through meditation on the Divine Love,

---

[10] I refer here to Institutional Christianity, as seen in the various churches with their rituals and dogmas. In my own mind, I differentiate between such institutional religion and the teachings of Christ.

in what is known as Mystic Union. Every branch of the human race doubtless includes persons gifted with such spiritual capabilities, but the Arabs of Arabia are, on the whole, a practical, down-to-earth people.

Mystics began to increase in numbers in Islam within a century of the Apostle's death, in Palestine, and in Kufa and Basra in Iraq. The most famous Muslim mystics, however, arose in Persia and, later on, in Spain. The Islam preached by the Prophet consisted primarily of the representation of God as infinitely Great, Glorious and Compassionate but as, on the whole, remote from man.

There are, however, here and there, a few verses suggesting the indwelling of the Divine Spirit in man and of His communing with the individual soul. For example, Qoran L, verse 16, says, "We certainly created man and We know what his soul whispers to him and We are nearer to him than the veins in his neck." The Muslim mystics made use of such verses as this to justify their belief in the indwelling of the Divine Spirit in man and in the possibility of the Mystic Union.

In the second century after the death of the Prophet, the Sufis made their appearance as the chief representatives of Islamic mysticism. The Shia sect in Persia developed a dogma of the indwelling of the Divine Essence in Ali and his descendants, a conception which seems to show signs of Christian influence.

Much of the writings of the Muslim *sufis* bears a close resemblance to the works of the Christian mystics. Indeed, at these spiritual heights, as they themselves state, dogma and ritual are left behind and all religions draw close to one another.

"Love Him whom saints and prophets all have loved; Through whom alone we all have lived and moved," writes one of the most famous of mystics, Jalal al Deen Rumi. And again:
"Immersed in the Beloved we shall be, when in one soul shall we be 'I' and 'Thee'."

But Christianity and Islam did not merely resemble one another in origin and then grow further and further apart. Mutual exchanges continued for many centuries, until the growing wealth and power of the West produced an ever-widening gap between the two communities. Perhaps the most striking example of the continuous exchanges between Islam and Christianity was that of Muhammad al Ghazzali, an Arabicised Persian, born in 1058, four hundred and twenty-six years after the death of the Messenger of God.

Ghazzali was one of the most brilliant intellects of his time and his lectures as professor of theology at the Nidhamiya College in Baghdad were attended by packed audiences. Then, suddenly, he abandoned a brilliant university career to become a penniless wandering ascetic seeking for Union with God. It was at this time that he began his most famous book, *Ihya Ulum al Deen*, the Revival of Religious Knowledge.

The aspect which interests us here is his give and take with Christianity, a religion with which he was familiar. To quote Professor Hitti,[11] "the Sermon on the Mount was drawn upon generously. In quotations from it we read about the 'blessed humble and blessed poor' (Matthew V, 5), 'the salt of the earth' (Matth. V, 13), 'the great in the kingdom of Heaven' (Matth. V, 19), and 'pearls on the necks of swine' (Matth. VII, 6)."

But the borrowings were not in one direction only. Thomas Aquinas, one of the greatest of Christian theologians, studied "Algazel" at the University of Naples. Dante, Pascal and Maimonides, the Jewish philosopher of Cordova, all borrowed from his ideas. The heart of Al Ghazzali's teaching may perhaps be expressed in a single phrase—"heavenly bliss is proportionate to the intensity of our love for God."

*   *   *

We set out to enquire into the causes of the rapid spread of Islam as a religion after the death of the Messenger of God. The reasons which we have discovered, while they do not in any sense cover the subject, may have sufficed at least to show that military coercion was not the sole, or even the principal reason.

The statement that Islam was propagated by the sword was true in one direction. If it had not been for the Arab conquests, large numbers of Muslims would not have arrived in Spain, Morocco, Persia or India. Once, however, the Arabs had reached these distant lands, they made little or no attempt to compel Jews, Christian or Zoroastrians to become Muslims. On the contrary, it was the tolerance shown by them which endeared them to their new subjects.

In the "desert belt" from Morocco to northern India, the un-

[11] P. K. Hitti, *Makers of Arab History.*

complicated simplicity of Islam was especially suited to the indigenous races. In Syria and Egypt Byzantine persecution of the nonconformist Christian sects drove them into the arms of the Muslims. Moreover, the staggering conquests achieved by the Arabs persuaded many peoples that God must be fighting on their side.

When, however, Islam reached peoples of more subtle intellect or more innate spirituality, it tended to become modified and adapted to the new spiritual climate and to acquire a local flavour more suited to the nature of the new converts.

*   *   *

In spite of these indisputable historical facts, Western writers still continue to claim that Islam was propagated by the sword.[12] These authors "prove" their case by quoting examples of massacres committed by Muslims throughout the ages. Such atrocities were perhaps committed by the Abbasids in Byzantine territory, by the Seljuq Turks, by Tamerlane, or by the Ottomans against the Armenians in the nineteenth century.

By careful selection of the incidents chosen as evidence, it can equally be "proved" that Christians employed massacre against members of other religions. When the First Crusade captured Jerusalem in 1099, great numbers of the Muslim defenders were massacred. In 1191, Richard Coeur de Lion caused some two thousand seven hundred Muslim prisoners-of-war to be butchered in cold blood. In 712, when the Muslims conquered Spain, they allowed the inhabitants complete religious toleration, subject to payment of poll-tax by Christians and Jews. But in the sixteenth century, when Christian kings were once again ruling Spain, the Inquisition imprisoned, tortured, executed and exiled some three million native Spanish Muslims.

The fallacy in such arguments lies once again in the attribution of one cause for one effect, whereas human affairs are infinitely complicated. The Crusaders did not massacre the Muslims because their religion required them to do so, but because the races of north-west Europe in the eleventh century were semi-barbarians. Tamerlane did not exterminate the people of Aleppo and Baghdad because Islam required him to do so, but because he and his followers were half-savages.

[12] See, for example, W. W. Cash, *The Expansion of Islam*.

In using such historical events as arguments, it is always necessary to distinguish, on the one hand, between the small numbers of Muslims and Christians who really try to practise their religion and, on the other, the vastly greater numbers of persons who are generally classified as belonging to one or other religion owing merely to the accident of their birth in Europe or in Asia.

A few years ago, I was staggered by a statement in a letter which I received from a Jewish friend, "Christianity", he wrote, "has always been the most cruel and bestial of religions." I could scarcely believe my eyes. Did not Christians believe that peacemakers are blessed, for they shall be called the children of God? Did not Christ say, "Love your enemies, bless them that curse you, do good to them that hate you?" But when my friend went on to describe the persecutions suffered by the Jews in Europe, I began to realise how easy it is to attribute crimes to other religions. Nothing in the New Testament can be taken to authorise the abominable treatment meted out to Jews in Europe. The nations concerned were savage, brutal, greedy and fanatical, and behaved in a way exactly contrary to the teaching of Christ.

On the whole, we are obliged to admit that, while Islam countenances war and, in certain circumstances, even orders it, the Muslim religion was not primarily propagated by the sword. On the contrary, the first Arab conquerors were conspicuous for their moderation and for the toleration which they showed for other religions.

Their military conquests were indeed rapid but the conversion of the conquered peoples to Islam was slow and was not achieved by force.

*   *   *

In this chapter we have compared Islam to official Christianity, thereby following a traditional pattern now fourteen centuries old. But our modern problem is basically different. Today the very existence of God himself is questioned by those who are unwilling to believe in anything which cannot be proved by their own powers of sight, hearing, touch, smell or taste.

This rejection of everything beyond the material world has deprived man of any object of loyalty outside the physical surroundings in which he lives. But man was created with a deep, if unconscious, longing to devote himself to some cause greater than himself.

As a result, we find him expressing his passionate desire for self-dedication by giving himself body and soul to political movements of this world such as Fascism, Communism, Nationalism or, more pathetic still, to passionate humanism seeking to find its outlet by material means alone. The failure of such hoped-for satisfaction compels him to resign himself to the loss of his own soul and to helpless acquiescence in a status of becoming a mere featureless automaton, a depersonalised number on a card.

The only answer to our modern dilemma is a return to personal religion, whatever creed or denomination we choose. All the mass movements of today reduce the individual to a faceless cypher, a microscopic molecule in an immense mass of machine fodder.

But God is able and willing to commune with the soul of the smallest human being. Only such communion as this can make men once more into free souls, into children of that God, whose service alone is perfect freedom from the physical or intellectual tyranny of men.

Epilogue

The extent of the Church Invisible is probably much wider than we imagine and in several places its horizons go beyond the possibilities of redemption known to the visible church. God can discern saints and the elect where our dull eye and our narrow understanding can only see the children of darkness

ABBÉ DE TOURVILLE, *Spiritual Letters*

God is love; and he that dwelleth in love dwelleth in God and God in him.

1 John IV, 16

> Nature's great secret let me now rehearse—
> Long have I pondered o'er the wondrous tale,
> How Love immortal fills the universe,
> Tarrying till mortals shall His Presence hail:
> When will ye cast the veil of sense aside,
> Content in finding Love to lose all else beside?
> JALAL AL DEEN RUMI (Trans. E. H. Palmer)

> My heart is capable of every form,
> A cloister for the monk, a fane for idols,
> A pasture for gazelles, the pilgrim's Kaaba,
> The tables of the Torah, the Qoran.
> Love is the faith I hold.
> MUHI AL DEEN IBN AL ARABI (Trans. R. A. Nicholson)

We end on the acknowledgement that all we can see and delight in, all that crushes and bewilders us, is nothing beside that we do not and cannot comprehend: "the mystery which from all ages hath been hid in God."[1]

EVELYN UNDERHILL, *Abba* (slightly abridged)

> Dear Lord and Father of Mankind
> Forgive our foolish ways;
> Reclothe us in our rightful mind,
> In purer lives Thy service find,
> In deeper reverence, praise.
> J. G. WHITTIER

[1] Ephesians III.

EPILOGUE

THE endless fighting and jealousy between the three great related religions—Judaism, Christianity and Islam—must surely be one of the greatest tragedies of human history. Judaism was the first world monotheism and hence contains few recommendations to respect other faiths. But Christianity claims to be the religion of love and Islam contains many injunctions in favour of Jews and Christians.

We must here distinguish once again between those few members of any religious group who really try to carry out the precepts of their faith and the vast majority who are Jews, Christians or Muslims in name only, but who pursue worldly aims and are swayed by human passions.

Pride is perhaps the human failing which has caused the most damage in history. For the rivalry between Muslims, Christians and Jews has been almost entirely due to human vanity rather than to genuine theological differences. For what can any of us understand of the immensity of God which could possibly justify us in killing, torturing or burning alive persons who hold a slightly different theory? Rather we gratify our own pride when we persuade ourselves that we alone possess the truth and that all the rest of the human race is in error.

It is difficult to avoid the impression that it was the Muslims who were the originators of wars of religion, although that was not their intention. It is interesting to speculate whether the decision of the Emigrants in Medina to attack Quraish caravans was not the origin of all religious wars. The ancient Greeks, the Romans and the Persians do not appear to have considered religious differences to be a cause for war. It is true that they sometimes persecuted religious communities within their own dominions, but these attempts at repression were normally caused by the belief that the sect in question was disloyal to the state.

In 633, however, the Arabs deliberately invaded the empires of Byzantium and Persia, fired with enthusiasm by the preaching of the Messenger of God. It is true that, when they conquered one country after another, they did not try to compel the Jews, the Christians or the Zoroastrians to become Muslims. Nevertheless, it was undoubtedly in the name of Islam that they set out to conquer the world. As a direct consequence of this fact, the counter-attack which came three centuries later was carried out in the name of Christianity, regardless of the fact that to love their enemies and not to return evil for evil were among the basic duties enjoined on Christians.

Nor only so, but in the Crusades the Christians were, at the beginning at least, more violent and brutal than the Muslims. This fact, however, cannot justly be ascribed to their respective religions but to the fact that the West European Christians were semi-barbarians, whereas the Muslims were in general members of an ancient civilisation. So many factors affect these historical movements that great care is needed to separate the many different causes involved.

Whether the Muslim-Christian religious wars were the cause of the subsequent inter-Christian religious wars is open to argument. The ancients suppressed religious sects which they believed to be subversive to the control of the government. The brutal repression of the Albigenses in the south of France in the thirteenth century was encouraged by the Pope because they were heretics, and by the King of France because they resisted his authority. In the same way, the Spanish persecution of the Protestants in the Netherlands was simultaneously religious and political.

In our own times, the rivalry between the Soviet Union and the United States partakes of the same dual nature. Partly ideological —capitalism against communism—it is also due to the national jealousies of the two Great Powers.

*   *   *

These unhappy political rivalries have left a deep rift of misunderstanding between Islam and Christianity. This is particularly true in the West. In the Middle East, indigenous Christians communities have survived in the midst of the Muslims, who have consequently never been so prejudiced against Christians as the Western nations were against Islam. In Western Europe and North America, the majority of the general public have a vague idea that Muslims are "just heathen", although they recognise a religious kinship with Judaism. In fact, ironically enough, Islam is nearer to Christianity than is Judaism.

*   *   *

I have already stated that I spent more than half my life entirely surrounded by Muslims. I frequently engaged in religious or semi-religious conversation with Muslims, as is inevitable for anyone living among Arabs, who constantly have the name of God upon their lips. Between us, we often accepted, rejected or advocated a certain course of action on the grounds that it would be acceptable or inacceptable to God. We were thus continually able to agree on the moral duties incumbent upon us.

In achieving this degree of religious co-operation, we discovered that nine-tenths of our religious obligations were identical. We would, of course, have differed, if we had attempted intellectual, theological definitions, but as none of us are able with our human brains to understand God, there did not appear to be anything to be gained by quarrelling over such a subject.

It always seemed to me to be an error to commence a discussion with Muslims by arguing about dogmatic differences. Both sides immediately champion their own beliefs, and anger and resentment inevitably flare up, resulting in increasing hostility and estrangement. Few missionaries I have known follow the example of Charles de Foucauld who held that we must first of all prove the superiority of our religion by the quality of our lives.

Some idea of the mixed origins of our ways of thought can be obtained by the realisation that the rather supercilious attitude of Western Christians towards Muslims seems to date from the industrial revolution. Before then there was plenty of hatred but less arrogance. It was during the Victorian age that the idea became general in the West that Islam inevitably led to poverty, backwardness and stagnation. The advocates of this theory enjoyed the comfortable feeling of superiority which they derived from it.

Unfortunately, however, they were ignorant of history and were unaware that, for seven centuries after the preaching of Islam, Muslim countries were far in advance of Western Christendom in wealth, culture and power. In the ensuing seven hundred years, their relative positions have been reversed. The Western Christian nations have forged as far ahead of the Muslim countries as the latter were formerly in advance of Europe. These are the normal rotations of the rise and fall of cultures and empires, which have been repeated again and again throughout history.

*   *   *

Even as children the belief that only Christians would be saved and all others condemned seemed to us unjust. It might be plausible enough in the case of those who had been instructed in Christianity and had then rejected it, but how could it be justified in the case of those who had never heard of it? The Messenger of God, of course, had taken the same stand, when he announced that the idolatrous ancesters of Quraish, to whom monotheism had never been preached, were nevertheless already burning in hell. I cannot help suspecting, as an old priest recently said to me in another context, "the good God is more broad-minded".

I am an ignorant person, quite untrained in theology. My long residence among Muslims has nevertheless convinced me that all persons who believe in God are trying to follow the same road. The differences in the methods they employ are principally due to the culture which they have inherited or the instruction which they received as children. If God is love, it does not seem, to our feeble intellects at least, that he would condemn to punishment persons who had never heard of a better way of life than that which they follow.

If we Christians believe that we are more nearly executing the will of God than are the adherents of other religions, it must surely be our duty to lead such lives as will draw all men of good will to ask the reason for our goodness. To treat them with arrogant contempt is more likely to convince them that ours is an intolerant and hard-hearted way of life.

A SHORT BIBLIOGRAPHY
FOR FURTHER STUDY

Andrae, Tor *Mahomet, sa Vie et sa Doctrine* (trans. from German by J. Gaudefroy-Demombynes)

Arnold, T. W. *The Preaching of Islam* (London 1896)

Arberry, A. J. *The Holy Koran* (London 1953)

— *The Doctrine of the Sufis*

Azzam, Abdul Rahman Pasha *The Eternal Message of Muhammad*

Athir, Izz al Deen ibn al *Al Kamil fi al Tarikh*

Baladhuri al *Futuh al Buldan* (Arabic) (Eng. translation, Leyden 1866)

Bichr, Fares *L'Honneur chez les Arabes avant l'Islam*

Blunt, W. S. *The Seven Golden Odes of Pagan Arabia*

Browne, E. G. *A Literary History of Persia*

Bukhari, Muhammad al *Al Sahih* (Arabic)

Bousquet, G. H. *El Bokhari, L'Authentique Tradition Musulmane* (Fr. trans) (Paris 1964)

Calverley, Rev. E. E. *Worship in Islam* (trans. from Ghazzali)

Caussin de Perceval *Essai sur L'Histoire des Arabes* (3 Volumes— Paris 1847)

Cragg, K. *The Call of the Minaret* (Oxford 1956)

Dermenghem, Emile *The Life of Mahomet*

De Boer, T. J. *The History of Philosophy in Islam*

Encyclopaedia of Islam

Field, Claud *Mystics and Saints of Islam* (London 1910)

Freeman, E. A. *History and Conquests of the Saracans*

Gabrieli, Francesco *Muhammad and the Rise of Islam*

Gaudefroy-Demombynes, M. *Mahomet* (Paris 1957)

Ghazzali, Muhammad al *Ihya Ulum al Deen* (The Revival of Religious Learning)

— *Mishkat al Anwar*

Gibb, H. A. R. *Mohammedanism. An Historical Survey* (Oxford, 1949)

— *The Arabs*

Gibbon, E. *Decline and Fall of the Roman Empire*

Guillaume, Alfred *Islam*

— *The Traditions of Islam* (Oxford 1924)

— *Life of Muhammad* (trans. of Ibn Ishaq, q.v. Oxford U.P. 1955)

Hamidullah, Muhammad *Le Prophète de l'Islam* (In French)

Hisham, Abdul Malik ibn *Sirat Rasulillah* (Edited version of Ibn Ishaq)

Hitti, P. K. *History of the Arabs*

— *Makers of Arab History*

Houdas et Marcais *Les Traditions Islamiques* (French trans. of Bukhari)

Huart *Histoire des Arabes*

Hughes, T. P. *Dictionary of Islam* (London 1935 Edn)

Ishaq, Muhammad ibn *Sirat Rasulillah* (Life of the Messenger of God)

Khalliqan, ibn *Biographical Dictionary*

Lammens, H. *L'Arabie Occidentale* (Rome 1914)

— *La Mecque à la Veille de l'Hégire* (Beirut 1924)

Lane Poole, Stanley *The Speeches and Table Talk of the Prophet Muhammad*

Lewis, Bernard *The Arabs in History*

Margoliouth, D. S. *Muhammad and the Rise of Islam*

— *Relations between Arabs and Israelites prior to the Rise of Islam* (Oxford Univ. Press 1924)

Masoodi, al *Muruj al Dhahab* (Meadows of Gold)

Muhammad Ali, Maulana *The Holy Qoran with Commentary* (Lahore 1920

Muir, Sir William *Life of Mahomet*

— *Annals of the Early Caliphate*

Nicholson, R. A. *A Literary History of the Arabs*

Noldeke, Theodor *History of the Qoran* (1860)

O'Leary, de Lacy *Arabia before Muhammad* (London and New York 1927)

— *Arabic Thought and its Place in History*

Qoran see Muhammad Ali

— trans. Richard Bell 1937

— trans. G. Sale

— see Arberry

Robertson-Smith, W. *Kinship and Marriage in Early Arabia* (Cambridge 1885)

Saad, Muhammad ibn al Zuhri *Al Tabaqat al Kabira* (4 volumes in Arabic)

Sale, G. *The Koran*

Sell, E. *Essays on Islam* (London 1901)

Stern, G. H. *Marriage in Early Islam* (London 1939)

Tabari, Al *Tarikh al Rusul wa al Muluk*
Tisdall, W. St. C. *The original Sources of the Qoran*
Waqidi, Muhammad al *Kitab al Mughazi* (4 volumes in Arabic)
Watt, W. Montgomery *Muhammad at Mecca*
— *Muhammad at Medina*
Wayriffe, U. *Arabica and Islamica* (London 1940)
Wellhausen, J. *Muhammad in Medina*

INDEX